Trade, Development and Political Economy

Anne O. Krueger

Trade, Development and Political Economy

Essays in Honour of Anne O. Krueger

Edited by

Deepak Lal
James S. Coleman Professor of International Development Studies
UCLA
Los Angeles
USA

and

Richard H. Snape
Deputy Chairman
Australian Productivity Commission
Melbourne, and
Emeritus Professor
Monash University
Australia

Editorial matter and selection © Deepak Lal and Richard H. Snape 2001
Text © Palgrave Publishers Ltd 2001

First published 2001 by
PALGRAVE
Houndmills, Basingstoke, Hampshire RG21 6XS and
175 Fifth Avenue, New York, N.Y. 10010
Companies and representatives throughout the world

PALGRAVE is the new global academic imprint of
St. Martin's Press LLC Scholarly and Reference Division and
Palgrave Publishers Ltd (formerly Macmillan Press Ltd).

ISBN 0-333-79034-0

This book is printed on paper suitable for recycling and
made from fully managed and sustained forest sources.

A catalogue record for this book is available
from the British Library.

Library of Congress Cataloging-in-Publication Data
Trade, development, and political economy : essays in honour
of Anne O. Krueger / edited by Deepak Lal and Richard H. Snape.
        p. cm.
    Includes bibliographical references and index.
    ISBN 0-333-79034-0
        1. International trade. 2. Commercial policy. 3. Economic
development. 4. International economic relations.
    I. Krueger, Anne O. II. Lal, Deepak. III. Snape, Richard H.

    HF1379 .T722 2001
    382—dc21
                                                00-066557

10   9   8   7   6   5   4   3   2   1
10   09 08 07 06 05 04 03 02 01

Printed and bound in Great Britain by
Antony Rowe Ltd, Chippenham, Wiltshire

Contents

v

List of Tables

List of Figures

List of Abbreviations and Acronyms

ACU	American Conservative Union
AFL	American Federation of Labor-Congress of Industrial Organizations
AITIC	Agency for International Trade Information and Cooperation
AMS	Aggregate measures of support
APEC	Asia Pacific Economic Cooperation
ASAs	Air service agreements
BoI	Boards of Investment
CE	Competitive equilibrium
CEPAL	United Nations Economic Commission for Latin America
COC	Chamber of Commerce
CV	Customs valuation
DA	Development assistance
DSM	Dispute settlement mechanism
DUP	Directly unproductive profit-seeking
ECA	Economic Cooperation Administration
ENT	Economic needs test
EP	Export promoting
ERPs	Effective rates of protection
ESF	Economic Support Fund
FDI	Foreign direct investment
FT	Free trade
FUSADES	Salvadoran Foundation for Economic and Social Development
GATS	General Agreement on Trade in Services
GATT	General Agreement on Tariffs and Trade
IBRD	International Bank for Reconstruction and Development
ICORs	Incremental capital–output ratios
IFS	International Financial Statistics
ILO	International Labor Organization
IMF	International Monetary Fund
IPR	Intellectual property rights
IPVC	Institute for Private Voluntary Cooperation

IS	Import substitution
ISTEC	Institute for Scientific, Technical and Economic Cooperation
ITU	International Telecommunications Union
LCV	League of Conservation Voters
LDCs	Least developed countries
MAI	Multilateral Agreement on Investment
MEA	Multilateral environmental agreements
MFN	Most-favoured nation
MISH	Market Information Survey of Households
NAFTA	North American Free Trade Agreement
NBER	National Bureau of Economic Research
NCAER	National Council of Applied Economic Research
NFIDCs	Net-food importing developing countries
NGOs	Non-government organizations
NICs	Newly industrialized countries
NRT	Net resource transfer
OECD	Organisation for Economic Co-operation and Development
PACs	Political action committees
PI–LC	Permanent income–life cycle
PPMs	Processes and production methods
PPP	Purchasing power parity
PTA	Preferential trade agreement
PVOs	Private voluntary organizations
QRs	Quantitative restrictions
RE	Rational expectations
RER	Real exchange rate
RTAs	Regional trading arrangements
S&D	Special and differential treatment
SITC	Standard International Trade Classification
SPS	Sanitary and Phyto-Sanitary Measures
TBT	Technical Barriers to Trade
TNCs	Transnational corporations
TRIMs	Trade-related investment measures
TRIPs	Trade-related intellectual property rights
TSLS	Two stage least squares
UNCTAD	United Nations Conference on Trade and Development
UPU	Universal Postal Union
UR	Uruguay Round
WHO	World Health Organization
WTO	World Trade Organization

Acknowledgements

The editors wish to express their considerable appreciation to Debra Lance who with efficiency and cheerfulness has undertaken a great number of editorial tasks, including preparing the manuscripts for submission to the publisher and liaising with contributors.

The editors and the publishers would like to thank: The Johns Hopkins University Press for kindly permitting Vernon Ruttan to make use of material drawn from his book *United States Development Assistance Policy*, pp. various (1996); Oxford University Press for kindly permitting W. Max Corden to make use of material drawn from his book *Trade Policy and Economic Welfare*, 2nd edn, pp. 262–4 and p. 267; The World Bank for kindly permitting W. Max Corden to make use of a table drawn from *Boom, Crisis and Adjustment* by I. M. D. Little, Richard Cooper, W. Max Corden and Sarath Rajapatirana, p. 268; and Kluwer Law International for kindly permitting Constantine Michalopoulos to use material drawn from 'Developing Country Strategies for the Millennium Round', *Journal of World Trade*, Vol. XXX, October 1999.

Notes on the Contributors

Robert E. Baldwin:	Hilldale Professor of Economics, Emeritus, University of Wisconsin-Madison
Jagdish N. Bhagwati:	The Andre Meyer Senior Fellow in International Economics at the Council on Foreign Relations (New York) on leave from Columbia University where he is the Arthur Lehman Professor of Economics and Professor of Political Science
W. Max Corden:	Chung Ju Yung Professor of International Economics, Paul H. Nitze School of Advanced International Studies, Johns Hopkins University
Meredith Crowley:	Department of Economics, University of Wisconsin-Madison
Sebastian Edwards:	Henry Ford II Professor of International Economics, University of California at Los Angeles
Ronald Findlay:	Ragnar Nurkse Professor of Economics, Columbia University
Herbert Giersch:	Emeritus Professor, Kiel University
Malcolm Gillis:	President, Rice University
Arnold C. Harberger:	Swift Distinguished Service Professor Emeritus, University of Chicago and Professor of Economics, University of California at Los Angeles
Helen Hughes:	Professor Emeritus, Australian National University
Ronald W. Jones:	Xerox Professor of Economics, University of Rochester

Deepak K. Lal: James S. Coleman Professor of International Development Studies, University of California at Los Angeles

Ronald I. McKinnon: William D. Eberle Professor of Economics, Stanford University

Michael Michaely: Aron and Michael Chilewich Emeritus Professor of International Trade, Hebrew University of Jerusalem

Constantine Michalopoulos: Senior Economic Advisor, World Bank

I. Natarajan: Chief Economist, National Council of Applied Economic Research, New Delhi

Sarath Rajapatirana: Visiting Scholar, American Enterprise Institute

Vernon W. Ruttan: Regents Professor Emeritus, University of Minnesota

Richard H. Snape: Deputy Chairman, Productivity Commission, Australia, and Emeritus Professor, Monash University

T. N. Srinivasan: Samuel C. Park Jr Professor of Economics, Yale University

Introduction

This volume is a tribute to Anne Krueger. Whom to invite to contribute was a real problem: to invite all who would have wished to do so would have filled a bookcase. So to narrow the field a little we decided not to open the gates on her two main country specialties – Korea and Turkey. But even within this restricted area we have risked offence, and to those who feel so offended, we apologize. But even publishers, who themselves hold Anne in high esteem, set limits.

Anne's parents emigrated from Australia to the United States in the early 1930s. The family is distinguished: her father was a psychiatrist (an author and an inventor of a new form of written music), two Australian uncles were knighted (Sir Roy Wright, an eminent Professor of Physiology and later Chancellor of the University of Melbourne, and Sir Reg Wright, an Australian Senator for three decades), while her sister June Osborn was Dean of the School of Public Health at the University of Michigan, now President of the Macy Foundation in New York. With such talent in the family, the pressure was on – or was it Anne who inspired her relations? She grew up in Buffalo, then to college at Oberlin, graduating soon after her nineteenth birthday. Thence to Wisconsin for graduate work and her PhD – by then she had decided not to pursue a career as a flautist, and a faulty knee had cut short competitive swimming at the highest level.

The next move was to the University of Minnesota where over a period of 23 years she was successively Assistant, Associate and then, from 1966, full Professor. For some of us living in other former British colonies, Anne first burst on the scene with her splendid 1969 *Journal of Economic Literature* survey article on balance of payments theory. But there were already papers in the *Journal of Political Economy* on the economics of discrimination (people, not price – a classic paper soon to be republished again) and on exchange control, in the *Review of Economic Studies* on labour supply curves, in the *Quarterly Journal of Economics* on exchange systems, in the *International Economic Review* (with Hugo Sonnenschein) on the gains from trade with changing terms of trade, and in the *Economic Journal* on income differences between countries. A great start for a career. And by then she had also launched her interests in India and Turkey (and learned to speak Turkish).

In the 1970s the flow continued: the famous 1974 *American Economic Review* article on rent-seeking (she invented the concept) being a milestone. By then she had extended her country specialization to Korea and had established the link to her parents' homeland – the first of a long series of visits (mainly to Monash University) being in 1973. Together with Jagdish Bhagwati she then launched the National Bureau of Economic Research multi-country study of foreign trade regimes and economic development, writing the volume on Turkey and one of the two overview volumes herself. Along with the studies by Little, Scitovsky and Scott and the work of Bela Balassa, these country studies and the overview volumes changed the predominant development paradigm from inward-looking to outward-oriented trade policies. Anne followed this up with another major multi-country series on the relation between trade and employment in developing countries.

As if this were not enough, over these years she also published books on import substitution in India and on trade and aid in Korea, and (in 1977) delivered an important Frank Graham Memorial Lecture, published in the Princeton Studies, which spawned new empirical research. But she was also making a major contribution to many people's lives, and to the profession, in her teaching and graduate supervision. A stream of students, now in senior positions in international agencies, national administrations – particularly in developing countries – and in universities, are evidence of her influence in these years at Minnesota. Her own apparently inexhaustible energy and professional and personal standards make a demanding and generous mentor, one that extracts the best.

All this provided the backdrop for the next step in Anne's career – as Vice President Economics and Research at the World Bank from 1982. She found herself embattled with people who were still living in the world of planning models and the economics of *dirigisme*. This was also the period when the Third World debt crisis was at its height. She convinced the powers that be of the need for the Bank to take macroeconomic adjustment and market economics seriously. This also meant the painful and thankless task of reorienting and restaffing the personnel under her charge. Despite endless meetings and ceaseless travel, with her unflagging energy she succeeded in making a major impact on the intellectual content of the Bank's work. One major achievement was the launching of four multi-country comparative studies of major issues in development, one of which she co-directed, which have produced major books. She also saw the launch of two new research journals by the Bank, which are still thriving. Her four-and-a-half years at the Bank left major legacies. The Bank acquired the intellectual resources to advise on macroeconomics and economic liberalization, which were to be the leifmotif of its work for the next decade. During her tenure, and as a consequence of her influence, the Bank was widely recognized as the intellectual leader in the field of development. Leaving the Bank at the end of 1986, Anne was appointed Arts and Sciences Professor of Economics at Duke. With her husband, Jim Henderson, also appointed to the Economics Department at Duke, a home with a tennis court and swimming pool and beautiful surroundings, life could be comfortable after the hectic atmosphere at the Bank. But Anne's energy and drive does not sit easily with comfort. The easy access to Washington, physical and personal, was used to the full, and the inputs into policy, the stream of publications, international visits, invited lectures and graduate students continued. In 1992 the anguish of Jim's cancer, and then death, brought this phase to an end.

And so to Stanford, where since 1993 Anne has been the Herald L. and Carolyn L. Ritch Professor of Humanities and Sciences. Immediately she decided to establish a research centre and after a few of the administrative battles which are endemic to universities, the Center for Research on Economic Development and Policy Reform was created, with Anne as Director.

The honours bestowed on Anne reflect her influence within the profession throughout the world: president of the American Economic Association (and earlier of the Minnesota and Midwest Economic Associations); honourary doctorates from Georgetown University, Hacettepe University (Turkey) and Monash University (Australia), Membership of the National Academy of Science, Fellowships of the American Academy of Arts and Sciences and the Econometric Society, recipient of the Robertson Prize of the National Academy of Science, the Bernhard–Halms Prize of the Kiel Institute, the Seidman Distinguished Award in Political Economy, and the Kenan Enterprise Award.

The multi-country origin of the contributors to this volume itself testifies to the international dimension of this international economist: six were born in the US, four in India, two in Germany, one in Australia (but there are three Australians), and one each in Burma, Canada, Chile, Sri Lanka, Greece, Israel and Czechoslovakia. Author or editor of 44 books, author of a host of articles, stimulating, considerate and compassionate colleague and friend, Anne, we salute you.

Deepak Lal
Richard H. Snape
March 2000

Part I
Trade

1
Outward-Orientation and Development: Are Revisionists Right?

T. N. Srinivasan and Jagdish Bhagwati

Introduction

Anne Krueger has been an influential thinker, researcher and policy adviser on economic development and its relationship with openness to international trade, investment and technology flows. Recently, in her presidential address (Krueger, 1997) to the American Economic Association, aptly titled 'Trade Policy and Development: How We Learn', she recalled that:

> Ideas with regard to trade policy and economic development are among those that have changed radically. Then and now, it was recognized that trade policy was central to the overall design of policies for economic development. But in the early days, there was a broad consensus that trade policy should be based on import substitution ... It was thought import substitution in manufactures would be synonymous with industrialization, which in turn was seen as the key to development.

She also noted how radically the different current thinking is by contrast. Thus, it is now widely accepted that:

> ... growth prospects for developing countries are greatly enhanced through an outer-oriented trade regime and fairly uniform incentives (primarily through the exchange rate) for production across exporting and import substituting goods ... It is generally believed that import substitution at a minimum outlived its usefulness and liberalization of trade is crucial for both industrialization and economic development. While other policy changes also are necessary,

changing trade policy is among the essential ingredients if there is to be hope for improved economic performance. (p. 1)

There have always been dissenting voices among academics and policy makers on the virtues of global integration. One of the most celebrated among them was that of Keynes who, after eloquently lamenting the demise of the golden era of globalization at the start of the First World War, argued heretically for protection in the 1930s.[1] Among development economists, Lance Taylor has been a persistent and articulate critic for several years. A more recent dissent comes from Dani Rodrik, whose impact has been greater because he is seen as more mainstream than Taylor and because today any argument against the trade liberalization that has been sweeping across the world in the last quarter of a century has many listeners.

In particular, Rodriguez and Rodrik (1999) have reviewed recent empirical studies that strongly supported the consensus on the virtues of openness. They claim to have identified several weaknesses endemic to this literature, making them sceptical 'that there is a strong negative relationship in data between trade barriers and economic growth, at least for levels of trade restrictions observed in practice' (p. 38). They further assert that 'the search for such a relationship is futile'. This assertion follows also from their finding that in most models of a small open economy,

there should be no theoretical presumption in favor of finding [an] unambiguous negative relationship between trade barriers and growth rates in the types of cross-national data typically analyzed... moreover an increase in the growth rate of output is neither a necessary nor a sufficient condition for improvement in welfare. (p. 5)

Rodrik (1999), in a policy-oriented analysis, goes further than Rodriguez and Rodrik (1999):

First, openness by itself is not a reliable mechanism to generate sustained economic growth. Second, openness will likely exert pressures that widen income and wealth disparities within countries. Third, openness will leave countries vulnerable to external shocks that can trigger domestic conflicts and political upheavals. (pp. 13–14)

The import substitution (IS) policies followed in much of the developing world until the 1980s were quite successful in some regards and their costs have been vastly exaggerated. (p. 64)

ISI worked rather well for about two decades. It brought unprecedented economic growth to scores of countries in Latin America, the Middle East, and North Africa, and even to some in Sub-Saharan Africa. (p. 99)

The evidence in favor of the small government/free trade orthodoxy is less than overwhelming. Investment and macroeconomic policies remain key. There is no magic formula for surmounting the challenges of economic growth. If there is, openness is not it. (p. 141)

...the economies that have done well in the post-war period have all succeeded through their own particular brand of heterodox policies. Macroeconomic stability and high investment rates have been common, but beyond that many details differ. (p. 47)

This is quite a handful of criticisms. The implication (and that is exactly how Rodrik's work has been widely interpreted) certainly is that the postwar case for openness in trade policy, especially when linked to improved economic growth performance and in turn to improvement in welfare, is to be rejected. For sure, it does seem to militate against Krueger's views. We have decided therefore to evaluate the Rodrik-style arguments. Briefly stated, we find that they amount to little that policy makers need to worry about when recommending a policy of trade openness. We proceed essentially in two steps.

First, we will argue that the criticism that, in theory, there is no presumption that openness in trade (that is, the Export Promoting (EP) strategy) will accelerate growth vis-à-vis the Import Substitution (IS) strategy, is both true and false.

At one level, Rodrik argues that the conventional belief among economists is that freer trade raises income once and for all but cannot raise its growth rate in a sustained fashion. But here he seems to fall victim to a common form of error: citing *one* popular model to argue that therefore we all believe only what is true in *that* model, or confining oneself to certain convenient parametric limits of the model to assert that this is what we must all regard as valid for policy discussions based on that model.[2] Thus, in the present instance, the standard Solow model will work for Rodrik's assertion, but not the Harrod–Domar model if labour remains slack throughout. Nor, as we discuss below, will the Fel'dman–Mahalanobis putty-clay model.

At another level, there are countless arguments, and models, that can be built, and indeed have been built (including by us), which show that free trade will reduce current income and even growth compared to autarky if market failures are present. Bhagwati (1958) showed that growth under free trade may even lower welfare. This can happen if there are distortions in place as growth occurs. (Contrary to Rodrik's presumption, however, we have used this finding to argue several years ago *against* the IS strategy. For, as we argue below, one reason why the IS strategy has not worked well is that it used quantitative restrictions (QRs) and other trade barriers to attract foreign investment which, given the trade distortion, reduced the social returns and may even have created social losses!)[3]

Sure enough, therefore, one can ingeniously construct anti-free-trade kinds of theorizing. But we must next ask the question: in formulating policy, do we view them as representing a 'central tendency' in the real world or merely 'pathologies'? These policy judgments cannot be avoided because otherwise one becomes a prisoner of the nihilistic view that 'because anything can be logically shown, nothing can be empirically believed and acted upon'.

We will return to this question below where we discuss the postwar empirical evidence on this question, arguing also that the cross-country regressions on which both Rodrik (who is sceptical of, if not hostile, to trade openness) and his foes such as Jeffrey Sachs (who cannot have enough of it) rely, are not the best tools for analyzing the problem of understanding the linkage between trade and growth. We will also argue that nuanced, in-depth analyses of country experiences in major OECD, NBER and IBRD projects during the 1960s and 1970s have shown plausibly, taking into account numerous country-specific factors, that trade does seem to create, even sustain, higher growth.

The danger of relying exclusively on cross-country regressions is manifest from Rodrik's remark that the best indicators of growth are macroeconomic stability and investment. For, without exception, the Soviet bloc countries that went steadily down before their collapse were marked by macroeconomic stability – a wit had remarked that Friedman and Marx were bedfellows – *and* by huge investment rates. Until the 1980s, India too had a stable macroeconomy and rising investment rates with an unusually poor growth record among developing countries.

There is no short cut to hard thinking and yet harder and patient analysis of countries in depth: a technique of which Krueger has been a pioneer. In fact, it would be astonishing if these cross-country regressions were by themselves able to settle so easily these difficult issues, for economics could then simply be handed over to unthinking robots. Alas, the reality is very different.

With these general remarks, we now proceed to our detailed analysis. The second section elaborates the familiar static and dynamic mechanisms through which openness influences economic performance including growth and welfare. We address the issue of trade–growth links in formal models, in particular whether freer trade can be expected to result in higher growth rates. We also emphasize the important distinction between openness of trade in goods and services and openness to foreign investment.

In the third section we first recapitulate the basic lessons on the adverse effects of IS strategy, as emerging (among other studies) from the NBER project directed by Bhagwati and Krueger, and then state some of the more recent arguments for openness.

In the fourth section we turn to empirical evidence and to the Rodriguez–Rodrik critique of the recent findings supporting the growth-enhancing aspects of trade openness. We conclude that the early embrace of freer trade by Anne Krueger, and the general acceptance of this prescription today, cannot be faulted.

Openness, growth and welfare

It is illuminating to analyze the benefits of openness from two alternative perspectives: first from the traditional trade-theoretic viewpoint of the efficiency-enhancing role of free trade in a static context, and second from the perspective of growth accounting and intertemporal efficiency and welfare.

Static efficiency of free trade

Foreign trade in goods and services offers yet another means, besides domestic technology, for obtaining goods and services for final use from domestic resource inputs. In autarky, an economy's *availability set*, that is, the set of vectors of goods and services available for final use, is the same as its *production possibility set*. But by using gainful trade to exchange goods and services produced at home for those produced abroad, the economy could add to its availability set under autarky. Also, using trade, an economy could augment its *utility possibility set* – that is, the set consisting of vectors of utilities enjoyed by consumers of the economy obtained by distributing available vectors of goods and services among consumers.

The above arguments for openness point to the *potential* benefits of openness, leaving it to the nature of institutions in an economy to determine whether or not the potential is realized and in what measure.

In contrast, the neoclassical case for free trade (FT) is based on institutional assumptions that include a market structure that is complete and a government that intervenes in the markets only to correct failures, if any, of the market. Under these assumptions, and others on technology and tastes, a competitive equilibrium (CE) under FT is a Pareto optimum. More precisely, in such an equilibrium an economy would be *productively* efficient (that is, it would operate on its *production* possibility frontier) and also *distributionally* efficient (that is, it would be at a point on the *utility* possibility frontier).

Clearly the efficiency characteristics of FT could fail to hold if any of the institutional or other assumptions underlying them fail to hold. For example, if externalities in production or consumption lead to market failures, and the government fails to correct them optimally, or more generally, if there are domestic distortions, a FT competitive equilibrium need not be efficient.

By the same token, under some departures from FT, efficiency in production could still hold. For example, consider a small open economy that imposes a tariff on an importable. In the cum-tariff CE, the economy would still be operating on its production possibility frontier and hence be productively efficient but it would be distributionally inefficient: there exists an equilibrium under FT that Pareto-dominates the cum-tariff CE. This important distinction, well-understood by trade theorists, between production efficiency and welfare (or distributional) efficiency has to be kept in mind. An analogous distinction arises in a dynamic context between growth effects and intertemporal welfare effects of trade liberalization.

Openness, growth and intertemporal welfare

The production efficiency and Pareto optimality of a FT competitive equilibrium for a small open economy can be shown, under similar assumptions, to hold in an intertemporal context by distinguishing commodities by the dates at which they are produced and consumed.

This said, the traditional growth accounting framework is more useful for discussing growth, which is a specific intertemporal phenomenon. In such a framework, the sources of growth are essentially three: growth in inputs of production, improvements in the efficiency of allocation of inputs across activities, and innovation that creates new products, new uses for existing products and brings about increases in the productivity of inputs. Openness to external trade, factor and technology flows has the *potential* to contribute to each of the sources of growth.

Being open to trade allows the economy to exploit its comparative advantage, thereby enhancing the efficiency of the allocation of domestic resources. Being open to capital, labour and other factor flows, enables an economy to augment those of its sources which are scarce relative to the rest of the world and also to use relatively abundant resources elsewhere for a higher return. Such freedom of movement would also enhance the efficiency of resource use (static as well as intertemporal) in each nation and the world as a whole. Finally, through openness to technology and knowledge flows, the fruits of innovation anywhere in the world could become available everywhere.

However, even these insights, under the given assumptions, need to be properly understood. Thus, as we have known since the findings of the 1950s, static and dynamic efficiency in resource allocation does not mean that the economy will grow in FT at an enhanced or even a positive rate in its *steady-state* equilibrium path. For example, in the absence of exogenously growing inputs, innovation and indefinite scale economies in production, and with the marginal return to any input declining to zero as its use increases indefinitely relative to others, there will be no steady-state growth. If there is an input that grows exogenously at a steady rate, then output will grow at the same rate in the steady state as that of the exogenously growing input. This is indeed the case in the celebrated closed-economy growth model of Solow (1956) with a fixed savings rate or in the optimal savings model of Cass (1965) and Koopmans (1965).

In these models, with the steady-state growth rate being exogenous, policy changes do not affect it. In the small open-economy, two-sector version of the Cass–Koopmans style optimal growth model such as that of Srinivasan and Bhagwati (1980), the steady-state growth rate of the economy is the same (*viz.* the exogenous rate of the growth of the labour force) in autarky, and not lower than in FT.

Nonetheless, it would be wrong to infer that, in all models, trade and growth will necessarily be unrelated. As is well-known (see Srinivasan, 1995), the insensitivity of the steady-state growth rate to policy, in particular to trade policy, in the Cass–Koopmans or Srinivasan–Bhagwati type models, arises from their strong assumption that the marginal product of capital inexorably declines to zero as the capital–labour ratio rises indefinitely. By contrast, in models such as the Harrod–Domar one-sector model or the Fel'dman (1928)–Mahalanobis (1955) two-sector model, the marginal product of capital is a constant with labour being in excess supply. As we reiterate briefly in the next subsection, in these models which may apply to many labour-surplus developing economies, even the steady-state growth rate is sensitive to policy and trade policy does favourably affect the steady-state growth rate.

There is also a subtler distinction between intertemporal welfare – that is, welfare along a growth path from given initial conditions – and steady-state welfare. As we pointed out long ago (Srinivasan and Bhagwati, 1980), for a small, open economy with no access to international borrowing or lending, it is possible that welfare is higher *at each point of time* in an autarky steady state as compared to a FT steady state. Nonetheless *intertemporal welfare* (that is, the discounted sum of the stream of utilities) is *always higher* in FT, the reason being that in moving to FT from an autarky steady state, the transitional gains outweigh the losses in the steady state.

A related distinction is between the level effect and the growth effect (that is, the effect on growth rates) of trade policies. For simplicity, if we consider a small, open economy producing traded goods, with world relative prices of these goods constant over time, with unchanging technology and no access to international capital markets, removing trade barriers will clearly raise the value of output (that is, factor income) at world prices at each point in time (and in the steady state assuming that the economy converges to one), if there is no change in the path of factor accumulation. This is the so-called level effect. Whether there will be a growth effect (that is, whether there is any change in the economy's steady-state growth rate) and, if there is, whether it will be transitory or permanent, depends both on the response of factor accumulation to the increase in income levels and whether the marginal returns to factor accumulation eventually diminish to zero. We show in the next section that it is possible to have level effects with no permanent growth effects and also to have both effects.

Next, it should be noted that market failures and distortions can undermine both efficiency and growth effects of trade policies. The general theory of distortions (Bhagwati, 1971) tells us that, if other distortions are present in the economy, trade liberalization *need not* lead to 'static' gains in the shape of a Pareto improvement. When it comes to the beneficial effects of growth, Bhagwati (1958, 1968a) showed equally that in the presence of distortions, growth under free trade *could* be immiserizing. By the same token, as Brecher and Diaz-Alejandro (1977) showed, foreign direct investment (FDI) that is attracted to a protected capital-intensive industry in a labor-abundant economy, will *surely* lead to a Pareto-inferior equilibrium as compared to an equilibrium with no such foreign investment and *might* lead to the same outcome if the expansion of the industry comes about through exogenous *domestic* investment.

Thus, if significant distortions are present when foreign trade (and investment) liberalization is undertaken, there is no presumption in theory that such liberalization would necessarily lead to a static Pareto improvement or to welfare-improving growth. But it is equally true that such static welfare gain and welfare-improving growth are not necessarily ruled out either.

Rodrik (1999), who essentially restates some of these well-known propositions and insights, seems to suggest that the proponents of FT are oblivious of these nuances and theoretical qualifications. The irony is that these nuances and qualifications have come from the *theoretical* writings of economists precisely such as ourselves who, in *policy* judgments, have opted progressively for freeing trade nonetheless, for reasons which we will discuss later in this chapter.

Effects of openness in growth models[4]

For the moment, however, we return to reiterating the fact that it is wrong to assert that, in steady state, the growth rate cannot be affected by trade policy. Indeed, the starting point of some, though not all, of the recent contributions to growth theory is a misleading characterization of neoclassical growth theory of the 1960s and earlier, as implying that a steady-state growth path always exists along which output grows at a rate equal to the exogenously specified rate of growth of the labour force in efficiency units. Thus, in the absence of labour-augmenting technical progress, per capita income does not grow along the steady-state path. Policies that affect savings (investment) rates have only transient effects on the growth rate of per capita output though its steady-state *level* is affected.

Even a cursory reading of the literature is enough to convince the reader that neoclassical growth theorists were fully aware that a steady state need not exist and that per capita output can grow indefinitely even in the absence of technical progress *provided the marginal product of capital is bounded away from zero by a sufficiently high positive number*. Moreover, they showed that once one departs from the assumption that the marginal product of capital *monotonically* declines to zero as the capital–labour ratio increases indefinitely – for example, if it initially rises and then falls – multiple steady-state growth paths are likely (only some of which are stable) and that the steady state to which a transition path converges would depend on initial conditions. Attempts at endogenizing technical progress were also made by theorists of the time.

Therefore, it should not surprise anyone familiar with neoclassical growth theory that the models in which the steady-state growth rate is not an exogenous constant could be used to generate growth effects from trade policy. Srinivasan (1999a,b) has done precisely this, using successively the two-sector Fel'dman (1928)–Mahalanobis (1955) model and then the Cass (1965)–Koopmans (1965) neoclassical model of optimal growth in their open-economy versions.

Rodrik (1996) therefore is mistaken in arguing that, in traditional theory, trade liberalization does not have a long-run growth effect, unless he means by 'traditional theory' any theory that confirms his statement.

Concluding observations

Thus, in conclusion of this section, we must reiterate that no *new* theoretical argument against the linkage of open trade with growth rates is to be found in Rodrik's recent critiques. In fact, his arguments are a subset of the *caveats* that sophisticated trade theorists have advanced, and diffused, to their students for a long time.

Indeed, even if one leaves the realm of graduate textbooks such as Bhagwati and Srinivasan (1983) and goes instead to the policy writings in the influential OECD, NBER and World Bank projects that played the critical role in shifting policies in several developing countries away from the IS strategy and in getting the World Bank to enforce trade reforms more fully, there is much evidence that the theoretical possibilities that could inversely relate growth to openness were not *forgotten*. Rather they were *discounted*, in light of the systematic in-depth and nuanced analyses of country experiences in projects, directed and written by economists who ranked among the leading trade and development economists of the time – among them, Ian Little, Tibor Scitovsky, Bela Balassa and Jere Behrman. Their political ideologies were spread along the entire spectrum and their economic views in many cases (including ours) evolved as a result of the research from a benign acceptance or mild skepticism of IS to a more enthusiastic embrace of EP.

Therefore, we reject the implied critique that the proponents, such as ourselves, of openness in trade are *either* unaware of the theoretical nuances and qualifications that can undermine the link between trade and growth – some of these reflecting our own work, as it happens – *or* have suffered from amnesia concerning them.[5]

The correct view of the matter is that the policy judgment that many of us were led to, in light of the many careful studies during the late

1960s through early 1980s, was that the EP strategy *in practice* was conducive to a significantly higher growth on a sustained basis, whereas the IS strategy produced, after an early IS period (what one of us has called Phase I) of often government-stimulated investments in several countries, an unsustainable growth path. The really interesting *empirical* question seemed to be to track down why. That is, (i) what ideas could we borrow from the huge theoretical literature on trade, efficiency and growth to explain this outcome; and (ii) were there new ideas that these studies suggested concerning the process or route by which openness in trade seemed to benefit the EP countries' growth rates?[6] To give the readers of this essay a flavour, and Rodrik a riposte, we now proceed to a short statement of what the findings on EP and IS strategies' relative merits were in these projects and associated writings.

Export promotion (EP) and import substitution (IS) strategies: empirical arguments and evidence[7]

The question of the wisdom of adopting an export-promoting trade strategy has recurred in the history of the developing countries. Development economics was born in an atmosphere of export pessimism at the end of the Second World War. By the late 1960s, however, the remarkable success of the few economies that pursued EP rather than IS policies swung the weight of academic opinion behind the EP strategy. Aiding this process were academic findings from several research projects which documented both these EP successes and the failures of the IS countries.

The role of export pessimism

The export pessimism following the Second World War, which had been a principal factor fuelling the IS strategy, was to prove unjustified by unfolding reality. At the outset, between the conclusion of the General Agreement on Tariffs and Trade (GATT) in 1947 and the first oil shock in 1973, world exports grew at an unprecedented average rate of 8.8 per cent per year. Although during the period of recovery from the first oil shock (1973–80) and from the second oil shock (1980–90), their growth rate fell to 4.4 and 4.3 per cent respectively, it has since recovered to 7 per cent during the period 1990–97 (GATT, *World Trade*, various reports, and World Bank, 1987, table A.8). The total exports of developing countries grew by 4.9 and 4.7 per cent per year on average respectively during 1965–73 and 1973–80.

The key question that remains at issue, therefore, is what has been called the 'fallacy of composition': how can all, or most, developing countries become successful exporters simultaneously? Or, focusing on the successful Asian exporters, the question may be put: can the Asian export model be successfully exported to all? The suspicion still lingers that the success of a few was built on the failure of the many and that, if all had shifted to the EP strategy, none would have fared well. But this worry is unnecessary.

First, the fear that world trade would have to grow by leaps and bounds if most developing countries pursued an EP strategy is unwarranted. The pursuit of an EP strategy simply amounts to the adoption of a structure of incentives which does not discriminate against exports in favour of the home market. This does not imply that the resulting increases in trade–income ratios will be necessarily as dramatic as in the Far Eastern case.

Second, the share of developing countries in the markets for manufactures in most industrial countries has been, and continues to be, small.

Third, a chief lesson of the postwar experience is that policy makers who seek to forecast exports typically understate export potential by understating the absorptive capacity of import markets. This comes largely from having to focus on known exports and partly from downward estimation biases when price elasticities for such exports are econometrically measured. Experience underlines the enormous capacity of wholly unforeseen markets to develop when incentives exist to make profits; 'miscellaneous exports' often represent the source of spectacular gains when the bias against exports, typical of IS regimes, is removed.

Fourth, trade economists have increasingly appreciated the potential for intra-industry specialization as trade opportunities open. There is no reason to doubt that intra-industry trade in manufactures among developing countries, and between them and the industrial countries, can also develop significantly.

Fifth, if we reckon with the potential for trade between developing countries where policies can change to permit its increase, and the possibility of opening new sectors such as agriculture and services to freer trade, then the export possibilities are even more abundant than the preceding arguments.

Sixth, some developing countries, as they grow, often will transit away from exporting labour-intensive goods, 'making room' for exports of the same goods from other developing countries. Ross Garnaut

(1996) has shown how Japan withdrew from such exports, 'accommodating' such newly growing exports from the Four Tigers, the NICs, during the 1970s. In the 1980s, and up to 1994, Garnaut shows the same phenomenon; but now the NICs withdrew and accommodated the huge entry of China.

Finally, as countries exporting more take markets out of the pot, they also put their own markets into the pot (unless they accumulate surpluses). The view of markets being a zero-sum game is, thus, simply wrong.

Therefore, although the postwar export pessimism was unjustified, it provided a rationale for the adoption of inward-looking trade policies in many developing countries. In addition, trade restrictions were adopted to protect the industries that had grown up fortuitously in Latin America because the Second World War had provided artificial inducements to set up domestic capacities to produce interrupted supplies from traditional, competitive suppliers abroad. Often, chiefly in Latin America, there was also a reluctance to devalue. Combined with high rates of inflation, this caused continuously overvalued exchange rates that amounted to a *de facto* IS trade policy.

Reasons for the success of EP

It is worth stressing again that the concept of EP, or outward orientation, relates to trade incentives (direct trade policies or domestic or exchange rate policies that affect trade) but does not imply that the EP strategy countries must be equally outward-oriented with regard to their policies concerning foreign investment. Hong Kong and Singapore have been more favourable in their treatment of foreign investors than the great majority of the IS countries, but the historic growth of Japan, presumably as an EP country, was characterized by extremely selective control on the entry of foreign investment.

Logically and empirically, the two types of outward orientation, in trade and in foreign investment, are distinct phenomena, though whether one can exist efficiently without the other is an important question that has been raised in the literature and is surrounded by far more controversy than the narrower question of the desirability of an EP strategy in trade.

Also, it is necessary to emphasize that the problems associated with capital account convertibility and related freedom of short-term capital flows, as underlined most recently by the Asian financial crisis, have no necessary relationship to FT's desirability, as noted in Bhagwati (1998a). Yet, in his recent article in *The New Republic* on fixing the world economy, Rodrik (1998) begins with the problems raised by the financial crisis and, in a non sequitur, goes on to argue that the *trading* regime needs a 'global fix'. This is, of course, a common method of false argumentation among anti-FT activists such as Ralph Nader but it is puzzling to find it in the policy writing of an economist of the considerable calibre of Rodrik.[8]

With the EP strategy then defined in terms of the incentive structure (see Bhagwati (1978) and Krueger (1978) for the definition most used), the substantive conclusion that emerged from the major research projects was that the economic performance of the EP countries had been remarkably strong, although they had no one rooting for their success when development efforts were being initiated in the early 1950s.[9] Here, as elsewhere, history turned up surprises.

In evaluating this outcome, we have to distinguish between two questions: (a) why should the EP strategy have been helpful in accelerating economic development, and (b) could the acceleration have been caused by factors other than the EP strategy? In answering these questions, the reflections emerging from the earlier-cited OECD and NBER projects are invaluable.[10]

Resource allocation efficiency. The first set of reasons for the success of the EP strategy relies on the fact that it brings incentives for domestic resource allocation closer to international opportunity costs and hence closer to what will generally produce efficient outcomes. This is true in the sense that there is no bias against exports and in favour of the home market (that is, $EER_x \approx EER_m$) under the EP strategy. Whereas in practice under the IS strategy the home market was substantially more profitable than the external market (that is, EER_m significantly exceeded EER_x). But it is also true in the sense that the IS countries seem to have generally had a chaotic dispersion of EERs among the different activities within export- and import-competing activities as well. That is, the degree of IS goes far and the pattern of IS reflects widely divergent incentives. By contrast, the EP strategy does better both on degree (since $EER_x \approx EER_m$) and on pattern.

Why is the degree of bias so large and the pattern wrong under IS? The answer seems to lie in the way in which IS is often practiced and in the constraints that surround EP. Thus IS *could*, in principle, be contained to a modest excess of EER_m over EER_x. But typically IS arises in the context of overvalued exchange rates and associated exchange controls. So there is no way in which the excess of domestic over foreign prices is being tracked by government agencies in most cases, and the excesses of EER_m over EER_x simply go unnoticed. The non-transparency is fatal. By contrast, EP typically tends to constrain itself to rough equality, and ultra-EP also seems to be moderate in practice, because policy-induced excesses of EER_x over EER_m often require subsidization that is constrained by budgetary problems.

In the same way, the pattern of EER_m can be terribly chaotic because exchange controls and QRs on trade will typically generate differential premiums and hence differential degrees of implied protection of thousands of import-competing activities. By contrast, the EP strategy will typically unify exchange rates, which avoids these problems and, when it relies on export subsidization, will usually be handled both with the necessary transparency and with budgetary constraints that would then prevent wide dispersions in EERs.

The chaotic nature of differential incentives among diverse activities in IS regimes has been documented by estimates of ERPs, effective rates of protection (though these estimates can be misleading in QR regimes where the import premiums may reflect effects of investment controls, indicating therefore resource denial rather than resource attraction to the high-premium and therefore, other things being equal, the high-ERP activities). The estimates of cross-sectional domestic resource costs (DRCS), which provide instead a guide to differential social returns to different activities, have also underlined these lessons.

Directly unproductive profit-seeking and rent-seeking activities. Yet another important aspect of the difference between EP and IS strategies is that IS regimes are more likely to trigger directly unproductive profit-seeking (DUP) activities (Bhagwati, 1982). These activities, of which rent-seeking activities (Krueger, 1974) are perhaps the most important subset, divert resources from productive use into unproductive but profitable lobbying to change policies or to evade them or to seek the revenues and rents they generate. The diversion of entrepreneurial energies and real resources into such unproductive activities tends to add to the conventionally measured losses from the high degree and chaotic pattern of IS.

Foreign investment. IS regimes have tended to use domestic resources inefficiently in the ways that were just outlined; the same applies to the use of foreign resources. This is perhaps self-evident, but (as we noted earlier) substantial theoretical work by Brecher and Diaz-Alejandro (1977), Uzawa (1969), Hamada (1974), Bhagwati (1973) and others has established that foreign investment that comes in over QRs and tariffs – the so-called tariff-jumping investment – is capable of immiserizing the recipient country under conditions that seem uncannily close to the conditions in the IS countries in the postwar decades. These conditions require capital flows into capital-intensive sectors in the protected activities. It is thus plausible that, if these inflows were not actually harmful, the social returns on them were at least low compared with what they would be in the EP countries where the inflows were not tariff-jumping but rather aimed at world markets, in line with the EP strategy of the recipient countries.

In addition, Bhagwati (1978) has hypothesized that foreign investments into IS countries will tend to be self-limiting in the long run because they are aimed at the home market and therefore constrained by it. If so, and there seems to be some evidence consistent with this hypothesis in recent empirical analysis, then IS countries could have been handicapped also by the lower amount of foreign investment flows and not just by their lower social productivity compared with the EP countries.[11]

Grey area dynamic effects. Although the arguments so far go a fair distance in enabling us to understand why the EP strategy does so well, dissatisfaction has continued to be expressed that these are arguments of static efficiency and that dynamic factors such as savings and innovations may well be favourable under an import-substituting trade strategy.

Of course, if what we are seeking to explain is the relative success with growth of the EP countries, this counter-argument makes little sense since, even if it were true, the favourable effects from these 'grey area' sources of dynamic efficiency would seem to have been outweighed in practice by the static efficiency aspects. But the counter-argument is not compelling anyway. Overall, it is not possible to claim that IS regimes enable a country to save more or less than EP regimes: the evidence in the NBER project, for instance, went both ways. Nor does it seem possible to maintain that EP or IS regimes are necessarily more innovative. It is possible to argue that EP regimes may lead to more competition and less-sheltered markets and hence more innovation. But equally, Schumpeterian arguments suggest that the opposite might also be true.

Again, in the matter of X-efficiency, the NBER project led some of us to argue that it is plausible that firms under IS regimes should find themselves more frequently in sheltered and monopolistic environments than those under EP regimes. X-efficiency therefore ought to be greater under the EP regime. Nonetheless, this is a notoriously grey area where measurement has turned out to be elusive.

Rate of investment. We may finally consider one particular 'grey area' matter, which relates to the rate of (productive) investment and where we think that something definite can be said empirically. We would contend (Bhagwati, 1996) that their EP strategy enabled the Far Eastern super-performers to sustain a higher inducement to invest, and hence higher investment rates (financed mainly by phenomenally high, often policy-induced savings), compared to IS strategy countries, chiefly India, where the inducement to invest was constrained by the growth of the domestic market (which, in turn, essentially meant the growth of the agricultural sector which, in practice, has rarely grown at more than 4 per cent annually anywhere over a sustained period exceeding a decade).

Here, we disagree with the implication of Paul Krugman's contention that the Asian economic miracle was not a miracle because it could be explained by extremely high rates of productive investment. The high rates of productive investment, sustained over a very substantial period, were themselves exceptional and were therefore a miracle in the sense of being off the charts. And, in criticism of Rodrik, they in turn reflected chiefly the EP strategy rather than any other plausible policy or accidental benefits from exogenous factors. Hence, Rodrik's contention that investment is correlated with growth, and not trade policy, ignores the fact that, at least in the case of the Four Tigers, the investment rates cannot be divorced from the trade policy these countries pursued. We have here yet another instance of the kind of folly that relying on cross-country regressions typically generates (as we argue more fully below).

Cross-country regressions: the RHS warriors engaged in mutual assured destruction

So, we conclude from these nuanced, in-depth studies of several countries, in the OECD and NBER projects in particular, in favour of trade openness. In fact, in our view, the most compelling evidence on this issue can come only from careful case studies of policy regimes of individual countries, and we argue below against the current resort (by Sachs, Rodrik and others) to cross-country regressions as a reliable method of empirical argumentation.

In *any* policy evaluation exercise, there is, of course, a largely insurmountable methodological problem dealing with counterfactuals. What one would like to know is what would have happened if a country had a set of policies different from the one it actually followed. There are several empirical approaches for answering this question. If some countries changed policies, one could use data from the same countries before and after their policy change (the so-called 'before and after' approach). Another approach is to compare the outcomes in countries which changed policies with those of a similar group of countries which did not (the so-called 'control group' approach). Other approaches include versions of a difference-in-difference approach in which one compares the difference in outcomes between countries which changed policies with the control group *before* the former changed policies with the difference *after* they changed policies, and simulations of the effects of a policy change in a country typically from an applied general equilibrium model. Each of these approaches has its own strengths and weaknesses, as is well known. Lastly there is the cross-country regression approach.

There has in fact been a proliferation recently of cross-country regressions as a method of analysis of issues relating to growth, trade and indeed other issues. Typically the recent opponents (for example, Rodrik) and proponents (for example, Sachs and Warner) of the view that openness in trade is linked to higher growth, are relying on such regressions to argue their respective cases. And, sadly, the media have cited such regressions as if they were 'scientific' evidence based on sound theoretical foundations, on reliable and comparable (over time and across countries) data that are free of measurement errors and biases, and on the use of appropriate econometric tools.

Unfortunately, there are reasons to be sceptical of the findings of most of these regressions for many reasons: their weak theoretical foundation, poor quality of their data base and inappropriate econometric methodologies. A typical regression of this genre will have some outcome variable (for example, average growth rate over some period) on the left-hand side (LHS) and a number of variables on the right-hand side (RHS) that are viewed as determinants of or factors influencing the LHS variable, the direction of influence being viewed as going from RHS variables to the LHS variable. In the openness context, the RHS variables will include a proxy for openness, other possible *systematic* determinants of growth such as rates of investment including proxies for human capital investments or stocks, dummy variables to capture country-, region-, or period-specific factors, even including dummies for civil wars, coups and revolutions, religion of the majority of the population, and a host of factors that are viewed as *idiosyncratic* influences on growth. There are a number of problems with the use of such regressions.

First of all, often though not always, the postulated relationship is not derived from any theoretical model. Even when it is, since economic theory rarely specifies the functional forms for the relationships, let alone the probability distribution of the stochastic error terms, the link in the econometric specification of the relationship between theory and the estimated regression is far more tenuous than is often realized.[12] As such, to assert that some hypothesis (for example, a positive relationship between growth and openness) is conclusively established or refuted by the regression is to claim too much.

Second, there is no reason to presume, even in theory, that the relationship is only from RHS variables to the LHS variable. If it runs both ways, then the LHS variable and a subset, if not all, of the RHS variables are jointly determined. The postulated regression is then *one* of a set of relationships characterizing the interrelationships among jointly determined variables. As such, unless treated econometrically in an appropriate way to take care of this simultaneity problem, parameters estimated from a single equation cannot be interpreted meaningfully. To be fair, a few careful empirical researchers do attempt to address the endogeneity of some of the RHS variables arising from simultaneity by using techniques of estimation other than ordinary least squares, such as two-stage least squares or instrumental variables. Nonetheless this remains an infrequent practice.

Third, many of the RHS variables often are not only poor empirical proxies for their theoretical counterparts but also subject to errors and biases of measurement. For example, defining a variable that captures the influence of a non-tariff barrier in a theoretical relationship and then finding a reasonable empirical proxy for it are not easy tasks. Measurement error in a RHS variable not only biases the estimate of its effect but also the effects of other RHS variables, the direction of bias not being predictable except in very simple situations. Also 'dummy' variables are best described as 'dumb' variables – they are introduced to capture the influence of factors (for example, civil war, revolutions, coups) of which the analyst has often no clue.

Fourth, in the context of relationships that have a temporal as well as cross-sectional dimension, there is the well-known problem that the estimated impact from a cross-section of an RHS variable on the LHS variable need not be the same as that from time-series data.

Fifth, it is highly unlikely that cross-country regressions, relying inevitably on simple proxies of critical explanatory variables such as trade policy, can really get reliably to the empirical reality of the trade-and-growth link in country experiences. In fact, even the LHS variable, the growth rate of GDP, needs to be handled with empirical and conceptual care. Not merely do we know that the estimated growth rates, and country rankings, are sensitive to whether one uses conventional or the Kravis–Heston–Summers estimates but we also know that, from a welfare-theoretic viewpoint, there is a good case for re-evaluating growth rates of each country at *its* international prices, as suggested by Little–Scitovsky–Scott (1970) and analyzed in Bhagwati and Hansen (1973). When this is done, we know from studies by Bela Balassa and others that the high, early growth rates under IS strategy in countries such as Brazil get revised drastically downwards. But the crude regressions on growth and trade almost never face up to these difficulties which can be, and were often, faced squarely in nuanced and intensive country-studies.

Nonetheless, one might observe, as one of us did earlier (Srinivasan, 1999b, pp. 25–6), that it is interesting and suggestive that vast numbers of such crude regression analyses have tended to be supportive of the notion that trade openness is associated with higher growth rates. Having observed that fact, we must still be wary of drawing any firm conclusions from them, especially in light of our foregoing criticisms of such an approach.

In fact, while such regressions can be suggestive of new hypotheses and be valuable aids in thinking about the issue at hand, we would reiterate that great caution is needed in using them at all as plausible 'scientific' support. This is particularly so since the regressions (and the conclusions based on them) are likely to be critically dependent on the period, sample of countries, and variables chosen. In fact, given these numerous choices, we can confidently expect that there are enough *de facto* degrees of freedom at an analyst's command to reverse any 'findings' that another analyst using similar regression methods has arrived at. So, the squabbles among the foes and the friends of open trade, based on these crude cross-country regressions, amount to little more than 'mutual assured destruction' by (or perhaps the MADness of) what we might characterize as the RHS warriors! But, as with all such wars, the fall-out is really what we should object to.

For the use of these cross-country regressions to argue the case for trade openness, when in fact nuanced and in-depth studies argue the case much more persuasively, is to lay open to attacks the case for trade openness, such as those of Rodrik, and therewith to create the illusion that the case for trade openness is illusory. It is ironic, for example, that *The Economist*, having for long given star billing to Sachs (through invited articles by him, heavily reliant on such regressions) and to the Sachs–Warner and other cross-country regressions (reported by its reporters and editors) in its recent support of trade openness, devoted an entire Economics Focus Column recently to discussing Rodrik's attack on them.[13] Perhaps it might have done better to have taken note of its own folly in highlighting these crude attempts at supporting trade openness in the first place!

In conclusion, therefore, we are happy to side with Anne Krueger's take on the positive link between open trade and growth performance, having found Rodrik's recent critique to be unpersuasive.

Notes

1. See, in particular, the discussion of this in Bhagwati (1994) and in Irwin (1996).
2. Recent instances include the common use of the Stolper–Samuelson model to argue that trade hurts real wages. But, even in that model, complete specialization will lead to the possibility that real wages improve even if the price of labour-intensive goods falls. This is a possibility that is in fact very real, since many labour-intensive goods are no longer produced in rich countries. Yet another example is his argument (Rodrik, 1997) that the labour demand curve becomes flatter under free trade than under autarky. But Panagariya (1999) has shown decisively that this cannot be asserted even in the 2×2 and 3×2 models, unless one makes special assumptions that Rodrik does not make.
3. See, for example, Brecher and Diaz-Alejandro (1977) for a formal demonstration; and Bhagwati's NBER synthesis volume (1978) for application of the argument to evaluate an IS strategy's demerits.
4. This section draws on Srinivasan (1999a,b).
5. This is not to say that *some* proponents of trade–growth linkage write, and get amply quoted even in magazines, as if no such nuances exist! But then Rodrik needs to say that, whereas these economists are wrong-headed, many others are not.
6. These types of questions and analyses are to be found in the study of India by us for the NBER project (Bhagwati and Srinivasan, 1975) and in Bhagwati's synthesis volume for that project (Bhagwati, 1978).
7. This section draws on Bhagwati (1988).
8. See also the Letter to the Editor by Bhagwati (1998b) on Rodrik in *The New Republic*.
9. The EP strategy is one which more or less equates the effective exchange rates on exports, EER_x, and on imports, EER_m.
10. It is odd that the young adversaries on the issue of openness in trade appear to be unfamiliar with these influential studies that deeply affected our thinking on the issue. Some of them must be equally unfamiliar with the literature on growth theory of the 1950s and 1960s; otherwise, it is hard to explain how the Harrod–Domar model of the earlier era has been rediscovered by them and named as the 'AK' model!

11. See Balasubramanyam and Salisu (1991) and Balasubramanyam, Salisu and Sapsford (1996).
12. Except in empirical studies such as, for example, those based on real business cycle models where it is integral to the model, the stochastic error term is added on to a purely deterministic theoretical equation – a practice that can be justified only if the RHS variable is the sum of its 'true' value and a stochastic measurement error.
13. Fortunately, the Economics Focus Column ('The Neverending Question', 3 July 1999) ended with a paragraph saying that the case for trade openness was best based on the in-depth and nuanced country studies. Unfortunately, the major projects of the OECD, NBER et al. that had done precisely this during the 1960s and 1970s were not cited.

References

Balassa, B., *The Structure of Protection in Developing Countries* (Baltimore: Johns Hopkins University Press, 1971).
Balasubramanyam, V. N., and Salisu, M. A., 'Export Promotion, Import Substitution and Direct Foreign Investment in Less Developed Countries', in A. Koekkoek, and L. B. M. Mennes (eds), *International Trade and Global Development: Essays in Honor of Jagdish Bhagwati* (London: Routledge, 1991) pp. 191–207.
Balasubramanyam, V. N., Salisu, M. A., and Sapsford, D., 'Foreign Direct Investment and Growth in EP and IS Countries', *Economic Journal*, 106 (434) (January 1996) 92–105.
Bhagwati, J., 'The Capital Myth', *Foreign Affairs*, 77 (3) (May 1998a) 77–112.
Bhagwati, J., 'Letter to the Editor: Global Fixes', *The New Republic* (14 December 1998b) 5.
Bhagwati, J., 'The "Miracle" That Did Happen: Understanding East Asia in Comparative Perspective', Keynote Speech at Cornell University Conference in Honor of Professors Liu and Tsiang, in E. Thorbecke and H. Wan Jr (eds), *Taiwan's Development Experience: Lessons on the Role of Government and Market* (Boston, Dordrecht and London: Kluwer Academic).
Bhagwati, J., 'Free Trade: Old and New Challenges', *Economic Journal*, 104 (423), (March 1994) 231–46.
Bhagwati, J., 'Export-Promoting Trade Strategy: Issues and Evidence', *World Bank Research Observer*, 3 (1) (1988) 27–57; reprinted in D. Irwin (ed.), *Political Economy and International Economics* (Cambridge: MIT Press 1991) pp. 491–526.
Bhagwati, J., 'Rethinking Trade Strategy', in J. Lewis and V. Kallab (eds), *Development Strategies Reconsidered* (Washington, DC: Overseas Development Council, 1986), pp. 91–104.
Bhagwati, J., 'Directly-Unproductive, Profit-Seeking (DUP) Activities', *Journal of Political Economy* (October 1982) 988–1002.
Bhagwati, J., *Foreign Trade Regimes and Economic Development: Anatomy and Consequences of Exchange Control Regimes* (Cambridge, MA: Ballinger, 1978).
Bhagwati, J., 'The Theory of Immiserizing Growth: Further Applications', in M. Connolly and A. Swoboda (eds), *International Trade and Money* (Toronto: University of Toronto Press, 1973), pp. 45–54.

Bhagwati, J., 'The Generalized Theory of Distortions and Welfare', in J. Bhagwati et al. (eds), *Trade, Balance of Payments and Growth: Essays in Honor of C. P. Kindleberger* (Amsterdam: North-Holland, 1971) pp. 69–90.

Bhagwati, J., 'Distortions and Immiserizing Growth: A Generalization', *Review of Economic Studies*, 35 (104) (October 1968a) 481–5.

Bhagwati, J., *The Theory and Practice of Commercial Policy*, Frank D. Graham Memorial Lecture, Essays in International Finance, 8 (Princeton, NJ: Princeton University, Department of Economics, 1968b).

Bhagwati, J., 'Immiserizing Growth: a Geometric Note', *Review of Economic Studies*, 25 (3) (June 1958) 201–5.

Bhagwati, J., and Hansen, B., 'Should Growth Rates be Evaluated at International Prices?', in J. Bhagwati and R. S. Eckaus (eds), *Development and Planning: Essays in Honour of Paul Rosenstein-Rodan* (Cambridge: MIT Press, 1973) pp. 53–68.

Bhagwati, J., and Srinivasan, T. N., *Lectures on International Trade* (Cambridge: MIT Press, 1983); second (revised) edn (1998) with Panagariya, A.

Bhagwati, J., and Srinivasan, T. N. *Foreign Trade Regimes and Economic Development: India* (New York: Columbia University Press, 1975).

Brecher, R., and Diaz-Alejandro C., 'Tariffs, Foreign Capital and Immiserizing Growth', *Journal of International Economics* (November 1977) 317–22.

Cass, D., 'Optimum Growth in an Aggregative Model of Capital Accumulation', *Review of Economic Studies*, 32 (1965) 233–40.

Fel'dman, G. A., 'K teorii tempov narodnogo dokhoda', *Planovoe Khoziaistvo*, (1928) 11, 146–70 and 12, 152–78.

Garnaut, R., *Open Regionalism and Trade Liberalization* (Singapore: Institute for South East Asian Studies, 1996).

Hamada, K., 'An Economic Analysis of the Duty-Free Zone', *Journal of International Economics* (August 1974) 225–41.

IMF, *World Economic Outlook* (Washington, DC: International Monetary Fund, 1999).

Irwin, D., *Against the Tide: an Intellectual History of Free Trade* (Princeton, NJ: Princeton University Press, 1996).

Koopmans, T. C., 'On the Concept of Optimal Economic Growth', *Study Week on the Econometric Approach to Development Planning* (Amsterdam, North-Holland for Pontificia Acad. Sci., 1965).

Krueger, A. O., 'Trade Policy and Economic Development: How We Learn', *American Economic Review*, 87 (1) (1997) 1–22.

Krueger, A. O., *Foreign Trade Regimes and Economic Development: Liberalization Attempts and Consequences* (Cambridge, MA: Ballinger, 1978).

Krueger, A. O., 'The Political Economy of the Rent-Seeking Society', *American Economic Review*, 64 (3) (1974) 291–303.

Little, I. M. D., Scitovsky, T., and Scott, M. F. G., *Industry and Trade in Some Developing Countries* (Oxford: Oxford University Press, 1970).

Mahalanobis, P. C., 'The Approach of Operational Research to Planning in India', *Sankhya: The Indian Journal or Statistics*, 16, parts 1 and 2 (1955) 3–62.

Panagariya, A., 'Trade Openness: Consequences for the Elasticity of Demand for Labor and Wage Outcomes' (University of Maryland, 1999) (mimeo).

Rodriguez, F., and Rodrik, D., 'Trade Policy and Economic Growth: a Skeptic's Guide to Cross-National Evidence', NBER Working Paper no. W7081 (April 1999).

Rodrik, D., *Making Openness Work: the New Global Economy and the Developing Countries* (Washington, DC: The Overseas Development Council, 1999).

Rodrik, D., 'The Global Fix', *The New Republic* (2 November 1998) 17–19.

Rodrik, D., *Has Globalization Gone Too Far?* (Washington, DC: Institute for International Economics, 1997).

Rodrik, D., 'Understanding Economic Policy Reforms', *Journal of Economic Literature* (1996).

Sachs, J. D. and Warner, A., 'Economic Reforms and the Process of Global Integration', *Brookings Papers on Economic Activity* (1995) 1–118.

Solow, R. M., 'A Contribution to the Theory of Economic Growth', *Quarterly Journal of Economics*, 70 (1956) 65–94.

Srinivasan, T. N., 'Trade Orientation, Trade Liberalization, and Economic Growth', in G. Saxonhouse and T. N. Srinivasan (eds), *Development, Duality, and the International Economic Regime: Essays in Honor of Gustav Ranis* (Ann Arbor: The University of Michigan, 1999a) pp. 155–96.

Srinivasan, T. N., 'As the Century Turns: Analytics, Empirics and Politics of Development', in G. Ranis, S.-C. Hu and Y.-P. Chu (eds), *The Political Economy of Comparative Development into the 21st Century: Essays in Memory of John C. H. Fei*, vol. 1 (Cheltenham, UK: Edward Elgar Publishers, 1999b) pp. 3–42.

Srinivasan, T. N. 'Long-Run Growth Theories and Empirics: Anything New?', in T. Ito, and A. O. Krueger (eds), *Growth Theories in Light of the East Asian Experience* (Chicago: University of Chicago Press, 1995) pp. 37–70.

Srinivasan, T. N., and Bhagwati, J., 'Trade and Welfare in a Steady State', in J. Chipman and C. P. Kindleberger (eds), *Flexible Exchange Rates and the Balance of Payments* (Amsterdam: North-Holland, 1980) ch. 18, pp. 341–53.

Uzawa, H., 'Shihon Jiyuka to Kokumin Keizai' ('Liberalization of Foreign Investments and the National Economy'), *Economisuto* (1969) 106–22 (in Japanese).

World Bank, *World Development Report 1987* (New York: Oxford University Press 1987).

2
Trade Policy and the Exchange Rate Regime[1]

W. Max Corden

The Mexican, Asian and Brazilian crises from 1994 to 1998 have led to a great debate about the choice of exchange-rate regimes for developing countries. In particular, 'fixed-but-adjustable' regimes have been shown to be incompatible with high capital mobility. This is not a new conclusion – and indeed is the principal explanation for the breakdown of the Bretton Woods system – but it is one that has been dramatically brought home by these more recent emerging market crises. At the same time, when the exchange rates have been reluctantly allowed to float as a result of crises, there has been excessive instability, as reflected in short-term overshooting of depreciations in the market. Again, the recognition of exchange-rate instability under floating rates is an old theme, stimulated especially by the extreme behaviour of the dollar and the yen during the 1980s and 1990s.

The current state of thought is that countries that have opened up to the world capital market cannot sustain fixed-but-adjustable regimes, and need to move either to floating, possibly with some management or soft targets, or to firmly fixed rates in the form of currency board regimes, dollarization or even monetary union with a major country (Eichengreen, 1994; Corden, 1994; Obstfeld and Rogoff, 1995). While recent examples of currency board regimes are fairly rare, the main cases being Argentina and Hong Kong, it is quite likely that more currency board regimes, or even dollarization, will be chosen. This is particularly so because recent experiences in East Asia of extreme exchange-rate movements under floating, following upon the breakdown of fixed-but-adjustable regimes, have led many people in the affected, and, indeed, other, countries to react against floating, often expressed as a hostility to 'speculators'.

This chapter, written in honour of Anne Krueger, discusses the trade policy implications of the choice of exchange rate regime in developing countries, and, more generally, the relationship between exchange rates and trade policy both in theory and in historical experience. Trade policy implications are generally ignored in the current discussion on exchange-rate regimes, even though there is an existing, and separate, literature on the exchange rate–trade policy relationship, a literature to which Anne has contributed in a classic study, namely, Krueger (1978).

The theoretical framework

To outline the theoretical framework, I draw on a fuller discussion in Corden (1997, ch. 15). If a country has a wide-ranging system of tariffs and quantitative import restrictions, and then eliminates the restrictions and reduces or eliminates the tariffs, and if the real exchange rate did not change, the demand pattern would shift towards imports while output of import-competing industries would decline. Hence, the current account would deteriorate, and employment would decline. A sufficient exchange-rate devaluation or depreciation in the market would increase exports as well as moderating the increase in imports and the decline in import-competing production. Trade liberalization should thus be part of a policy package which includes adequate real depreciation.

Consider the small country or 'dependent economy' model with three goods, or categories of goods, namely, importables (*M*), exportables (*X*) and nontradables (*N*). *M* and *X* combined are tradables. The foreign currency prices of *M* and *X*, namely, p_m^* and p_x^*, are given from outside. The price of *N* is p_n. The nominal exchange rate is *e*, an increase in *e* being a depreciation. A single tariff, *t*, applies to *M*. The domestic prices of *M* and *X*, namely, p_m and p_x, are thus, respectively, $ep_m^*(1+t)$ and ep_x^*. The 'switching ratio', *S*, is defined here as the relative domestic price of tradables to nontradables. While this is sometimes called the real exchange rate, I use this term for a slightly different concept below. The domestic price of tradables is a weighted average of p_m and p_x, the weights being α and $(1-\alpha)$. These weights are not necessarily constant. For given real expenditure, production functions and domestic demand functions, *S* determines the current account and the excess demand–supply situation in the market for nontradables.

Hence,

$$S = [\alpha ep_m^*(1+t) + (1-\alpha)ep_x^*]/p_n \tag{2.1}$$

It can be seen that, with p_m^*, p_x^* and p_n constant, a decline in t (trade liberalization) requires a rise in e if S is to stay constant.[2] It may be a realistic assumption that p_n can rise but not fall. In that case, while a decline in t would still require a rise in e to keep S constant, a rise in t could be associated with either a fall in e (appreciation) or a rise in p_n.

The next step is to allow for the possibility of changes in p_m^*, p_x^*, and p_n. The concept of the *real exchange rate* must then be introduced. Assume realistically that there is some given rate of inflation abroad, causing p_m^* and p_x^* to rise continuously, and also some underlying rate of inflation in p_n at home. The relative rates of inflation are then crucial. For given t and e, S will fall if a weighted average of p_m^* and p_x^* rises more slowly than does p_n. A compensating steady rise in e can then keep S constant. Once-for-all trade liberalization (fall in t) will require e to rise faster than this for a short period, and then depreciation would have to return to its steady compensating rate.

I define the real exchange rate here as the relative price of tradables *excluding tariffs and their various equivalents* to nontradables. Defining R as the real exchange rate in this sense, holding constant the terms of trade, so that p_m^* and p_x^* always rise to the same extent, we can simply write p^* for the foreign price-level and we get

$$R = ep^*/p_n \tag{2.2}$$

Hence, from (2.1) and (2.2)

$$S = R(\alpha t + 1) \tag{2.3}$$

It follows that (in order to keep S constant) trade liberalization (fall in t) will require a real depreciation (rise in R), the latter depending not just on e but also on the changes in p^* and p_n. If p_n is rigid downwards because of downward nominal wage rigidity, and p^* is constant, a fall in t requires a rise in e – that is, nominal depreciation.

The literature

Until the 1960s, trade policy and exchange-rate policy were kept in separate compartments in textbooks and the theory literature. Trade policy belonged to microeconomics – or to general equilibrium real trade theory – and the exchange rate to Keynesian macroeconomics. When discussing the effects of tariffs, the implications for the exchange rate were not explicitly discussed, essentially because the assumption was made either that the general equilibrium effects were small – so that a partial equilibrium approach was justified – or that price and wage flexibility would ensure necessary general equilibrium at 'full employment.' In one part of the textbook the neoclassical assumptions were made, and in the other part, the Keynesian assumptions.[3]

At a more practical level, in most or all developed countries the exchange-rate issue in connection with trade policy hardly arose because large-scale unilateral trade liberalizations by high-protection countries were hardly under consideration. Either trade liberalization was reciprocal under the various GATT rounds, or it involved small changes with no significant effects on the balance of payments or overall employment. It was the experience or possibility of significant unilateral liberalizations by high protection developing countries (and also by Australia, which was somewhat similar in this respect to developing countries) that gave rise to a new literature linking trade policy and the exchange rate.

As far as I am aware, the first theoretical papers linking trade policy (actually tariffs) to the exchange rate were Corden (1966) and Johnson (1966), and the fullest exposition was in Corden (1971, ch. 5). The historical experience in developing countries of 'reluctant exchange-rate adjustment' leading to increases in protection, and sometimes to decreases, within the framework of the fixed-but-adjustable regimes that existed at the time was described first in Bhagwati (1968), and then in much detail in Krueger (1978). The influential book by Little, Scitovsky and Scott (1970) argued the need for unilateral trade liberalizations to be accompanied by devaluations, though this theme was only developed in a few pages.

Anne's book drew on the nine country studies which were the outcome of the National Bureau of Economic Research project on Foreign Trade Regimes and Economic Development (the 'Bhagwati–Krueger') project. She showed how trade policies and devaluations interacted. For example, what was the effect of a devaluation when there were existing (and maintained) quantitative restrictions, or when simultaneous partial liberalization took place? Most relevant for the present discussion was her strong conclusion that 'failure to devalue by a sufficient margin will prevent sustained liberalization; and inflation after devaluation at a fixed exchange rate will prevent sustained liberalization. A realistic real exchange rate ... [is] ... an essential condition for sustained liberalization' (p. 231). As a framework for her analytical descriptions of what had happened as a result of devaluations by the nine countries – with experiences varying a great deal – she divided the developments into five 'phases'. Possibly these phases were somewhat artificial concepts but they did give some coherence to complicated stories.

The focus on the need for devaluations to accompany or precede unilateral trade liberalizations emerged clearly in Papageorgiou et al. (1991), which was a summary book based also on a series of country studies conducted this time under World Bank auspices. The theme could also be found in several papers by Bela Balassa before that date. In the present paper I shall draw mostly on empirical material in Little et al. (1993). This book was the outcome of another comparative countries studies project, this time dealing with the macroeconomic experiences of 18 developing countries, including almost all large developing countries, other than China, and many others. It was initiated by Anne and by Deepak Lal when she was Vice President for Economics at the World Bank and Deepak was Research Advisor. The relevant material comes from a chapter entitled, 'Trade Policies: Tightening and Liberalization', and the research for that chapter was done by one of the co-authors, Sarath Rajapatirana.

The historical experience

Table 2.1, which comes from Little et al. (1993), sums up some of the principal results. In the eighteen countries in the period from 1965 to 1990 there were 59 episodes when trade policies were significantly changed, consisting of 26 episodes of trade policy 'tightening' (usually the expansion of the range of imports to which quantitative import restrictions applied) and 33 episodes of trade policy liberalization.[4] The key fact that emerges is that in 29 of 33 liberalization episodes, the exchange rate was devalued or was flexible during that episode. Liberalization without devaluation was quite rare, with only four such cases.[5]

The 29 episodes included altogether eight episodes of major trade regime changes (Korea 1965–67, Chile 1974–79, Sri Lanka 1977, Turkey 1980, Morocco 1984, Indonesia 1986–89, Mexico 1985–90 and Nigeria 1986–88). These cases consisted of substantial, often drastic, trade liberalizations, but also of sustained efforts not to use trade policy tightening in the future to counter balance-of-payments problems. In all but one case (Mexico), liberalization was associated with significant, sometimes very large, devaluation.

Sometimes the two policies of trade policy tightening and devaluation were used together in response to a current account problem. As shown in Table 2.1, this was so in 13 cases, of which seven were in the

Table 2.1 Trade policy episodes, trade regime changes and the exchange rate, 1965–90

	1965–73	1974–79	1980–83	1984–90	1965–90
Trade policy tightening	6	9	8	3	26
Exchange rate devalued or flexible during episode	3	1	7	2	13
Exchange rate fixed during episode	3	8	1	1	13
Trade policy liberalization	9	7	5	12	33
Exchange rate devalued or flexible during episode	9	4	5	11	29
Exchange rate fixed during episode	0	3	0	1	4
No changes in trade policy	6	4	10	5	22
Trade regime changes	1	2	1	4	8
	Korea 1965–67	Chile 1974–79 Sri Lanka 1977	Turkey 1980	Morocco 1984 Indonesia 1986–89 Mexico 1985–90 Nigeria 1986–88	

Source: Little et al., *Boom, Crisis and Adjustment: the Macroeconomic Experience of Developing Countries* (New York: Oxford University Press, 1993), p. 268.

period 1980–83. Current account problems were, of course, severe in the 1980–83 period because of the debt crisis. But a fixed exchange rate clearly increased the likelihood of trade policy tightening. In the period 1965 to 1979, there were 11 episodes when the exchange rate was fixed but there was trade policy tightening, but only three episodes (out of four for the whole period 1965–90) when the exchange rate was fixed but there was liberalization.

It is worth looking closely at how policies responded to a balance-of-payments crisis or deterioration as reflected in the current account situation. It is shown in the chapter (by probit analysis) that in the first three periods – that is, from 1965 to 1983 – current account deficits were likely to lead to trade policy tightening the following year. This is not at all surprising. What is surprising is that in the last period (1984–90) current account deficits were more likely to lead to trade liberalization.

These liberalization episodes preceded by current account crises are examples of what is described in Little et al. (1993) as 'the new liberalization'. (There are also a few examples from before 1984.) In these cases, a balance-of-payments crisis led both to a substantial devaluation *and* to trade liberalization, sometimes indeed to a regime change. The crisis created the shock environment in which trade liberalization and other radical policy changes became politically possible. The 'new liberalization' also reflected ideological shifts and the influence at times of crisis of the International Monetary Fund and the World Bank. The most important point is that in the 1980s the new willingness of many developing countries to alter exchange rates – the abandonment of 'reluctant exchange rate adjustment' – made this new liberalization possible.

Is a revival of protectionism likely?

Countries may deprive themselves of the exchange-rate instrument by joining a monetary union, by establishing a credible currency board regime, or by giving up their own currency in favour of a foreign currency – such as dollarization. These can all be described as methods of monetary integration. The advantage of such integration is that the possibility of exchange-rate crises of the kind that fixed-but-adjustable regimes are prone to is ruled out. This is currently the main reason why one can expect more developing countries to choose the monetary integration option. But the option of trade liberalization combined with devaluation is then also ruled out unless it is undertaken at the outset of the regime change. There are many arguments for and against monetary integration. These need not be rehearsed. The main point here is that the implications for trade policy need also to be considered.

Much unilateral trade liberalization by developing countries has by now taken place. Hence it might be argued that a potential problem hardly remains. But there is still a considerable way to go in many cases.[6] The practical suggestion must then be that any country that chooses to shift to a regime of monetary integration should *first* engage in unilateral trade liberalization to bring it closer to free trade, and combine or precede this with a substantial devaluation.

Even when trade is substantially liberalized, the possibility of a return of protectionist measures cannot be ruled out once a country has lost the exchange rate instrument. The country may suffer an adverse terms-of-trade shock, or a sudden decline in capital inflow or increase in capital outflow. These are adverse 'asymmetric' shocks which would have led in the past, at least since the 1980s, to devaluation or to depreciation of the exchange rate in the market. With monetary integration this would not be possible, and the only remaining possibilities would be to borrow abroad temporarily, to suffer a deep recession, to rely on downward wage and price flexibility, or to increase protection, perhaps combining the last with some Keynesian fiscal expansion. In the Bretton Woods period, when exchange-rate adjustments were reluctant, trade policy 'tightening' was the common response. It is likely that in such circumstances protectionist pressures would again increase.

Actual increases in protection may be limited by obligations incurred by membership of the World Trade Organization, or perhaps by membership of a free-trade area. Here it has to be borne in mind that WTO obligations do not always constrain countries' tariff policies because tariffs may have been 'bound' at high levels above existing rates. For example, Brazil has bound rates as high as 70 per cent. Aside from this, there are always loopholes, the main ones at present being anti-dumping measures. Developing countries, especially in Latin America, have even now been following the example of the advanced countries in the extensive use of anti-dumping tariffs. Governments may find it difficult to resist protectionist pressures, and may not wish to resist. Of course, they might take a long-term view. If the shocks are expected to be temporary, they may be willing to live with a temporary recession for the sake of avoiding the long-term costs of revived protection. But the pressures will be there.

The issue is not only a matter of political economy – that is, of pressure group politics. In addition one must at least take note of the optimal short-term policy from a pure efficiency point of view. When the exchange rate is fixed or unavailable as a policy instrument, when foreign inflation is low and there is significant downward inflexibility of domestic prices and wages – as is usual – and when short-term foreign borrowing is not possible, optimal short-term policy might involve the use of some exchange-rate substitutes, such as a uniform tariff, perhaps combined with a uniform export subsidy. I do not advocate such policies, which have notorious costs, especially in the long term, and when they are not uniform. Flexibility downwards of domestic wages and prices, or short-term foreign borrowing, if possible, would clearly be preferable.

But one conclusion clearly emerges. The possibility of a revival of protection – with all its long-term costs – provides an argument against monetary integration. This must be set against various other arguments in favour. The arguments in favour may still be strong – depending on the degree of openness of the economy, the need for monetary discipline on the basis of previous inflation experiences, the unlikelihood of adverse asymmetric shocks, and the flexibility of prices and wages – but here we have an argument against.

Perhaps the days of fixed-but-adjustable regimes are indeed coming to an end because of high capital mobility and the difficulty of controlling international capital movements, especially outflows. In that case, if the concern is to avoid a revival of protectionism, it may be better to move to floating rate regimes, no doubt with some exchange-rate management. And yet, it must be admitted that floating rates also have problems, though probably less from this point of view than permanently fixed rates.

Do floating rates stimulate protection?

It is a common argument that sharp or prolonged appreciations of real exchange rates generate pressures for protection. The obvious explanation is that real appreciations reduce the competitiveness of import-competing industries. This is an adverse effect which protection is then designed to offset. Of course, an increase in protection would add to the adverse effect that real appreciation has on export industries, which would thus be hit twice. It is a consequence which advocates of protection at times of real appreciation always ignore.

I am not aware of any systematic empirical support for the view that real appreciations actually increase protectionist measures. But it is certainly plausible, and there is some anecdotal evidence from episodes of real appreciations of the US dollar. The view that real appreciation leads to increases in protection became common during the episode of severe real appreciation of the US dollar (up to 50 per cent) in the early 1980s. In any case, here we have another possible link between exchange rates and trade policy.

From the point of view of developing countries, there are actually two distinct cases to consider, namely, the Dutch Disease and the anti-dumping cases. In the Dutch Disease case a boom in a developing country – whether in productivity or in export prices – in one part of tradables, the booming sector B, leads to a decline in the domestic price of the lagging tradables sector L, relative to the price of nontradables, N. Thus the boom has an adverse effect on the L sector. This is the familiar Dutch Disease effect, and may generate pressures to protect that sector. In a fixed exchange-rate regime, where the price of L is constant (apart from the effect of inflation abroad), the adverse effect on sector L would be brought about by a rise in the price of N resulting from increased spending on N, while in a floating rate regime, where the price of N is possibly held constant, it would be brought about by a decline in the domestic currency price of L resulting from nominal appreciation.

A similar Dutch Disease effect would result from capital inflow into a country, associated with a domestic consumption or investment boom. In a fixed-rate regime real appreciation would be brought about by a rise in domestic wages and prices owing to the spending boom, while in a floating rate regime it would be brought about directly, when capital inflow appreciates the currency. Many examples could be given from the emerging markets booms of the early nineties.

The important point to note here is that real appreciation in these cases reflects an economy's adjustments to what might be called 'fundamentals'. In the capital inflow case the absorption or transfer of foreign savings, in the form of capital inflow, requires the generation of an appropriate current-account deficit, and real appreciation combined with increased domestic spending bring this about. The outcome does not finally depend on the nominal exchange rate regime, since there would be real appreciation both with a fixed rate and a floating or flexible rate regime. The most one can say is that, for given capital inflow, real appreciation would probably emerge faster in the floating rate regime. This is because domestic prices in a fixed exchange-rate regime are likely to be slower to rise in response to increased spending on domestic goods and services than the nominal exchange rate would be to appreciate in a floating rate regime in response to increased demand for domestic currency.

The 'anti-dumping' case, by contrast, is different. It concerns the effect of depreciations of the exchange rates of developing countries on the trade policies of developed countries. Thus it only applies when the developing country has a floating or flexible rate regime. This time the developing country's nominal and real exchange rate depreciates, rather than appreciating. Such a depreciation may wholly reflect a necessary adjustment to a decline or cessation of capital inflow or to sudden capital flight. Alternatively, it may additionally result from exchange-rate overshooting not justified by 'fundamentals.' We have seen such depreciations, notably overshooting, in recent emerging markets crises. In any case, the sudden increase in competitiveness of the developing country's exporters brought about by depreciation generates protectionist pressures in other countries. In practice, in recent years, these have taken the form of pressures for anti-dumping measures in developed countries, especially the United States and the European Union. In this case a floating exchange-rate regime does tend to stimulate protectionism, though not in the developing country itself but rather in its export markets.

The central problem is extreme exchange-rate instability. The special problem of the floating rate regime compared with the fixed-but-adjustable one is that floating may lead to exchange-rate overshooting. Indeed, the exchange rate may depreciate or fluctuate sharply because of herd behaviour or self-justifying expectations in the capital and foreign exchange markets, when there would have been no exchange-rate changes at all in the old-style fixed-but-adjustable regime.

Conclusion

In summary, large-scale unilateral trade liberalization requires generally an associated devaluation or a depreciation in the market. Furthermore, a revival of protection in response to adverse asymmetric shocks is more likely if a country does not have the exchange rate instrument available. The empirical evidence from Little et al. (1993) reported here shows pretty clearly that under the fixed-but-adjustable exchange rate regimes, broad unilateral trade liberalization in developing countries took place almost always in conjunction with devaluations. When devaluations were reluctant, current-account problems were more likely to lead to the expansion of the scope of quantitative import restrictions. Exchange-rate flexibility made possible liberalizations.

But the fixed-but-adjustable exchange-rate regime is not compatible with high capital mobility and the avoidance of crises. One way out that has been widely canvassed is to move to currency board, dollarization, or monetary union arrangements. There are some very good arguments in favour of countries moving to currency board, or other monetary integration, regimes. These arguments apply primarily to very open economies (as we learned from the theory of optimum currency areas) and to countries that have been unable to generate their own anti-inflation discipline. But against this must be set the concerns stressed in this chapter. Will large-scale unilateral trade liberalization still be feasible when it is no longer possible to devalue beforehand or at the same time? And, more important, is there a likelihood of a revival of distorting trade policy measures in response to adverse asymmetrical shocks? If such measures are to be avoided, more reliance will have to be placed on downward flexibility of nominal wages and of prices of nontradables.

The extreme opposite is the floating exchange-rate regime, this being the regime that many developing countries have been forced to choose – or involuntarily found themselves in – as a result of recent crises. This regime also has great disadvantages – notably the inconvenience of short-term exchange-rate instability, adverse distributional effects and, above all, the tendency to overshooting. In addition, when depreciations overshoot, protectionist pressures may be generated in countries that provide the markets for the exports of the developing countries concerned. Nevertheless, one may conjecture that this last problem is much less severe than the danger for trade policies posed by monetary integration regimes.

Perhaps a compromise can be found, involving flexible exchange rates without excessive instability and overshooting. Such an outcome would depend on the maintenance of stable and cautious monetary and fiscal policies and some judicious interventions and 'soft' exchange-rate commitments. Alternatively, if monetary integration is chosen, more reliance may eventually have to be placed on domestic wage and price flexibility. In any case, the discussion of the choice of exchange-rate regimes needs to take into account the implications for trade policies. This is the principal message of this chapter. The cause of trade liberalization and the avoidance of the revival of widespread protection in developing countries, will, I hope, not be set back by changes in exchange-rate regimes. This is a cause to which Anne Krueger has devoted so much effort, and in support of which she has been so influential.

Notes

1. I am indebted to very helpful comments from Sarath Rajapatirana and Richard Snape. Sarath Rajapatirana has also supplied me with detailed information on trade policies.
2. This conclusion is obviously true if the weights (α and $(1-\alpha)$) also stay constant. But it is likely that α would change when t changes. I have not resolved this theoretical problem, but it seems intuitively quite implausible that a change in α would reverse the conclusion.
3. These remarks, and further remarks below on the theoretical literature, should be qualified as follows. Economists were, of course, aware that, given a fixed exchange rate, import controls, exchange controls, or tariffs, would or should be used to deal with balance-of-payments problems, and the details of controls

and their consequences were discussed at length in an extensive literature. See particularly Meade (1951, ch. 21) and, for a full review, Yeager (1966, ch. 7).

4. The countries covered in the project were: Argentina, Brazil, Cameroon, Chile, Colombia, Costa Rica, Côte d'Ivoire, India, Indonesia, Kenya, Mexico, Morocco, Nigeria, Pakistan, Republic of Korea, Sri Lanka, Thailand and Turkey.

5. The four cases were Kenya, Korea and Nigeria in the 1974–79 period, and Côte d'Ivoire in the 1984–90 period. Kenya had devalued two years before the liberalization process, and liberalization actually took place in the middle of the coffee boom. Nigeria liberalized at the start of the oil boom.

6. In 1996, the following developing countries had still high levels of protection – with high nominal tariff rates and relatively large coverage of quantitative restrictions in their import regimes: Egypt, India, Kenya, Malawi and Zimbabwe. Possibly others, notably Brazil, should be included in this list.

References

Bhagwati, J., *The Theory and Practice of Commercial Policy: Departures from Unified Exchange Rates* (Princeton: International Finance Section, Princeton University, 1968).

Corden, W. M., 'The Structure of a Tariff System and the Effective Protective Rate', *Journal of Political Economy*, 74 (1966) 221–37.

Corden, W. M., *The Theory of Protection* (Oxford: Clarendon Press, 1971).

Corden, W. M., *Economic Policy, Exchange Rates and the International System* (Chicago: The University of Chicago Press, 1994).

Corden, W. M., *Trade Policy and Economic Welfare*, 2nd edn (Oxford: Oxford University Press, 1997).

Eichengreen, B., *International Monetary Arrangements for the 21st Century* (Washington, DC: The Brookings Institution, 1994).

Johnson, H. G., 'A Model of Protection and the Exchange Rate' *Review of Economic Studies*, 33 (1966) 159–63.

Krueger, A. O., *Foreign Trade Regimes and Economic Development: Liberalization Attempts and Consequences* (Cambridge, MA: Ballinger, 1978).

Little, I. M. D., Scitovsky, T., and Scott, M., *Industry and Trade in Some Developing Countries* (London: Oxford University Press, 1970).

Little, I. M. D., Cooper, R. N., Corden, W. M., and Rajapatirana, S., *Boom, Crisis and Adjustment: the Macroeconomic Experience of Developing Countries* (New York: Oxford University Press for the World Bank, 1993).

Meade, J. E., *The Balance of Payments* (London: Oxford University Press, 1951).

Obstfeld, M., and Rogoff, K., 'The Mirage of Fixed Exchange Rates', *Journal of Economic Perspectives*, 9 (1995) 73–96.

Papageorgiou, D., Michaely, M., and Choksi, A., *Liberalizing Foreign Trade: Lessons of Experience in the Developing World* (Oxford: Basil Blackwell, 1991).

Yeager, L. B., *International Monetary Relations: Theory, History, and Policy* (New York: Harper & Row, 1966).

3
Some Insights from Real Exchange-Rate Analysis

Arnold C. Harberger

It is likely that very few contemporary economists would recognize the real exchange rate as a very recent arrival on the list of important economic concepts, or would realize that real exchange-rate analysis, as we know it today, was not part of the standard preparation of international trade economists, even as late as forty or fifty years ago. It has been my good fortune to witness the arrival of this new offspring of our intellectual heritage and to observe at close hand its development over recent decades.

As is the case with most new ideas, a certain aura of haziness has surrounded the concept and the analysis, as different professionals with different backgrounds tried to use them in approaching and solving different problems. This haziness persists even to this day, though I believe I sense a gradually emerging consensus. I hope that in this chapter I will be able to help push this process along.

As an illustration of the haziness surrounding the concept of the real exchange rate (RER), let me list the titles of six different panels of the table on 'Real Effective Exchange Rate Indices', as they appear in the IMF's *International Financial Statistics (IFS)* (August, 1999, pp. 54–5). There is one panel giving indexes 'based on relative unit labour costs', another 'based on relative normalized unit labour costs', another 'based on relative value-added deflators', another 'based on relative wholesale prices', yet another 'based on relative export unit values', and still another 'based on relative consumer prices'.

This plethora of definitions very clearly reflects the diversity of opinion that must have arisen as the Fund's panel of experts tried to decide on what series the IMF should publish under the real exchange-rate label. I think that readers can easily imagine, going over the Fund's six panel headings, that each of them was thought to give evidence relative to one class of questions or another. I do not want to take space at this point to explore precisely what questions these may have been. Rather, I want to show that there is a 'natural' definition for the real exchange rate – one that flows quite directly from the theory of international trade. Moreover, and quite surprisingly (to me), this 'natural' definition is not included among the six alternatives presented in *IFS*!! Still further, this 'natural' definition can be considered as one of the absolutely key relative prices of macroeconomic analysis. Hence for sure, it is not one that should have been overlooked. I conclude, then, that the failure of this key definition to appear on the IMF's list is a reflection of the general haziness, referred to above, that seems still to surround the concept of the real exchange rate.

The demand and supply of foreign currency

In this section I shall try to build the base for the above assertions, concentrating on the flow demand and flow supply of foreign currency.

Consider first how one would approach the problem of empirically analyzing developments in the market for any ordinary good (say tomatoes) or service (say plumbing services). One would surely want quantity and price data with which to explore the movements of supply and demand in the market in question. But if the analysis covered any significant period of time, the nominal price of tomatoes or wage of plumbers would not be the relevant price. We would instead want to express this price in real terms, by deflating it by some numeraire price or price level. Now, while a standard text on general equilibrium theory will probably tell us that we can choose 'any given price' out of the set $P_1, P_2, \ldots, P_n$ as our numeraire, no empirical worker would proceed down that path. The reason is that we want our empirical numeraire to reflect movements in the general level of prices, not the idiosyncratic movements of some individual commodity's market. Imagine trying to do a serious monetary analysis in which real cash balances were expressed by dividing the nominal quantity of money by the price of sugar! Or trying to study cyclical movements in which real GDP was obtained by dividing the nominal GDP by, say, the price of petroleum! In these cases, huge amounts of unwanted 'noise' would be introduced into our time series. Half one's energy in conducting an analysis in such terms would have to be devoted to explaining away or correcting for the idiosyncratic movements of one's ill-chosen numeraire.

I believe most empirical workers in economics would agree that there are only two readily available candidates for an all-purpose numeraire – these are the GDP deflator and the Consumer Price Index (CPI). Each of these has a sound conceptual base – using the one, all deflated series are expressed in terms of general 'production units'; using the other, they are expressed in terms of general 'consumption units'. Neither of these two series is subject to the type of idiosyncratic movements that characterize the price of many individual goods and services (though one must always be alert to possible manipulation, particularly of the CPI).

Now turn to the market for foreign currency. Here, too, we have a situation of supply and demand, and the relevant price is obviously the exchange rate. The nominal exchange rate E (in a peso country) is the nominal peso price of the nominal dollar. If any sort of inflation is going on in the peso country, we would want to correct for it in the same way we would if we were analyzing the market for tomatoes or for plumbing services. That is, we would want to express it in terms of the standard empirical numeraire $\bar{P}_d$. This yields $E/\bar{P}_d$ as the real peso price of the nominal dollar.

What is the relevant quantity to be juxtaposed to this price? A little thought should make it clear that it is not the quantity of US dollars, but rather the quantity of *foreign exchange* being demanded and/or supplied, that is relevant. We must think of a country's exports as being its major continuing source of flow supply of foreign exchange, and of its imports as the major source of its flow demand for foreign exchange. There is no sense whatever, in a market economy, in thinking of an exchange rate with the US dollar that equilibrates Mexico's exports to and imports from the US, and of another exchange rate with the pound sterling that equilibrates Mexico's trade to and from the UK, and so on. In a world of convertible currencies the relative exchange rates of the dollar, the pound, the franc, and so on, are set in a world market that is, for practical purposes, beyond being influenced by events in Mexico. So when we develop the demand and supply for foreign currency, we take the total foreign currency demanded by the Mexican market and express it all in dollars using the contemporaneous world-market rates for the conversion.

Thus we are using an exchange rate expressed in pesos per dollar as the price which equilibrates the market for foreign exchange, with other currencies being converted to dollars at the prevailing set of cross-rates with the dollar. It is important to realize that the choice of the dollar as the standard unit of foreign currency has no special meaning, nor does it assign to the dollar any special status. If instead of using the dollar we chose to express our picture of supply and demand for foreign currency in terms of pounds, we could do so by a simple relabeling of the axes. We could multiply the quantity axis by £/$, thus expressing total foreign currency supplied or demanded in terms of pounds, and would simultaneously multiply by $/£ the vertical axis, which was previously in units of real pesos per dollar, thus rendering it in new units of real pesos per £. Hence the very same diagram used to express the supply and demand for foreign currency (measured in dollars) as a function of $E/\bar{P}_d$, where E is measured in pesos per dollar, can be used to depict supply and demand for foreign currency measured in pounds as a function of $E/\bar{P}_d$, where E' is measured in pesos per pound. A given point, expressing, say, $3 billion of foreign exchange against a price of 10 real pesos per dollar, can be relabelled as expressing £2 billion of foreign exchange against a price of 15 real pesos per pound. This change reflects nothing more than the fact that $1.50 was the relevant dollar price of the pound at that 'moment'.

In the same way as was shown above, the demand and supply for foreign currency could be expressed in francs, deutschmarks, euros or yen, without modifying anything except the quantity and price yardstick used in the measurement.

The real exchange rate as the key equilibrating variable for a country's international trade and payments

We are for the moment working with $E/\bar{P}_d$ (the real price of the nominal dollar) as our concept of the real exchange rate. The best way to focus on this as the relevant variable is to assume that all world prices (measured in dollars) are given – that is, beyond the control of the country in question. In this case, the real price of the nominal dollar is equal to the real price of the real dollar, independent of the weights used in the index that defines the real dollar. (I want to postpone the question of how to choose this index until later, precisely because that choice depends very heavily on the issues treated in this section.)

The main point of this section is that the natural response of any country's economy to any of a whole host of 'international trade disturbances' is an adjustment of the real exchange rate, through movements either of the nominal exchange rate E, or of the general price level $\bar{P}_d$, or of both. A partial list follows:

(i) The introduction of new *import restrictions* will typically shift the demand curve for foreign exchange to the left, causing the equilibrium real price of the dollar to fall.

(ii) The introduction of *export restrictions* will typically shift the supply curve for foreign exchange to the left, causing the equilibrium real price of the dollar to rise.

(iii) A change in the rate of inflow of foreign capital will typically add more to the supply of foreign exchange than to its demand, thus causing the equilibrium real price of the dollar to fall.

(iv) A rise in the world price of an export good will cause the supply curve of foreign currency to shift to the right, thus causing the equilibrium real price of the dollar to fall (causing Dutch Disease, if the positive shock to foreign currency receipts is sufficiently large).

(v) A rise in the world price p^*_j of an import good M_j can shift the demand for foreign exchange in either direction depending on the price elasticity of local demand for M_j, as a function of its internal relative price $P_j/\overline{P}_d$. With an inelastic demand, the demand for foreign exchange will shift to the right, and its equilibrium real price will rise. With an elastic demand these effects are reversed.

(vi) A reduction in the real cost of producing a tradable good will typically add to the supply of foreign exchange if that good is an export product, and will typically subtract from the demand for foreign exchange if the good in question is an import substitute. In either case the natural consequence is a fall in the equilibrium real price of the dollar.

(vii) A reduction in the real cost of producing a nontradable good will tend to work in the opposite direction (that is, to raise the real price of the dollar), subject to some qualifications. The broad theorem is that an equal reduction in the real cost of producing all goods and services is equivalent to an increase in real income. If, then, the equilibrium real exchange rate is invariant to changes in real income, then reducing the real unit cost of nontradables production by α per cent must have the opposite effect on the equilibrium real exchange rate from a reduction, also of α per cent, in the real unit cost of producing all tradables.

I use the word 'typically' in characterizing the natural response to a disturbance because there are significant exceptions to the rule. For example, a tariff on a good (condensers) that is an input into import-substitute production (refrigerators) will tend to raise the local cost of producing the end-product in question (refrigerators). All this will lead to a reduction in imports of the input (condensers) and an increase in importation of the final product (refrigerators). With fixed proportions the latter effect will outweigh the former, so the net effect on the country's demand for imports will be positive. Here is a case where a rise in the particular tariff rate (that on condensers) is trade creating! This is not, however, the place to explore such nuances in detail, or even to try to provide an exhaustive list. Our focus here is not on the source of the disturbances but on the response. Whatever may cause a shift in the supply and/or demand for foreign exchange, so as to open up a breach between them at the 'old' real exchange rate, will cause a movement of the real exchange rate that will work to close that breach, via movements either in E, or in $\bar{P}_d$, or in both.

This, to me, describes the key role that the real exchange rate plays in the economics of international trade. It is a role that can be occupied by no other variable, and is at the same time one that is utterly essential in bringing about full adjustment in the face of all kinds of disturbances. It then follows, I firmly believe, that our empirical definition of the real exchange rate should be one that is compatible with, sensitive to, and hopefully reflective of this role.

Converting foreign currency from nominal to real units

The world is never so kind as to present us with a pattern of world prices that stays constant while an economy like Mexico's or Indonesia's receives and responds to some major international shock. One must simply recognize that world prices P_j^* have their own movements through time, and that even broad averages of them typically exhibit significant amounts of drift over quinquennia and decades, less often over years, and rarely over quarters or months. This means that the issue of converting foreign currency to real terms is not always critical. For example, the overshoots of the real exchange rate of Argentina (1982), Mexico (1983, 1995) and Indonesia (1998) took place in a sufficiently short span of time, within which $E/\bar{P}_d$ moved so dramatically (over a factor ranging from two to six) that one could simply forgo adjusting for the comparatively minuscule contemporaneous adjustments of $\bar{P}^*$ (the world price level), much less lose sleep over precisely what index to use in constructing $\bar{P}^*$.

But there are plenty of problems (for example, the analysis of the real exchange-rate history of a country over, say, three or four decades) for which an adjustment is needed to take us from $E/\bar{P}_d$ (the real price of the nominal dollar) to $E\bar{P}^*/\bar{P}_d$ (the real price of the real dollar). For such exercises one would have to choose a specific index for $\bar{P}^*$. Here we try to examine some of the main considerations that should guide this choice. Let me approach this discussion by showing how our own intellectual history may have led people astray, in at least two important ways.

Consider first the way international trade theory was traditionally taught. Who will ever forget country A and country B, which constituted the whole world in countless exercises covering everything from comparative advantage, to the theory of tariffs, to the gold-standard, specie-flow adjustment mechanism? Well, I believe that this grounding in a two-country world is what led many people to think of the real exchange rate as a symmetrical concept – with country A's real exchange rate with country B being the reciprocal of country B's real exchange rate with country A. It only takes a little reflection to see that a real exchange-rate measure defined in a symmetrical way will not, *even in* an old-fashioned two-country model, perform the equilibrating function that we identified in the previous section as its principal role. One gets to that result only when our model has not only just two countries but also just two goods. Then the RER is just the relationship, in one currency or another, between the prices of the two goods, that is, EP_b/P_a or $(P_a/E)/P_b$.

But once nontradables enter the picture we must recognize that their prices in country A play a major role, while their prices in country B play no role at all in A's own adjustment to a given disturbance. From these two conclusions it follows that the price level of nontradables in A must be reflected somewhere in A's RER measure, while the price level of nontradables in B (and, more generally, in other countries) should *not* be reflected. *How, then, can any proper real exchange rate be symmetrical, in the sense of using the same type of index in the numerator (for $\bar{P}^*$) and in the denominator (for $\bar{P}_d$)?* Yet please note that every one of the IFSs six definitions of the real exchange rate *is* symmetrical in this sense.

The theoretical literature of modern, real-exchange-rate economics does not fall into this trap. Here the most common norm is to work with a single country producing two or three goods. If two, they are tradables and nontradables. If three, they are exportables, importables and nontradables. In either case, the price level of nontradables, P_n, plays a key role in the resulting models, where typically the RER is defined as P_t/P_n.

The problem here is that we *have no direct empirical counterpart to the concept of the nontradable good.* I tell my students that for the most part nontradables are like quarks or black holes – things we never really observe directly but whose existence we can both deduce from our theory and infer from our observations. It is really very simple. All internationally traded goods can be said to have international prices at which they are traded, prices that can be adjusted to an appropriate cost, insurance, and freight (CIF) or free on board (FOB) basis for any country. But not so for nontradables, where nearly all the standard examples fail. Restaurant meals contain nontradable services, but tradable dinnerware, kitchen equipment and food items. Taxi rides likewise are built up from nontradable services and tradable cars, tyres, and fuel.

If we use the index i to refer to nontradable inputs and the index j to refer to tradable inputs, any given final product price can be represented as a weighted sum of the prices of its inputs, that is, $P_f = \sum_i \alpha_{if} P_i + \sum_j \alpha_{jf} P_j$. For a true, tradable final product, P_f will be determined in the world marketplace and an increase in the world price will give rise to increased rents (P_i) to one or more domestic factors. I think that the products that we commonly call nontradable have the characteristic that P_f is determined mainly or exclusively by the equilibrium of domestic supply and demand. But this does not stop it from being an average of tradable and nontradable components.

So we can think of the GDP deflator, or any other weighted average of final-product prices, as being a weighted average of tradable and nontradable prices, even though we never (or hardly ever) really see a final good or service that reflects only nontradable prices. Thus if our final product price index is $\bar{P} = \sum_f \lambda_f P_f$, this transforms into $\bar{P} = \sum_f \lambda_f \sum_i \alpha_{if} P_i + \sum_f \lambda_f \sum_j \alpha_{jf} P_j$, and can thus be said to be a weighted average of tradable and nontradable components.

The consequence of all of this is that we really cannot produce, out of direct observations, the empirical counterpart to P_t/P_n. But that is no problem as we can easily obtain something like $P_t/\bar{P}_d$, which can alternatively be expressed as $P_t/(\lambda P_n + (1-\lambda)P_t)$, where λ and P_n are not observed. (In all these price-level formulations, units are assumed to be defined such that all base-period prices are equal to one.)

Thus if $\bar{P}^\star$ represents a relevant index of the world price of tradables, one can say that for *given* world prices $\bar{P}^\star$, when our measure of RER $(=E\bar{P}^\star/\bar{P}_d)$ goes up or down, this reflects a rise or fall in a sort of P_t/P_n variable.

The real problem is, in my opinion, that even though we are obviously free to define things as we wish, *we do not really want to define the real exchange rate as something that moves up or down with the price level of the country's own tradables.*

Consider first a definition of $\bar{P}^\star$ that was some sort of weighted average of the world prices of the exports and imports of the country in question. Now, let the world price of petroleum rise for Mexico or Indonesia, or the price of coffee for Brazil or Colombia. In the first instance this would cause the index $\bar{P}^*$ to rise. Of course, the greater availability of foreign exchange would cause the real price of the nominal dollar $(E/\bar{P}_d)$ to fall, but this would only help turn a 'perverse' effect on the RER into an ambiguous one.

I use the word 'perverse' not because of some anomalous reaction (as with Giffen goods) but rather in a sort of semantic sense. All (or at least most) of us are completely at home with the idea of Dutch Disease. It is natural, therefore, for us to think that an oil boom in Indonesia or a coffee boom in Colombia will lead to a reduction in the real cost of the real dollar, that is, in a reduction of the RER defined in this way. Yet if we choose to use an index of the world prices of the country's exports and imports as our measure of $\bar{P}^*$, we do not get a clear-cut result, even in a very obvious Dutch Disease situation. The answer is *not to include the country's export prices in the index for $\bar{P}^*$*, at least not with weights corresponding to their importance in that country's trade.

Import prices do not give us the same kind of trouble, in part because the change in the world price of any particular import good will in any case have an uncertain effect on the RER, depending on the price elasticity of demand for imports of that good. Thus, a weighted average of the world prices of a country's imports is a more plausible candidate for the index $\bar{P}^*$.

But before leaving the topic of import prices, let me note that they, too, can lead us into trouble if we choose a definition of the RER that reflects the *internal price of tradables* relative in theory to nontradables, in practice to some general index $\bar{P}_d$. The source of trouble here is the mirror image of the Dutch Disease case. We are all aware that new import restrictions cause the demand for foreign currency to shift to the left, and its equilibrium real price to fall. But those very import restrictions cause the affected import and/or importable-goods prices to *rise*. Hence an index $\bar{P}^*$ that included the gross-of-tariff world prices of import goods would tend to rise with the imposition of a new tariff, thus tending to offset its 'natural' effect of causing $(E/\bar{P}_d)$ to fall. Once again, we get an ambiguous outcome in place of the 'normal' one. This exercise leads us to insist that if an import price index is used for $\bar{P}^*$, it should be an index of CIF prices in the open world market, and not of internal (for example, tariff-inclusive) prices for this set of tradable goods.

The preceding discussion makes clear that there are significant problems with many commonly-used country-specific definitions of $\bar{P}^*$. This by itself suggests that it may be worthwhile to seek a definition that is not country-specific. There are many precedents for this in economic analysis. On the whole, when we define real wages across occupations, regions, and so on, we do not typically seek separate consumer price indexes according to the specific consumer baskets of each occupation or region. Instead, we typically treat the national CPI as a general numeraire for the purpose of defining real wages.

In a similar way, we can think of defining $\bar{P}^*$ as a generalized bundle of tradable commodities, priced, as I like to put it, in the middle of the Atlantic and Pacific Oceans. I believe that it would be a worthwhile use of the research resources of the IMF and/or the World Bank to institutionalize the building and maintenance of such an index. The weights attaching to the different goods and services entering this index could correspond to their relative importance in world trade, though I believe a better case could he made for using weights that correspond to their relative importance in world production. Such an index would serve the purposes of being a world-price numeraire for tradable goods generally.

I was led to think in these terms by working with the World Tables and the individual country balance-of-payments data presented in *International Financial Statistics*. Consider the World Tables presenting time series covering some thirty-odd years of current dollar value of exports and imports of member countries. For most purposes, these series would be far more useful if they were expressed in real terms. The same is true for series on balance-of-payments deficits and surpluses, on international debt, and so on. Of course, there is always the possibility of converting these various series into real terms on a country-by-country basis, using country-specific dollar-price indexes for the purpose. But not only is that a lot of work; one also runs into serious problems of comparability among researchers. To me, the potential advantages of a well-defined, widely-accepted world numeraire are so great as to be essentially beyond dispute.

But what to do in the meantime, that is, before the IMF or the World Bank creates this numeraire? Here I have an interim suggestion that has at least the merit of having been tested by experience. This is an index that I call the SDR-WPI. I and many of my students have been using it for some 15 years, in many different international and domestic applications where something like a world price level numeraire is called for. So far the snake has not risen up to bite us, not even once.

What then, is this SDR-WPI? Conceptually it is very simple. It builds on the notion that on the whole, indexes of wholesale and producer prices are heavily weighted with internationally-tradable goods. Consider, then, that the WPIs of the US, Japan, Germany, France and the UK are each a separate local-currency price of a basket of tradables. If we are to define $\bar{P}^*$ in terms of US dollars, we then want to convert these local currency prices to dollar prices by multiplying them by $/¥, $/DM, and so on. We then convert the results to an index basis with, say, 1990 equal 100, and combine the five indexes using the same weights as the IMF uses in defining the SDR. These weights have changed gradually over time, mainly to reflect the growing relative importance of the Japanese economy. In our own uses of the SDR-WPI, we have typically selected the set of weights that defined the SDR for our particular base year, and used that set of weights to define a constant-weight SDR-WPI for that particular exercise or study. I believe, however, that if one were to build an SDR-WPI for general, profession-wide use, it would be convenient to build into it the changing weights used by the Fund for the SDR. The simplest way to do this would be to build the index Divisia-style, with each year's percentage changes in the component WPIs being weighted by that year's SDR weights.

Defining real-exchange-rate equilibrium

The most natural approach to defining real-exchange-rate equilibrium is to work with the demand for imports and the supply of exports, with the quantity units defined as real dollars (or other currency of choice) and with the price axis representing the RER defined as real pesos per real dollar.

Thus we start with a demand for foreign currency derived from the demand for imports, and a supply of foreign currency derived from the supply of exports. Their crossing point gives us the equilibrium RER if there are no international capital movements or losses of reserves by the Central Bank or payments of interest and dividends in what the *IFS* classifies as 'income items' and no current transfers. All these items taken together comprise the 'net resource transfer' to or from the country, and it is this net resource transfer that in the end can finance an excess of imports over exports or that can be financed by an excess of exports over imports.

Happily for us economists, there is a very convenient identity between $(M^d - X^s)$ and $(T^d - T^s)$. The first parenthesis represents the excess of import demand over export supply in a period; the second represents the excess of the country's total demand for tradable goods and services over its total supply of them. If I_{pd} represents the flow of importables produced and demanded at home and E_{pd} represents the flow of exportables produced and demanded at home, we have $T^d = M^d + I_{pd} + E_{pd}$, and $T^s = X^s + I_{pd} + E_{pd}$. From this the identity $(M^d - X^s) \equiv (T^d - T^s)$ follows directly. The equilibrium RER can then be seen to be that which generates a zero excess demand measured either as $(M^d - X^s)$ or as $(T^d - T^s)$. (To permit the necessary aggregation, all these flows must be expressed in a common unit – the 'dollar's worth'.)

This works very well as long as we are dealing with a net resource transfer of zero. But if the net resource transfer (NRT) is different from zero, it must be presumed to have an effect on the underlying demand pattern. If an inflow of $1000 is spent on tradables it will by itself cause $(T^d - T^s)$ and $(M^d - X^s)$ to increase by $1000, so the extra supply of foreign exchange in this sense creates its own demand, and there is no need for the RER to change.

If, on the other hand, the net resource transfer is spent on nontradables, it creates an excess demand in the nontradables market matched by an excess supply of foreign exchange. In this case the equilibrating function of the RER is called into play, and the real price of the real dollar must fall to close the gap.

The easiest way to build up loci of potential equilibrium positions, under different amounts of net resource transfer, is to consider the excess demand $(T^{do} - T^{so})$, where T^{do} and T^{so} are the demand and supply of tradables, each measured in units of real dollars' worth and built on the assumption of a zero net resource transfer. If there is in fact a zero net resource transfer, the equilibrium RER is determined by the intersection of these curves. The T^{do} and T^{so} curves will shift due to disturbances like import and export restraints, technological advances, and so on, and the equilibrium RER will shift with them. But we are here focusing on disturbances represented by the NRT itself, or by changes in it.

The key proposition here is that the NRT is not itself the relevant variable. One needs to know how the NRT is divided into its two components, $B_t + B_n$. We have seen that B_t (borrowing spent on tradables) does not affect the equilibrium RER, while B_n (borrowing spent on non-tradables) does. Our key conclusion is that one finds the equilibrium RER by inserting a wedge equal to B_n (measured in real dollars) between the T^{do} and T^{so} loci defined above.

Unfortunately, to implement this concept empirically one must know how the NRT of any given period is divided into B_t and B_n. This is easy to do for a company's borrowings but very difficult for a nation's. One really ought to work with all the separate items of gross inflow and gross outflow that constitute the NRT, and find B_{tj} and B_{nj} for each of them before finally aggregating these component flows into B_t and B_n for the nation. To my knowledge nobody has done this. Most analysts, including myself, have instead worked with the NRT itself, or with capital account data. The preceding paragraphs should serve to warn us how potentially treacherous it is to take these common short-cuts. Bad results are to be expected from using NRT or capital flow data to explain movements in the RER whenever there are (usually unknown to us) substantial changes in the fraction of net flows that is spent in nontradables.

Specifying demand functions in international trade

Let me begin this section by setting out my favourite specification for the demand function for 'tradable good j'.

$$T_j^d = a_0 + a_1 y + a_2 RER + a_3 (P_j / E\bar{P}^*) + B_{jt} + a_5 (M^s - M^d)/\bar{P}_d \qquad (3.1)$$

There is a great deal of international trade economics imbedded in this simple function. Not much need be said about the income term, y, which is 'standard'. But the price terms contain an important subtlety. We have seen that the RER is the key variable that moves to eliminate potential disequilibria in the market for foreign exchange. In so doing it represents a movement in the price of what I call 'the greatest real-world composite commodity' – a country's tradables. It is as if the prices of all tradable goods and services were in a huge elevator, moving up and down *together*. We can learn nothing about the elasticity of wheat demand with respect to the RER if we fit a standard function in which the price variables are of the standard type $P_j/\bar{P}_d$ for wheat and its main substitutes. That function has interest of its own but tells us nothing about a_2. In theory, a_2 should be obtained from an 'elevator experiment', where in fact we move all tradables prices up and down together. In practice we have to use a measure like $E\bar{P}^*/\bar{P}_d$ to try to capture (imperfectly) the same effect.

What we're really doing with the coefficients a_2 and a_3 is a sort of nesting of substitution terms. One could broaden this nesting and have one term representing the price of wheat relative to the prices of grains, another reflecting the price of grains relative to the price of food, yet another showing the price of food relative to the price of tradables, and finally the RER itself (the price of generalized tradables relative to $\bar{P}_d$).

The main point is to focus on a_2. The elasticity here is bound to be extremely low. Estimates of price elasticity for an aggregate like food typically hover in the range of -0.25 to -0.50. But the substitutability between food and non-food has to be substantially greater than that between food and the mysterious aggregate we call nontradables. This latter would be a plausible guide to the magnitude of the own-price elasticity of tradables demand.[1]

Now since the demand for tradables is, for the reason indicated, likely to be 'everywhere and always' of very low elasticity, this puts the supply of tradables into a very critical position. If the elasticity of supply is also low, even moderate shocks can lead to high volatility of the RER. If, on the other hand, the supply of tradables is quite elastic, this can help keep the RER within a relatively modest range, even in the face of substantial shocks. I believe we have real-world counterparts to these situations. The overall supply of tradables is almost certain to be quite inelastic in countries whose tradables sector is dominated by agriculture, mining and fishing. These would include Argentina, Brazil, Chile and Indonesia, among many others. Countries whose tradables sector is dominated by manufacturing and services would include Hong Kong, Korea, Singapore and Taiwan, plus the great bulk of the advanced industrial countries. All would tend to have a reasonably elastic supply of tradables. The reason is that these are activities whose outputs can be as much as doubled, simply by adding another shift. This entails some premium in real costs, but not, in general, a huge one. Hence we expect the volatility of a country's real exchange rate to depend quite critically on its industrial structure.

The coefficient a_3 has no real counterpart in the macro-trade literature, since it is really tracking the idiosyncratic movements of the price P_j of a particular tradable good (or subset). But it surely belongs in the demand equation for that good. The term in B_{jt} appears without a coefficient. This simply represents how much of foreign borrowing (or better, of the net resource transfer) was spent on good j. We can adjust this term in steps, and perhaps get some additional insights at each step. In my own work, I used to represent this term as $a_4 NRT$, making the net resource transfer the explanatory variable and then emphasizing that the coefficient a_4 could vary a lot from event to event, even in the same country in adjacent periods. I now prefer to put just B_{jt} because that presentation makes the same point, louder and clearer.

Going still another step, we get to the practice, frequently found in the literature, of making demand depend not on real income but on total real expenditure. This treats $(y + NRT)$ as the relevant explanatory variable, and implicitly assumes that we spend borrowed money the same way we spend income. That may sometimes be true, but certainly not reliably so. Country borrowing has sometimes fed construction booms (largely nontradable), sometimes gone to buy capital and consumer goods (largely tradable). The mix depends on who is borrowing and for what purpose. Readers will sense immediately the link of the B_{jt} term to the income–expenditure approach to the balance of payments, where one finds quite extensive use of expenditure variables similar to $(y^* + NRT)$.

The final coefficient in equation (3.1) is a_5. It is aimed at capturing the type of adjustment emphasized in the monetary approach to the balance of payments. It is built in the style of disequilibrium economics, with increments to flow demand arising whenever unwanted stocks are present. I believe this is a far better way to represent the monetary approach than through continuous-equilibrium models, but that is another story. Here I only want to emphasize that the coefficient a_5 is dependent on our choice of period. An excess holding of $1000 of real monetary balances could give rise to extra spending of $50 within a week, $150 within a month, $300 within a quarter and $600 within a year, so a_5 could go from 0.05 to 0.60 for total spending, which in turn would be divided between tradables and nontradables.

There is clearly a kinship between the income–expenditure and the monetary approaches to balance-of-payments analysis. In putting the two together in the same model it is therefore important to avoid any implicit double-counting of effects. This could, for example, entail defining B_{jt} so as to exclude $a_5(M^s - M^d)/\bar{P}_d$. The best way to check on this is to set up a simple dynamic model and work through a series of simulations.

I want to keep the two approaches separate because I truly believe that we have learnt different important things from each. The monetary approach, in my view, called attention to a 'new' adjustment mechanism, whereby equilibrium could be restored (after, say, the printing of ΔM^s in a fixed-exchange-rate world) without there being any significant resort to either price adjustment or interest-rate changes. In the end, of course, this all happens through an induced loss of international reserves – that is, through a net resource transfer carried out through reducing the nation's foreign assets rather than increasing its foreign liabilities.

Is foreign borrowing an adjustment mechanism?

I cannot conclude this chapter without addressing an issue that has haunted me for some thirty years. I was very glad to be present as the monetary approach was unveiled and evolved at the University of Chicago in the late 1960s and early 1970s. I savoured every step of this development, feeling I was learning something both new and important. But in the end there was one troubling 'conclusion' – namely the sense that one got from many representatives of the monetary approach that somehow the RER didn't exist, or if it existed its equilibrium didn't vary much (or at all). As one who believes that real exchange-rate analysis brought in equally important new insights, I have always resisted this overtone in the monetary approach literature. But to confirm its existence consider the following recent citation: 'The equilibrating mechanism with financial integration is not the RER. Rather it is changes in banks' net financial position.'[2]

There is no question that a healthy capital market can do a lot to smooth out potential fluctuations in the short- or medium-term equilibrium RER. This is what private sector arbitrage (over time) would do; it is also what well-placed Central Bank intervention in a floating exchange-rate system would try to accomplish. In this way, borrowing can be used to spread the real costs, say, of a natural disaster, over a number of years. So yes, international borrowing operations have the capacity to smooth out RER fluctuations, and hold the RER to a time path that mainly reflects its long-term upward or downward drift. But this, to me, only says that borrowing helps when serious RER adjustment is not needed.

But what about the case of Japan, from the 1950s to the 1980s? Here a continual appreciation of the real exchange rate was *required* by differential productivity advances as between tradables and nontradables. Here, to prevent appreciation, that is, to make foreign currency more costly, would call for the country to lend, not borrow, abroad. This is precisely what Japan did, and massively so, being the principal supplier of funds to the international capital markets for decades – yet even that did not prevent a huge equilibrium appreciation of the yen.

Similarly, high levels of financial integration have not prevented very significant upward and downward movements in the real exchange rates of Germany, France and the United Kingdom.

The coefficient a_2 reflects the focus of the traditional 'elasticities approach'. The only thing to bear in mind here is that most of the elasticities literature deals with elasticities of demand for imports and/or of supply of exports, and not the elasticity of demand for tradables as such. So one would have to effect the requisite transformation. As a result, I would propose that the profession simply accept that foreign borrowing operates to reduce the equilibrium RER at times, while acts of repayment operate to raise it at times. A big current rise can be prevented by accepting a long series of imperceptible future increases, but when the true long-term equilibrium level of the RER changes, acts of borrowing cannot prevent fundamental RER adjustments from taking place through variations either in the nominal exchange rate E or in the domestic price level $\bar{P}_d$.

Notes

1. When all goods are divided into two composites C and G, the own-price elasticity of C consists of (minus) the unweighted *sum* of the cross-elasticities of C with respect to the prices of all components of G, or equivalently, of (minus) the value-weighted *average* of the cross-elasticities of all components of C with respect to the price of G. The elasticity of food w.r.t. the price of nontradables is thus one member of a set which, when averaged over all components of tradables, yields the own-price elasticity of tradables.
2. Juan Luis Moreno-Villalaz, 'Lessons From the Monetary Experience of Panama: a Dollar Economy With Financial Integration', *The Cato Journal*, 18 (3) (Winter 1999) p. 438.

4
Limiting Moral Hazard and Reducing Risk in International Capital Flows
The Choice of an Exchange-Rate Regime[1]
Ronald I. McKinnon

The current consensus in the academic literature, endorsed by the IMF and other international organizations, is that one of the main lessons of recent financial crises in East Asia and Latin America is the need for more flexible exchange-rate arrangements. Stanley Fischer, the Deputy Managing Director of the International Monetary Fund, stated the matter thus:

> There is a tradeoff between the greater short-run volatility of the real exchange rate in a flexible rate regime versus the greater probability of a clearly defined external crisis financial crisis when the exchange rate is pegged. The virulence of the recent crises is likely to shift the balance towards the choice of more flexible exchange rate systems, including crawling pegs with wide bands.
>
> (Fischer, 1999)

In her 1997 paper, 'Nominal Anchor Exchange Rate Policies as a Domestic Distortion', Anne Krueger agrees. She analyzes how pegging the exchange rate in order to slow ongoing domestic inflation creates a distortion in the capital market. As long as the peg holds and domestic inflation continues, the effective real rate of return (cost of capital) seen by domestic investors falls below the real return being garnered by foreign creditors. So, absent exchange controls, this differential encourages excess inflows of capital – as in Mexico before the 1994 crisis.

Although Krueger is surely right for the 'bad' fixes which she identifies, not all exchange rate fixes distort the international capital market. This chapter analyzes the choice of an exchange rate regime for 'emerging-market' economies – that is, those that are both less developed and net absorbers of private foreign capital. But it does not focus directly on the exchange rate's role in macroeconomic stabilization. Instead, I focus on how interest differentials between the centre country (the United States) and the periphery (emerging-market economies) influence the incentive to hedge against currency risk, hedging which limits the undue absorption of foreign capital. The underlying risk minimization problem is considered in two dimensions.

First, suppose that the term structure of domestic and international debt finance is quite short – as is now the case throughout the developing world, such as in East Asia and Latin America. Do fixed or floating exchange rates minimize the incentives for banks and nonbank corporations to borrow *without* covering forward their short-term foreign currency debts? Here, I shall distinguish between 'good' fixes and 'bad' fixes.

Second is the question of whether the term to maturity of private debt finance is itself endogenous to the nature of the exchange rate regime. Instead of accepting short-term bank deposits, borrowing internationally by issuing long-term bonds is itself a hedge against currency crises – and permits a faster recovery once such attacks occur. Here, I shall argue that a credible domestic monetary programme for stabilizing the exchange rate in the long run can lengthen the term to maturity of both national and international finance, and thereby reduce the exposure of an emerging-market economy to sudden reversals of investor sentiment leading to financial panics. But no exchange-rate regime, no matter how well chosen, can avoid the need for prudential regulation of domestic banks to hedge their short-term foreign exchange risks – regulation which, on occasion, could extend to exchange controls over short-term international capital flows. The regulatory problem of getting banks to hedge their foreign exchange risk is, of course, aggravated by moral hazard from deposit insurance – and from other sources of domestic and international bailouts should the payments mechanism be threatened by collective bank failures.

The exchange rate as nominal anchor:
the regulatory dilemma

With the important exception of Japan, a common East Asian monetary standard existed before the crises of 1997 (Frankel and Wei, 1994; Ohno, 1999). By keying on the dollar, the macroeconomic policies of the crisis economies – Indonesia, Korea, Malaysia, Philippines and Thailand were (loosely) tied to each other – and to those of the non-crisis economies of

Hong Kong, Singapore and Taiwan. Their dollar exchange rates had been fairly stable for more than a decade and, by the purchasing power parity criterion, were more or less correctly aligned with each other and with the American price level (McKinnon, 2000). Besides insulating each other from 'beggar-thy-neighbour' devaluations, these informal dollar pegs had successfully anchored their domestic (wholesale) price levels during their remarkably rapid economic growth in the 1980s through 1996. (Similarly, a credible peg of 360 yen to the dollar was the monetary anchor in Japan's own great era of high growth and rapid financial transformation in the 1950s and 1960s.)

In more open financial systems without exchange controls on capital accounts, is moral hazard from using the dollar exchange rate as a nominal anchor too high? Before the 1997 crisis, banks in the East Asian economies faced substantially higher nominal deposit rates in domestic currency than if they accepted eurodollar or euro-yen deposits. Figures 4.1–4.4, displayed on pages 60–3 for Indonesia, Malaysia, Thailand and Korea respectively show differentials between three-month deposits in domestic currency and those in eurodollars of the order of 2 to 10 per cent. (And these spreads would be 4 to 5 percentage points higher if the very low short-term euro-yen rates were compared to deposit rates in rupiahs, ringgits, baht, won, and so on.)

Wouldn't banks have greater incentive to borrow *unhedged* in dollars if the domestic exchange rate was pegged rather than floating? Superficially, it seems plausible that, for a given interest differential and short-term finance, a pegged exchange rate would encourage banks with moral hazard and other risk-loving agents to take the risk of borrowing in foreign exchange hoping that the exchange rate will not change within their short time-horizons. Whereas, if the exchange rate was floating, they would be more hesitant to do so.

> The Asian experience shows that a potential problem with using a nominal exchange rate anchor is that while the private sector is supposed to base its wage and price decisions on the assumption of a fixed nominal exchange rate, the supervisory authorities may want the private sector to hedge its external liabilities just in case the exchange rate cannot be held fixed.
>
> (Adams et al. 1998, p. 79)

The dilemma is a real one. Given that domestic interest rates in developing countries on the periphery are naturally higher than those in the centre country (the United States), then regulatory authorities must

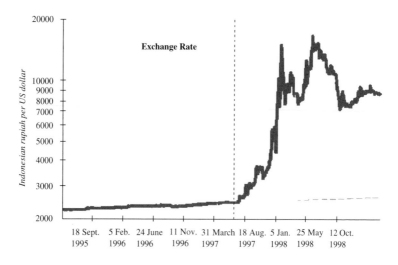

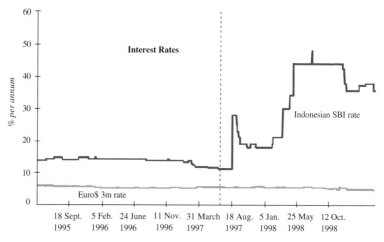

Figure 4.1   Indonesia

be ever-vigilant to prevent unhedged borrowing by individual banks (or even nonbank firms) in dollars and in other foreign currencies. Otherwise, as unhedged foreign currency liabilities cumulate, risk premia (to be defined below) in domestic interest rates may increase for the country as a whole. As domestic interest rates rise, further adverse

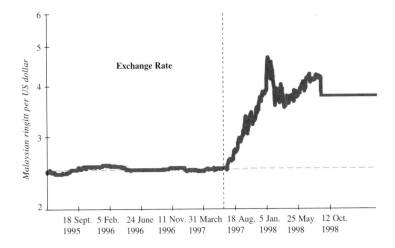

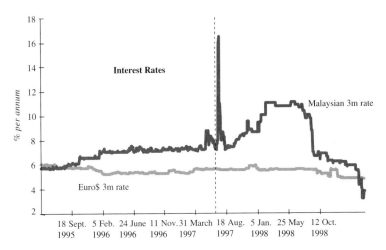

Figure 4.2 Malaysia

selection is triggered as more banks are tempted to borrow by accepting low interest foreign currency deposits. Because no interest rate can be found to price currency risk properly, the international capital market breaks down in the presence of a multitude of national monies.

Floating the exchange rate need not mitigate this regulatory dilemma. Under floating, the temptation to borrow unhedged at short term would

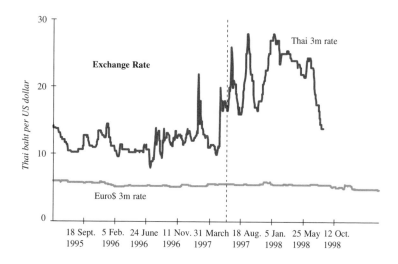

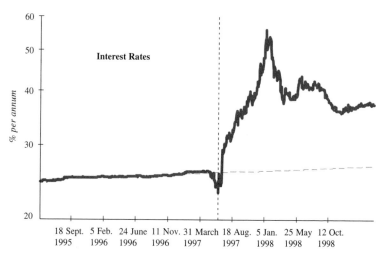

Figure 4.3   Thailand

still be there, and could even be augmented. For the East Asian economies, giving up on the dollar as a collective nominal anchor, and the considerable long-run benefits deriving from that, may yield no offsetting regulatory advantages to help contain moral hazard in domestic banks and other institutions. A simple algebraic model can show this trade off more precisely.

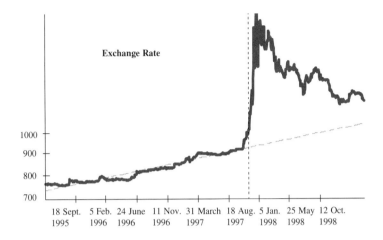

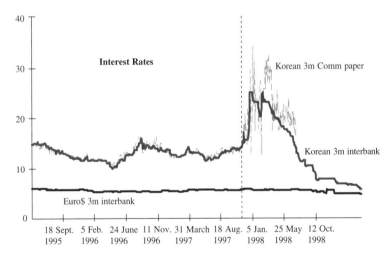

Figure 4.4 Korea

Modelling the super risk premium

Consider some interest rate identities for a given, fairly short, term to
maturity. Suppose no government controls on international payments
or domestic interest rates so that a well-organized market in currency
futures can exist. Then, by covered interest arbitrage, the (deposit)

interest differential is equal to the forward premium, that is,

$$i - i^* = f > 0 \qquad (4.1)$$

where

i = the domestic nominal (deposit) interest rate

i^* = the dollar (deposit) interest rate in the international capital market

f = the forward premium on dollars in domestic currency.

If domestic banks accepting dollar deposits at the low interest rate i^* cover by buying dollars forward, the cost of the forward cover per dollar so borrowed is simply f. Thus, the effective interest rate on hedged dollar deposits is $i^* + f$

$$i_{hedged} = i^* + f = i \qquad (4.2)$$

So, with forward covering, there is no net interest gain from accepting dollar deposits over accepting higher interest deposits in domestic currency. Hedged borrowers in foreign exchange see the same cost of capital as domestic banks accepting deposits denominated in the domestic currency.

Banks without moral hazard would voluntarily cover the exchange risk. They may well have accepted dollar deposits simply for convenience in clearing international payments. In contrast, poorly capitalized banks prepared to gamble on the basis of government deposit insurance might well accept low-cost dollar deposits as an ongoing source of finance for loans denominated in the domestic currency – unless a vigilant regulatory authority forces them to hedge.

But how much of the interest differential in equation (4.1) represents a 'margin of temptation' where banks with (latent) moral hazard will try to avoid regulatory sanctions and borrow in dollars anyway? Let us partition the interest differential into:

$$i - i^* = E\hat{e} + \rho_{currency} \qquad (4.3)$$

$\rho_{currency}$ is the currency risk premium as ordinarily defined. Apart from any unidirectional expected movement in the exchange rate, it represents the extra return required by investors to hold domestic rather than foreign currency assets. In the specific East Asian context, it represents domestic financial volatility – in interest rates or domestic price levels – measured against similar risk(s) prevailing in the markets of the centre country – that is, the United States. Thus $\rho_{currency}$ increases with that country's exchange rate volatility against the US dollar.

In the 'peripheral' Asian debtor countries, $\rho_{currency}$ is (was, before 1997) normally greater than zero. But it can be reduced toward zero if there is financial convergence with the United States, that is, the dollar exchange rate has been credibly stabilized through proper price-level alignment (PPP) so that interest rate volatility also approaches American levels.

The other component of the interest differential – the expected depreciation of the domestic currency, $E\hat{e}$ – can be decomposed into two parts. First, within a managed exchange rate regime with a crawling or constant peg (typical of a few South East Asian countries, Mexico, Brazil, and several emerging-market economies), the exchange rate can change predictably and smoothly according to government's policy announcements and commitments – such as the downward crawl in the Indonesian rupiah before the 1997 crash (Figure 4.1). Second, is the small probability of a 'regime change': a large, sudden devaluation whose timing is unpredictable.

$$E\hat{e} \equiv E\hat{e}_{predictable} + E\hat{e}_{regime\ change} \qquad (4.4)$$

Although both types of expected change in the exchange rate in (4.4) widen the nominal interest differential in (4.3), it is plausible that $E\hat{e}_{regime\ change}$ is part of the margin of temptation for banks with moral hazard to overborrow, while $E\hat{e}_{predictable}$ is not. If the exchange rate was expected to depreciate smoothly through time, even banks with very short time horizons will account for the higher domestic currency costs of repaying short-term foreign currency deposits. Therefore, we exclude $E\hat{e}_{predictable}$ from our measure of the *super risk premium*:

$$\rho_{super} = \rho_{currency} + E\hat{e}_{regime\ change} = i - i^* - E\hat{e}_{predictable} \qquad (4.5)$$

The super risk premium, ρ_{super}, represents the margin of temptation for banks to overborrow in foreign exchange beyond what they might do if forced to hedge. (Even if banks were required to hedge their foreign exchange exposure, McKinnon and Pill (1996, 1997) show that international overborrowing could still occur because banks with moral hazard assume too much domestic credit risk.) ρ_{super} has two components: the currency risk premium, as defined above; and the possibility that the regime could change through a discrete devaluation. The latter source of upward pressure on the interest rate on assets denominated in the domestic currency is sometimes called 'the peso problem'.

By borrowing unhedged in foreign currency, the domestic banks with deposit insurance and other government guarantees ignore downside bankruptcy risks implied by large devaluations whose timing is uncertain. They also ignore ongoing volatility in the exchange rate as measured by $\rho_{currency}$. In setting domestic nominal lending rates, the banks will only cover the 'predictable' component of the expected depreciation within the currency regime. In the special case where the nominal exchange rate is fixed, unhedged banks on lend at the international *nominal* interest rate plus a normal profit margin. For ease of macroeconomic exposition in this chapter, this profit margin between deposits and loans is simply set at zero.

The basic idea here is that the decision-making horizon of the bank with moral hazard is sufficiently short that it ignores unpredictable changes in the exchange rate. The managers of the bank simply hope that anything drastic, if it happens at all, won't happen 'on their watch'. The super risk premium in the interest differential then defines their margin of temptation to gamble and accept foreign currency deposits unhedged.

This incentive to gamble by a poorly supervised bank also extends to incurring undue risks with its domestic loan portfolio. McKinnon and Pill (1998, 1999) show how this domestic credit risk interacts with foreign exchange risk to lead to (potentially) enormous overborrowing in international markets. Using a large cross-country data base, Kaminsky and Reinhart (1999) link the prevalence of domestic banking (credit) crises to foreign exchange crises, that is, runs on the currency.

'Good' fixes versus 'bad' fixes versus floating

The debate over fixed versus floating exchange rates has been going on since the end of the Second World War and has many dimensions – not all of which can be covered here. For any emerging-market country where the dollar remains the safe-haven and reference currency as in Asia, Latin America, and elsewhere, the optimal choice of an exchange rate regime can be narrowed down to an exercise in minimizing the super risk premium. Assuming that there is potential moral hazard in banks, what exchange rate regime would minimize the margin of temptation to overborrow?

Like almost all protagonists in the debate, I initially abstract from term-structure considerations. That is, consider interest rates, exchange rates, risk premia, and so on, as if there was only one, fairly short, term to maturity – as in the algebraic framework developed above. (This assumption is relaxed below.) Under this analytical ground rule, did the Asian-five crisis economies make a mistake in pegging to the dollar before 1997?

The $E\hat{e}_{regime\ change}$ component of the super risk premium would seem to be higher under a pegged than under a floating exchange rate. Fixed exchange rates tend to break down on occasion. Even though the probability of a large discrete devaluation is small in any one decision interval, domestic interest rates can be driven up in the face of this possibility. Thus, at first glance, one might conclude that the margin of temptation, as measured by ρ_{super}, is higher when the exchange rate is being used as the nominal anchor. And for post-crisis East Asia, influential commentators, for example, the deputy managing director of the IMF, Stanley Fischer (1999), Barry Eichengreen (1999), Martin Wolf (1999) and George Soros (1999) have argued for greater exchange-rate flexibility.

But this line of argument overlooks $\rho_{currency}$, the other component of the super risk premium. For any given peripheral country, $\rho_{currency}$ depends on the stability of its exchange rate cum monetary regime – which largely depends on the robustness of its link to the world dollar standard. In times of crisis, the dollar is viewed as the safe-haven currency or definitive money; and, correspondingly, the yield on US Treasury bonds defines (in the argot of the finance literature) the 'risk-free' return. So if a country on the periphery of the dollar standard credibly integrates monetary policy with that of the United States – convergence in rates of price inflation to secure the exchange rate without the threat of using exchange controls – such a 'good fix' will be rewarded with a lower $\rho_{currency}$, and a low $E\hat{e}_{regime\ change}$. Before 1997, Malaysia seems to have come closest to this nirvana of using a good fix to minimize ρ_{super}. Figure 4.2 shows its short-term interest rate was closest (within 1 or 2 per cent) of the American.

Not under duress, now suppose a country voluntarily decides to 'abandon' the dollar standard as the nominal anchor and float its exchange rate. As long as the great mass of internationally tradable goods and services are dollar-invoiced and stable-valued, this experiment in monetary independence is somewhat difficult to define. Suppose the central bank does not directly key on its dollar exchange rate but aims to stabilize the domestic price level by other means. Then, in a dollar zone, success must still lead to a nearly stable exchange rate with the dollar (McKinnon, 2000).

But suppose our monetary authority is a more determined floater. Concerned with the potential moral hazard in banks from the exchange rate remaining stable, the Central Bank arranges policy so that the exchange rate continually moves like a 'random walk' per month or even per quarter. Then, because random exchange rate movements increase volatility in domestic-currency prices and interest rates, $\rho_{currency}$ also increases. And this increase in $\rho_{currency}$ will be aggravated if the country in question is a large foreign currency debtor.

In summary, moving from a 'good fix' to a floating exchange rate need not reduce the super risk premium and the margin of temptation for international overborrowing *ex ante*, that is, before any major attack on the currency. Under greater exchange rate flexibility, $\rho_{currency}$ will increase even if $E\hat{e}_{regime\ change}$ declines. (But even a floating exchange rate can be attacked, so $E\hat{e}_{regime\ change}$ is not negligible.)

Of course, a 'bad fix', that is, one which is obviously unsustainable because of, say, ongoing domestic fiscal deficits likely to be monetized (Russia and Brazil in 1998), or just with ongoing inflation as Krueger identified for Mexico before the 1994 crash, will make $E\hat{e}_{regime\ change}$ very large. Correspondingly high domestic interest rates relative to those prevailing in safe-haven-currency countries create a huge margin of temptation for unhedged international borrowing that could completely undermine the domestic system of prudential bank regulations (McKinnon and Pill, 1999). Here a more flexible but controlled exchange rate, perhaps a downward crawl which matches the internal rate of inflation, coupled with controls over international capital flows seems more likely to be the best way of coping with such an unfortunate situation.

But before the 1997 currency attacks, the East Asian pegs to the dollar looked like good fixes with purchasing power parity, price level stability, and fiscal balance. The problem wasn't with their exchange rate policies but with the weak prudential regulation of their financial systems. In defence of the regulators, however, the resulting overborrowing was aggravated by the erratic behaviour of the yen/dollar exchange rate and the extremely low nominal interest rates on borrowing in Japan in yen (McKinnon, 2000).

The restoration rule and the long-run confidence problem

In comparing 'good fixes' to floating to 'bad fixes', our short-run analysis of the super risk premium proceeded without specifying the term structure of interest rates and exchange-rate expectations into the more distant future. In common with the literature on the subject, we focussed on the incentives to overborrow *ex ante*, that is, before any speculative attack. Moreover, also in common with the literature, we did not specify the exchange-rate obligations of the authorities *after* a (successful) attack had occurred. In a model that had only one term to maturity, we defined a good fix to be one where any peripheral country maintained nominal exchange rate stability and purchasing power parity against the centre country's currency *ex ante*.

However, implicit in the ideal of a good fix is that it is sustainable in the more distant future. Even if a surprise speculative attack upsets the fixed rate system in the short run, the macroeconomic fundamentals and the determination of the authorities would still allow the economy to recover its nominal exchange-rate and price-level equilibrium in the long run. If such a favourable long-run expectation could be sustained, this would prevent – or at least limit – the kind of fundamental loss of confidence in their currencies that the five Asian countries actually experienced in late 1997 and early 1998.

The behaviour of countries operating under the international gold standard before 1914 is instructive. In the face of a liquidity crisis, a country would sometimes resort to gold devices – that is, it would raise the buying price for gold or interfere with its exportation. This amounted to a minor, albeit temporary, suspension of its traditional gold parity. In more major crises, including wars, a few outright suspensions for some months or years occurred. After any suspension and devaluation, however, the gold standard generally succeeded in having countries return to their traditional mint parities. The resulting long-run stability in exchange rates helped anchor the common price level and long-term interest rates. In early 1914, exchange rates, wholesale prices, and interest rates in the industrial countries were virtually the same as they had been in the late 1870s.

This gave the pre-1914 gold standard great long-run resilience. After any short-run crisis that forced the partial or complete suspension of a gold parity, the country in question was obliged to return to its traditional parity as soon as practicable (Bordo and Kydland, 1995). I have dubbed this unwritten obligation of the classical gold standard 'the restoration rule' (McKinnon, 1996, ch. 2). Even when a currency crisis undermined the government's ability to sustain convertibility in the near term, longer-term exchange-rate expectations remained regressive with respect to the country's traditional gold parity. Because of the restoration rule, long-term interest rates showed little volatility by modern standards (McKinnon and Ohno, 1997, ch. 8); and, without significant financial risk, their levels also remained low: about 3 per cent in the UK and 4 per cent in the United States.

For the pre-1914 gold standard, Goodhart and Delargy (1998) studied how high-growth debtor countries on the periphery of Britain responded to speculative attacks. Their sample included Austria, Argentina, Australia, Italy and the United States (which experienced several attacks). They conclude:

> The onset and initial context of the Asian crisis, involving an inter-
> action between a toppling investment boom and a febrile banking
> system, should not have been surprising. From an historical point of
> view, it was depressingly familiar. Moreover, it will happen again
> and again. Much of the pattern is, probably, an inherent feature of
> development.
>
> What, however, differed from our pre-1914 crises and the Asian cri-
> sis was the international monetary regime and the consequential
> implications for post-crisis monetary conditions in the affected coun-
> tries. Confidence in the maintenance of the gold standard, pre-1914,
> led to stabilizing mean-reverting expectations, and hence a rapid
> restoration of gold reserves, liquidity, and low interest rates alongside
> the maintenance of continued price stability. In the main case in our
> pre-1914 sample where there was no such confidence (Argentina),
> pressures on the exchange rate were eased by a (debt) moratorium,
> allowing a sharply improving trade balance to bring about the needed
> monetary expansion.
>
> (Goodhart and Delargy, 1998, p. 285)

The parallel for a restored East Asian dollar standard is quite clear. Each
central bank sets its long-run monetary policy to be consistent with
maintaining a 'traditional' exchange rate against the dollar within a narrow band, which amounts to having the same long-run rate of price
inflation (optimally zero) in its producer price index as in the United
States. (This does not rule out slowly gliding bands as followed by
Indonesia and Singapore before 1997.) Each central bank also announces
that it will normally adjust short-run interest rates and intervene to keep
its exchange rate within the band. But faced with a massive speculative
attack, the central bank may well suspend the fixed rate temporarily by
temporarily floating – and not raise short-term interest rates to exorbi-
tant levels to defend it.

However, this is not the end of the story. As soon as practicable after
the speculative attack, the distressed country's central bank would begin
nudging its exchange rate back up toward its traditional dollar parity.
Allowing for temporary crisis-based suspensions of the fixed exchange
rate, followed by (gradual) restoration of the traditional parity, poses
problems for speculators. They don't have any clear point at which
to get out of their short position in the domestic currency in order to

realize speculative profits. In contrast, a more or less discrete devaluation in response to a speculative attack, with no attempt at restoration, makes it easy for speculators to get out safely. Paradoxically, even though speculators know that temporary suspensions of the fixed exchange rate are possible, speculative attacks may diminish if they also know in advance that the restoration rule is in place.

In highly indebted economies, the worst possible trade-off is sharply higher domestic interest rates and deep devaluations that cause massive bankruptcies throughout the economy. The forced suspension of the exchange rate peg is accompanied by such policy disarray that people see *no* future for the dollar value of their currencies, and lose confidence completely – as more or less happened in the Asian five.

To stem this loss of confidence, each affected Asian government should have announced their intention to restore their traditional dollar parities as soon the dust settled. To be sure, renegotiating the external debt to greatly lengthen its term structure while improving the prudential regulation of the banks would be an important part of the necessary reforms. So would keeping the lid on actual and prospective fiscal deficits. (Remember Keynesian counter-cyclical policies can't work, or work perversely, in a confidence crisis.) All would contribute to the credibility of restoring the traditional exchange rate.

Even better to have the restoration rule in place before any speculative attack. It should be one of the 'normal' operating rules of the International Monetary Fund. Once a group of neighbouring countries, as in East Asia, all have the same commitment to exchange stability in the long run, contagion would be better contained. Indeed, a speculative attack on any one of them becomes less likely to begin with.

By late 1998, Thailand and Korea had already made substantial progress in nudging their exchange rates back up, and have been rewarded by their domestic interest rates coming back down to single-digit levels (Figures 4.3 and 4.4 respectively). But, by delaying the implementation of this 'restoration rule', their currencies were left undervalued for too long – leading to so much domestic price inflation that the original exchange rate 'parities' became too difficult to retrieve.

Perhaps because France had suffered from numerous confidence crises since the Second World War, in the early 1990s it provided the best modern example of a country more promptly following the restoration rule. The massive speculative attack against the franc in September 1993 forced a virtual suspension of the ERM bilateral parity grid: official exchange rate margins were widened from 2.25 per cent to a ridiculous ± 15 per cent. Yet, within a few weeks, the franc–mark exchange rate quickly returned to its traditional level; and French short- and long-term interest rates closely tracked German ones in the 1990s. So quickly was the mark–franc exchange rate restored that the devaluation had a negligible effect on the French price level. Because France's monetary and fiscal 'fundamentals' were not misaligned with Germany's, restoration was easy – even though defending against the initial massive attack was impossible.

Lengthening the term structure of finance: general lessons

Is there a general lesson here about the feasibility of freely floating exchange rates among different classes of economies? In his chapter titled 'The Confidence Game', Paul Krugman (1999) identifies the differences thus:

> It seems, in other words, that there is a sort of double standard enforced by the markets. The common view among economists that floating rates are the best, if imperfect, solution to the international monetary trilemma was based on the experience of countries like Canada, Britain, and the United States. And sure enough, floating exchange rates work pretty well for First World Countries, because markets are prepared to give those countries the benefit of the doubt. But since 1994 one Third World country after another – Mexico, Thailand, Indonesia, Korea, and most recently, Brazil – has discovered that it cannot expect the same treatment. Again and again, attempts to engage in moderate devaluations have led to a drastic collapse in confidence. And so now markets believe that devaluations in such countries are terrible things; and because markets believe this, they are.
>
> (Krugman, 1999, p. 111)

Krugman makes an important distinction. To cushion the effects of the fall in primary products prices caused by the Asian crisis, Australian and Canadian exporters of primary products could let their currencies float downwards without capital controls and not be attacked. Why? Because expectations for the Australian and Canadian dollars were already regressive: during the course of the downward float, people expected the rates to come back. Both were mature-market economies with (1) credible internal monetary policies (independent central banks) for targeting their domestic price levels over the long run; and (2) relatively long terms to maturity for their internal and external debts. (In Asia, the non-crisis creditor countries of Taiwan and Singapore were (are) more like mature capitalist ones in these respects.)

Of course, (1) and (2) are complementary. Only with long-term confidence in the purchasing power of domestic money (against the centre country's) would exchange-rate expectations be naturally regressive, and are long-term bond and mortgage markets possible to organize. And having finance at longer term bolsters the credibility of the central bank to hit its inflation targets over the longer term. However, even in Canada – where the structure of finance is fairly long and where the Bank of Canada had, by 1991, put a highly credible domestic monetary regime not dissimilar to the American for limiting inflation in place – medium-term misalignments of the Canadian dollar with the American have created unhappiness.

The run up of the Canadian dollar from 1988 to peak at 89 cents in 1991 seemed to many observers to overvalue the Canadian dollar and aggravate the recession of 1991–92. Similarly, the fall of the Canadian dollar to touch 63 US cents in early 1999 seems to be all out of proportion to Canada's now modest dependence on primary products exports. Because of the high degree of trade dependence with the United States, feeling was widespread that this fall reduced Canadian living standards. In June 1999, in a report from the C. D. Howe Institute in Queens University, two of Canada's most distinguished economists wrote:

> Canada's experience with a floating exchange rate has been disappointing. The floating dollar has been prone to major misalignments, as its current weakness demonstrates, that put Canada at a disadvantage in the North American competition for physical and human capital investment. As the Canadian economy becomes more open to trade and investment flows, and those flows become more focussed on the United States, the benefits of greater fixity with the US dollar are growing.
>
> (Courchene and Harris, 2000, p. 1)

To be sure, there are influential critics of the Courchene–Harris report: Laidler (1999) and Murray (2000) believe that the Canadian dollar should continue to float. Nevertheless, the Canadian experience suggests that, while 'First-World' countries can allow their exchange rates to float freely without being attacked as most 'Third-World' would be, the resulting swings in the exchange rate may still be uncomfortably wide in the absence of any firm long-run exchange rate objective. Even with a stable internal monetary standard in place (a believable set of monetary procedures for targeting and stabilizing the domestic price level), regressive exchange rate expectations are not strong enough to prevent damaging medium-term fluctuations.

Now return to our 'emerging-market' debtor economy where the term structure of finance is short and where there is no history of central bank independence. Its government would be even more hard pressed than Canada's to put a purely internal monetary standard in place that convincingly pinned down the domestic price level (relative to the centre country's) over the long run. Indeed, in most Third World economies – including the Asian five – the central bank has often been commandeered to provide cheap credit for promoting exports, subsidizing commercial banks, and otherwise directing credit in line with the government's development programme. Sometimes, this strategy has been facilitated by ringing the country with capital controls.

Correspondingly, there is a potential lack of confidence in the long-term exchange rate *unless* the government can effectively restrain itself. By credibly pegging to the dollar, the central bank shows the market that it is prepared to limit growth in domestic base money and avoid future inflation despite its lack of independence. Before 1997, during their 'miracle' growth phases, the East Asian economies successfully pegged to the dollar as the nominal anchor for their domestic price levels. With the benefit of hindsight, however, we now know that this policy was seriously incomplete. First, and most obviously, there was the failure to properly regulate the financial system – including the central bank itself in some cases – against undue risk taking including short-term foreign exchange exposure.

Second, and more subtly, the East Asian debtor economies had not committed themselves to long-term exchange-rate stability in the mode of the nineteenth century gold standard – even though they seemed to be securely pegged in the short and medium terms. Because of the short-term structure of finance, each was vulnerable to a speculative attack on its currency; but none had a long-run exchange-rate strategy in place to mitigate the worst consequences of any such attack. That is, there was no restoration rule for keeping exchange-rate expectations regressive.

In part, the problem arose because the pre-1997 East Asian dollar standard was informal rather than formal. With exception of Hong Kong, none of the countries involved had formally declared a dollar parity – and each had been classified by the IMF as following some variety of 'managed floating' rather than being a dollar pegger (McKinnon, 2000). After any forced suspension, there was no traditional (gold) parity in the nineteenth-century sense to which the government was obviously bound to return.

Probably the biggest problem, however, was philosophical. In the endless debate on fixed versus floating exchange rates, academic economists on either side have failed to take the term to maturity of the exchange rate into account. Given the great asymmetry among national monies, I have been arguing that countries on the periphery of the dollar standard will always be subject to speculative attacks and (attempted) flight into dollars. (The small countries in Eastern Europe are similarly situated on the periphery of the euro standard.)

But emerging-market economies whose macroeconomic fundamentals are sound so as to permit a 'good fix' for their exchange rates should extend the maturity of that commitment to the distant future, that is, adopt the restoration rule explicitly – and, ideally, collectively. (Of course, those that must rely on the inflation tax, and cannot credibly commit to long-run exchange rate stability, should not try it.) Indeed, the benefits from having the exchange rate pinned down in the long run exceed those from having a hard short-term fix. With regressive exchange-rate expectations and the future price level more secure, the authorities can seriously encourage the lengthening of the term structure of domestic and foreign finance. As long-term bond issues in the nineteenth-century mode begin to displace short-term bank finance, the government's commitment to long-term exchange rate stability is naturally reinforced.

In summary, suppose that the long-run monetary, fiscal and price-level fundamentals of an 'emerging-market' country could be sustainable. Nevertheless, the national currency is subject to a massive speculative attack – possibly aggravated by contagion from neighbouring countries. Then temporary suspension of official intervention should be coupled with the promise of eventually restoring the initial par value of the currency. Despite some unavoidable temporary currency depreciation, our restoration rule would maintain regressive expectations and limit capital flight.

This has several advantages:

In the *short run*, the government under attack isn't forced to increase near-term interest rates so sharply in a cyclical downturn – or when its banks are particularly weak from maturity mismatches. The expectation of eventual exchange-rate appreciation minimizes (but need not eliminate) the need to increase short-term interest rates to assure the markets that restoration is in prospect.

In the *medium run*, when the errant exchange rate is nudged back up, the contagion from 'accidental' competitive devaluation is mitigated. Despite a temporary devaluation at the outset of the attack, the other countries within the Asian dollar standard need not worry about persistent 'beggar-thy-neighbour' policies. Moreover, within the domestic economy, the bankruptcy threat to foreign-currency debtors is diminished.

In the *long run*, the central bank can keep the domestic price level consistent with eventually restoring its 'traditional' dollar exchange parity. Domestic inflation would not spiral out of control. If the domestic bond market were open, long-term interest rates would remain fairly stable at levels close to those in the United States. Indeed, only with a credible commitment to long-term exchange rate stability in place, is it possible to develop a long-term domestic bond market – so vital for reducing term-structure risk in a reformed banking system.

Note

1. I would like to thank Huw Pill of the Harvard Business School and the ECB for his ideas and help in preparing this paper.

References

Adams, C., Mathieson, D. J., Shinasi, G., and Chada, B., *International Capital Markets: Developments, Prospects and Key policy Issues* (Washington, DC: International Monetary Fund, September 1998).

Bordo, M., and Kydland, F., 'The Gold Standard as a Rule: An Essay in Exploration', *Explorations in Economic History*, 32 (October 1995) 423–64.

Courchene, T., and Harris, R., 'North American Monetary Union: Analytical Principles and Operational Guidelines', *The North American Journal of Economics and Finance*, 11(1) (August 2000) 3–18.

Eichengreen, B., 'Building on a Consensus', *Financial Times* (2 February 1999).

Fischer, S., 'On the need for a lender of last resort' (New York: address to the American Economic Association, 3 January 1999).

Frankel, J. A., and Wei, S. J., 'Yen Bloc or Dollar Bloc? Exchange Rate Policies in the East Asian Economies', in T. Ito and A. Krueger (eds), *Macroeconomic Linkage: Savings, Exchange Rates, and Capital Flows* (Chicago: University of Chicago Press, 1994).

Goodhart, C., and Delargy, P. J. R., 'Financial Crises: Plus ça Change, plus c'est la Même Chose', *International Finance*, 1 (2) (December 1998) 261–88.

Kaminsky, G., and Reinhart, C., 'The Twin Crises: Balance of payments and banking crises in developing countries', *American Economic Review*, 89 (3) (June 1999) 473–500.

Krueger, A. O., 'Nominal Anchor Exchange Rate Policies as a Domestic Distortion', *Center for Research on Economic Development and Policy Reform*, Working Paper no. 2 (February 1997).

Krugman, P., *The Return of Depression Economics* (New York: W. W. Norton, 1999).

Laidler, D., 'The Exchange Rate Regime and Canada's Monetary Order', Bank of Canada, working paper 99–7 (March 1999).

McKinnon, R. I., 'The East Asian dollar standard, life after death?', *Economic Notes*, 29(1) February 2000.

McKinnon, R. I., *The Rules of the Game: International Money and Exchange Rates* (Cambridge, MA: MIT Press, 1996).

McKinnon, R. I., and Ohno, K., *Dollar and Yen: Resolving Economic Conflict Between the United States and Japan* (Cambridge, MA: MIT Press, 1997). (Japanese Translation, Nihon Keizai Shimbun, 1998.)

McKinnon, R. I., and Pill, H., 'Credible Liberalizations and International Capital Flows: the Overborrowing Syndrome', in T. Ito and A. O. Krueger (eds), *Financial Deregulation and Integration in East Asia*, NBER (University of Chicago Press, 1996) pp. 7–48.

McKinnon, R. I., and Pill, H., 'Credible Liberalizations and Overborrowing', *American Economic Review* (May 1997) pp. 189–93.

McKinnon, R. I. and Pill, H., 'International Overborrowing: A Decomposition of Credit and Currency Risk', *World Development*, 26 (7) (July 1998) 1267–82.

McKinnon, R. I. and Pill, H., 'Exchange Rate Regimes for Emerging Markets: Moral Hazard, and International Overborrowing', *Oxford Review of Economic Policy*, 15 (3) (Autumn 1999), pp. 19–38.

Murray, J., 'Why Canada Needs a Flexible Exchange Rate', *The North American Journal of Economics and Finance*, 11(1) (August 2000) 41–60.

Ohno, K., 'Exchange Rate Management in Developing Asia: a Reassessment of the Pre-crisis Soft Dollar Zone', ADBI Working Paper 1, Asian Development Bank, Tokyo (January 1999).

Soros, G., 'To Avert the Next Crisis', *Financial Times* (4 January 1999).

Wolf, M., 'Pegging Out', *Financial Times* (January 1999).

5
Developing-Countries' Trade Policies in the 1990s: Back to the Future[1]

Sarath Rajapatirana

Introduction

Developing-countries' trade policies in the 1990s owe much to the events of the 1980s. Many events had helped to shape trade policies of developing countries in the 1980s. Of these, the economic crises of that decade, which led some to condemn it as the 'lost decade', spawned unprecedented policy reforms.[2] The reforms that began in the 1980s continued in the 1990s. Despite the East Asian crisis that began at the end of 1997, the 1990s were less turbulent than the 1980s. However, the participation of developing countries as full members in the Uruguay Round (UR) negotiations was a decisive factor in their 1990s liberalizations.

Anne Krueger has provided the profession with a comprehensive framework to analyze trade policies in her celebrated work with Jagdish Bhagwati. Their National Bureau of Economic Research (NBER) project (Bhagwati, 1978) that studied trade policies of developing countries in the 1960s and 1970s has changed the ways that the profession looks at trade regimes. In addition, she played a singular role as Vice President of Economic Research Staff during in the early to mid-1980s to persuade the World Bank to place trade reforms at the top of its structural adjustment programmes.[3]

The work of Anne Krueger and of many contributors to this volume strengthened the theoretical and empirical case for more open trade policies that eventually led to widespread trade liberalizations. Their work provides us with the basis to judge the trade regimes that have come into being in the 1990s. Despite the reforms, these regimes are still far from the ideal regime of low levels and low variance in protection based on tariffs and characterized by transparency. Hence there is an unfinished agenda for trade reform. Meanwhile, new challenges to further reform have arisen and new forms of trade restrictions have begun to appear as the old forms of restrictions were being reined in. A new round of multilateral trade negotiations is needed to lay the basis to address the unfinished agenda of domestic trade reforms and to meet the new challenges to liberal trade policies. A period of reforms much like the 1980s is needed, which suggests a back-to-the-future strategy. There are, of course, many other items that go beyond the domestic agenda. They are not discussed in this chapter.

This chapter is divided into six sections. The next section places developing-countries' trade trends in the 1990s in a global context. Then, the chapter recounts the factors that led to the reforms. This is followed by a discussion of the main trends in reforms at the country level in relation to a twenty-country sample. The fifth section reviews the main issues that arise from the reforms and the new challenges, and then identifies a future agenda for reforms. Finally, some conclusions are drawn.

Developing-countries' trade trends

During 1990–97, world trade (export and import volumes) grew by 6.5 per cent per year and developing-countries' exports by 8.7 per cent per year. While 1997 saw the East Asian Crisis that led to a reduction in export growth in that region, the growth rate of exports of developing countries in the first seven years of the 1990s has been substantial. World output grew at 2.3 per cent per year over the 1990–97 period and developing-countries' output grew at 3.1 per cent per year (World Bank, 1999). These economies also became more integrated with the world economy. Estimates of developing-countries' trade openness (as indicated by their trade ratios) show an equally good performance (Drabek and Laird, 1998). Meanwhile, the value of world trade in services grew at an annual rate of 8 per cent during the 1990s. The export of services, which started from a low base, grew faster than goods trade during the same period. Still, developing countries remained as net importers of services. These averages mask many differences in the performances of individual countries and regions during the 1990s. The East Asian countries led the way in the growth of exports and changed the patterns of trade between developed and developing countries permanently. First, manufactured goods exports from developing countries were the fastest growing component of trade, led by East Asian countries. They averaged around 12–15 per cent growth per year during the 1990s, continuing a trend that started in the late 1960s when these countries began to liberalize their trade regimes. Second, there was a decline in trade in mining products from developing countries following the fall in oil prices. The previous decade had started with the second oil shock in 1979–80, when oil prices rose to unprecedented levels. Third, there was an increase in intra-regional trade among developing countries, in part due to the unilateral liberalizations and in part due to the reduction in trade barriers against one another on a preferential basis under regional trading arrangements (RTAs). Latin America led the developing world in rejuvenating and creating RTAs. Finally, Africa had the slowest growth in trade in the 1990s due to a combination of its slower liberalization and its commodity composition concentrated in primary products.

Developing-countries' trade policies in the 1990s differed from those of the 1980s in terms of dominant themes and policy experiences of different groups of countries. Anne Krueger has analyzed the trade policies of the 1980s with her characteristic depth and insight. That analysis provides us with a sound starting point to examine the trade policies of developing countries in the 1990s. She found that trade policies of developing countries in the 1980s were less restrictive than those of the 1970s (Krueger, 1990, p. 102). On the same basis, we can say that the trade policies of the 1990s are less restrictive than those of the 1980s and, for that matter, than anytime in the post-Second World War period for most developing countries.

There is no better way to demonstrate these differences than to contrast the emerging themes of the 1990s with the themes that Anne Krueger had identified for the 1980s (see Krueger, 1990). First, in contrasting the trade regimes of the 1980s with the period 1950–80, she noted that there was increased differentiation in trade policies among the developing countries. This followed from the fact that many East Asian countries took the lead in liberalizing their trade regimes while nearly all other developing countries had maintained restrictive trade regimes. In the 1990s, there is less differentiation since nearly all the developing countries had begun to liberalize their trade regimes.

Second, she observed a long-term trend towards less restrictive trade regimes. In the 1990s, trade reform has become a unifying goal; the differences lie only in the speed of liberalizations. The responses to reforms have differed among countries depending on the strength and credibility of the initial reforms and the different country settings. A third aspect of the trade reforms of the 1980s she noted was that developing countries were becoming more integrated with the world economy in both trade and capital flows than in the previous three decades. This is certainly the case in the 1990s. Measured by trade intensity indexes (exports and imports as a ratio of GNP), developing countries are more closely integrated in trade than ever before. And they are also closely integrated into the world capital market. The amount of net private capital flows to developing countries rose by five fold from the mid-1980s to the mid-1990s (IMF, 1998). While it is beyond the scope of the present analysis to explore the consequences of integration into the world capital market, manufactured exports from the developing countries have become closely linked to private foreign direct investment (FDI) in the export sectors. That has become possible with the reduction of bias against exports due to trade liberalization and to the more hospitable environment created for private FDI in most of the developing countries through the reform of their regulatory regimes in the 1990s.

Finally, in the early 1980s, real oil prices reached a peak and mining products had a large share of the total exports of developing countries. In the 1990s, many developing countries moved from a position of primary products exporters (agriculture and mining products) to become exporters of manufactures on a wider scale than before. This happened in part due to the changed economic environment of the 1990s and in part due to the decline in the real price of oil, which fell to its lowest level since the early 1970s and reduced the size of oil exports in total exports. In the mid- to late 1990s, agriculture export prices also fell, giving greater weight in value to manufactures. The success of manufactured exports from developing countries can be seen in the increase in their share in total exports of developing countries from 17 per cent in 1980 to 24 per cent in the 1990s.

As noted above, despite the East Asian crisis of 1997, the decade has been less turbulent than the 1980s. Many of the countries that were in desperate situations in the 1980s have been able to stage good recoveries due to reforms and the return of private FDI to developing countries. The irony is that some of the East Asian countries, such as Malaysia, South Korea and Thailand, that had been setting a strong pace of export growth, fell victim to their own success in the late 1990s. The crisis was mainly due to the weaknesses in their financial systems, a lack of vigilance in the conduct of macroeconomic policies which led to the appreciation of exchange rates, and the recession in Japan that reduced the demand for their exports.

Factors that led to the policy reforms

If the 1980s was the decade of initiating reforms, the 1990s was a decade of continuing them. There was less urgency to undertake reforms in the

1990s compared to the 1980s. Nevertheless many developing countries undertook trade reforms in the present decade that led to more liberal trade regimes than before, for a host of factors discussed below.

The 1980s was a decade of crises, starting with the second oil shock of 1979–81, a debt shock that began when Mexico was unable to service its debt, the rise in interest rates as United States' monetary policy was targeted to reduce double-digit inflation, and the worldwide recession that ensued. While these negative shocks led to crises in the majority of developing countries except for the oil exporters, they were not wholly external in origin. In many cases the crises were mainly home grown following consumption and investment booms in the mid- to late 1970s. Irrespective of the origin of the crises, they led to reforms, which are now termed 'new liberalizations' (see Little et al., 1993, and Corden, this volume). The crisis broke existing coalitions that had supported the protectionist regimes and also led to the emergence of new coalitions led by reformist leaders. Consequently, policy makers found it easy to push through reforms when the alternative of not reforming became increasingly politically costly. In a sample of twenty countries discussed in the fourth section of this chapter, there was only one case in which reforms were undertaken without crisis. That was Colombia in 1991. The impetus for it came from a leadership change, when Cesar Gaviria assumed office as President of Colombia. He was deeply committed to trade reforms and reduced a planned four-year programme of trade reform into 18 months (Rajapatirana et al., 1997).

A second factor that led to the continuation and consolidation of trade reforms in the 1990s was that the intellectual case for it was being strengthened by new research. New lines of research have been particularly supportive of trade policy reforms. These are the creation of endogenous growth models by Romer (1986), Lucas (1988) and others that permitted the analysis of policy reforms within a growth model. The other was the empirical work associated with Dollar (1992), Sachs and Warner (1995), and Edwards (1997), among others. Their work built on the foundation of empirical work of Little, Scitovsky and Scott, and Balassa, Bhagwati and Krueger in the 1970s. Both new ideas and empirical results have been carried through to policy makers in different forms and channels.

In the 1980s many of the policy makers were well-versed in theoretical and empirical work on trade. Perhaps the best example of this is from Latin America where many of the trade and finance ministers were economists trained in the United States. Also in the process of discussing trade components in structural adjustment loans between

World Bank staff and developing-country policy makers, there was an important transfer of knowledge and experience (Edwards, 1997). Moreover, the results of trade reforms were easy to see in the East Asian economies where trade reforms had been associated with the region's remarkable output and export growth.

There were detractors from the line of argument that liberalized trade regimes based on neutral incentives were at least in part responsible for the stellar economic performance. Amsden (1989), Wade (1990) and Lall (1996) prominently have advanced the idea that it was selective promotion of specific sectors and well-targeted public investment that led to economic success. Dani Rodrik (1992) has also been very sceptical about across-the-board trade liberalizations, although he has not advocated the selective promotion of specific industries. However, the case for selective intervention does not seem to have convinced policy makers in many other parts of the world. In Latin America, for example, strong reforms were undertaken in the 1990s that followed the mainstream paradigm of neutral incentives. In addition, the case for strong reforms was supported by the negative lesson arising from the collapse of the Soviet model that had in the past been emulated by countries like India.

A third factor that facilitated trade reforms of the 1990s was the negotiations leading to the signing of the Uruguay Round (UR) Agreements. The preparation for the round brought trade issues to the centre stage and helped provide an external force to bear on domestic policies of developing countries, committing them to reduce trade barriers and bind their tariffs. While domestic crises created the impetus for trade reform, the UR provided a mechanism to reduce barriers and to link it to an external guard against slippage. To be sure there are many aspects of the round that could have served a liberal trade environment better, but it did create the atmosphere for trade reform in the 1990s.

Developing countries had been reluctant to participate in previous rounds since many items of interest to them such as textiles, clothing and agriculture were not included in the agenda for negotiations. On the other hand, they could have influenced the agenda by participating in the multilateral trade negotiations. Instead, they had preferred to 'free ride' when developed countries had reduced barriers on a most-favoured-nation (MFN) basis. They had invoked 'special and differential' treatment as the reason for not entering into reciprocal negotiations with developed countries. That position thawed in the 1990s for several reasons: (i) Given the increasingly strong intellectual position that liberalized trade was good for developing countries, multilateral trade negotiations that could lead to liberalized trade became attractive. (ii) Developing countries realized that they would lose out by not participating, since they could influence the agenda for negotiations. (iii) There was increasing realization by developing countries that the benefits of 'special and differential' treatment they received under the Generalized System of Preferences were not great, nor were these concessions bound. (iv) Since many developing countries had become important players in world trade, particularly in manufactures, they would not be allowed to 'free ride' by the developed countries. Consequently, developing countries joined GATT and later WTO in larger numbers than ever before. By 1998, WTO had some 132 members and some 32 countries were in the process of negotiating entry. Almost all the new members who are still waiting in the wings are developing countries and transition economies. In other words, the 1990s saw an unprecedented increase in the participation of developing countries in the multilateral trading system, accepting its laws and processes and attempting to secure increased access to the world market on a bound basis.

A fourth factor facilitating increased trade liberalization in the 1990s was the adoption of flexible exchange rates by many developing countries. Changes in domestic prices came to be reflected in the exchange rates, thus removing a constraint on trade liberalization that had existed in the 1960s and 1970s. Very few trade liberalizations by developing countries were associated with fixed exchange rates for reasons that are clearly articulated in Max Corden's contribution to this volume.

Finally, the international financial institutions (the World Bank and the IMF) along with the GATT/WTO continued their support for trade reform. The World Bank had led the way in the 1980s with its support for trade reforms, though this support declined in the 1990s with the decline in structural adjustment lending (Krueger and Rajapatirana, 1999). On the other hand, the IMF (1998) has increasingly included trade policy conditions in its Stand-by programmes. The creation of the WTO, the bringing of agriculture and services within a multilateral trade discipline, the establishment of the trade policy review mechanism, as well as the newly refurbished dispute settlement mechanism have all contributed to a more favourable environment for further trade liberalization.

Reform trends in the 1990s in a twenty-country sample

In this section, we look at a twenty-country sample to identify the main trends in trade policy reforms in the 1990s at the individual country level. The sample is sufficiently diverse to represent developing countries in general. It includes the relatively rich developing countries (middle income as defined in the World Bank atlas) such as Argentina, Chile, South Korea and Venezuela, and poor countries such as India, Kenya, Nigeria, Sri Lanka and Pakistan. It also includes countries with large populations such as India, Indonesia and Brazil, and less populous countries such as Bolivia and Costa Rica. There are relatively more industrialized countries such as Brazil, Mexico and South Korea, and countries that are mostly agricultural such as Côte d'Ivoire, Kenya and Thailand. Three countries out of the twenty are oil exporters – namely Cameroon, Indonesia and Mexico. Moreover, the countries in the sample are from four continents.

The time period chosen to identify the trends in developing-countries' trade policies is 1985–96. As noted above, many countries had begun trade reform earlier in the 1980s in response to crises. Many others had begun reforms even earlier in the 1970s and some, such as South Korea, in the 1960s. If we had limited the period to the 1990s, we would not have been able to identify the main trends for the decade since many countries had already undertaken reforms. Consequently, it would give the impression that these countries did not undertake reforms when, in fact, they had undertaken strong reforms one or two decades before.

Many countries in the sample undertook reforms in the 1990s (years of reforms are indicated in parentheses). These were Argentina (1991–93), Brazil (1990–92), Cameroon (1990–94), Colombia (1990–91), Costa Rica (1992), Côte d'Ivoire (1994), India (1991–92), Kenya (1991–95), Nigeria (1995), Pakistan (1994), Thailand (1990) and Venezuela (1996).

One group of countries in the sample undertook strong reforms in the 1970s and 1980s which qualify them not only as early reformers but also as strong reformers compared to the mild and weak reformers identified in Table 5.1. Countries in the stronger reformer group are Bolivia (1985), Chile (1974), Sri Lanka (1977), Turkey (1980) and Mexico (1985–90). Bolivia and Chile undertook reforms that amounted to complete regime changes ending with low protection as well as very low variance in protection. Bolivia has a two-tier tariff system of 5 per cent and 10 per cent, and Chile has a 10 per cent uniform tariff. In both these countries, quantitative restrictions (QRs) apply to less than one per cent of their imports. There are five countries in this group of strong reformers. They have low protection (in the 11 per cent to 13.5 per cent range) and low variance in tariffs (measured by tariff dispersion) and QRs apply to less than 10 per cent of their tariff lines.

Table 5.1 Trade reforms, 1985–96: twenty-country sample

Countries	Reform Years Before 1985	Reform Years 1985–96	Type of reforms[1]	Overall outcome % per annum Ave. GDP growth 1985–96	Overall outcome % per annum Ave. GDP growth post-reform[2]
Bolivia	—	1985–87	S	3.26	3.70
Chile	1974–79	1992–93	S	7.03	6.70
Colombia	1984–87	1991–92	S	4.23	4.70
Korea	1966–71	—	S	8.44	8.60
Mexico	—	1985–90	S	2.03	2.50
Sri Lanka	1977–80	1989–90	S	4.40	5.10
Turkey	1980	1985–86	S	4.73	4.40
Mean				*4.87*	*5.10*
SD				*2.19*	*2.01*
(Mean/SD)[3]				*2.23*	*2.54*
Argentina	1976	1991–93	M	2.17	3.30
Brazil	1968	1990–92	M	2.94	3.20
Indonesia	—	1986–89	M	7.19	8.00
Thailand	—	1988–91	M	8.72	8.50
Mean				*5.26*	*5.75*
SD				*3.20*	*2.89*
(Mean/SD)				*1.64*	*1.99*
Camaroon	—	1989–93	W	−0.61	−0.70
Costa Rica	—	1986–89	W	3.85	3.90
Côte d'Ivoire	—	1986–89	W	2.15	2.00
India	1980–85	1991–92	W	5.91	7.00
Kenya	—	1991–92	W	3.72	2.90
Morocco	1984–85	—	W	3.96	3.70
Nigeria	1973–74	1986–90	W	4.59	4.80
Pakistan	1972–73	1987–88	W	5.41	4.70
Venezuela	—	1989–90	W	2.58	2.80
Mean				*3.51*	*3.46*
SD				*1.96*	*2.13*
(Mean/SD)				*1.79*	*1.62*

Notes:
[1] S = strong, M = mild, W = weak.
[2] Estimated with one-year lag after initiation of reforms.
[3] Mean/standard deviation = coefficient of variation.
Source: World Bank 1997 data base.

All the countries in the group entered the 1990s with liberalized trade regimes. It may be noted that the coefficient of variation for GDP growth is higher among stronger reformers than in the other two groups. While we cannot attribute causality between GDP growth and the strength of reforms, due to the difficulties of creating a proper counterfactual, the high coefficient of variation for GDP growth for the strong reformers suggests that the association is more than casual.

We have defined a group of mild reformers in the sample. They are Argentina, Brazil, Indonesia and Thailand. With the exception of Indonesia, the countries in this group undertook their trade reforms in the early 1990s. Indonesia attempted to cope with the sharp decline in oil prices with a package of reforms that began in 1986. Thailand began the reform process in 1988, but the more substantial reforms came in the early 1990s. For the group as a whole, tariffs are between 13.5 and 33 per cent range. Tariff dispersion ranges from zero to 80 per cent. Their QRs coverage is between 11 and 30 per cent of their tariff lines.

The third group, which we identify as weak reformers, comprises the largest number in the sample. They are Cameroon, Costa Rica, Côte d'Ivoire, India, Kenya, Morocco, Nigeria, Pakistan and Venezuela. Like the other two groups, this group includes countries that began the reform process in the mid-eighties. Their reforms were limited in scope and were implemented slowly compared to the strong reformers. Their levels of protection as measured by nominal tariffs range from 19 to 70 per cent. Tariff dispersion among them is wide and ranges from 19 to 134 per cent. QRs still cover a large part of the tariff lines. They are as high as 30 per cent for India and 50 per cent for Pakistan.

Several generalizations can be made about trade reforms and the trade regimes they evolved into in the 1990s, based on the sample. They help us in identifying an agenda for future trade reforms.

First, while the 1990s saw further progress in trade reforms that had begun in the 1980s for most countries in the sample, the trade regimes that have evolved still have high as well as wide variance in protection. It is true that many countries liberalized their trade regimes and protection is lower than it had been at any time in the last five decades. Yet, all the countries in the mild and weak reformer groups have a considerable distance to move towards a fully liberalized trade regime. If we use Chile as the yardstick, since it has low protection, low variance and hardly any QRs, the other 19 countries all have a large, unfinished agenda to attend to. Among the three groups, those in the strong reformers group have less distance to cover to catch up with Chile, compared to those in the mild and weak categories of countries. Chile itself had resolved to reduce its uniform tariffs to 7.5 per cent in 1996. It postponed that decision and has now resolved to adopt a 6 per cent uniform tariff by 2003. Similarly, Sri Lanka had earlier decided to move towards a uniform 15 per cent tariff in 1998 – a decision which it has now postponed indefinitely. The reason for both these countries to postpone further liberalization is unclear to outside observers. But it does indicate some slowing down of the reform effort.

Second, the variance in protection in some countries may have increased in the 1990s. There are several reasons for this. Firstly, many countries have continued to protect agriculture even when they have reduced overall protection, much like developed countries. High agriculture protection is a key feature of present trade regimes in the majority of developing countries: in tariff structures in the sample countries, agriculture carries higher than average protection. For example, Nigeria has tariffs of over 100 per cent for agriculture. Others have bound tariffs on agriculture at much higher rates than for manufactures. Brazil has bound agricultural tariffs in the 80–230 per cent range, while India has bound its agriculture tariffs at a 0–300 per cent range.[4] However, many of these rates have been reduced over time and the applied tariff rates for agriculture are at present much lower than these bound rates. Nevertheless, there still exits the possibility that the applied rates could be raised in the future. In addition, there are various non-tariff barriers which are more common in agriculture than in industry, such as state trading, where the importing entity can reduce or ban imports altogether. Colombia uses a domestic procurement scheme (*convenios de absorcion*) in agriculture for some products, which treats imports as a residual. The Andean Group as a whole uses a price band system for some agricultural products, which incorporates a variable levy. This levy can rise to very high levels, above the bound rates, when international prices of agricultural goods decline. This in fact happened in late 1990s. Another reason for increasing variance in protection is RTAs. Their tariff preferences have led to zero or low tariffs among the member countries, widening the variance between both high and low tariffs, and between member and non-member country import tariffs.

Third, most of the reforms in the 1990s were confined to export rather than import liberalization. A typical sequence has been to reduce barriers on exports such as export duties, provide duty drawbacks and credit subsidies, and to compensate for tariffs on imported inputs used in the production for exports. This is followed by more direct subsidies based on performance criteria and in many instances they go beyond providing 'free trade status' for exports. There is less emphasis on reducing import protection. Brazil, India, Indonesia, Nigeria, Thailand, Turkey and Venezuela have followed this sequence. Venezuela has gone to the extent of identifying 'sector leaders' and targeted them for special concessions, such as energy subsidies. Concessional credit is extended in many of these countries to small and medium-sized exporters. While it is true that many of the subsidies have to be phased-out (with an eight-year time horizon for developing countries under the Uruguay Agreement), they nevertheless introduce a distortion into the trade regime. There is a bias against exports arising from the prevailing import protection which cannot be corrected through export subsidies without incurring additional costs, such as the cost involved in administering a subsidy system, the incentives it would create for rent-seeking, and inducing countervailing actions by importing countries. In many countries the presence of the bias is not appreciated. Part of the problem can be traced to the attempt by countries to follow the so-called 'Japanese–Korean model', in which import liberalization was held up for a few years until export success was achieved (see Clements and Sjastaad, 1984). This view presupposes that import tariffs do not harm exports, that a period of import protection is not only harmless but necessary, and that there are clever bureaucrats who can implement a system of targeted export subsidies efficiently and be immune to corruption.[5] This view has been challenged strongly by Little (1994), and Lal and Myint (1996), among others. In addition, more recent research, as well as recent observations from East Asia, suggest that a sequence that neglects import liberalization has led to lower total productivity growth in the protected industries of Japan and Korea (see Beason and Weinstein, 1996; Lawrence and Weinstein, 1999).

Fourth, many developing countries have begun to use anti-dumping on a wider scale than in the past, as they have reduced protection through tariffs and QRs. In the twenty-country sample, Argentina, Brazil and Colombia have increased their anti-dumping initiations, although not to the same extent as their developed-country counterparts. Interestingly, anti-dumping duties have been imposed within RTAs as other barriers to trade have been reduced. In their increased use of anti-dumping, developing countries are beginning to imitate developed countries. Australia, the European Union and the United States have led the way in the use of anti-dumping and it has become the weapon of choice for protection. The UR left anti-dumping open to abuse, even though it did tighten the circumstances in which it could be used. One irony is that some countries that did not have anti-dumping, countervailing duty, or safeguards laws have introduced them in the 1990s following the UR and have begun to use them as protectionist devices. Colombia, which had strict constraints on anti-dumping and safeguard actions, made them less strict after the Marrakesh Agreement. It has become easier to initiate anti-dumping and safeguards actions (Rajapatirana, 1998).

Finally, one important feature of trade regimes in the 1990s is the increasing number of RTAs. Their number has quadrupled since the 1970s. Just over 100 regional trading agreements have been notified to the WTO and earlier to GATT. There are others not notified when such agreements are established under the 'enabling clause' of the Tokyo Round. The character of RTAs has changed since the 1960s and 1970s, particularly in Latin America, where they were used as protectionist devices. In the 1990s they have become devices that restrict trade, not deliberately but by the sheer difficulty of implementing them. The chances that they become stepping stones for multilateral free trade seem less likely than devices that restrain trade across different trading arrangements. Their main problem arises from rules of origin. To give one example, Bolivia has signed 28 regional agreements with a variety of rules of origin, giving customs officials wide choices to use their discretion in classifying imports and providing opportunities for rent-seeking.[6] RTAs have the potential for trade diversion, which is welfare reducing. Such instances have been documented.[7]

Main issues arising from the trade reforms in the 1990s and a future agenda

From the above analysis it seems clear that there is a future agenda to be addressed by developing countries to move towards more liberalized trade regimes. Among them, the following are crucial.

First, a 10 per cent uniform tariff such as Chile now has would be ideal and within the reach of the majority of the developing countries. Reducing variance in protection is as important as reducing the level of protection. Wide variances in protection distort resource allocation. There is now much evidence that the replacement of QRs with tariffs and the eventual reduction of tariffs when combined with a devaluation (as is needed in most cases) does not necessarily lead to reduction in tariff revenues, a common reason given by many developing countries for not reducing tariffs. There is also little justification to impose

QRs on balance-of-payments grounds (GATT, Article XVIII) for the simple reason that they do not work. Instead they lead to inefficiencies and rent-seeking. Only regimes based on tariffs can assure that variance in protection is kept within known limits. Tariff reductions are easy to accomplish and provide a signal to economic agents that a country is on the path of reform and that its protection levels become predictable. It is noteworthy that despite the East Asian crisis of 1997, Korea and Indonesia did not introduce new trade restrictions. Instead, they have resolved to reduce protection in the near future. However, some countries (Argentina, Brazil, India and Thailand) did increase protection when they were confronted by negative shocks in 1994 and 1997. These increases have been relatively small and have not changed the character of their trade regimes.

Second, reducing barriers on the export side while maintaining import protection does not lead to the realization of full benefits of a trade liberalization as confirmed by new evidence (Lawrence and Weinstein, 1999). Imports provide an efficient and significant channel for learning and acquiring technological knowledge. Before the UR, there were no strong strictures against export subsidies. This allowed countries to liberalize on the export side while maintaining import restrictions. This alternative may not be available in the future, given the challenges to export subsidies through countervailing duties and through the dispute settlement mechanism, which will be used by trading partners more than in the past.

Third, as mentioned above, developing countries have begun to use anti-dumping more than ever before, even though their use is less than that of some developed countries. Argentina initiated 15 anti-dumping cases in 1997, Brazil 11 cases, India 13 cases, Korea 15 cases, and Malaysia 8 cases, as reported to the WTO (1998). Anti-dumping has increased in the 1990s although the main users of this measure are developed countries, led by Australia, the European Union and United States. Except in the case of predation, there is hardly a sound economic basis to use anti-dumping. In most cases, anti-dumping measures are less appropriate than safeguards. As a temporary measure, safeguards are preferable to anti-dumping given that they are imposed on a MFN basis. They require a more strict burden of proof and are limited in duration.

Finally, the best way to minimize trade diversion within RTAs is to lower tariffs on non-member countries and keep these arrangements open to new members. Theoretically, common markets do not require rules of origin as they rely on a common external tariff. However, many common markets have used differential rules of origin as temporary measures until agreement is reached on common external tariffs. To that extent, the adverse effects of rules of origin are found in both free-trade agreements and common markets. There is also the danger that the need to agree on a common external tariff could lead to higher tariff rates than an individual country would adopt on its own. In addition, further liberalization becomes more difficult if the stronger members resist it. A short-term palliative for regional arrangements is to adhere to Article XXIV of GATT and avoid the use of the 'escape clause' under which developing countries are exempt from Article XXIV provisions. Moreover, in a world where major trading nations are forming trading blocs, strengthening the rule-based WTO system gives a better balance of power between the strong and the weak countries.

While macroeconomic crises in the 1980s helped to break protection-supporting coalitions, in the 1990s such an impetus is absent in the developing world outside of East Asia. In any case, East Asian economies entered the 1990s with lower protection and the crises in those countries have created the impetus for further liberalization. For other developing countries, an external impetus such as a new round is needed to achieve their remaining agenda for reforms. Meanwhile, sufficient support may be forthcoming from successful exporting lobbies to complete the agenda for reforms.

To achieve many if not all of these future agenda items, a new round of multilateral trade negotiations is needed. That would bring trade issues to the fore again and provide opportunities to address many of the issues discussed above, such as eliminating export subsidies earlier than promulgated by the UR, reforming anti-dumping rules, and changing the law with respect to the 'escape clause' in RTAs. A new round could open areas for negotiations going beyond the 'built-in agenda' of the UR to realize many of the areas that developing countries are interested in by virtue of their comparative advantage. These are the full implementation of the Agreement on Textiles and Clothing, preferably accelerating the process, addressing agriculture protection that has remained high in developed countries, providing for the movement of natural persons under the General Agreement on Trade in Services as well as increasing access to developed-country service markets in such activities as construction. Some leading developing countries such as India have argued that a new round is not warranted until the UR agreements are fully implemented.[8] These countries were less than fully enthusiastic about the UR to begin with. However, the suggested delay of multilateral trade negotiations implies delaying a means to achieve higher growth and living standards.

Conclusions

Developing countries have more liberal trade regimes in the late 1990s compared to any time since the Second World War. However, theoretical and empirical work on trade points to greater benefits that could be achieved with more liberalized trade regimes.

Developing countries could do well to reduce protection and its variance, rely on tariffs and avoid imitating the protectionist stances of developed countries in their use of anti-dumping and continued protection of agriculture, and opt for MFN-based trade over regional arrangements.

The agenda for reform could be best addressed by a starting a new round of multilateral trade negotiations sooner rather than later. It would facilitate further liberalization and allow developing countries to realize many of the areas of interest to them. Short of a multilateral trade negotiation, there will be sectoral negotiations which will advance only the agenda of the more powerful countries in trade, as it will give them an opportunity to 'cherry-pick' from an agenda that may not be beneficial to developing countries. Once developed countries accomplish their agenda through this process, they may be unwilling to negotiate measures to reduce barriers in areas of interest to developing countries. Of course, developing countries could, and some have indeed already, liberalize their trade regime unilaterally, Chile being the prime example of a country that has implemented unilateral trade liberalization. That strategy still remains the best option for developing countries. However, a multilateral trade negotiation such as the suggested 'Millennium Round' should allow developing countries to gain over and above their unilateral trade liberalization and also allow wider choices in addressing items of interest to them. Additionally, it would help to provide a guard against domestic protectionist interests, which may resist further liberalization.

Developing-countries' trade reform agenda could follow a back-to-the-future strategy to initiate a period of reforms such as those of the 1980s. During that period reforms were crisis-driven. A more efficient way to induce reforms without crises is to initiate a round of multilateral trade negotiations where a proper give and take can make all parties benefit from trade reform, even beyond what could be achieved unilaterally.

Notes

1. The author, a visiting scholar at the American Enterprise Institute, thanks Migara de Silva and Cherian Samuel for their comments on an earlier version of this chapter. Thanks are also due to Deepak Lal and Richard Snape, the editors of this volume, for their help to improve the essay. Any errors that remain are entirely the author's.
2. This expression was used often by Mr Barber Conable, the Republican congressman who became the President of the World Bank in 1986. Yet, it was a decade of reform and not one of loss, even in terms of GDP growth, if the proper long-term trend rates were applied to measure developing country growth during the decade.
3. The author was Chief of Policy Analysis in the Economics and Research Staff in the World Bank, when Anne Krueger was Vice President of Economics and Research. He was able to observe first hand Anne Krueger's role in persuading the World Bank's senior management, as a member of that group, to support trade liberalization in developing countries, while relentlessly exposing protectionist practices in developed countries.
4. In India the presence of state trading in agriculture acts as a quantitative barrier to imports.
5. This view is associated with Amsden, Wade, Lall et al., as well as the World Bank's *Miracle* study (1993).
6. The extent of the choices can be gauged by the fact that with some 7200 tariff lines, 28 different agreements with different rules of origin, and three phases of implementation, there is a theoretical choice-set for a single country that exceeds 600 000! While a yard of cloth cannot be classified as a live animal, the choice-set still remains large to give enormous discretion to customs officials.
7. Yeats (1998) demonstrated that trade diversion was likely in the automotive sectors in the Mercosur agreement.
8. Second Ministerial Conference (Address by Ramkrishna Hedge – Minister of Commerce, India), WTO (1998).

References

Amsden, A., *Asia's Next Giant: South Korea and Late Industrialization* (New York: Oxford University Press, 1989).

Beason, R., and Weinstein, D. E., 'Growth, Economies of Scale and Targeting in Japan 1955–1990', *Review of Economics and Statistics*, 78 (1996) 286–95.

Bhagwati, J. N., *Foreign Trade Regimes and Economic Development: Anatomy and Consequences of Exchange Control Regimes* (Cambridge, MA: Ballinger Press, 1978).

Clements, K., and Sjastaad, L. A., *How Protection Taxes Exporters*, Thames Essay no. 39 (London: Gower Press, Trade Policy Research Centre, 1984).

Dollar, D., 'Outward-oriented Developing Economies Really Do Grow More Rapidly: Evidence from 95 LDCs, 1976–85', *Economic Development and Cultural Change*, 40 (3) (1992) 523–44.

Drabek, Z., and Laird, S., 'The New Liberalism: Trade Policy Developments in Emerging Markets', *Journal of World Trade*, 32 (5) (1998) 241–69.

Edwards, S., 'Trade Liberalization Reforms and the World Bank', Papers and Proceedings, *American Economic Review*, 87 (2) (New Orleans, 1997) 43–8.

International Monetary Fund, *World Economic Outlook* (Washington, DC, 1998).

Krueger, A. O., 'Trends in Trade Policies of Developing Countries', in C. S. Pearson and J. Riedel (eds), *The Direction of Trade Policy: Papers in Honor of Isaiah Frank* (Cambridge, MA: Blackwell, 1990) pp. 87–107.

Krueger, A. O., and Rajapatirana, S., 'The World Bank Policies Towards Trade and Trade Policy Reform', *The World Economy*, 22 (6) (1999) 1–24.

Lawrence, R. Z., and Weinstein, D. E., 'Trade and Growth: Import Led or Export Led? Evidence from Japan and Korea', paper presented to the World Bank Workshop on 'Rethinking the East Asian Miracle' (San Francisco: February 1999) (mimeo).

Lal, D., and Myint, H. U., *The Political Economy of Poverty Equity and Growth: a Comparative Study* (New York: Oxford University Press, 1996).

Lall, S., 'Paradigms of Development: the East Asian Debate', *Oxford Development Studies*, 45 (2) (1996) 147–74.

Little, I. M. D., 'Trade and Industry Revisited', *Pakistan Development Review*, 33 (4-1) (1994) 359–89.

Little, I. M. D., Cooper, R. N., Corden, M. W., and Rajapatirana, S., *Boom, Crisis and Adjustment: the Macroeconomic Experience of Developing Countries* (Oxford: Oxford University Press, 1993).

Lucas, R., 'On the Mechanics of Economic Development', *Journal of Monetary Economics*, 22 (1) (1988) 3–42.

Rajapatirana, S., 'Evaluating Integration Choices: the Case of Bolivia', *Journal of Economic Integration*, 12 (3) (1997) 298–324.

Rajapatirana, S., 'Colombian Trade Policies and the 1996 WTO Trade Policy Review', *The World Economy*, 21 (4) (1998) 515–27.

Rajapatirana, S., de la Mora Sanchez, L. M., and Yatawara, R. A., 'Political Economy of Trade Reforms 1965–94: Latin American Style', *The World Economy*, 20 (3) (1997) 208–24.

Rodrik, D., 'The Limits of Trade Policy Reform in Developing Countries', *Journal of Economic Perspectives*, 6 (1992) 87–105.

Romer, P. M., 'Increasing Returns and Long-Run Growth', *Journal of Political Economy*, 94 (5) (1986) 1002–37.

Sachs, J., and Warner, A., 'Economic Reforms and the Process of Global Integration', *Brooking Papers on Economic Activity*, 25th Anniversary Issue (1995) 1–95.

Wade, R., *Governing the Market: Economic Theory and the Role of the Government in East Asian Industrialization* (Princeton, NJ: Princeton University Press, 1990).

World Bank, *Global Economic Prospects and the Developing Countries 1998/99* (Washington, DC, 1999).

World Bank, *The East Asian Miracle* (New York: Oxford University Press, 1993).

World Trade Organization, 'India and the WTO', Commerce Minister's Message, Second Ministerial Conference of the WTO (Geneva, 18 May 1998).

World Trade Organization, *Annual Report* (Washington, DC, 1998).

Yeats, A. J., 'Does Mercosur's Trade Performance Raise Concerns about the Effects of Regional Trade Arrangements?', *World Bank Economic Review*, 12 (1) (January 1998) 1–28.

6
Developing-Country Issues for WTO Multilateral Trade Negotiations[1]

Constantine Michalopoulos

Introduction

The failure of the World Trade Organization (WTO) 3rd Ministerial Meeting in Seattle to launch a new round of multilateral trade negotiations was a setback for the development of a liberal international trade system governed by multilaterally agreed rules. This failure should be a cause of concern to developing countries since they benefit greatly from a rules-based trading system. The lack of agreement in Seattle to review existing rules that are not helpful to development will not cause the problems faced by developing countries to disappear; nor will their reasonable concerns be addressed about the implementation of the Uruguay Round (UR) agreements or their needs for additional assistance. At the same time, WTO negotiations on Agriculture and Services, already mandated under the UR, will go forward, as will a review of the Trade Related Intellectual Property Rights (TRIPs) Agreement, scheduled for 2000. Thus, in the months and years ahead, developing countries will need to develop strategies regarding the ongoing negotiations, identify topics that they themselves want to bring to the WTO as well as positions on issues that others propose for multilateral trade negotiations. No single strategy will suit them all. Their varying trading interests require that they develop different strategies and pursue them in the context of coalitions with other WTO members.

The purpose of this study is twofold: (i) to analyze the issues of interest to developing countries that should be included in future WTO negotiations; and (ii) to suggest developing-country strategies for multilateral trade negotiations which would also result in their greater integration into the multilateral trading system. The analysis will draw on insights Anne Krueger developed in the context of the Uruguay Round

(Krueger and Michalopoulos, 1985) as well as more recently (Krueger, 1998, 1999) on how multilateral trade negotiations can contribute to more liberal trade policies for development.[2]

The chapter is organized as follows: first, there is a review of the agenda for negotiations and reviews already mandated under the UR – agriculture, services and TRIPs. The next section contains an analysis of the many new subjects that have been proposed for negotiation and suggests developing-country positions on each.[3] Then the possible strategies for developing-country participation in future negotiations are discussed. The final section summarizes the conclusions and recommendations.

The built-in agenda for negotiations and reviews

Agriculture

Developing-countries' interests in agricultural trade vary considerably. There is a group of major exporters of agricultural commodities (for example Argentina, Thailand) which are members of the Cairns Group. The position of these countries is clear. They will be looking to: (i) early, total elimination and prohibition of export subsidies which tend to undermine the competitive position of efficient producers, and in the same connection, seek to regulate the provision of export credits; (ii) deep cuts in tariffs, removal of non-tariff barriers and increase in trade volumes under tariff quotas so as to enhance market access prospects; and (iii) elimination of trade-distorting domestic support measures (WTO, 1998a).

Next, there is a large group consisting of the net-food-importing developing countries (NFIDCs) and others with a significant agricultural sector, which produce but also import food and export various agricultural products.[4] Past policies in many of these countries tended to penalize rather than support agriculture. Two kinds of issues have been raised by several of these countries. First, while supporting reductions in export subsidies and trade-distorting domestic support in developed countries, they are concerned that the limits to aggregate support and export subsidies contained in the agreement (and their possible further tightening in the new negotiations) would limit their capacity to increase support to agriculture, should they in the future decide to do so.[5] Second, they argue that although reduction in export subsidies by developed countries will be beneficial to their own domestic agricultural production, the resulting increase in prices of foodstuffs would increase foreign exchange outlays for least developed countries (LDCs) and NFIDCs which can ill afford them.

While the UR Agreement on Agriculture focused on distortions primarily introduced to agricultural trade by developed-country practices, it contains provisions which permit developing countries to increase support to agriculture (and to poor consumers) through means not available to developed countries. For example, direct and indirect investment and input subsidies to poor farmers are excluded from the calculation of aggregate measures of support (AMS); reduction in support commitments by developing countries can take ten years to be implemented while LDCs are totally exempt; food subsidies to urban and rural poor are excluded from the calculation of support. Moreover, there is considerable difference between the applied and bound tariff rates in agriculture for these countries. Applied tariffs in agriculture averaged 25 per cent compared to 66 per cent for bound rates for 31 developing countries (excluding Cairns Group members), which suggests there is considerable scope for increases in their protection of agriculture, should they wish to do so (Michalopoulos, 1999b).[6]

It can be argued, however, that the exception of investment and input subsidies provided to poor rural households from the calculation of the AMS is subject to the 'peace clause' – Article 13 of the Agreement on Agriculture, and thereby limited to the 1992 levels of support (Kwa and Bello, 1998). This may indeed result in unreasonable restraints for low-income developing countries which may wish over time to increase their support for the rural poor. To eliminate this ambiguity, such subsidies could be included in the 'Green Box' of measures which are permitted under all circumstances, or in a new 'Development Box' as suggested by some developing countries in the preparations for the Seattle Ministerial. But, on the whole, and with the exception noted above, it is difficult to visualize circumstances where the Agreement seriously constrains the efforts of developing countries to pursue policies that would efficiently promote their agricultural sector.

There is little evidence that the export subsidy reductions of the UR Agreement have led to an increase in import expenditures of poor NFIDCs. Even so, it is legitimate to ask what might happen in the future and what is the proper international response to such a potential problem.

The problem relates to the possible adverse short-term effects of eliminating trade-distorting measures on poor NFIDCs, which are likely to be outweighed by the longer-term worldwide efficiency gains. Actually the short-term effects are also likely to spread out over time – as the distortions are bound to be phased out rather than eliminated at once. And it would be very difficult to isolate the impact of the resulting price increases from other factors, including the policies of developing countries. It is for this reason that the International Monetary Fund (IMF) did not provide automatic financing from its Compensatory and Contingency Financing Facility but drawings from it were included in the overall IMF programme to individual countries.

The Food Aid Convention (International Grains Council, 1999) stipulates that, when allocating food aid, priority should be given to LDCs and low-income countries. Other NFIDCs can also be provided with food aid 'when experiencing food emergencies or international recognized financial crises leading to food shortage emergencies or when food aid operations are targeted on vulnerable groups'. But there is nothing – and there should be nothing – automatic about the assistance provided. Indeed, if a need can be shown to exist, the international response should not be limited to food aid but extended to all kinds of general-purpose financing on appropriate terms. The latter would be better than food aid, which is frequently tied to procurement from a particular donor and determined by food stock availability of the donor, rather than by the needs of the recipient.

In sum, the large number of developing countries for which the agriculture sector is an important source of income and employment, especially for the poor, would benefit from a further liberalization of the sector and should join the Cairns Group members in their efforts to: (i) seek a very substantial reduction in export subsidies; these subsidies, which are primarily extended by developed countries, tend to undermine the efforts of developing countries to stimulate increases in their own agricultural output; and (ii) seek to improve market access for their potential agricultural exports by negotiating for tariff reductions (probably through a formula approach that can best deal with tariff peaks and escalation) and opening up of tariff quotas. At the same time they need to safeguard those aspects of the Agreement which permit them to extend assistance of various types to poor farmers as well as maintain programmes of assistance and food security to the poor. But these measures should not introduce distortions between selling to the domestic market and abroad, or between sectors.

Finally, the matter of increasing costs to net-food importing countries is better addressed in the context of the overall availability of concessionary finance to these countries, rather in the context of food aid.

Services

In the aftermath of the great confrontations between developed and developing countries over the inclusion of services in the UR, the implementation of the Agreement has resulted in comparatively little controversy. GATS involves commitments through a combination of positive and negative lists which has permitted countries to exclude modes or sectors in which they wish to avoid foreign competition. In addition, many developing countries have recognized the adverse effects that protection of inefficient service sectors can have on the rest of the economy. Many have liberalized their service sectors autonomously and have participated actively in the successful conclusion of two additional sectoral negotiations since the end of UR, on financial services and telecommunications. One problem, identified by some countries as a constraint to greater liberalization, is the absence of a suitable safeguard clause in the GATS. While Article X of GATS requires negotiations whose result should enter into effect no later than three years after the entry into force of the WTO agreement, that is by 1998, this has not happened.

What is the appropriate strategy for developing countries in this setting? There are no obvious developing-country groupings as is the case for example, with agriculture. Rather, there is a large range, from the LDCs with scarcely any modern domestic service providers, to middle-income countries with some very advanced service sectors concerned about market access in the developed countries, and many countries in between. There is, however, one mode of supply and two sectors that hold special interest for many developing countries: movement of natural persons, and maritime and construction services.

Movement of natural persons

While some progress has been made regarding the movement of qualified professionals to work abroad, developed-country restrictions inhibit increased service earnings for developing countries through this mode of supply. The commitments on trade in services have tended to emphasize measures regulating commercial presence – which is important for foreign direct investment – rather than 'mode four' involving movement of natural persons.

The commitments made regarding the movement of natural persons have primarily involved intra-corporate transferees, business visitors, as well as independent professionals, including those providing services within service contracts. One of the limitations imposed by a large number of countries is an economic needs test (ENT). This typically involves judgments by government agencies based on non-transparent criteria as to market conditions, availability of local service providers and so on, regarding which foreign service providers to permit and which not. Indeed, of the 54 countries which have made commitments subject to a needs test, only three have stated criteria for ENT. Frequently, the result is to nullify access commitments involving mode four supply of services. Developing countries may wish to press both for liberalization of mode four supplies in more professional categories and through limiting the use of ENT in specific sectors, and making the ENT criteria transparent and consistent.

Construction services

In addition to overall liberalization in mode four commitments, specific sector-based liberalization involving the movement of natural persons may be important in the area of construction services. Several developing countries, especially in Asia, which have the capacity of exporting such services, or other services based on their comparative advantage in labour-intensive activities, are constrained by restrictions on 'movement of natural persons'.

Maritime services

Efforts to reach agreement in this sector failed in 1995–96 and the negotiations were suspended with a view to resuming them in the wider context of the service negotiations, starting in 2000. This should be a major area of interest for developing countries: 'the oceans are populated by cartels known as shipping conferences'. These cartels set prices and pursue other collusive activities in 85 per cent or more of maritime services they control. They are often exempted from anti-trust law in developed countries (Francois and Wooton, 1999, p. 4).

Their impact in raising transport costs to poorer developing countries, especially to low volume, high distance destinations – in Africa and poorer island economies, can be even more important than further tariff liberalization. Maritime transport costs on merchandise trade in Sub-Saharan Africa exceed 8 per cent compared with OECD tariffs (after preferences are taken into account) of less than 3 per cent (Francois and Wooton, 1999). Liberalization in this sector, which would lead to increased competition and reduced costs, may be of great importance to many of the small-economies members of the WTO. Also, liberalization could lead to increases in the provision of maritime shipping services by some developing countries themselves.

In addition to these specific areas of interest, developing countries need to press for the establishment of a suitable transparent and non-discriminatory safeguard mechanism. While further liberalization of their service sector would in many cases be in their own interest, the political economy of trade reform requires that a suitable safeguard mechanism is put in place for trade in services, just as it is for trade in goods.

In sum, the service negotiations offer opportunities for developing countries to further open up their own service sectors, which many may wish to do in any case in order to reap the benefits of increased efficiency, as well as to bind liberalization they have already undertaken. In exchange they should seek liberalization in certain sectors and modes of supply of interest to them.

TRIPs

Perhaps no other agreement of the UR has generated more concerns in the developing world than TRIPs. The review of TRIPs mandated for 2000 offered an opportunity for the developing countries to propose changes in the existing rules which would tend to be beneficial to development. They were, as it now appears likely, resisted by entrenched interests in developed countries. If they fail to achieve their objectives in the Review, developing countries may wish to make this topic part of a subesequent larger multilateral trade negotiation.

There are several sets of problems that the Agreement poses. There is a general concern that the efficiency losses – resulting, for example, from significantly increased prices in pharmaceuticals – would exceed any dynamic gains resulting from increased research and development or larger flows of foreign direct investment (Braga, 1996; Correa, 1998; Deardorff, 1992), or that the length of time provided for patent protection is excessive. There are also concerns that the Agreement does not provide for a reasonable balance between the rights of producers and users of knowledge and technology and that it is based on an outdated concept of 'knowledge' which does not take into account the externalities of knowledge dissemination. But there is little agreement on how these broad issues can be addressed.

The patent system itself poses problems for many poorer developing countries with an agricultural-based economy, despite Article 27.3(b) which provides them with flexibility in terms of Intellectual Property Rights (IPR) protection through *sui generis* systems in agriculture. The system is unlikely to work as an incentive to local innovations – except in countries with a significant private scientific and technological infrastructure. At the same time, the Agreement, by not recognizing community proprietary rights to traditional knowledge, has led commercial firms in developed countries to seek proprietary rights to traditional medicines or product varieties ('basmati' rice and the bark of the *neem* tree are the best-known examples). The Agreement may also result in constraints on farmers' use of their own seeds saved from harvest for replanting and it has tended to encourage patents in processes involving biotechnology aimed at providing substitutes for existing developing country exports. Last, but not least, developing countries have experienced difficulties in implementing the procedural and legal commitments required by the Agreement (Duran and Michalopoulos, 1999). Changing a number of these provisions to make the Agreement more 'development' friendly will not be easy because of the strength of the commercial interests in the developed countries which it protects. Developing-country priorities during future negotiations should include the following:

- Maintenance of the flexibility they now have within the Agreement. To this end, they must try to ward off efforts by developed countries to limit flexibility regarding what is considered a *sui generis* system or expand the basic provisions on IPR protection already included in the TRIPs Agreement.

- Securing developed-country commitments in support of concrete and effective ways to: (a) render operational TRIPs provisions involving technology transfer to developing countries and in particular to LDCs, and (b) share the benefits of R&D undertaken in the developed countries but originating in knowledge available to indigenous people and local communities.[7]

- Obtaining reasonable time extensions for implementing the Agreement. It would probably be unrealistic to seek a general extension of the transition period for implementation of the Agreement by developing countries. On the other hand, since few developing countries have put in place suitable *sui generis* legislation, it may well be reasonable to argue very strongly for additional time to implement Article 27.3(b).

- Increasing, where possible, developing-country flexibility under the Agreement. Some specific amendments of 27.3(b) that developing countries may be willing to pursue include the exclusion from patents of naturally occurring substances – including genes and naturally occurring micro-organisms, as well as essential drugs on the World Health Organization (WHO) list.

Other potential subjects for negotiations

Many developing countries feel that before they consider any issue – beyond the three agreed areas – they would like to obtain developed-country commitments on aspects of implementation of the UR which they consider unsatisfactory. On the other hand, there is a variety of other subjects which developed countries have suggested for future multilateral trade negotiations. For some – for example, environment, competition and investment – preparatory work has been under way based on previous WTO Ministerial decisions. For others – trade facilitation and electronic commerce – work has started more recently. Finally, there are subjects such as industrial tariffs on which many countries want to negotiate, and others such as labour standards which are favoured by only a few.[8]

This is a vast array of subjects on which to negotiate. The criteria which countries use in deciding on a position should include (i) the net benefits they would expect to obtain for their economies both through their own liberalization and through improved access in the markets of others; (ii) the net benefits that would result from setting new rules and reinforcing existing ones, or changing them, where appropriate; and (iii) the institutional capacity needed to implement whatever new agreements are reached. Based on these criteria different developing countries may well reach different conclusions about their stance. An attempt is made to reach some broad conclusions from the standpoint of developing countries as a whole, recognizing that such generalizations need to be carefully scrutinized in the case of individual countries or groups of countries.

Issues of special interest to developing countries

Implementation

In the period leading to the Seattle Ministerial, developing-country concerns in this area focused on two issues: (a) inadequate implementation by developed countries of commitments they had made under the UR, usually in special and differential treatment (S&D) of developing countries, but also in adhering to the letter but not the spirit of UR commitments, for example in the Agreement on Textiles and Clothing; and (b) limitations in developing-countries' institutional capacity to implement UR Agreements in many areas, but especially in TRIPs, Sanitary and Phyto-Sanitary Measures (SPS), Technical Barriers to Trade (TBT), and Customs Valuation (CV) (Michalopoulos, 1999a; UNCTAD, 1998; WTO, 1997–98).

A very large number of provisions have been introduced into the GATT/WTO agreements to provide S&D treatment (WTO, 1999a). Many developed-country commitments in this regard have been articulated in such general terms as to be nearly meaningless. It is quite appropriate that more meaningful and concrete steps are elaborated in some areas – for example, technology transfer in the context of TRIPs. However, the past reliance of developing countries on some S&D provisions – for example, their right to non-reciprocity and non-adherence to various WTO disciplines – has had negative effects on their trade and development prospects. By not participating in the exchange of reciprocal reductions in trade barriers they also have missed the opportunity of gaining reductions in the trade barriers in developed countries on products of specific export interest to them – as evidenced by the fact that tariffs of developed countries are higher than average on manufactures of special interest to the developing countries. Moreover, the permissiveness of WTO provisions has enabled developing countries to maintain higher levels of domestic protection. But this protection has introduced distortions in domestic resource allocation, encouraged rent seeking and waste, and adversely affected growth in productivity and sustainable development (Finger and Winters, 1998; Srinivasan, 1998).

On the other hand, the institutional capacity of developing countries to implement their UR commitments was overestimated. Many are finding it either too difficult or too costly to implement the changes needed on a timely basis (Finger and Schuler, 1999). And their technical assistance needs far exceed the present capacity of the WTO to address them. Thus, there is a clear and urgent need to come up with concrete proposals on how to help developing countries, especially the LDCs, meet their WTO obligations through technical and other assistance and to provide suitable extensions to the transition periods for implementation provided for this purpose in current agreements. But extensions should not be provided in other areas, for example in subsidies, where the issue is not the lack of institutional capacity but unwillingness to reform.

Industrial tariffs[9]

Both developed and developing countries called for new negotiations on industrial tariffs in the context of the preparatory process for the Seattle Ministerial meeting. The average, trade-weighted most-favoured-nation (MFN) applied tariffs facing developing-countries' exports of manufactures in OECD markets, though small in absolute terms (3.4 per cent), tend to be almost four times as high as those faced by other OECD countries (Hertel and Martin, 1999).[10] Negotiations on industrial tariffs also offer opportunities to address the continuing problem of tariff peaks that are still present in developed-country markets for products of interest to developing-country exporters.

In order to obtain such reductions, however, developing countries would need to provide increased opportunities for access to their own markets for manufactures. Applied industrial tariffs in developing countries are typically higher and with a greater degree of dispersion – that is, there are also tariff peaks in developing countries. Moreover, developing-countries' exports of manufactures are directed increasingly to other developing countries rather than to developed-country markets.

But, except for Latin America, a large number of developing countries have not bound significant portions of their industrial tariffs. Even those that have done so often use 'ceiling bindings', with bound rates much higher than applied rates. To achieve reductions in tariff peaks a formula approach could be used that results in greater proportional reductions of high bound tariff rates in both developed and developing countries (Laird, 1999). Other approaches may also be feasible but in such cases developing countries may be at a disadvantage because few of their markets are individually large enough to be of 'interest' to developed countries participating in the negotiations.

While such a negotiation is, in principle, of considerable interest, the difficulties in reducing tariff peaks should also be recognized. Tariff peaks in developed countries – defined here as products on which tariffs are at least 12 per cent, or roughly three times their average MFN tariff on manufactures – are present in the following product groups: (a) major agricultural staple food products such as meat, sugar, milk and cereals; (b) cotton and tobacco; (c) fruits and vegetables; (d) processed food products – canned meat, fruit juices and so on; (e) textiles and clothing; (f) footwear and leather products; and (g) selected automotive and transport equipment products (UNCTAD/WTO, 1997). Product groups (a) to (d) are agricultural commodities which would be the subject of negotiations in agriculture. It will be difficult to get developed countries, especially the United States, to negotiate their tariff rates on textiles, and clothing, which, under the Agreement on Clothing and Textiles, should be the only mechanism of protection of this sector (against WTO members) after 2005. But, clearly, an effort should be made. After all, the developed countries may be asking developing countries to make commitments in a number of 'sensitive sectors' as well. Finally, leather and footwear and transport equipment are important to producers in a number of developing countries but obviously to fewer than those affected by tariff peaks in agriculture and textiles.

Despite the difficulties, a potentially mutually-beneficial negotiation could occur in which developing countries reduce ceiling bindings – and perhaps some applied rates as well, in exchange for further reductions in industrial tariffs of developed countries – which, however, included significant reductions in peak tariff rates. Such a negotiation could yield benefits to the developing countries in a variety of ways.

They would benefit both from their own liberalization – which typically accounts for the bulk of the estimated welfare gains – as well as improve stability in their own trade regimes through binding more products and doing so closer to applied rates. And they would benefit greatly from increased market access in other developing and developed country markets (Hertel and Martin, 1999).

Good ideas, but can they be implemented?

This group of topics contains three issues – government procurement, electronic commerce and trade facilitation – in which new agreements may result in welfare improvements for developing countries, but which have institutional requirements that may be a serious burden for many WTO members to shoulder.

Government procurement

Few developing countries have joined the plurilateral agreement already in place. Some (including Chile and Hong Kong) agree with the objectives of the agreement but find its implementation provisions to be cumbersome. Participation in the agreement has become almost mandatory for newly acceding members, with the United States insisting on all acceding countries making a commitment in this regard (Michalopoulos, 1998).

Developing countries can benefit significantly from participating in the agreement – not so much because of their capacity to gain international contracts but in terms of improved resource utilization through more transparent and competitive government procurement practices. The question of increased transparency, in particular, received a great deal of attention in the discussions preceding Seattle.

As most government purchases relate to services rather than merchandise trade, the issues have essentially to do with liberalization and national treatment of foreign service providers. Indeed, a recent study (Evenett and Hoekman, 1999) suggests that it is important to eliminate preferences in government procurement *before improved competitive practices* are put in place. This is because if the opposite sequence is followed, preferences on government procurement could lead to an increased resource misallocation.

For developing countries the issues have to do with implementation: can the agreement be simplified – especially in its operation on the basis of bilateral reciprocity? Is this an important enough area for developing country WTO members to adopt new multilateral rules? Can they be assured that the technical assistance that they will need to implement the new provisions, and probably the new legislation required, would be forthcoming?

Trade facilitation

This topic has generated considerable interest in the private sector and is being considered as one of the areas in which new 'rules-making' efforts may be desirable. As formal trade barriers have gone down, procedural requirements of various kinds impede the flow of goods and services: innumerable and non-standardized documentation requirements exist for exports and imports. On average, about 60 documents are used in an international trade transaction – and they often differ from country to country. These are compounded by antiquated official clearance procedures. Lack of transparency and predictability is a major source of uncertainty in terms of the costs and time for delivery of commercial transactions. The problems are much greater in developing countries where automated procedures in customs administration do not exist.

The WTO work so far has identified the following areas in which proposals have been made for improvements and revisions: (i) government mandated information requirements; (ii) procedures for customs clearance; (iii) transparency and review; and (iv) transport and transit. There are at least eight international conventions and agreements guiding these areas, of which the most important is the 1973 International Convention for the Simplification and Customization of Customs Procedures (Kyoto Convention of 1973) but in which no more than half of WTO members participate.

Developing-countries' trade would benefit significantly from improved trade facilitation measures. Few, however, have the technical capacity to adhere meaningfully to multilateral rules regarding such procedures without significantly strengthening their institutions. While technical assistance would obviously be needed, such assistance may not be sufficient to modernize their institutions in a reasonable period of time. As a consequence, meaningful progress in this area may best be made by keeping the subject outside the 'single undertaking' (see below). If there is enough support to conclude a multilateral agreement, developing countries should have an option of joining at a later time when they have the institutional capacity to meet its requirements.

Electronic commerce accounts for a small but rapidly growing proportion of world trade in goods and services. This growth has occurred in a legal vacuum with few accepted rules and disciplines. Moreover, the cross-border nature of the transactions has made the issue of legal jurisdiction unclear. Over time, a framework of global rules for transactions over the Internet will have to be established. The key issue is whether there is enough understanding of the issues and enough international consensus to attempt to reach an agreement as part of a new round of WTO negotiations.

The topic was first raised in the context of the WTO Geneva Ministerial meeting of 1998. At that time, WTO members committed to a standstill; that is, 'to continue their current practice of not imposing customs duties on electronic transmissions' and to produce a report that may contain recommendations for action (WTO, 1998b). In subsequent discussions, developing countries raised a variety of concerns. Some thought that such a commitment would result in countries foregoing future opportunities to collect customs revenue; others were concerned as to whether the electronic mode of service supply should be given preferential status relative to other modes which were being regulated. Most were unwilling to commit because they felt that they did not have enough understanding of the issues and because of uncertainties about the policy implications of future technological change.

Developing-country concerns about foregone tariff revenues are clearly an exaggeration – after all, most countries provide large-scale exemptions to their existing tariff schedules. Further WTO discussions, while reaching consensus on a few points, also identified a large number of issues: a consensus is emerging that the electronic delivery of services falls within the scope of the GATS and all GATS provisions are applicable to it, and that the 'technological neutrality' of GATS means that electronic supply of services is permitted unless specifically excluded. There are many uncertainties, however: (i) how to classify internet access and services, including new ones; (ii) whether certain products electronically transmitted should be classified as goods; (iii) what are the proper links to the Telecommunications Agreement; (iv) how to ensure privacy of transactions and how to value encrypted data; and (v) what are the links to TRIPs – for example, copyright protection for electronic and database material. And finally, there are many standards-related issues which need to be addressed involving interconnection and interoperability of systems, to ensure that standards set by governments do not impede electronic commerce (WTO, 1999b).

The major concern that most developing countries should have on electronic commerce is that they do not have the technical capacity to meaningfully negotiate a multilateral agreement at this time. To do so, in most cases, may result in assuming commitments which they do not have the capacity to implement. Thus, it may well be that, at present, developing countries agree simply to continue the standstill on tariff-exempt electronic transmissions and defer multilateral negotiations on this issue to a later time.

Some difficult issues

The environment

Issues involving the various links between trade and the environment have been extensively discussed in the WTO since 1995[11] The issues are thorny and complex, driven by two concerns: on the part of the developed countries, a desire to be responsive to strong pressures exerted by domestic environmental groups to preserve global biodiversity and prevent environmental damage through all possible measures – including trade restrictions; and on the part of developing countries, concerns that developed countries violate WTO rules when they act to restrict access to their market on environmental grounds, sometimes unilaterally determined, and especially when the alleged environmental damage occurs beyond the developed-countries' own borders, and extends to the processes and production methods (PPMs) of the traded merchandise.

There are several interrelated issues that have formed the basis of the debate so far and the positions on these issues vary both among developed and developing countries:

- The relationship between trade provisions of Multilateral Environmental Agreements (MEA) and the WTO. This includes questions such as which MEAs to include; what to do in case the measures are incompatible with the WTO; what to do regarding countries which are not members of a particular MEA; and which dispute settlement mechanisms to use.

- Whether and how to take into account process and production methods as they relate to the environment in the framing of trade rules; and in this connection what weight to put on multilateral agreements (for, example on ozone-depleting substances) or unilateral judgements, such as those used by the United States in the tuna-dolphin case; or the precautionary principle used by the EC. Also, what to do about proliferating eco-labelling schemes, which could adversely affect exports from developing countries, and how to bring them in conformity with broader WTO rules on standards; and, finally, how to deal with emerging issues such as those related to trade in genetically modified organisms.

● The general relationship between trade, the environment and development: this has many facets, ranging from the formal recognition that poverty is a major cause of environmental degradation, to provision of assistance to developing countries to promote sustainable development, to issues related to the impact of new environmentally motivated standards imposed by developed countries on the competitiveness of developing-countries' exports, and to the broad relationship of different trade liberalization measures and the environment (Bhagwati and Srinivasan, 1996).

Developing countries face a basic dilemma: do they negotiate an agreement covering the various complex trade and environment issues, which could involve legitimizing through explicit, detailed understandings different market access restraints on environmental grounds but would limit the more blatant unilateral developed-country abuses; or do they leave the system as it is, where developed countries can use the broad language of GATT Article XXb to restrain trade on environmental grounds (recently interpreted very broadly by the Appellate Body of the Dispute Settlement Mechanism (DSM) of the WTO in the shrimp–turtle case), and rely on dispute settlement to curb developed-country abuses? Various developing countries would respond to this dilemma differently. But on balance, it may well be, given the difficulties developing countries have in accessing the DSM, they may wish to negotiate an interpretive statement on Article XXb.

Competition

The issue was originally placed on the WTO agenda by the United States as a means of promoting greater market access, especially in the Japanese market, where it felt that poorly enforced competition laws disadvantaged United States exporters; but the United States has cooled off in its advocacy of a WTO agreement on this issue.

There is no consensus on how to proceed in the WTO. The alternatives include: (a) the establishment of minimum anti-trust standards that would prohibit certain practices while applying notification requirements on others, but which would be administered by national authorities; (b) linking competition policy to limitations in the use of other WTO practices – for example, anti-dumping; and (c) extending the coverage of WTO rules under Article XXIII of the GATT which allows WTO members to challenge practices which, while not illegal under WTO rules, result in nullification of benefits negotiated in trade agreements.

For small developing economies, an open trade regime and liberal policies toward foreign investment may be sufficient to cope with most problems arising from domestically generated restrictive business practices. For those that have enacted competition laws, implementation capacity is often limited. The highest priority for many is to establish and implement proper national competition policies which need to focus on facilitating new entry, eliminating administrative obstacles to the establishment of new firms, reducing transport costs which create local monopolies and so on – rather than establishing and implementing an anti-trust machinery.

Moreover, for small developing countries the key issues regarding restrictive business practices may involve primarily activities of transnational corporations (TNCs) (Hoekman and Holmes, 1999; Low and Subramanian, 1996). These corporations have the potential to dominate small economies or reduce the benefits that accrue to host countries – for example, through transfer pricing and related actions that stem from the large proportion of international trade which involves intra-firm transactions. Unless such activities are brought under the competition rules proposed, which has not been the case so far, there is little reason to focus on multilateral rule-making for developing countries in this area.

Although tightening anti-dumping rules would benefit all countries, neither the United States nor the EU is interested in introducing competition mechanisms to deal with issues covered by anti-dumping. And the recent upsurge of anti-dumping actions by many developing countries suggests that many of them are of the same view. There is also little to be gained by developing countries in improved market access in developed-country markets by multilateral rules covering anti-trust. Most of these markets already have reasonably-functioning anti-trust systems which could be used by developing countries. For all these reasons, a multilateral agreement on competition is not of high priority for most developing countries.

Foreign investment

Foreign investment *is* of great importance to developing countries. But the key questions are not its importance to development but whether a balanced agreement can be reached on the issue, which reflects both the interests of developing countries and those of TNCs and foreign investors, and whether the WTO is the right institution in which to pursue it. The recent history of international negotiations suggests a negative answer to both questions.

The issue was raised in the Uruguay Round, only to be limited to the trade-related aspects of investment measures (TRIMs) because of developing-country opposition. A WTO working group on investment was established following the Singapore Ministerial. In parallel, there was an effort to conclude an agreement within the OECD, the so called Multilateral Agreement on Investment (MAI). When that failed, the EU proposed that the issue be pursued in the WTO. It should also be recalled that the issue was included in the Havana Charter for the International Trade Organization, and that in the 1970s, much before the MAI, there were several efforts initiated by UNCTAD and backed by many developing countries to reach an international understanding on restrictive business practices of TNCs – which also failed, because of opposition by the developed countries.

The effort to pursue an agreement within the OECD – which excluded developing countries – was ill-advised. In addition, developing countries and many NGOs have argued with reason that the draft MAI was both too ambitious and did not contain a proper balance between the rights and responsibilities of TNCs, nor between the rights and responsibilities of the TNCs on the one hand and those of the governments receiving foreign investment, on the other.

In the last two decades, there has been a great deal of analysis focusing on the enormous potential that foreign private investment carries for development, but also of the potential problems and pitfalls of a totally unregulated foreign private investment regime for developing countries with weak supervisory institutions. Over the same period, developing countries liberalized capital markets and regulations governing foreign private investment – both direct and portfolio – which led to spectacular increases in the volume of private capital flows to developing countries – all this without a multilateral agreement. Private capital flows have been concentrated and many countries, for example in Sub-Saharan Africa, have not been able to attract significant flows of foreign private investment. It is doubtful, however, that a multilateral agreement to increase the future inflow of foreign investment is a priority for such countries.

Given the previous history of international negotiations on this topic, there should be little optimism that a formal agreement is achievable which balances the interests of foreign private investors and developing countries. Notwithstanding a generally more favourable attitude towards foreign private investment in developing countries, recent private capital volatility has, if anything, made such an agreement even more difficult. And it is not clear that such an agreement, while potentially helpful, is actually necessary for developing countries wishing to attract foreign private investment.

Various aspects of foreign investment are already addressed in the GATS, which offers the opportunity for voluntary commitments. As Hoekman and Saggi (1999) argue, there is potential for further such commitments by countries in this area. A more general agreement is neither needed nor feasible.

Labour standards

Despite being repeatedly rebuffed, most recently at the Seattle Ministerial, the United States continues to bring up labour standards as a topic for possible WTO negotiations. In this it has enjoyed the support of a few developed countries in the EC which, however, have advocated a 'softer' position involving the establishment of joint working groups between the WTO and the International Labour Organization (ILO). But most countries have been of the view that the issue belongs, and should be addressed solely, in the ILO. The proposal is intended to placate protectionist attitudes, primarily of US labour unions. It is also being supported by a number of well-meaning NGOs, whose legitimate concerns in this area – for example, regarding child labour – indirectly provide 'cover' and support to protectionists. It can lead to no plausible benefits to developing-countries' trade. Therefore, it should be strongly resisted as a topic for inclusion in any WTO negotiations.

Strategic options

The above analysis of the topics for WTO negotiations of interest to developing countries has reached several conclusions: first, that in addition to the already agreed negotiations on Agriculture and Services and the review of TRIPs, action on strengthening the implementation capability of developing countries should be a high priority in the immediate future. Second, there are two other topics, industrial tariffs and the environment, which for different reasons should also be of interest to many developing countries. Third, there are several other topics (government procurement, trade facilitation, electronic commerce) on which multilateral negotiations may either be premature or in which developing countries require considerable assurances that the necessary capacity to implement them is put in place before an agreement is reached. Finally, there are several topics (labour standards, competition, foreign investment) in which future negotiations to establish new rules are neither in the interest of nor a priority for most developing countries.

There continue to be strong political-economy arguments for a new WTO Round of multilateral trade negotiations involving a single undertaking, but for a relatively small number of topics so that it does not severely tax the negotiating or institutional capacity of countries, and which can be concluded over a reasonable time-frame. The basic reason why a single undertaking is needed is to permit trade-offs across topics.

Developing countries have important interests in having developed countries liberalize agriculture, reduce tariff peaks in industrial products, modify TRIPS, as well as liberalize some specific service sectors and modes of supply. On the other hand, developed countries would be looking for additional developing-country commitments in the form of more bindings and reductions in the bound and applied rates of industrial products, as well as additional commitments in service sectors. The only way developing countries can overcome the opposition of entrenched protectionism in developed countries – for example, in agriculture, maritime services, or textiles – is to take advantage of the pressure that export interests in the developed countries will bring to bear on their own governments to negotiate, in order to open up developing-country markets. Countervailing pressure from export interests of developed countries on their governments is critical to opening up developed-country markets in areas of interest to developing countries (Krueger, 1999). This pressure and linkages may exist within a particular topic – for example, industrial tariffs – but are maximized if there are opportunities for linkages across a wider set of negotiations.

The danger of a large set of negotiations for developing countries is that it will tax their institutional capacity to negotiate and implement new agreements. This is an important reason why developing countries should try to negotiate no more than four to five topics: agriculture, services, TRIPS, industrial tariffs and, possibly, the environment. To use the old bicycle analogy: the momentum of a new Round is needed to push the bicycle forward, but we should not to load the bicycle with so much baggage that it collapses from the excessive weight.

Developing countries would also need to decide on the scope and nature of S&D treatment they would seek in any new agreements. The two elements of S&D that developing countries should insist on in any new agreements are the same as those which are necessary for implementation of their existing commitments: effective technical assistance and reasonable transition periods to permit countries to develop the institutional capacity needed to implement WTO obligations.

A similar approach is needed to deal with the special problems of LDCs. Already, there are indications that developed countries may be prepared to go further in extending voluntary preferences to these countries, perhaps even extend a commitment to duty-free and quota-free access to virtually all LDC exports. Such commitments are relatively easy to make, as LDCs account for very small fractions of developed-country-imports in most product categories. As a consequence, LDCs may not have to 'offer' any new liberalizing commitments in order to obtain improved market access.

The main constraints to LDC export expansion, however, derive from weaknesses in institutional capacities as well as supply-side factors (UNCTAD, 1998; WTO, 1998c). Thus, the key issue for LDCs is how to ensure concrete and effective support for trade-related capacity-building measures in such areas as agriculture, services or TRIPS. At the same time it is important for LDCs to recognize the pitfalls of past developing-country experience with the flexibility provided under WTO rules and disciplines. Existing S&D provisions permit LDCs the most freedom of policy choice possible, in areas such as subsidies, that they can least afford. Tighter WTO disciplines in some policy areas may be helpful to LDC governments that wish to introduce and gain domestic consensus for trade policy reform.

Finally, the question of the 'credit' that developing countries could get as a consequence of their own autonomous liberalization of trade in goods or services should also be considered in this context. This issue was raised first by the World Bank in 1984, when it became apparent that a number of developing countries were liberalizing their trade regimes, and the question was how to obtain 'credit' for such liberalization in the upcoming Round (Michalopoulos, 1985; Krueger and Michalopoulos, 1985). There was no general provision in the UR to deal with this issue. But the principle received explicit support in the Joint Statement issued in Seattle by the heads of the IMF, World Bank and WTO. However, the only way developing countries can use it in practice is by converting trade liberalization which they have autonomously undertaken – because it was in their interest to do so – into legally bound tariff schedules or service commitments which can then be used to obtain improved market access for their own exports or for any other benefits they seek to obtain in future negotiations.

Conclusions

Developing countries can derive significant benefits from a new WTO Round of negotiations. While the interests of different groups of countries will differ, there are a number of important issues beyond agriculture and services, on which developing countries as a group may wish to reach agreement in a new Round, especially those of TRIPs (on which a Review is already envisaged) and industrial tariffs. It may also be advantageous that an agreement on some linkages between trade, environment and development be explored.

The failure of the Seattle Ministerial should be viewed as a temporary setback to efforts to reach multilateral agreements in a number of areas of importance to the world economy and to the prospects of developing countries. It is unclear how long it would take to organize the political consensus in both developed and developing countries in support for a new Round of multilateral trade negotiations, especially in view of the lack of a 'fast track' authority in the United States. But an effort is needed to develop such support over time in order to combat the protectionist sentiments that are constantly present in all countries. Despite the difficulties in reaching agreement among the many WTO members, multilateral negotiations which are linked as a 'single undertaking' are preferable to individual negotiations. This is because they maximize the opportunities for trade-offs across issues and permit liberalizing forces in both developed and developing countries to exert pressure on governments for a liberalized trade environment worldwide. But a new Round should not contain too many issues, as it would strain the institutional and implementation capacity of many developing countries.

Developing countries should be prepared to exchange mutually liberalizing trade concessions, because that is the only way to maximize the benefits they obtain from multilateral trade negotiations and because of the increasing importance of intra-developing-country trade. Their focus on special and differential treatment should be on the establishment of realistic transition periods and technical assistance to help them deal with institutional weaknesses, not to avoid needed policy reforms. But they should not be prepared to accept commitments they cannot implement within the context of existing institutional capacity, in exchange for vague offers of technical assistance. Explicit developing-country commitments in areas in which they have implementation difficulties should be balanced with explicit developed-country commitments to fund the needed technical or other assistance.

Notes

1. The author is Senior Economic Advisor in the World Bank. The views expressed in this essay are solely those of the author and should not be in

any way attributed to the World Bank. He wishes to thank Sam Laird and Frank Wolter of the WTO, Otto Genne of the Netherlands delegation to the WTO, Esperenza Duran of AITIC, Will Martin of the World Bank and Richard Snape for helpful comments on earlier drafts of this chapter.

2. The chapter draws in part on work of the author published under the title 'Developing Country Strategies for the 'Millennium Round' in the *Journal of International Trade*, 33 (5) (October, 1999) 1–30, with the kind permission of Kluwer Law International.

3. Croome (1998) contains a review of the various topics and their origin – that is, unresolved issues from the Uruguay Round (UR), decisions of previous WTO Ministerial meetings, and so on. See also Anderson (1999).

4. There is also a third group of countries with small non-diversified agricultural sectors – for example, small island economies – which are not likely to be significant participants in these negotiations.

5. Some also point to the 'unfairness' of the agriculture agreement since it still permits greater support levels for developed countries – which had in the past given a great deal of assistance to their agricultural sector – as opposed to the developing countries which penalized agriculture in the base period (Das, 1998).

6. Although there may be some problems for LDCs regarding the limits on AMS after the expiry of the transition periods (UNCTAD, 1998).

7. For details see Duran and Michalopoulos (1999).

8. Many other topics have been under consideration, especially regional agreements, and anti-dumping. They are not considered here either because there is no widespread support or because there is active opposition by some WTO members for a modification of existing arrangements.

9. The term 'industrial' is a slight misnomer: it includes all tariff lines other than those classified as 'agriculture' defined in the UR as HS 1-24 and a few additional lines from other HS categories (WTO, 1995).

10. The actual tariffs developing countries face are likely to be lower because of the existence of various preferential schemes. But the very proliferation of such schemes makes a calculation of the actual tariffs they face problematic.

11. A useful summary of the main WTO issues from a developing country perspective is presented in Shahin (1997); see also OECD (1999).

References

Anderson, K., 'The WTO Agenda for the New Millennium', *Economic Record*, 75 (228) (March 1999) 77–88.

Bhagwati, J., and Srinivasan, T. N., 'Trade and the Environment: Does Environmental Diversity Detract from the Case from Free Trade?', in J. Bhagwati, and R. Hudec (eds), *Fair Trade and Harmonization* (Cambridge, MA: MIT Press, 1996) pp. 159–224.

Braga, C. A., 'Trade-related Intellectual Property Rights: the Uruguay Round Agreement and its Economic Implications', in W. Martin and L. A. Winters (eds), *The Uruguay Round and the Developing Countries* (London: Cambridge University Press, 1996) pp. 341–79.

Correa, C. M., *Implementing the TRIPS Agreement* (Penang: Third World Network, 1998).

Croome, J., 'The Present Outlook for Trade Negotiations in the World Trade Organization', *Policy Research Working Paper*, no. 1992 (Washington, DC: World Bank, 1998).

Das, B. L., *The WTO Agreements: Defficiencies, Imbalances and Required Changes*, (Penang: Third World Network, 1998).

Deardorff, A., 'Welfare Effects of Global Patent Protection', *Economica*, 59 (1992) 35–51.

Duran, E., and Michalopoulos, C., 'Intellectual Property Rights and Developing Countries in the WTO "Millennium" Round', *The Journal of World Intellectual Property*, 2 (6) (November 1999) 853–74.

Evenett, S., and Hoekman, B., 'Government Procurement: Do Border Barriers Matter?', CEPR Workshop (London, 19–20 February 1999).

Finger, J. M., and Winters, L. A., 'What Can the WTO Do for Developing Countries?', in A. O. Krueger (ed.), *The WTO as an International Organization* (Chicago: University of Chicago Press, 1998).

Finger, J. M., and Schuler, P., 'Implementation of Uruguay Round Commitments: the Development Challenge', *Policy Research Working Paper*, no. 2215, World Bank (October 1999) pp. 365–97.

Francois, J., and Wooton, I., 'Trade in International Transport Services: The Role of Competition', Rotterdam University (processed, August 1999).

Hertel, T., and Martin, W., 'Developing Countries Interests in Liberalizing Manufactures Trade', CEPR Workshop (London, 19–20 February 1999).

Hoekman, B., and Holmes, P., 'Competition Policy, Developing Countries and the WTO', *Policy Research Working Paper*, no. 2211, World Bank (October 1999).

Hoekman, B., and Saggi, K., 'Multilateral Disciplines for Investment-Related Policies?', paper presented at the Conference on Global Regionalism, *Instituto Affari Internazionali* (Rome, 8–9 February 1999).

International Grains Council, Food Aid Committee, 'Food Aid Convention' (London, 24 March 1999).

Krueger, A. O. (ed.), *The WTO as an International Organization* (Chicago: University of Chicago Press, 1998).

Krueger, A. O., 'The Developing Countries and the Next Round of Multilateral Trade Negotiations', *The World Economy*, 22 (7) (September 1999).

Krueger, A. O., and Michalopoulos, C., 'Developing Country Trade Policies and the International Economic System', in E. Preeg (ed.), *Hard Bargaining Ahead: US Trade Policy and Developing Countries* (Washington, DC: Overseas Development Council, 1985) pp. 39–57.

Kwa, A., and Bello, W., 'Guide to the WTO Agreement in Agriculture', Chulalong University (processed) (1998).

Laird, S., 'Multilateral Approaches to Market Access Negotiations', in M. R. Mendoza, P. Low and B. Kotschwar (eds), *Trade Rules in the Making* (Washington, DC: Brookings, 1999).

Low, P., and Subramanian, A., 'Beyond TRIMS: a Case for Multilateral Action on Investment Rules and Competition Policy', in W. Martin and L. A. Winters (eds), *The Uruguay Round and the Developing Countries* (London: Cambridge University Press, 1996) pp. 380–408.

Michalopoulos, C., 'Non Tariff Measures', *Trade and Development*, no. 6 (Washington, DC: Development Committee, 1985).

Michalopoulos, C., 'WTO Accession for Countries in Transition', *Post-Soviet Prospects*, VI (3) (1998). Available at www.csis.org/html/psp.html

Michalopoulos, C., 'Developing Countries in the WTO', *The World Economy*, 22 (1) (1999a) 117–43.

Michalopoulos, 'Trade Policy and Market Access Issues for Developing Countries', *Policy Research Working Paper*, no. 2214, World Bank (October 1999b).

OECD, 'Trade Measures in Multilateral Environmental Agreements: Synthesis Report of Three Case Studies', COM/END/TD(98) 127FINAL (Paris: OECD, 1999).

Shahin, M., *'Trade and the Environment in the WTO: a Review of its Initial Work and Future Prospects'* (Penang: Third World Network, 1997).

Srinivasan, T. N., *Developing Countries and the Multilateral Trading System: From the GATT to the Uruguay Round and the Future* (Boulder and Oxford Westview Press, 1998).

UNCTAD, 'Post-Uruguay Round Tariff Environment for Developing Country Exports', UNCTAD/WTO Joint Study, TD/B/COM.1/14 (October 1997).

UNCTAD, *The Least Developed Countries 1998 Report* (Geneva: United Nations, 1998).

WTO, *The Results of the Uruguay Round of Multilateral Trade Negotiations: the Legal Texts* (Geneva: WTO, 1995).

WTO, 'Trade-Related Technical Assistance Needs-Assessment', Committee on Trade and Development, WT/COMTD/IF/1-38 (1997–98).

WTO, *Cairns Group Ministerial Meeting, Communiqué*, WT/L/263 (April 1998a).

WTO, 'Declaration on Global Electronic Commerce', WT/MIN/(98)/DEC/2 (26 May 1998b).

WTO, 'Market Access for Exports of Goods and Services from the LDCs: Barriers and Constraints', WT/COMT/LDC/W/11/REV.1 (4 December 1998c).

WTO, 'Developing Countries and the Multilateral Trading System: Past and Present', Development Division, Background Document for High Level Symposium on Trade and Development (Geneva, 17–18 March 1999a).

WTO, 'Work Programme on Electronic Commerce', S/C/8 (March 1999b).

7
Assessing the Promise of a Preferential Trade Agreement

Michael Michaely

Introduction

This chapter intends to contribute to the methodology of assessing *ex-ante* the potential for welfare expansion of a contemplated preferential trade agreement (PTA): to analyze salient issues involved in such assessment; and, in view of this analysis, to clarify the meaning of some conventional yardsticks used for the purpose, or suggest several new tools.

The discussion will take place predominantly within the Vinerian framework; that is, it will address the issue of the impact of a PTA through changes in trade flows and, in conjunction with them, in domestic economic activity. It is probably worthwhile to be explicit on what the analysis will not do: (i) By implicitly assuming a free-trade area rather than a customs union, it will avoid the issue of establishment of a common external tariff. Yet, as a matter of convenience and focus, it will also ignore the issue of the rules of origin, which are inherent in a free-trade area and which may distort its operation (see Krueger, 1993). (ii) It is a 'static' analysis, referring to the impact of a PTA within an existing system and avoiding 'dynamic' issues which have formed a substantial part of recent discussions. It also overlooks potential economies of scale. (iii) It will not go into 'political-economy' considerations – again, an important element of recent analyses which refer to the extent and direction to which the conclusion of a PTA would affect other trade-policy decisions (such as the introduction of multilateral or unilateral tariff changes, or the conclusion of other PTAs). (iv) Finally – as the chapter's title implies – the analysis will refer strictly to trade, and not to issues such as free labour mobility, integration of capital markets, harmonization of taxation systems or monetary policies, and the like. And, although the analysis applies in principle to trade in services as well as in goods, many of the issues involved refer in fact only to the latter.

In the rest of this section, the conventional list of attributes involved in the assessment of a PTA will be briefly re-stated. Following this, the plan of the discussion will be laid out.

Viner's (1950) pioneering analysis concluded, roughly, that so far as the welfare outcome of a PTA is concerned, everything is possible. Viner's followers, primarily Meade (1955) and Lipsey (1960), have developed the major considerations by which the likelihood of one outcome rather than another should be judged. The Meade–Lipsey criteria, which have long been the conventional wisdom, will be listed here in the briefest way, since their rationale is only too well known. Some of these criteria are not entirely independent: they may be related to others or even be components of others. The order in which the list is organized does not necessarily reflect importance: rather, it is intended to serve the order of the following discussions.

A home-country welfare expansion rather than a contraction, following a PTA, is more likely:

   (i) the higher the level of the home-country's (geographically uniform) tariffs prior to the agreement;
  (ii) the higher the tariff level of the contemplated partner;[1]
 (iii) the larger the economic size of the partner;
  (iv) the higher the share of the partner in providing the home-country's imports;
   (v) the lower the ratio of imports from the rest of the world to the home-country's aggregate economic activity;
  (vi) the closer the relative prices in the partner's economy are to those of the rest of the world. This is partly related to (iii) above – economic size – and to the following criterion, namely:
 (vii) the more similar the partner to the rest of the world in the structure of its economic activity.[2]

The first three attributes listed here – (i), (ii) and (iii) – will be addressed in the following section, 'Clarification of criteria and indication for measurement'. The third section, 'The intensity of trade flows', will then discuss one measure related to attributes (iii) and (iv); whereas the fourth section, 'Indices of compatibility', will refer primarily to aspects of attributes (vi) and (vii).[3] The final section will draw some conclusions.

Clarification of criteria and indication for measurement

We shall now turn to the analysis of the first three criteria just listed: clarify them where clarification is needed and specify the concepts in some detail, in view of the principles following which the criteria have been formulated. Part of this analysis will not reveal much that is new; but in other parts issues will be exposed which have been paid little attention to and consideration of which should make the application of the criteria involved more meaningful.

Level of the home-country's pre-agreement tariffs

The higher the tariff level the more likely will trade creation rather than trade diversion follow a PTA, and the stronger would be the (favourable) consumption effect due to the reduction of the home price to the consumer.[4] But a few issues must be raised:

(i) What is the home-country's (aggregate) 'tariff level'? The term is, as is rather well known, far from being straightforward and a considerable amount of attention has been paid in the literature to its ramifications.[5] Using a weighted average to indicate the aggregate level in which import values of the individual goods are used for weights must yield an outcome which, for well-known reasons, would be biased downwards – in most cases, probably drastically so. A non-weighted average, on the other hand, though free of bias, would resemble the 'true' average only by accident. For the purpose at hand, however, the relevant question is not primarily whether the definition, or index, used is a good approximation of the 'true' concept but whether a bias is introduced, in some way, in the use of one index or another for the assessment of a PTA. That is, when we compare aggregate tariff levels in the context of the statement that starting from a higher tariff level makes a PTA more promising, does the use of a proposed index lead to a bias? The answer appears to be in the negative. Though either a weighted average (by imports) or a simple arithmetic mean are poor approximations of the 'true' average level, the absence of bias should make legitimate the use of either of these indices for *ordering* alternative starting levels of tariffs.

(ii) A related issue arises in this context – namely, the degree of *dispersion* in the home-country's tariff system. Suppose, for simplicity, that we use an unweighted, arithmetic mean as our index of aggregate tariff level and that by this measure two tariff systems are found to be equal. But one system involves a higher level of dispersion of individual tariff levels than the other. The promise of a welfare expansion rather than contraction, following a PTA, should be higher when the more-dispersed tariff system is involved. This could be seen from the following reasoning. It is well known that the welfare loss from the existence of a tariff system is a function not just of the average tariff level but also of the degree of dispersion in it.[6] Hence, the gain from trade creation as well as the (positive) consumption effect following a PTA would be higher the higher the dispersion (given the average level). The loss from trade diversion, on the other hand (again, of course, ceteris paribus), is a function of the tariff level alone and not of the dispersion. Hence, taken together, these considerations should lead to a higher expectation for a welfare improvement when the tariff system is more highly dispersed. We thus reach the conclusion that in assessing the significance of the pre-agreement (home-country's) tariff system, levels should be indicated not just of the average tariff but also of the system's degree of *dispersion*.

(iii) Yet another issue should be raised in this context – namely, whether a tariff level *specific* to the partner should be used. Although by assumption the home-country's tariffs are *geographically* uniform prior to the PTA, no uniformity by *commodities* would be found (except by chance, so rare as to have never been observed – and if this does happen, all the discussion of averages and dispersion would become redundant). Unless – again by chance, whose probability must be zero – the commodity structure of imports from the partner happens to be identical to that of the home-country's imports from the rest of the world, the average tariff level of the former must be different from that of the latter. Is it of any relevance, in the present context, that such difference exists? Consequently, should we be concerned only with the home-country's aggregate tariff level or also with the average tariff level on imports from the partner?

The answer is that the latter tariff level is of much significance, although we do not know whether particularly low or particularly high tariffs on the partner's imports is a factor more conducive to welfare expansion or its contraction.[7] When, say, this particular tariff level is low, it should be presumed that: (1) To the extent that trade creation takes place, the gain from it should be low. (2) When trade diversion is the outcome, its loss would, again, be low. (3) Finally, the (favourable) consumption effect would also be low. Thus, all welfare effects – positive and negative – are likely to be low.

Hence, (this is *not*, though, a logical inevitability!) the agreement is likely to be of smaller consequence – one way or another – than had the tariff level under consideration been high. To cite an extreme case: when this tariff level is zero, the agreement would be meaningless (but with a proviso to be specified shortly). We do not know, however, whether in the general case this (smaller) impact is more or less likely to be positive or negative.[8]

The discussion thus far suggests that 'the' level of the home-country's tariffs prior to the PTA should be represented by a specific average concerned with tariffs on imports from the partner. This, however, should be qualified: it may be expected that following the PTA import patterns would change – even that new imports altogether should be forthcoming from the partner (once more, in the Vinerian context this is the *only* way in which imports change!). Hence, other tariffs on goods which are not imported from the partner, or not to any significant extent, should also be relevant. Thus, the attribute on hand, namely the home-country's tariff level prior to the PTA, should be indicated by *both* the aggregate tariff level and by a measure specific to the partner.

(iv) Finally, an issue exists of which type of tariffs should be the subject of observation. Specifically, should it be *nominal* tariffs – nominal rates of protection – or *effective* protection rates? The answer is that *both* sets of protection rates are relevant. For the extent of a potential trade diversion, it is the set of nominal tariff rates which matters.[9] For the *potential* for trade creation, the *nominal* rate is again the relevant variable. But once trade creation does take place in any given activity, it is the *effective* protection rate which would determine the size of the gain from it to the economy. For the consumption gain the *nominal* tariff rate is applicable. Both sets of rates should hence be used. (This also applies – as could be seen, even more forcefully – to the specific average tariff level related to the structure of imports from the partner.) In pragmatic terms, one should probably construct two indices. One, to represent the level of nominal tariffs, would be an arithmetic, unweighted average of tariff rates. The other – certainly more difficult to construct – would be a weighted average of effective protection rates where the size of *value added* should be used as the weight of each activity.

The level of the partner's tariffs

In considering this factor, no ambiguity is involved. Removal (or reduction) of these tariffs would definitely be a source of gain to the home country – whether for the partner trade creation or trade diversion follows, and whether it leads for it to a net gain or loss. And, again unambiguously, the gain to the home country would be higher the higher the size of removal of the partner's tariffs (whether due to a higher initial tariff level or, when the tariff is only lowered rather than fully eliminated, to a higher proportion of tariff reduction).[10] With complete tariff elimination, the gain per unit of trade translates simply to the rate of tariff imposed by the partner on any good imported from the home country.

As in the earlier case discussed, *two* separate 'average levels' of tariffs are relevant. The first applies to *existing* exports of the home country to the partner. Here, unlike other instances discussed thus far, the index used would be both *precise* and provide a *cardinal* outcome.[11] It should be a weighted average of tariff levels where the values of exports of each good to the partner are used for weights. The use of this measure in the present context would be free of the biases normally involved in estimating the 'average' tariff level. Combining the use of this measure with the total value of the trade flow involved – multiplying one by the other – would yield the aggregate gain, in money terms, of the home country from the partner's tariff removal.[12] To give it any meaning, this size should obviously be presented as a ratio of the country's aggregate economic activity.

Another index belongs again to the family of indicators of an *ordinal* outcome. This will be an average (once more, perhaps a simple arithmetic average would serve) of the partner's tariffs on its imports in general (that is, not specifically from the home country). This would be an indication of the potential of expansion of the home-country's exports, through displacement of the partner's imports from others, not necessarily where imports from the home country already exist (or, where they do, beyond their present size).

It should be noted that in this instance – that is, when the partner's tariffs are discussed – it is only the *nominal* tariff rates which are of concern: effective rates of protection are relevant to the welfare impact of the agreement on the partner, but not on the home country.

The partner's size and economic diversification

It had been considered an important and undisputed criterion of assessment for many years that the larger the economy of a partner the more successful a PTA was likely to be. Recently, however, doubts have been raised; hence, a need exists for some clarification on this matter.[13]

The rationale for this criterion is rather simple, and is related to criteria (v) and (vi) on the list presented in the Introduction. The larger the size of the partner (whether this is due to a large size of a single economy or to a large number of countries which constitute the partner), the less distinct it is likely to be. That is, the more its economic structure will resemble that of the rest of the world (unless the 'rest of the world' itself becomes only a small fraction of the world) and the more relative prices in its tradable sector will resemble those of the rest of the world. Hence, trade diversion towards it would be less costly and the fall of domestic prices of imports in the home country would be larger, following the agreement. In an extreme case in which the partner is large enough to constitute most of the world (in terms of economic activity), a PTA would become almost identical with a complete move of the home country to free trade.

An objection to this line of reasoning has been raised in recent years by Bhagwati and Panagaryia – both separately and jointly.[14] They argue, to the contrary, that 'small is beautiful' for a partner; the smaller the partner, the less would be the deterioration of the home-country's terms of trade following the PTA and the smaller, hence, its (certain) loss.

This, indeed, is a valid argument when the partner country falls in the range of what I have termed 'ultra-small' economies; that is, when the partner is small enough for the home country to fully absorb the partner's exports, following the agreement, and still import some of the good from others. Thus, this becomes a valid and relevant consideration when agreements are contemplated among the world's smaller economies.

'Size' may obviously be interpreted in more than one way. In the present context both the (partner) country's *trade* and its aggregate economic activity should be considered (the two should be different in the general case – unless the ratios of trade to aggregate activity happen to be similar among economies). The size of both aggregate activity and trade provide an indication of the ease with which the partner's goods may potentially replace imports from others as well as the home-country's own production.

Diversification of the partner's economy is strongly related to its size – and is, indeed, a major element in leading one to consider size as an important attribute. Diversification of economic structures must be predominantly a function of two factors: size and level of development. And the more diversified the economy, the less 'unique' it should be; that is, the more it should resemble the rest of the world and, hence, the more promising should a PTA with it be.

Although this inference has not, apparently, been disputed in the literature, the just-discussed qualification concerning size should hold here as well. When the partner's economy is both small and highly diversified, its actual and potential export goods thus being many rather than few, it is more likely to become 'ultra small' in reference to the markets of its individual goods. Thus, when the partner is a small economy, diversification beyond some range would make an agreement with it less rather than more promising.

The intensity of trade flows

For the assessment of a concrete (contemplated) PTA, the observed size of trade with a partner (that is, its share in the home-country's aggregate flow) – referring to criterion (iv) above – is sufficient, with no need to go beyond it and inquire about the origins of this size. For generalizations, on the other hand (such as for assessing the role of 'regionalism'), a separation of contributing factors would be required.

The simplest, and most common, instrument used for such separation is the 'intensity ratio' of trade flows. This is defined – say, for country j's imports from country k – as:

$$I_{jk} = \frac{M_{jk}}{M_j} \Big/ \frac{X_k}{X_w},$$

where
j = home country
k = partner country
I_{jk} = intensity ratio of the partner's provision of the home-country's imports
M_{jk} = country j's imports from country k
M_j = aggregate imports of country j
X_k = aggregate exports of country k
X_w = aggregate world exports.[15]

An index of unity indicates a perfect 'neutrality': the share of the partner in providing the home country's imports is identical with the former's share in world exports (hence in world imports). An index above unity indicates a 'preference' to the partner – the stronger, the higher the index; whereas an index below unity would indicate, to the contrary, some constraining element. The intensity ratio is thus a summary measure of all factors other than the partner's size (that is, its share in world trade) which contribute to the bilateral trade flow – presumably, factors related to 'proximity', in its broad sense.

The 'intensity ratio' is a rather straightforward instrument of assessment. But two issues deserve some consideration. First, as it is presented here, the share of one country in the trade of the other is fully explained – by definition – by its size and by the intensity ratio of the trade flows involved (that is, by a multiplication of the two measures). In recent literature, a measure appears which does not have this attribute. This has been suggested by Summers (1991), whose (implied) definition of the intensity ratio is $I^s_{jk} = (M_{jk}/M_j)/(G_k/G_w)$, where G_k and G_w stand, respectively, for the partner's and the world's incomes (GDP) rather than, as before, the respective trade flows. The difference between the two measures lies, of course, in the fact that trade ratios (the share of trade in income) differ among economies (as well as over time in any given economy). Hence, to fully explain (in the accounting sense) the size (that is, share) of a given bilateral trade flow, one would have to add to the suggested intensity ratio another factor – the 'internal' trade share (in income). It is hard to see why this index should be used, rather than the one defined in its conventional manner.

An interesting issue is concerned with the possible relationship of the geographic pattern of a country's trade with its commodity structure. With a given size (of trade) of two economies, their bilateral trade flows may be large or small not because of factors (such as proximity, common language and the like) which facilitate one country's trade with another but (or, in addition to) due to the commodity structure of these flows. Thus, if one country's imports consist in a particularly high proportion of a good of which the other country exports a lot and of which it is (out of proportion) a large world supplier, imports of the former from the latter would tend to be high, regardless of proximity or distance. Hence, if the intensity ratio is presumed to indicate just the impact of factors which facilitate (or constrain) trade between two partners it has to be abstracted from or standardized for the impact of commodity composition of the trade flows of the countries involved – one's imports and the other's exports. This would be done through an adjusted index in which the intensity ratios are calculated separately for each good then aggregated using the appropriate weights.

Thus, the adjusted intensity ratio in country j's imports from country k is defined as:

$$\bar{I}_{jk} = \sum_i \left[\frac{M^i_{jk}}{M^i_j} \Big/ \frac{X^i_k}{X^i_w} \right] \frac{X^i_k}{X_k} = \frac{1}{X_k} \sum_i \left[\frac{M^i_{jk}}{M^i_j} . X^i_w \right],$$

where

$\bar{I}_{jk}$ = commodity-adjusted intensity ratio of country j's imports from country k

M^i_{jk} = imports of good i by country j from country k
M^i_j = aggregate imports of good i by country j
X^i_k = aggregate exports of good i by country k
X_k = aggregate exports of country k, and
X^i_w = aggregate world exports of good i.

Note that the weights used are the shares of each good in the exports of country k – the *partner* country.

The adjusted intensity ratio will, indeed, be an indicator of the impact of factors which have a geographic interpretation. The two indices – the adjusted and the unadjusted ratios – will differ from each other in the general case and either one could be larger or smaller than the other. The two will tend to be more similar when both the import structure of one country and the export structure of the other resemble those of the world flows. The two would thus tend to be far from each other when commodity structures of the two flows involved are more distinct. The adjusted ratio would be far below the unadjusted when both trade flows (one country's imports, the other's exports) are heavily concentrated in the same goods. The reverse relationship would be observed when the two flows are concentrated in different goods. Be that as it may, if our interest lies in geographic explanations the adjusted rather than the unadjusted intensity ratio should be used as an appropriate instrument for assessment.[16]

Indices of compatibility

Purpose of the indices

The 'indices of compatibility' to which we shall now turn are designed to address the prospects of trade expansion between two partners on the basis of the commodity structures of the countries involved – a feature which has been referred to repeatedly in our earlier discussions. They incorporate the effects of a variety of elements. Some of these are mentioned in or implied by the list of attributes presented in the Introduction; in particular, the degree of similarity of a partner – as well as of the home country – to the rest of the world and the level of commodity diversification in the partner country's trade and production flows. These are *general* attributes of an economy. But in addition the indices of compatibility, like the index of trade intensity we have just discussed, refer to the *specific* relationship of two concrete economies to each other. In other words: a knowledge of the general attributes of two economies would give us a clue as to what levels may be expected for the indices of compatibility between them; but the indices would still be materially different between different pairs of countries possessing the same attributes.

We shall suggest here three different indices, all of which have the same basic structure. Their definitions and formulations will first be presented, following which their meanings and implications will be explored. All three indices are designed to describe the similarity – or its absence – between the commodity structures of two flows, of either trade or production, between two partners for which the prospects of a PTA would be of concern.

Formulation[17]

The first index refers to compatibility of the trade flows of the two partners – one's imports and the other's exports. It is defined as:

$$Sm_j x_k = 1 - \frac{\sum_i |m_{ij} - x_{ik}|}{2} \quad \text{and} \quad Sx_j m_k = 1 - \frac{\sum_i |x_{ij} - m_{ik}|}{2},$$

where
$Sm_j x_k$ = index of compatibility of imports of country j with exports of country k (partner)
$Sx_j m_k$ = index of compatibility of exports of country j with imports of country k
$|\;|$ = indicates absolute values (that is, regardless of sign)
x_{ij} = share of good i in total exports of country j
m_{ij} = share of good i in total imports of country j
x_{ik} = share of good i in total exports of country k
m_{ik} = share of good i in total imports of country k.

The range of values of this index of compatibility (say, between j's imports and k's exports) is between zero and unity. It will be zero when the trade flows have no similarity whatsoever: there is no good imported at all, by one country, which is exported to any extent by the other. On the other hand, the index will reach unity, its maximum level, when the structures of the two trade flows are identical: in proportion of each aggregate, one country exports precisely what the other imports.

Second, the index of compatibility between the home-country's production and the partner-country's exports is defined as:

$$Cx_j q_k = 1 - \frac{\sum_i |x_{ij} - q_{ik}|}{2},$$

where

Cx_jq_k = index of compatibility of exports of country j with production of country k

x_{ij} = (as before) share of good i in total exports of country j

q_{ik} = share of good i in total production of tradables of country k.

Once more, the index ranges potentially from zero to unity. It will be zero when one country exports none of what the other country is producing and unity when the structure of one country's exports is identical with that of the other's production.

The third index describes the compatibility of the structures of the two export flows – one of the home country and the other of its partner. It is defined as:

$$Tx_jx_k = 1 - \frac{\sum_i |x_{ij} - x_{ik}|}{2},$$

where

Tx_jx_k = index of compatibility of exports of country j with exports of country k

x_{ij} = (as before) share of good i in total exports of country j

x_{ik} = (as before) share of good i in total exports of country k.

As is self-evident by now, the index ranges from zero – where no good is exported jointly by the two countries – to unity, when the structures of exports of the two countries are identical.

Interpretation and implications

We shall now address the meaning of the three proposed indices, each in its turn. The first index of compatibility (S), which matches the import flow of one country (home) with the export flow of the other (the partner), yields important information about the potential of a PTA for trade *diversion* (of the home-country's trade towards the partner). The higher the index, the more similar is the structure of the partner's exports to that of the home-country's imports; hence, the stronger the potential of displacement of imports from the rest of the world by imports from the partner. Also, presumably, the less costly is such displacement (for any given amount of it) – that is, the smaller the welfare loss to the home country from any given size of trade diversion.

As stated earlier, the match-up of these two trade flows would be *partly* a reflection of the peculiarities of the two economies involved and would thus be specifically related to these two economies: one country's exports may just happen to fit well the import requirements of another and be a poor match to the imports of a different partner. But, in another part, the degree of compatibility should reflect some fundamental economic attributes affecting the partner equally in its relationships with any other economy. In terms of our criteria, the less of an exception the partner is – that is, the more alike it is to the rest of the world – the better should be the match of its exports with the import structure of any foreign country. The absence of uniqueness should in turn primarily reflect several attributes, partly related to each other, some of which we have already addressed: the *size* of the economy – the larger it is, the closer it should be to the rest of the world; the degree of *diversification* of the structure of economic activity and, in particular, of the economy's trade flows; the degree of the economy's *industrialization* (which must, in turn, also be an important determinant of the degree of diversification) – the larger the role of manufacturing (and services) and the weaker the reliance on raw materials and other primary goods, the less distinct must the economy's features be; and finally (again, partly related to other attributes), the level of economic *wealth* – the richer the economy, the fewer its unique attributes.

All these assertions make, I believe, strong *a priori* sense; but I have also made an attempt of empirical verification. Table 7.1 presents the findings of a study of a large sample of countries.[18] The level of the index of compatibility is the dependent variable and four attributes are the independent, explanatory variables: (i) the country's size – represented by aggregate GDP; (ii) the commodity diversification of its exports;[19] (iii) the economy's wealth, represented by the level of *per capita* GDP; and (iv) the level of industrialization, represented by the share of the manufacturing sector in aggregate GDP.

The findings of Table 7.1 indicate that: (i) taken together, the four attributes presumed to explain the level of the index of compatibility

Table 7.1 Determinants of the index of export–import compatibility

Explanatory variable	Regression coefficient	T-statistic
Constant	0.326	4.748
Aggregate GDP	1.46 E-14	1.167
Concentration of Exports	−0.587	−5.417
Per capita GDP	8.22 E-06	5.383
Share of manufacturing	0.461	2.168
Adjusted R^2	0.807	
D-W statistic	2.137	

do, indeed, with an R^2 around 0.8, provide a major explanation; (ii) all four attributes have impacts in the expected directions: the index is negatively related to the intensity of commodity concentration (that is, positively related to the level of diversification) and positively related to all other variables; and (iii) the confidence levels of the estimates suggest, however, that only three of these inferences have strong credibility, whereas the fourth, concerning the impact of the variable of *aggregate GDP*, received (with a confidence level of 0.25 for this regression coefficient) only a more hedged support. The latter finding is somewhat surprising. It seems to suggest that when an economy is highly developed – rich, industrialized, and with a highly diversified economic structure – its *size* does not matter much.

The second index of compatibility suggested here (C) addresses the similarity of the structures of the home-country's *production* (rather than imports) and the partner's *exports*. Although its interpretation is less self-evident than that of the earlier index, it would be clear, upon reflection, that this index provides an indication of the potential of a PTA for trade *creation*. The creation of trade is, by definition, in the present context, a replacement of home production by imports from the partner; and this should be easier the more similar the pattern of the partner's exports is to that of the home-country's own production (with a proviso to be mentioned shortly). To cite an extreme case: when the partner exports nothing which the home country produces, no displacement of production by imports could take place at all.[20] At the other extreme, replacement should be easiest – ceteris paribus, of course, including a given size of the partner – when the partner's export structure matches perfectly the home-country's own production pattern.

Like the earlier index, the one discussed now must reflect some element of chance, concerned with specific and unique features of both the home country and its partner. But beyond it, like its predecessor, it would originate again from basic economic features of the partner, all contributing to the absence of 'uniqueness' of the structures of its production and trade: large economic size, wealth, degree of diversification, and intensity of industrialization. In other words, the same attributes which make a partner country a candidate for providing a large amount of trade of the diverting character would also make it a potentially large provider of trade of a creating nature. These same attributes make the partner's production and trade appropriate for displacing either imports from the rest of the world or the home-country's own production.[21]

The third index (T), which matches the *export* structures of both countries, is actually of an auxiliary nature – without, that is, much life of its own. It mostly serves to qualify inferences drawn by the use of the other two indices; in particular, those based on the just-discussed index of production–exports compatibility. The higher the exports-exports compatibility, the *less* should a PTA lead to new trade between the two partners through either trade creation or trade diversion. When the two economies are found to specialize in their export flows in the same range of goods, either partner should not be expected to provide much of the imports of the other; hence, a PTA discriminating in favour of such partner would not lead to much displacement of either imports from the rest of the world or of the home-country's own production. This inference should be of particular strength if the two countries display a high degree of commodity concentration of their exports and, *a fortiori*, when these exports consist mainly of primary rather than manufactured goods – intra-industry trade being much less likely in the trade among economies specializing in the former category of goods.

Concluding remarks

Following a discussion of criteria by which an idea of the likely outcome of a PTA should be formed, methods of constructing an assessment have been suggested and analyzed. A few concluding remarks about the nature of this assessment, and its limitations, are now in order.

First, it should be re-emphasized that the focus of this analysis is the *ex-ante* evaluation of the *promise* of a contemplated PTA. Thus, the methods developed and discussed here are *not* appropriate for the analysis of the *outcome* of an agreement. The latter is, needless to say, an important issue and it would involve several elements common with the *ex-ante* analysis; but it is nevertheless a separate matter.

Second, a *variety* of indices, or instruments of measurement, has been discussed here. Some of these refer to different aspects altogether of the general issue; others have areas of tangencies, referring (partly and implicitly) to the same basic criteria. All of these instruments are, hopefully, of some use (as would be others that may come up) and all should be applied *in conjunction* with others. A warning should be sounded against an endeavour – always tempting – of making some composite index out of the separate instruments to provide a single number which might be used for the assessment on hand. Even more than Fisher's now-defunct 'ideal' index, any averaging of the separate measures, done in one way or another, would lack an appropriate economic interpretation. Desirable as it would be, a short-cut is not available. This also implies that *judgement* must, at the end, play a part: with the same set of measurements, different users may reach different conclusions. This is unfortunate, but at least the use of 'objective' measurements such as those discussed here would make the inferences less arbitrary.

Third, all the yardsticks analyzed here are intended to suggest potential sizes of trade flows – trade creation, trade diversion or trade expansion. Although this knowledge is required, at some point, to draw welfare implications, the latter are definitely *not* measured by any of the methods discussed here. Moving from changes in quantities (and prices) to welfare gains or losses is a topic loaded with potential hazards and which is, in any case, beyond the scope of the present discussion.

Finally, and related to the last point, we should not even make the claim that the analysis is designed to provide estimates of trade flows; it is less than that. The measurements analyzed here would not provide cardinal answers, only *ordinal*. They would not tell us whether a contemplated agreement would lead to one or another change in trade flows (and certainly not whether the agreement would be 'good' or 'bad'). They would, instead, tell us whether a potential agreement given a certain set of circumstances is more or less likely than other (actual or potential) agreements to yield a favourable outcome; hence, whether it is more or less worthy – *if at all* – of being concluded.

Notes

1. This consideration has been absent in Viner's analysis as well as in most of the following literature, since only *imports* were analyzed as the source of change; it is thus not strictly a 'Meade–Lipsey' criterion, although Meade did pay passing attention to the export side. A major contribution to the incorporation of exports into the analysis is that of Wonnacott and Wonnacott (1981). See also Michaely (1977, pp. 216–17).

2. Another attribute, which will not be addressed here directly but will be implied in some of the analysis, is the degree of 'complementarity', rather than 'competitiveness' of the home-country's and the partner's economies. This issue has not been fully resolved in the literature (see Michaely, 1977, pp. 205–7).

3. Due to space limitations, a fuller discussion of criteria (iv) and (v) – which is often conducted today under the term of 'natural trade partners' – will remain beyond the scope of the present essay.

4. This has been an undisputed element of the conventional wisdom; in fact, many of the other criteria are strongly related to this attribute. Yet it runs counter to the perception expressed quite commonly in recent years – in both deliberations of policy makers and in the professional literature – which asserts that PTAs contemplated at present (say, in Latin America) stand a better chance of success in comparison with those of a generation

ago because they start from a more favourable position: they come on the heels of a major (unilateral, non-discriminatory) trade liberalization, with a dramatic reduction of trade barriers (tariffs and NTBs alike).

5. A thorough discussion of the concept may already be found in Haberler's (1936) classic. See also Corden (1966) and Michaely (1977, ch. 5).

6. For one exposition, see again Michaely, *ibid.*

7. The analysis here is suggestive and intuitive, rather than formal. The Vinerian context assumes that prior to the PTA *no* imports from the partner exist (or, put differently, where they do exist, the PTA would be immaterial) Hence, implicitly, we deviate here from this context.

8. Deviating somewhat from the present context, we may note that the inferences just drawn should apply also to the case in which a low tariff level on imports from the partner originates not from the latter's specialization in goods which carry low tariff tags in the home country but, instead, to a discrimination in favour of the (future) partner *prior* to the PTA: it is immaterial for the outcome whether the initial level of tariffs is low due to dispersion of the tariff system or to a geographic discrimination. The latter possibility will be referred to again below.

9. It should be noted, though, to avoid confusion, that once trade diversion does take place, the size of the loss from it, for a unit of diversion – the terms-of-trade deterioration – is *not* a function of the tariff level but only of the price differential between imports from the partner and those from the rest of the world.

10. The relationship between the extent of tariff removal by the partner and the home-country's gain should be understood as follows (assuming, for simplicity, constant costs; that is, a fixed supply price of the home country of exports to its partner). First, over some range when the rate of tariff removal is small enough, the preference given by the agreement would be ineffective – no change would take place. With a tariff reduction beyond this range, exports from the home country would replace the partner's imports from the rest of the world: when just this takes place, no gain to the home country is yet involved. From here onwards, any further tariff reduction by the partner would be a source of further gain to the home country. In reference to *existing* imports (of the partner from the home country) prior to the PTA, it is obviously just the latter range which is relevant. If the supply price of either the home country or the partner is *not* fixed, the analysis would become more complicated and the inferences should be hedged.

11. Strictly speaking, this statement applies again to the case in which the home-country's supply price is fixed.

12. This outcome could obviously be yielded by foregoing any estimate of an 'average': by instead estimating, separately, the gain for each tariff item and aggregating the results.

13. The following draws on my recent contribution in Michaely (1998).

14. See Bhagwati (1993), Panagaryia (1995, 1996), and Bhagwati and Panagaryia (1996a,b).

15. In principle, $X_w \equiv M_w$, but in concrete estimates, the two would normally differ somewhat from each other.

16. To illustrate the difference between the two indicators, Table 1 provides an example of two alternative trade structures. In one, the commodity composition of the two trade flows is 'atypical' and the two are concentrated

Table 1   Trade flows of two partners: alternative commodity compositions

Common data to two alternatives

X_w = world exports (= imports) consists of:

		Value
Good A	=	100
Good B	=	600
Good C	=	900
Total	=	1600
M_j (aggregate imports of j)	=	100
X_k (aggregate exports of k)	=	150
M_{jk} (aggregate imports of j from k)	=	80

Case 1

Good	J's imports from			K's exports to		
	K	ROW	Total	J	ROW	Total
A	78	2	80	78	10	88
B	1	9	10	1	20	21
C	1	9	10	1	40	41
Total	80	20	100	80	70	150

Case 2

Good	J's imports from			K's exports to		
	K	ROW	Total	J	ROW	Total
A	4	1	5	4	3	7
B	28	7	35	28	22	50
C	48	12	60	48	45	93
Total	80	20	100	80	70	150

I_{jk}	=	Intensity ratio (unadjusted)	=	8.53		
I_{jk}	=	Commodity-adjusted intensity ratio	Case 1		=	1.65
			Case 2		=	8.53

in the same commodities (good A); in the other, commodity structures are 'typical' (that is, close to those of the world at large).

We see that in the atypical case, the adjusted ratio is far below the unadjusted; in comparisons involving many countries, the two could provide entirely different indications. In the typical case, the two measures are practically identical.

17. The indices of compatibility have been developed in my recent paper (Michaely, 1996). They are, however, a modification of the 'index of similarity' I designed, many years ago (Michaely, 1962a), to assess the chance of diverging price movements of a country's exports and imports. I have then applied it, with a slight variation (Michaely, 1962b), to the *geographic* rather than the commodity structure of trade flows, as a measure of the intensity of multilateral balancing of trade (this index has then been adopted by Grubel and Lloyd (1975) to refer again to *commodity* structures, to indicate the extent of intra-industry trade). As a tool of predicting future trade flows following a radical policy change, I first used the index for the purpose on hand, roughly in the way it is presented here, in a paper (1980, in Hebrew) analyzing the trade implications of the peace agreement between Egypt and Israel.

18. This is taken from my earlier-noted recent paper (1996). The data cover 44 countries as follows: Argentina, Australia, Belgium, Bolivia, Brazil, Canada, Chile, China, Colombia, Costa Rica, Denmark, Ecuador, El Salvador, Finland, France, Germany, Greece, Guatemala, Honduras, Hong Kong, Indonesia, Italy, Jamaica, Japan, Korea, Malaysia, Mexico, the Netherlands, New Zealand, Nicaragua, Norway, Panama, Paraguay, Peru, the Philippines, Portugal, Singapore, Spain, Sweden, Thailand, UK, the United States, Uruguay, and Venezuela. For each of these countries, the index of compatibility of its exports with the imports of, *separately*, all other 43 countries was estimated. Following that, an unweighted average of the 43 indices was taken, to represent 'the' index of compatibility of the country's exports with the imports of foreign countries. This index serves, then, to represent the country's observation as the dependent variable in the regression run here (that is, the regression is based on 44 observations).

19. Represented here by its *inverse* – the level of commodity concentration – which is, in turn, measured by the Gini–Hirschman index of concentration and is based, like the index of compatibility itself, on the three-digit level of the SITC.

20. As on an earlier occasion, this statement must be qualified by the observation that the partner's potential is assessed through what it *actually* exports. It is possible that with the introduction of discrimination in its favour, the partner would be found to export some new goods to the home country, displacing the latter's own production.

21. No regression analysis similar to the one represented in Table 7.1 has been tried in this case. The construction of the production–exports index is a much more demanding task than that which is required for the estimate of the imports–exports index, and a mass production of the former is not feasible. The difficulties originate mostly in the scarcity of production data classified in sufficient detail, as well as the need to then match classifications of trade and production.

References

Bhagwati, J. N., 'Regionalism and Multilateralism: An Overview', in J. de Melo and A. Panagaryia (eds), *New Dimensions in Regional Integration* (Cambridge, MA: Cambridge University Press, 1993) pp. 22–51.

Bhagwati, J. N., and Panagaryia, A., 'Preferential Trading Areas and Multilateralism: Strangers, Friends or Foes?', in J. Bhagwati and A. Panagaryia (eds), *The Economics of Preferential Trade Agreements* (Washington, DC: American Enterprise Institute, 1996a) 1–78.

Bhagwati, J. N. and Panagaryia, A., 'The Theory of Preferential Trade Agreements: Historical Evolution and Current Trends', *American Economic Review*, 86 (1996b) 82–7.

Corden, W. M., 'The Effective Protective Rate, the Uniform Tariff Equivalent and the Average Tariff', *Economic Record*, 42 (1966) 200–16.

Grubel, H. G., and Lloyd, P. J., *Intra-Industry Trade: the Theory and Measurement of International Trade in Differentiated Products* (London: Macmillan, 1975).

Haberler, G., *The Theory of International Trade* (London: Hodge & Company, 1936).

Krueger, A. O., 'Free-Trade Arrangements as a Protectionist Device: Rules of Origin', *NBER Working Paper* no. 4342 (1993).

Krugman, P., 'The Move toward Free Trade Zones', *Policy Implications of Trade and Currency Zones* (Kansas City: Federal Reserve Bank of Kansas City, 1991) 7–40.

Lipsey, R. G., 'The Theory of Customs Unions: a General Survey', *Economic Journal*, 70 (1960) 496–513.

Meade, J. E., *The Theory of Customs Unions* (Amsterdam: North-Holland Publishing, 1955).

Michaely, M., *Concentration in International Trade* (Amsterdam: North-Holland Publishing, 1962a).

Michaely, M., 'Multilateral Balancing in International Trade', *American Economic Review*, 52 (1962b) 685–702.

Michaely, M., *Theory of Commercial Policy: Trade and Protection* (Oxford: Philip Allan; and Chicago: University of Chicago Press, 1977).

Michaely, M., 'The Economic Significance of Peace with Egypt', *Economic Quarterly* (in Hebrew), 105 (1980) 116–22.

Michaely, M., 'Trade preferential Agreements in Latin America: An Ex-Ante Assessment', *World Bank Policy Research Working Paper* no. 1583 (1996).

Michaely, M., 'Partners to a Preferential Trade Agreement: Implications of Varying Size', *Journal of International Economics*, 46 (1998) 73–85.

Panagaryia, A., 'Rethinking the New Regionalism', *World Bank Conference on Trade Expansion* (1995).

Panagaryia, A., 'The Free Trade Area of the Americas: Good for Latin America?', *The World Economy*, 19 (1996) 495–515.

Summers, L., 'Regionalism and the World Trading System', *Policy Implications of Trade and Currency Zones* (Kansas City: Federal Reserve Bank of Kansas City, 1991) 295–301.

Viner, J., *The Customs Union Issue* (New York: Carnegie Endowment for International Peace, 1950).

Wonnacott, P., and Wonnacott R., 'Is Unilateral Tariff Reduction Preferable to a Customs Union? The Curious Case of the Missing Foreign Tariffs', *American Economic Review*, 71 (1981) 704–14.

8
Reciprocity in Trade Agreements[1]

Richard H. Snape

Introduction

International trade agreements have been around for centuries, if not millennia. They take innumerable forms, but all involve reciprocity in one form or another, explicit or implicit. Whether a country should enter into trade agreements can be and is debated; if it does enter into such agreements, the form and terms of reciprocity are at the heart of the issue.

Reciprocity can be viewed in at least two dimensions: number of countries and number of products. Reciprocity may be between a single pair of countries or it may be on a more generalized basis; it may be in respect of a particular product, or it may be across a whole range of products. A particular trade agreement may comprise a combination of both – for example, a framework agreement between a number of countries and covering a wide range of products, but with provisions for agreements with more specific reciprocity involving smaller sets of countries and products.

In viewing the options, a pair of axes can be envisaged, one being the number of countries, the other the number of products. Within this plane a bilateral and wide-ranging free-trade agreement (such as that between Australia and New Zealand) rates high on the product scale but low on the country scale. On the other hand, the Universal Postal Union agreement rates very high on the country scale but low on the product scale.

The WTO's 'single undertaking' set of agreements rates close to being highest on both scales – country and product. The WTO embraces the broadest set of trade agreements with in-principle coverage of all goods, services and intellectual property, all forms of trading and all countries (currently 139 members). These agreements incorporate reciprocity in its most expansive form.

In contrast to the WTO agreements, nearly all the commitments and entitlements in international aviation are negotiated and agreed on a bilateral approach between pairs of countries. These agreements are product-specific and country-specific: they rate very low on both scales.

Economic analysis of reciprocity has concentrated almost entirely on the country dimension: thus there is a huge literature on preferential trade agreements. Little analytical attention has been given to choices on the product dimension. But popular demands for 'reciprocity' most commonly seek reciprocity on both a country- and product-specific basis. Such calls are recurring themes in the popular domain of trade policy. In 1982, William Cline referred to thirty bills being before the US Congress at that time aimed at achieving 'reciprocity' in international trade (country and product), largely to sanction retaliation by the United States against other countries that were perceived as refusing to open their markets. In 'The Return of the Reciprocitarians', Bhagwati and Irwin (1987) referred to the surge of support for reciprocity (including retaliation) in the UK in the closing decades of the nineteenth century, comparing it with a similar surge in the United States a century later. In Australia, as in many other countries, some of the old populist advocacy of 'protection all round' has moved to reciprocitarianism either on a retaliatory basis – 'open up or take the consequences' – or cooperative basis – 'we'll open up if you do'.

What has not been appreciated, perhaps, by many of the proponents of product-specific and country-specific reciprocity is that in international aviation there is a worldwide set of examples of just this type of agreement. In this chapter, after describing the main properties of the WTO, I turn to international air services agreements, describing their structure and consequences, and the difficulty of any country breaking out of the mould. Other sectors which have characteristics or agreements similar to international aviation are then briefly considered. The focus is not on reciprocity in the sense of threats or retaliation (see Krueger, 1995, ch. 4, or Bhagwati and Patrick, 1990); but rather on attempts to open markets in a more cooperative framework. The concluding section attempts to draw some lessons.

Of course, trade agreements have dimensions other than product and country, including the nature of the entitlements and commitments and the manner in which these are specified – in particular, whether a positive or negative listing approach is taken – and whether the agreement is open to other parties, and on what terms. Some of these aspects are also addressed.

This chapter relates not only to Anne Krueger's work on trade agreements, but also to her status as international aviation consumer *par excellence.*

The GATT/WTO multilateral multi-product approach

Since 1947, world trade has been liberalized to an extent that probably seemed impossible when the process began. The General Agreement on Tariffs and Trade (GATT), and the reciprocity incorporated in it, has been at the core of this liberalization. Lest this be questioned, one can reflect that with very few exceptions, the United States has not reduced any tariffs since the early 1920s other than in the context of negotiations with other countries, and that from 1947 to the mid-1980s all of these negotiations were under GATT or embraced by the principles of the GATT.

The key to US liberalization from the 1930s was the Reciprocal Trade Agreements Act of 1934, but this built on the decision taken in 1923 that conditional MFN (most favoured nation) would be replaced by unconditional MFN (Diebold, 1988, p. 3; Destler, 1986, ch. 1). For the United States, once the GATT came into existence, liberalization under the GATT replaced liberalization initiated on a bilateral basis.

The GATT (and now the WTO) rule of unconditional MFN treatment for GATT members has ensured that all negotiated, and unilateral, trade liberalizations by GATT members have been passed on to all other GATT members. Any particular negotiation may involve a limited set of products, and initially be between a small set of countries, but the liberalization for any specific product is extended to all members. Each member knows that it will benefit, unconditionally, from the liberalization of all other members: the only condition for obtaining MFN treatment for all goods and now (most) services is membership of the WTO. The unconditional MFN rule has ensured that country discrimination does not occur in the application of restraints to trade, including restraints that are applied to 'safeguard' particular industries. The GATT covers all goods and all forms of trade in goods, except government procurement, and except if there are explicit waivers or similar exceptions. It effectively prohibits all forms of governmental barriers to trade (other than on an exceptions basis), apart from import tariffs. Discrimination among products is thus allowed, but in general only in the forms of tariffs. Increasingly the tariffs have been 'bound' and reduced.

The General Agreement on Trade in Services (GATS) is in some senses even broader than GATT (Snape, 1998). For example, it covers trade for which investment or enterprise establishment is necessary, and some aspects of competition policy. Like the GATT it embraces all the members of the WTO, and in principle it covers all services. It is more complicated than GATT in the manner in which it addresses barriers to trade, adopting a combination of positive and negative listing. Once a country schedules a service sector (positive listing), all forms of barriers are prohibited unless the barriers themselves are scheduled (negative listing). As is well known, a major advantage of this broad multilateral, multi-product approach of the GATT and now the WTO is that wide-ranging trade-offs or reciprocity can be achieved both within countries and between countries. Within countries, countervailing political forces – associated with those industries that expect to gain exports from the reduction of barriers in other countries – can be marshalled against import-competing industries that see their future prospects being eroded by trade liberalization. And similarly between countries, trade-offs involving many countries with diverse interests can be achieved which would be impossible if negotiation were confined to bilateral product-specific reciprocity.

It is also well known that a disadvantage of this approach is that progress can be constrained by the slowest moving member of the 'convoy', or 'foot-draggers'. Under GATT, progress on occasion has been secured only by effectively excluding some sectors of political sensitivity to many developed countries from the negotiations – agriculture from the mid-1950s and textiles and clothing from the early 1960s – and by providing special, more permissive, rules for developing countries.

These products and countries were only brought back into the general negotiated reciprocity when the scope of the possible trade-offs was increased. This occurred in the Uruguay Round with the inclusion of services and intellectual property in the negotiations for the first time, and in the reopening and expansion of some old issues such as subsidies, safeguards, dumping, and the use of quantitative restrictions by developing countries. The resistance of the agricultural and clothing industries in developed countries was countered by the pressure in the same countries to secure international agreements to open markets for their services exports and to protect intellectual property: the domain in which reciprocity could be exercised was increased. Similarly, the reluctance of many developing countries relating to protection of intellectual property was in part overcome by the prospects for increased clothing, textile and, for some, agricultural exports.

A feature of the GATT, and now the WTO, is that a means is provided to overcome some of the problems associated with 'foot-draggers'. This is through the provisions for clubs within the club, or more restricted reciprocity in the country dimension: that is for customs unions and free-trade areas. Like-minded countries can go further in more limited reciprocal liberalization if they so desire, provided they go, or say that they intend to go, all the way – that is for free trade among the participants. But this of course cuts across the non-discrimination principles on which the WTO agreements are built, introducing a form of conditional MFN, or more limited reciprocity. Whether these more limited agreements promote or hinder broader liberalization depends (*inter alia*) on the membership, the nature of the agreements and exceptions, and on whether they are open to new members.

As noted above, the non-discrimination principle of the GATT and now GATS refers to countries, but not products, though in general the only form of discrimination permitted among goods under GATT is in the form of tariffs. It is a nice twist that when discrimination among (developed-country) members is permitted under the GATT and GATS, discrimination among products is not permitted (or at least it is discouraged). A free-trade area agreement or customs union is supposed to provide for free trade among the parties in 'substantially all products' (GATT, Article XXIV) or to have 'substantial sectoral coverage' and provide 'for the absence or elimination of substantially all discrimination … in the sectors' (GATS, Article V). Country-specific discrimination and reciprocity thus comes on the condition that product-specific discrimination and reciprocity will be limited.

Pressures for more specific reciprocity has been growing strongly in many quarters in recent years. Some of this has resulted in the formation of free-trade areas and other regional trade agreements. For example, the United States did not have any mutual preferential trade agreements until the 1980s; now it has NAFTA (North American Free Trade Agreement), an agreement with Israel, and is promoting 'Free Trade in the Americas'. The European Union, starting from an embryonic common market of six members in 1957, now has 15 members, is set to increase further, and has more and more association and other agreements (Snape, 1996). There are now only three members of the WTO (Hong Kong, Korea and Japan) which are not parties to a mutual preferential trading arrangement. Two of these three are exploring preferential arrangements while all are parties to the non-preferential APEC (Asia Pacific Economic Cooperation) agreement.

As well as preferential arrangements between countries, there has also been pressure in some quarters for sector-specific agreements with reciprocity confined to the sector. To a significant extent the structure of the GATS encourages such sector-specific (though not country-specific) reciprocity: both financial services and telecommunications have achieved agreements in which the negotiations and trade-offs have been sector-specific (though once negotiated the benefits have been extended to all members of the WTO). The GATS also encourages mutual recognition of standards (but on the basis that such agreements are open to other members with similar standards) as do some other WTO agreements. The nature of the plurilateral Government Procurement Agreement under the WTO also encourages sector-specific reciprocity, particularly in services. Under the WTO, the movement for 'zero for zero' agreements for some sectors is another manifestation of the sector-specific emphasis, as is the 'early voluntary sectoral liberalization' in APEC.

Obtaining product-specific reciprocal liberalization in the sectors which are relatively easy to liberalize means that these bargaining levers, and reciprocity offers, are no longer available when the more difficult sectors are being considered.

I now turn to international air services. I do so to highlight characteristics and implications of a set of trade agreements which incorporate reciprocity very narrowly defined – that is of the form which appears to be advocated in some quarters for other products.

International air services

For international air services there is a multilateral agreement covering aircraft flying through countries' airspace and for landing for technical purposes – for example, refueling. But for the last fifty years virtually all other aspects of international air services have been conducted within a structure of bilateral agreements. There are now about 3000 such agreements throughout the world.

Reciprocity in air services extends beyond country and product specificity, to reciprocity in the forms in which trade can take place. Thus the framework agreement under which the bilateral air service agreements (ASAs) are negotiated provides a taxonomy of 'freedoms'. In contrast, the GATT and GATS focus on barriers to trade, not on categories of permission to trade. These freedoms involve the conditions (including total capacity, frequency of flights, types of aircraft, cities that can be served, and fares) under which the designated airlines of partner countries can provide services between and beyond each other, the routes they can take, including intermediate points, whether and on what conditions they can carry foreign and domestic traffic within each other's territories, whether they can 'codeshare' on each other's and/or third parties' aircraft, and who can provide ground services in each country.

Central to any preferential agreement, and thus to bilateral reciprocity, is a rule of origin. Who is 'us'? Importantly, this decision cannot be taken unilaterally, for partner countries are not obliged to accept the definition of national designation by a country. Thus when Iberian Airlines bought into Aerolineas Argentinas, the United States threatened to refuse to recognize Aerolineas as an Argentinian airline, that is until it had extracted concessions from the Argentinians for US airlines flying to Argentina. The general standard for national airline designation – that is so that an airline can use the rights which have been negotiated by 'its' government – is national ownership and control, with the ceiling on foreign ownership varying between countries. (For example, it is 25 per cent in the United States and 49 per cent in Australia.)

Thus governments are negotiating maximum volumes of production and trade of international aviation, the nature of the trade, and the conditions under which trade may take place. They are also specifying who can produce and undertake the trade. It is almost inevitable then that governments will involve national airlines heavily in the negotiations of ASAs and that the interests of the airlines will receive considerable weight, more than those of specific industries in GATT or even GATS negotiations. Governments may – and do – feel an obligation to ensure that what has been negotiated for carriers of its country is, at least in part, produced by the carriers. Trade-offs of the liberalization of international air service for the liberalization of other sectors rarely occur; indeed it would be difficult for these to occur even if they were desired.

Another feature is that the agreements themselves – or key parts of them – are often confidential. (Such confidentiality does not exist with respect to the ASAs of the United States due to disclosure requirements in the United States.) In part, this is because negotiations do not occur simultaneously. Negotiators may not want a third party to know what 'concessions' they have granted to a partner if they soon will be conducting negotiations with that third country. This may be particularly so if a country has negotiated 'beyond' rights with the partner which could enable its airlines to carry traffic between the partner and the third country if the third country grants it rights to progress to that country. Such secrecy is not conducive to good governmental processes.

With ASAs structured in this way it is hardly surprising that comparative advantage has little to do with the provision of international air services. Very few international airlines have been driven out of the industry by international competition in the last fifty years; those that have left the industry usually have been in situations in which there has been more than one designated national airline (for example, in the UK and United States) and where the competitive pressure has come largely from other airlines of the same country.

It may be instructive to reflect for a moment on the situation which would prevail if the same trading conditions applied to shoes. There would be 3000 or more bilateral agreements in the world controlling the export and import (and indeed the production for home use) of shoes. Australia would have an agreement for shoes – and only shoes – with, say, Japan, for the trade between Australia and Japan. The agreement would specify a maximum number of shoes which could be imported into Australia from Japan and *a similar* maximum number of shoes that could be exported from Australia to Japan. It may specify the types of shoes that could be traded. It may specify the approval processes for the prices to be charged and which companies could load and unload the shoes – possibly giving a monopoly on unloading and distribution to the local shoe manufacturers. It would specify the national ownership conditions for nationally designated shoe manufacturers. It would restrict the re-export of a country's shoes from the partner country to other countries. Japanese tourists would have to wear Australian shoes when walking in Australia, and similarly Australians would be required to wear Japanese shoes in Japan (this is as close as I can get to cabotage restrictions).

Liberalization under product-specific bilateral reciprocity

I now turn to some of the implications for countries attempting to liberalize within the context of product-specific bilateral reciprocity. In recent years there has been very substantial liberalization of international aviation, but the bilateral system imposes severe constraints on what can be achieved and the manner in which liberalization can occur.

First, it is apparent that if a country attempts to liberalize unilaterally, it may achieve nothing. Indeed it could be worse off, particularly in the opportunity cost sense, in the future. This is because there can be no additional capacity between countries unless the countries at the ends of any route agree to it. (Taking the shoe analogy, there would be no additional Japan–Australia shoe trade unless the Japanese government agreed to it, even if Australia had removed all restrictions to trade.) Existing traffic rights on a route to and from a liberalizing country could be reduced, and the protection for foreign carriers on that route increased by their government. Even if existing capacity were not altered on a route, the foreign government could allocate all increases in future capacity to its own national carriers. Passengers could face a market with less competition, reduced services, and higher fares. Third country carriers would not be able to offer direct competition unless the country at the other end of a route allowed it. It was for these reasons that the Productivity Commission (1998) – although it generally sees unilateral liberalization as being the preferred trade policy option – did not recommend general unilateral liberalization of international aviation for Australia.

Second, the system imposes capital market constraints both in the raising of equity capital from foreigners and in discouraging, almost to the extent of preventing, mergers across countries. (The formation of the European Union is having implications for European carriers in this regard, and for the air service agreements of European countries with countries outside Europe. There is conflict between individual governments and the European Commission as to whether these agreements should be negotiated by European governments individually or by the European Commission for the EU as a whole.)

Third, airlines which desire to compete and expand are induced to find ways around the constraints. One form in which this is being manifest is through the development of codesharing and more extensive alliances. Alliances are now proliferating – Oneworld, Star, Wings and others. While many of the benefits of mergers may be achievable by forming alliances, and alliances could still be chosen as a form of business coordination if there were no national designation rules that depend on ownership, the point remains that the merger option is ruled out by these rules. The leaders in these alliances have been the airlines of countries in which governments have been withdrawing from airline ownership or control or, as in the case of the United States, were not owners of airlines.

Fourth, airlines in some countries tend to dissuade their governments from entering into liberalizing agreements with foreign countries not only because such liberalization may mean greater competition from the airlines of the foreign country (or countries). If there is, or could be, more than one designated international airline in its own country, liberalization could imply greater competition from its own nationals as well as from foreigners.

Fifth, a large liberalizing country will tend to develop a hub and spoke network of ASAs which can provide benefits to its airlines greater than those under multilateral (or plurilateral) liberalization. The airlines may therefore resist more general liberalization. This point may need some elaboration.

In recent years the United States has negotiated thirty bilateral 'open skies' agreements. These agreements by and large remove all capacity and other constraints on flying between and beyond the United States and the partner country. They incorporate a significant movement towards liberalization and the negative listing of restrictions. (However, ownership and control requirements for national designation are not relaxed, nor is cabotage by foreign airlines allowed.) As a result of this series of agreements, US airlines are able to carry traffic on any routes in the network. But partner country A will only be able to carry traffic between A and B if it has an agreement with B to do so, and only between B and the US if it has an agreement with B to carry beyond B. (Rights to carry passengers or cargo beyond the partner country generally are quite restricted.) Again A will only be able to carry between B and C if it has beyond (and intermediate) rights with both countries. With bilateral agreements it would require 465 ($=\frac{1}{2}n(n-1)$) bilateral open skies agreements (on the US pattern) between the 31 countries for the airlines of each of the countries to have the same rights in the network which the US airlines have, and to provide full competitive pressures on the US airlines. Alternatively, and much more simply, the same network opportunities for all the countries and the same competitive pressures on the US airlines could be exerted if there were a single plurilateral open skies agreement covering the 31 countries. Having liberalized first, the US airlines have an incentive to resist such a plurilateral agreement.

Sectoral reciprocity in other sectors

What is it about international aviation that has led to bilateral, product-specific reciprocity? It is instructive to consider other industries that come closest to international aviation, either in the form of the service or the nature of international trade agreements. In this context, shipping, telecommunications, postal services and government procurement are worthy of attention.

Maritime

The maritime industry provides a service similar to aviation, and like international aviation requires access to domestic territory for a foreign carrier for international trade to occur. While no general maritime agreement has been concluded under GATS, the GATS Annex on maritime transport does not limit the application of GATS to shipping as does the Annex on air transport to aviation.[2] (The latter Annex excludes all air traffic rights and services directly related to traffic rights from all GATS constraints.) Shipping lines have long been supported in a variety of ways by governments, but government ownership has not been a significant feature of the industry in most countries. Unlike aviation, bilateral reciprocity has not been the rule in shipping. The United Nations Conference on Trade and Development (UNCTAD) 40:40:20 rule, under which the source and destination countries would share 80 per cent of the traffic and the rest would be available for third parties, which was developed in the late 1970s, comes closest to the aviation type of arrangement, but this was undermined by many developed countries, led by the US, and the code has not been widely adopted (Feketekuty, 1988, p. 261).

Telecommunications

The industry which perhaps has been closest to aviation in the form of international agreements is basic telecommunications. The International Telecommunications Union (ITU) has a long history – its forebears date to 1865 – having been designed to coordinate telecommunications, networks and charging. In principle, the regulations establish a system under which 'every relationship between carriers for the exchange of traffic must be agreed by the national administrations in the countries of origin and destination' (DOCITA, 1999, para. 54). But revolutionary technological change, active liberalization by many governments and changing ownership structures of former government monopolies – to some extent associated with the technological change – have rendered the old regulatory structures indefensible or irrelevant for most countries. In most major countries the pressures against those who would seek to defend old interests have been too great. Between liberalized countries, many of the old bilateral agreements (often between carriers) have broken down even without explicit government negotiations. The old structure of bilateral reciprocity is disappearing.

While negotiations for a new international agreement on telecommunications were not completed before the birth of the WTO in 1994, the Trade Negotiation Committee agreed to continue negotiations beyond that date. Like similar negotiations in financial services, but unlike those in maritime and the movement of natural persons, agreement was reached. With commitments by (now) more than eighty governments, the agreement, within the context of GATS, came into effect on 5 February 1998. The commitments by most governments are on an unconditional MFN basis, the MFN status being extended to all members of the WTO and not just to the signatories to the telecommunications agreement. (Some countries have taken MFN exemptions, including the United States for some satellite-based services.) These unconditional MFN commitments supersede the bilateral arrangements of the ITU: what remains on a bilateral basis for non-liberalized countries in particular are settlement rates for traffic imbalances between countries, with the rates at which settlement occurs often bearing little relation to the costs (accounting or opportunity) of the services (Productivity Commission, 1999, ch. 3). (Value-added services also lie outside the WTO Agreement.) As they are now within the WTO processes, basic telecommunications are in a situation in which they can more easily be incorporated into reciprocity deals that embrace other sectors and products in the context of future WTO negotiations.

Post

Formed in 1874, what is now the Universal Postal Union (UPU) comprises almost 200 countries which have agreed to 'the formation among all member countries of a single postal territory for the reciprocal exchange of letter-post items' with 'the abolition of the sharing of charges between the country of origin and country of destination, each administration retaining the entire amount of the charges which it collects' (subject to the payment for transit at intermediate points).[3] This principle of 'source collects all' was compromised in 1969 to allow destination countries to require payment from source countries if the annual weight of mail received was greater than that which was sent. The rates of payment are determined by the UPU and are the same for each country. In this regard the charging mechanism has moved closer to that which operated for telecommunications.

Where post and basic telecommunications now differ is in the handling of 'messages' when they arrive at the frontier of the destination country. Conditions of such access to internal distribution systems have been the core of the telecommunications negotiations and many of these conditions are now liberalized under the WTO. But while various stages of the international postal chain are now being contracted-out to private enterprises by national postal authorities, the decisions on how distribution will be handled within destination countries is still decided by the national postal authorities of the destination countries, subject to the UPU requirement that postal administrations of the member countries must deliver all international items in the same way that they deliver similar domestic mail (Industry Commission, 1992, ch. 6).

With the recent development of private services carrying mail between and within countries, some stresses are being placed on the UPU regulations. Should destination countries refuse to accept mail from countries of whose distribution processes they think do not accord to with the provisions of the UPU – as they are entitled to under the UPU – bilateral agreements could develop.

Government procurement

Bilateral sectoral reciprocity is playing a large role in the WTO's Government Procurement Agreement. Government procurement was excluded from the provisions of the GATT from the outset in 1947, as it has been from the beginning of the GATS in 1994. A Code was formulated in the Tokyo Round of GATT negotiations, this code being developed further (and renamed an Agreement) in the Uruguay Round. It is now one of only two remaining plurilateral agreements under the WTO, the distinguishing feature of the plurilateral agreements being that they are binding only on those WTO members that sign them. The Agreement thus incorporates a much more limited member-reciprocity than do the rest of the WTO agreements. Of the 134 members of the WTO, only the members of the European Union, together with the United States, Canada, Japan, Korea and seven other countries, are signatories. But even among these members there is some product-specific reciprocity, particularly in services including construction services. Thus, for example, the commitments of the United States include the provision that 'A service listed in Annex 4 is covered with respect to a particular Party only to the extent that such Party has included that service in its Annex 4' (Annex 4 refers to the procurement of services). The EU commitments list many exemptions of a bilateral and product-specific nature, these to be maintained as long as the stated member country maintains a similar exclusion against the EU. It may be that no liberalization of government procurement would have been possible, particularly in services and construction, without these country and product limitations on reciprocity, but it may also have been the case that broader trade-offs would have been possible on a wider canvas.

Some lessons

While there does not appear to be a single simple answer to the question as to why international aviation is characterized by bilateral, product-specific reciprocity, these examples suggest that the limitations on reciprocity and liberalization are associated with government involvement in the market place. The implication is that it is the close involvement of governments in production of international air services that is a key factor.[4] All government procurement was excluded from the general disciplines, including MFN, of the GATT and GATS. The Government Procurement Agreement that has emerged is relatively modest, with low membership, high threshold values and aspects of sector- and product-specific reciprocity. Telecommunications, although multilateral in terms of technical standards under the ITU, has only recently started to break out of bilateral arrangements for other matters into a multilateral framework, and this has been associated with retreats in public ownership in many countries. For international postal services the international agreement is multilateral in important aspects (mainly of a technical rather than an economic nature), but it reserves internal carriage for control by domestic postal authorities, where public ownership is virtually ubiquitous.

International shipping interests in the main trading countries, and in the United States in particular, have so far been able to resist any major international agreements, but non-discriminatory access generally has been the practice. The major forms of protection have been subsidies and the reservation of certain cargoes (generally some government cargoes) and cabotage for nationally owned ships; protection has not been based on the provisions of international agreements as in aviation. Many of the countries that promoted the UNCTAD Liner Code had government-owned shipping lines: had such government ownership been more widespread it seems probable the UNCTAD Codes would have been applied more widely.

In international aviation, government ownership (or ownership by interests close to governments) has been very common in most countries other than the United States, and designation of national carriers to exercise the rights under bilateral air service agreements has been ubiquitous. The United States sought a liberal multilateral framework for air services at the conclusion of the Second World War, an arrangement that clearly would have suited its airlines, but the wishes of other governments prevailed. Many of these governments now wish for a more liberal system, but are constrained by the entrenched bilateral approach.

Thus government involvement in production or procurement appears to be a key factor in the development of product-specific bilateral agreements. What other lessons may be drawn?

First, with respect to incorporating air services into wider trade negotiations, for many countries the prestige attached to having a national flag carrier, owned by nationals, is such that encompassing air services into a broader framework of negotiations may inhibit the other negotiations, rather than provide a basis for mutually beneficial trade-offs. If no trade-offs are feasible, it is best not to make other liberalization conditional on liberalizing air services. But are there other sectors against which the interests of international air services may be set, so that the terms of reciprocity can be broadened? Shipping may be a possibility, if not on its own but in a broader package. The Asian crisis and increasing airline debts may be weakening the attachment to national airlines in some countries, and this may help. On the other hand, and as noted above, the advantages which US airlines are obtaining from the United States moving first in bilateral open skies agreements may dampen their enthusiasm to apply a countervailing force, in a multilateral multi-product context, against US maritime interests.

Second, with regard to the implications for the adoption of bilateral reciprocity for other products, bilateral reciprocity leads down a path from which, particularly if it is on a product-specific basis, it is hard to escape. Even with the drive to liberalization in international aviation in recent years, the constraints which the existing system imposes on *unilateral* liberalization are such that the liberalization has essentially been bilateral. Far from facilitating unilateral or multilateral liberalization in international air services, bilateral product-specific reciprocity has obstructed it.

Third, governments are more likely to engage in cross-sector reciprocity, that is to trade off the losses to one sector's producers against the gains of other sectors' producers and of consumers, when the governments themselves are not involved in production. Privatization thus may increase the set of products across which liberalization trade-offs can be achieved in the context of international negotiations. In international aviation the ownership and designation provisions provide the crucial stumbling block in escaping from bilateral reciprocity.

Fourth, rapid technological and other changes, and the consequential development of products and modes of transacting, can lead to the erosion of product-specific reciprocity. This has happened through technology in telecommunications and in Europe political changes are imposing stresses on aviation agreements. Technological changes may not be independent of ownership or government guarantees of survival. Appropriate incentive structures are important for innovation; bilateral product-specific trade agreements and government participation in industries may not provide the best environment for such innovation.

Notes

1. This chapter draws on the (Australian) Productivity Commission's Inquiry into International Air Services. The views are those of the author, and should not be attributed to the Commission or the Australian Government. Without implicating them, I am grateful to my fellow Commissioner on the Inquiry, Helen Owens, and to the staff who worked on it, led by Geraldine Gentle and

Paul Belin. For comments on a draft, I am grateful to Gary Sampson, Mike Woods, Jim Roberts and Keith Trace.
2. Some countries have scheduled commitments in the maritime sector.
3. Web site:http://www.upu.int/manuals/AN/Constitution/APEHIS_001.html
4. Of course, there are special characteristics, such as how to marry the limited availability of landing slots, and the times available, with unconditional MFN obligations, but these are not insoluble.

References

Bhagwati, J., and Irwin, D. A., 'The Return of the Reciprocitarians: US Trade Policy Today', *The World Economy*, 10 (2) (June 1987) 109–30.
Bhagwati, J., and Patrick, H. T. (eds), *Aggressive Unilateralism: America's 301 Trade Policy and the World Trading System* (Ann Arbor: University of Michigan Press, 1990).
Cline, W. R., ' "Reciprocity": a New Approach to World Trade Policy?', *Institute for International Economics, Policy Analyses in International Economics*, no. 2 (September 1982).
Destler, I. M., *American Trade Policies: System under Stress* (Washington, DC: Institute for International Economics, and New York: the Twentieth Century Fund, 1986).
Diebold, W. Jr, 'The History and the Issues', *Bilateralism, Multilateralism and Canada in U.S. Trade Policy* (Cambridge, MA: Ballinger for The Council on Foreign Relations, 1988) chapter 1.
DOCITA, *Submission by the Department of Communications, Information Technology and the Arts to the Productivity Commission Inquiry into International Telecommunications Market Regulation* (Canberra, May 1999).
Feketekuty, G., *International Trade in Services: an Overview and Blueprint for Negotiations* (Cambridge, MA: Ballinger for American Enterprise Institute, MA, 1988).
Industry Commission, *Mail, Courier and Parcel Services*, report no. 28 (Canberra, 30 October 1992).
Krueger, A. O., *American Trade Policy: a Tragedy in the Making* (Washington, DC: The AEI Press, 1995).
Productivity Commission, *International Air Services*, Inquiry report no. 2 (Melbourne, 1998).
Productivity Commission, *International Telecommunications Market Regulation*, position paper (Canberra, June 1999).
Snape, R. H., 'Trade Discrimination – Yesterday's Problem?', *The Economic Record*, 72 (219) (December 1996) 381–96.
Snape, R. H., 'Reaching Effective Agreements Covering Services', in A. O. Krueger (ed.), *The WTO as an International Organization* (Chicago: University of Chicago Press, 1998) pp. 279–92.

Part II
Development

9
Economic Development from an Open Economy Perspective[1]

Ronald Findlay and Ronald W. Jones

Anne Krueger's career, which we celebrate in this volume, has straddled two of the 'fields' of our discipline – International Trade and Economic Development. The intersection of these two fields, which in the language of set theory is a subset of their union, has been particularly rich and fertile for both of them. Concerns about 'development' and the closely related issue of 'growth' have inspired a large and growing volume of work on the dynamization of the traditionally static corpus of pure trade theory and also on the role of skills, externalities, infrastructures and numerous other factors. Our concern in this chapter, however, will be to look at this intersection from the opposite direction. What difference does a 'global' or 'open economy' perspective make to how the problems of the development and growth of a national economy are perceived?

It is fair to say that the field of Economic Development began its modern existence in 1943 with the publication of Paul Rosenstein-Rodan's famous article on the 'Big Push'. It is useful to remember that the subject of his creative effort was a problem that is now highly topical once again – the reconstruction of South-Eastern Europe. This article, and the subsequent work of Ragnar Nurkse (1953) and Arthur Lewis (1955), basically looked at the problem of development from the standpoint of a single *closed* economy, relying solely on its home market. The experience of the Great Depression of the 1930s and the dislocation of the 1920s convinced these economists that trade, which had been the 'engine of growth' in the nineteenth century up to 1914, was an unreliable option for the less developed countries of the world in the post-Second World War era. Hence they chose to emphasize 'national' as opposed to 'international' paths of development, leading to the doctrines of the 'big push' and 'balanced growth'. The

159

apparently successful Soviet industrialization drive under the first Five Year Plan also inspired many policy makers and planners in the Third World, such as Nehru and P. C. Mahalanobis in India, to follow autarkic paths.

Albert Hirschman (1958) began with import substitution and the creation of 'linkages' as the key to successful development in his doctrine of 'unbalanced growth'. Hollis Chenery (1979), in his influential work for USAID and later the World Bank, also stressed a rigid 'foreign exchange constraint' on development that could be loosened only by foreign aid and not by exports. Also supporting the tendency towards 'inward-looking' development strategies was the work for the UN of Raul Prebisch (1950) and Hans Singer (1950) on the alleged secular tendency of the terms of trade to shift against primary products in favour of manufactures. In the light of all of these distinguished voices raised against the classic route of growth through international specialization, it is not surprising that the great majority of developing countries adopted a variety of policy measures that restricted their exposure to foreign trade and inflows of foreign capital.

Ranged on the other side of the debate were only a few figures of comparable distinction. Jacob Viner (1953) and Gottfried Haberler (1959), the two leading specialists in the international trade field, were each invited to give a lecture on the topic of trade and development – Viner in Rio de Janeiro and Haberler in Cairo. Both staunchly defended the applicability and relevance of the concepts of comparative advantage and international specialization to the problems of development. Viner was particularly cogent in his critique of the concept of 'disguised unemployment' which was so strongly espoused by Rosenstein-Rodan, Nurkse and Lewis, and Haberler vigorously disputed the Prebisch–Singer thesis of the secular deterioration of the terms of trade for primary products.

In his Inaugural Lecture at the London School of Economics, Hla Myint (1967) coined the terms 'outward- and inward-looking countries' in contrasting the success of Thailand, Malaysia and Indonesia, which continued their profitable international specialization on primary products, with the failure of the more autarkic policies of Burma and Sri Lanka. These differences in performance, already notable by the late 1960s, grew even more pronounced in the subsequent decade. It was only by the late 1980s, however, when Anne Krueger went to the World Bank as Research Director, that the conventional wisdom could be said to have shifted decisively from inward to outward orientation in development policy.

A critique of early development theory

Two decades ago Albert Hirschman (1981) lamented the decline of 'high development theory' after its promising beginnings in the 1940s and 1950s. He acknowledged that much useful work was being done on many aspects of the problems of the less developed countries in relation to labour markets, income distribution, foreign trade and so on, but complained that all of this was within standard universalistic 'monoeconomics' rather than based on any special theory of development as such. He put forward a characteristically subtle cultural explanation for this failure of development economics to emerge as a unique field, attributing it to disappointed expectations about the performance of developing countries themselves. He argued that economists with their liberal faith in *interests* as the sole motive of social behaviour failed to recognize the power of the *passions*, that resulted in disruption of smoothly linear development by dictatorship, rebellion, civil war and so on.

Recently, however, Paul Krugman (1995) has put forward a different and simpler explanation. He says that the insights of early development pioneers all required a framework of imperfect competition in order to model them adequately, a framework that did not exist at the time. As a major example he cites the case of the 'big push' argument, which received an adequately rigorous formulation only with the publication of the article by Murphy, Shleifer and Vishny (1989) in the last decade.

He considers an economic system in which all goods are initially produced by a 'traditional' low-productivity technology under constant returns to scale. For simplicity, labour is the sole factor of production. The utility function of consumers in the aggregate is Cobb–Douglas and symmetric – that is, the same fraction of total income is spent on each good. However, each commodity can also be produced by a 'modern' technology that requires a fixed cost after which output is proportional to labour input at a higher level than in the corresponding traditional technology. Furthermore, to induce labour to move to the modern sector from the traditional sector, a wage premium à la Arthur Lewis must be paid. Consider an entrepreneur in any single potential modern sector. To protect himself from competition from the traditional sector he would have to charge the same price as that sector charges, equal to its unit cost. The size of the market would be determined by the total income generated by the entire economy, which operates with traditional technology. The entrepreneur might well find that the lower marginal cost of production does not compensate sufficiently for the fixed costs and wage premium that must be paid. If so, production is not undertaken. Suppose, however, that the entrepreneur was assured that *all* sectors would simultaneously consider modern production. The market for his product would then be significantly larger and it is possible that now he, and therefore every modern producer in a symmetric situation, would find it profitable to undertake production. These 'demand spillovers' from each sector to the others are thus the vital 'external economies' necessary to validate the 'big push' argument rigorously.

Krugman notwithstanding, however, 'high development theory' does not appear to have been revived by the infusion of models constructed by the intrepid few who have the 'courage to be silly' as he charmingly puts it. Perhaps common sense gets in the way. The fatal flaw of the original 'big push' theory, in our opinion, was not the lack of clever tricks of formal model-building but the assumption of a closed economy. Whatever excuse there may have been for that assumption in the aftermath of the Great Depression and the Second World War there is clearly none today. With the world market out there for any competitively priced output of a 'modern' technology, why is it necessary for a bigger *home* market to be created by a coordinated series of simultaneous investments as advocated by this doctrine? The only justification could possibly be some collective version of the infant industry argument in which there is a better case for a creche of infants taken together than each one individually. All the familiar criticisms of the infant industry argument, notably for example in Baldwin (1969), would apply to this case as well.

Development as a logistic process

Our position in this chapter is that any viable interpretation of 'development theory' must explicitly consider the opportunity to engage in international trade and other transactions across national borders at every stage of the development process. This process itself we conceive in terms of the familiar 'logistic' curve which shows per capita income as first rising at an accelerating rate from an initial persistently low real amount and then levelling off once a phase of 'maturity' is reached. In terms of the rate of growth as a function of the level of per capita income, the curve would rise from near zero at low levels to a peak at some intermediate level, then fall to a lower but steadily positive rate thereafter. While this logistic pattern of 'modern economic growth' has been noted by many distinguished authorities, including Arthur Lewis (1955), Walt Rostow (1960) and Simon Kuznets (1966), our interpretation here will be different, since it emphasizes the importance of international trade and investment, the nature of competition in markets, the role of reputation effects, the possibility of imitation in technology and the necessity of research and development.

This formulation of the development process starkly poses the question of what forces generate the initial transition from relative stagnation to growth at an accelerating rate, that is, the 'take-off' as Walt Rostow famously dubbed it. He associated the take-off with a sharp increase in the proportion of national income saved and invested and with the emergence of a 'leading sector' that pulled the rest of the economy in its wake. Our contention is that the 'leading sector' in almost all cases was associated with some sort of primary export to the world market. One thinks naturally of rubber and tin in Malaysia, cocoa in Ghana, tea in Sri Lanka, coffee in Brazil, rice in Burma and Thailand, sugar in the Philippines and so on. As Myint (1958) convincingly argued, these export sectors can be viewed in many cases as arising out of a 'vent for surplus' being created for underemployed natural and human resources rather than the conventional movement along a given production possibility frontier as in the familiar textbook diagrams. Some economy-wide fixed costs had to be incurred for the establishment of ports, harbours, railways and associated infrastructure in each of the new 'export economies', the financing for which was provided by capital exports from London and other European centres. Migration was also extensive, consisting of a European stream to the Americas and Australia and largely Chinese and Indian streams to colonial territories in Southeast Asia and the Caribbean. The period 1870–1914 was truly an era of 'globalization' on a massive scale, which continued after the First World War but was stopped in its tracks by the onset of the Great Depression of the 1930s. Only the United States, Canada and Australia attained West European levels of per capita income before 1930. Latin America, Asia and Africa, despite being drawn into the 'world wide web' of trade and factor movements during this period, still lagged substantially after the end of the Second World War.

Primary exports were indeed an 'engine of growth' for these countries but the growth that did occur was not appreciably ahead of that of the already industrialized countries. Profits, employment and the capital stock were all constrained by the rate at which exports could grow. If the supply of primary exports grows faster than does the national income of the industrialized countries, or the 'North', and hence on average of the demand for these products, the terms of trade would deteriorate and 'Southern' supply growth would be brought down to equality with demand in the North. The bulk of the supply of these primary exports, close to one hundred per cent for many tropical products such as coffee, rubber and sugar was concentrated in the South itself and so there was no space created for further absorption of these exports by displacement of import-competing production within the North.

In more recent times, a different story emerges in the case of labour-intensive manufactured exports of standardized products, such as textiles and steel. As the original four Asian 'tigers' demonstrated during the last three to four decades, open markets in the North could absorb effectively unlimited supplies of these exports without any significant negative impact on the terms of trade and hence profitability and growth. As real wages and costs rose in these rapidly growing economies they were able to 'climb the ladder of comparative advantage' by changing the product mix towards increasingly capital-intensive and technologically sophisticated goods. Taiwan, Hong Kong, South Korea and Singapore all had close to double-digit growth for about three decades up to 1990 and all have achieved the transition to economic and industrial maturity in a single generation, an unparalleled feat in economic history and one impossible to achieve without open and expanding world markets and a willingness to enter them.

The four 'tigers' were followed on the path of export-oriented growth by some traditional primary exporters such as Malaysia and Thailand. These countries supplemented their historical reliance on primary products such as rice, rubber and tin with manufactured exports of increasing capital-intensity and technological sophistication. Even though primary exports expanded quite rapidly they were outstripped by manufactures which are now over 80 per cent of the total exports in each case. The Philippines and Indonesia also followed a similar pattern.

The concept of a 'ladder of comparative advantage' is not just a vivid metaphor but a precise analytical construct. To demonstrate this we extend the Solow neoclassical growth model to an open economy setting of a multi-good, two-factor Heckscher–Ohlin economy. The familiar HOS (for Heckscher–Ohlin–Samuelson) trade model can now also stand for Heckscher–Ohlin–Solow. Drawing on our earlier work (Findlay, 1973, 1984; Jones, 1974) it is possible to construct a synthetic or surrogate production function for 'foreign exchange' or units of equal purchasing power in world markets. Given constant returns to scale technology for N goods as functions of capital and labour we can draw isoquants in capital–labour space for units of each of these goods that have the same value (say, a million dollars) at a given set of world product prices. These N goods can be ranked in order of capital-intensity. The 'convex hull' of these N isoquants can then represent the synthetic isoquant for a unit of international purchasing power at the given world product prices. By the constant returns to scale assumption for each of these N goods the surrogate production function will exhibit constant returns to scale as well. This aggregation connects the one-good closed economy Solow model to an N-good 'small open economy' Heckscher–Ohlin–Solow model. Labour in efficiency units can be assumed to grow at a constant rate, as in the original model, and savings behaviour can also be defined similarly as either a constant fraction of income or a constant rate of time preference. In a more open setting the local savings rate no longer restricts the volume of capital formation because of the possibility of foreign investment.

The surrogate production function has (N − 1) linear facets, each with an upper- and lower-limiting capital–labour ratio. If the economy's initial capital–labour endowment ratio is very low it will be located on the most labour-intensive of these facets, so that the economy will produce one or at most two of the most labour-intensive of the N goods. As the capital–labour ratio rises over time as a consequence of saving, leading to capital accumulation at a higher rate than labour force growth, it traverses increasingly capital-intensive facets. In other words its comparative advantage evolves towards more capital-intensive goods; the developing country ascends the 'ladder of comparative advantage'. Eventually the economy reaches a capital–labour ratio that is stationary at a long-run steady-state level, defined by the equality of the rate of return to capital with the given rate of time preference.

Anne Krueger (1977) herself looked at the evolution of comparative advantage in a very similar fashion, in her widely influential Graham Lecture. Her basic model has three goods, one natural-resource product using land as a specific input and two manufactured goods, both using capital, with labour used in all three sectors. One of the manufactured goods is more capital-intensive than the other. The model permits a rich interplay between endowment patterns and their changes over time with production and the structure of trade. Abundant supply of the specific natural resource and the accumulation of capital push manufacturing production in an increasingly capital-intensive direction. Countries that are initially labour-abundant concentrate on labour-intensive exports but climb the ladder of comparative advantage as they save and accumulate capital.

How does this open economy evolution differ from that of a closed economy? One difference is that the return to capital at any given capital–labour ratio will always be higher, or at least no lower, than in the closed economy because the economy can switch production towards more capital-intensive goods without experiencing a decline in the return to capital so long as the economy remains on the same facet. The return to capital does eventually fall, but more gently, so that the steady-state capital–labour ratio of the open economy, and therefore per capita utility, will be higher than in the corresponding closed economy. Secondly, the nature of the world market in many of the labour-intensive manufactures is highly competitive. A number of countries produce textiles, steel and footwear, and if a new entrant can get its workforce to produce a reliably consistent product, it can compete by manufacturing at lower cost than existing producers. Furthermore, its output is not constrained either by its own demand or by the average rate of growth in the North because it will not be the only supplier. Capturing, say, 3 per cent of the world market could reflect a significant local rate of activity. International trade allows a strong imbalance between local demand and local supply, and thus fits neatly into a scenario of 'unbalanced growth'. Furthermore, not only need local production not be constricted by local demand, real capital accumulation need not be constrained by a low local savings rate. We comment later on the important role of foreign investment in this depiction of early stages of the development process. Finally, note that in an open economy a consistent 6 or 7 per cent aggregate growth rate can mask quite a significant churning of activity at the micro level. Some industries can be expanding at 35 or 40 per cent yearly while others, in which the country is losing its comparative advantage as real wages rise, are in significant decline. In his Presidential Address to the American Economic Association, Arnold Harberger (1998), who succeeded Anne Krueger in this position, stressed the uneven growth rates at the micro level between 'sunrise' and 'sunset' sectors.

What we have depicted so far as a smooth process of breaking out of initial stagnation to eventual industrial maturity is in practice, of course, a much more difficult affair. The earlier stages of industrialization involve rising capital-intensities of production, but so long as products are standardized and competition is based mainly on cost considerations, the developing economy can make the successive incremental ascents of the ladder of comparative advantage relatively easily. Matters are not so simple, however, when further progress requires the producer to have a reputation for the quality and reliability of 'brand name' products. Marketing and advertising become crucial, once we depart from the simple 'price-taking' hypothesis of perfect competition.

It is at this stage that the imperfect competition approach advocated by Krugman undoubtedly comes into its own. Korea, Taiwan, Hong Kong and Singapore were all 'world champions' of initially labour-intensive and subsequently more capital-intensive standardized production. When it comes to computers, automobiles and other such sophisticated products, however, success becomes more problematic. The 'big push' argument, which we have rejected for the initial phase of development and industrialization, now becomes relevant. If these NICs or 'newly industrializing countries' are to compete with already well-established firms in the United States, Western Europe and Japan, consumers all over the globe need to become familiar with new names such as Acer, Hyundai and Samsung. Establishing a brand name for one product naturally carries over to other products that may not at all be closely related technologically or functionally. Thus the German trusts, the Japanese *zaibatsu* and the Korean *chaebol* can all be seen as institutions that incur the fixed costs of establishing reputation for quality and reliability for all of the wide range of products that their firms try to sell in world markets. The 'coordination problem' that smaller and more specialized firms would each face in trying to establish themselves in world markets can be solved by the establishment of such multi-product enterprises.

Of course, it is necessary to balance the pooling of fixed costs across a wide range of products with the actual expertise involved in the manufacture of each product. The current crisis in Korea has revealed that the *chaebol* in many instances attempted to enter too wide a range of products and services, emphasizing the acquisition of market share and entry into new fields above prudent considerations of cost. The fact of such excesses, however, does not detract from the legitimacy of the extension of the 'big push' argument to exports of up-scale products at the appropriate stage of development.

At this point it may be useful to recapitulate our discussion of the role of international trade in the logistic process of economic development. Subsequent to the Industrial Revolution, the first growth impulse to reach the developing countries came through the demand from the North for primary products, many of them specific to the geographic and climatic conditions of the tropics. With the bulk of world supply coming from the exports of relatively few nations, prospects for growth led by primary exports were constrained to approximate equality with the growth rate of the North, with declining terms of trade if supply from the South exceeded this rate bringing the growth rates back into balance. This meant that the 'gap' could at best be maintained, not closed. The opportunity for accelerating growth rates in the South was provided by labour-intensive manufactured exports, which could not only meet incremental demand in the North but could also *displace* the extensive production of these goods in the North. The resources thus freed up in the North could then be used to produce more technologically sophisticated consumer and capital goods in greater demand throughout the world. Eventually, as capital–labour ratios and technological capability grew in the most successful of the NICs they could themselves begin to enter the ranks of the producers of these 'up-market' goods, but at decelerating rates of growth until they gradually approach the lower but steadily positive growth rates of the North itself. 'Convergence' would thus occur, but by a different and more roundabout route than the simple mechanics of the neoclassical growth model of the closed economy, in which all countries mechanically follow the same track but at later and later dates.

The currently deep and ongoing Asian economic crisis might seem to cast doubt in some quarters about the efficiency and desirability of this outward-looking sequence that we have described. In our view, however, such a contention would be mistaken. Indeed it is even possible to argue 'dialectically' that the crisis itself is a demonstration of the success of the open economy route and the failure of the autarkic alternative. China, after following an extreme version of the isolationist path with disastrous results, abandoned this strategy and enthusiastically adopted the Deng Hsiao Ping 'open door' policy. Exports of labour-intensive manufactures from China grew at explosive rates for well over a decade. Added to the supply from the much smaller original East Asian tigers, however, the world economy, in our view, ran into a glut of output and capacity for a wide range of standardized products exported by all these economies. Since very heavy borrowing had also taken place on world capital markets to finance not just these projects but also 'non-traded' highly expensive real estate ventures as well, the crisis of overproduction manifested itself more dramatically as a 'financial' crisis when the lenders attempted to recall their loans. The situation is aggravated by the current stagnation in Japan but there is no reason to believe that the world economy will not resume a more robust growth path in the not too distant future.

Foreign investment, technology transfer and fragmentation of global production

Our examination of the role of the open economy in the logistic process of development has so far been confined mostly to trade in goods. Foreign investment, however, has often been almost as important a factor in this process. Just as differences between nations in factor endowments or technology can create the incentive for trade in goods due to differences in relative costs, these same differences lead to divergence in rates of return to capital that create mutually beneficial opportunities for borrowing and lending. It is only when the severe requirements for the factor price equalization theorem are satisfied that trade in goods alone eliminates the need for factor mobility to supplement trade if full efficiency in the allocation of resources on a global basis is to be achieved. In the 'Golden Age' from 1870 to 1914, as we have seen, there was a massive flow of capital from the industrialized nations of Western Europe to much of the rest of the world, not only Asia, Africa and Latin America but North America, Russia and Eastern Europe as well. The movement of capital into the economies breaking out of stagnation and underdevelopment accelerates their growth in this transitional process, enhancing the logistic pattern of development itself, since otherwise growth of these countries would be constrained by their own domestic savings. Particularly noteworthy was the fact that much of this borrowing was for long-term public infrastructure projects such as urban construction, public utilities and transportation. Primary production, from plantations and mines, was also a major sphere in which foreign investment was concentrated during this period.

Direct foreign investment in the first decade after the Second World War had a very different character. In many countries import-substitution policies made manufacturing sheltered by tariffs and other trade restrictions the popular avenue for foreign investment to enter. As demonstrated by a number of papers, notably Brecher and Diaz-Alejandro (1977), Brecher and Findlay (1983) and Jones (1984), foreign investment in this situation has a *negative* impact on the welfare of the recipient country. It draws domestic resources into less efficient import-competing production and out of potentially efficient exportable production. Another way of making this point is that the host country loses because the market price paid for a unit of foreign capital exceeds the shadow price of capital to the domestic economy because of the presence of the distortionary tariff. In addition the borrowing of public authorities during the 1870–1914 era was largely confined to infrastructure projects by fiscally prudent governments. In the case of the many postcolonial newly independent developing countries many of the public sector projects turned out to be of the 'white elephant' variety.

It is fortunate that uncompetitive import-substitution industries are not the only sectors that have attracted direct foreign investment into manufacturing in the developing countries. Labour-intensive products, components and processes, as we have seen, are all manufacturing activities in which developing countries have a genuine comparative advantage. Particularly when supported by good physical and social infrastructure, and a stable macroeconomic environment, projects in these types of manufacturing activity have attracted large and growing volumes of direct foreign investment. Perhaps even more important than the capital itself has been the transfer of technology from the multinational firms of the advanced countries to the host economies that they enter.

Levels of technology clearly differ enormously between the most advanced countries of the North at the top of the spectrum and the developing countries just beginning their transition. As Thorstein Veblen (1915) noted long ago, however, in his classic book on *Imperial Germany and the Industrial Revolution*, this gap itself presents a huge opportunity to the relatively more backward country. It can exploit existing innovations made in the North by the much less costly process of imitation and also avoid the mistakes made in the more uncertain environment that existed when the innovations were first made. In Veblen's famous example the original narrow gauge British railway tracks were inadequate for the unexpected high volume of traffic, while Germany was able to install the more appropriate broader gauge when it built its own railway system. Currently China can avoid the construction of thousands of miles of telephone lines by making use of satellite technology. Prod-uctivity growth in less developed countries that have the necessary skills and institutions to exploit the gap effectively can therefore be very high, once again accelerating the higher growth of the transitional countries relative to the original pioneers at the top, who may suffer from what Veblen called the 'penalty of taking the lead'.

The 'technology gap', while positive at any moment of time, is clearly something that evolves over time. The technological level of the North grows relatively slowly at some rate determined by the scale and effectiveness of their research and development (R&D) efforts. The follower countries can grow much faster since their own productivity growth is an increasing function of the size of the gap itself – as postulated in the well-known article by Nelson and Phelps (1966). The narrowing of the gap would clearly be facilitated if there are some human or institutional links between the source and recipient countries for the transmission of technology. Historically, the movement of skilled individuals and entrepreneurs has been an important factor in this regard. The major role, however, is played today by multinational corporations. As argued in Findlay (1978), the exposure of the follower country to trade and foreign investment is also a key variable determining the extent of technology transfer.

In most of the 'technology gap' literature the leader and the follower never change positions. The best the follower can do is to come closer and closer to the moving level of the leader – he can never catch up entirely or overtake. An alternative scenario involving 'leapfrogging' is sketched out in some recent models. For example, Ohyama and Jones (1995) analyze a situation in which the leader on the basis of current technology can be overtaken by a laggard, even though the leader has an absolute technological advantage in *both* technologies. As with trade, in this case it is comparative rather than absolute advantage which counts. The current leader's superiority with the new technology may be too small relative to its existing technology for it to be worthwhile to adopt the new technology if the present discounted value of the additional profits are too low, while the opposite could be true for the laggard. Thus there could be a rotation of leadership or 'leapfrogging' in technological leadership as has happened in fact throughout history.

Finally we note a phenomenon of major significance that is increasingly manifesting itself in the pattern of global production. This is the breaking up of hitherto vertically integrated production within a single country into a series of separate processes or stages, which may be assigned to different countries. This is termed 'fragmentation' in Jones and Kierzkowski (1990, 2001). Fragmentation as such is not unknown in earlier times, but it has obviously been given a tremendous boost by the enormous reduction in the costs of communication and information processing that have occurred recently. This phenomenon has clearly opened up even greater possibilities for trade, specialization, investment and learning than was the case before. The logistic process of development, as we have argued in this chapter, is a truly global phenomenon and is becoming more so every day. It is something that Anne Krueger recognized at the very outset of her brilliant career.

Note

1. We thank Richard Snape for helpful comments.

References

Baldwin, R. E., 'The Case Against Infant Industry Tariff Protection', *Journal of Political Economy*, 77 (1969) 295–305.

Brecher, R. A., and Diaz-Alejandro, C. F., 'Tariffs, Foreign Capital and Immiserizing Growth', *Journal of International Economics*, 7 (1977) 317–22.

Brecher, R. A., and Findlay R., 'Tariffs, Foreign Capital and National Welfare with Sector-Specific Factors', *Journal of International Economics*, 14 (1983) 277–88.

Chenery, H. B., *Structural Change and Development Policy* (Oxford: Oxford University Press, 1979).

Findlay, R., *International Trade and Development Theory* (New York: Columbia University Press, 1973).

Findlay, R., 'Relative Backwardness, Direct Foreign Investments and Technology Transfer: a Simple Dynamic Model', *Quarterly Journal of Economics*, 92 (1978) 1–16.

Findlay, R., 'Growth and Development in Trade Models', in R. W. Jones and P. B. Kenen (eds), *Handbook of International Economics*, vol. 1 (Amsterdam: North-Holland, 1984) chapter 4.

Haberler, G., *International Trade and Economic Development* (Cairo: National Bank of Egypt, 1959).

Harberger, A. C., 'A Vision of the Growth Process', *American Economic Review*, 88 (1) (March 1998) 1–32.

Hirschman, A. O., *The Strategy of Economic Development* (New Haven: Yale University Press, 1958).

Hirschman, A. O., 'The Rise and Decline of Development Economics', *Essays in Trespassing* (Cambridge University Press, 1981) chapter 1.

Jones, R. W., 'The Small Country in a Multi-Commodity World', *Australian Economic Papers*, 13 (1974) 225–36.

Jones, R. W., 'Protection and the Harmful Effects of Endogenous Capital Flows', *Economic Letters* (1984).

Jones, R. W., and Kierzkowski, H., 'The Role of Services in Production and International Trade: a Theoretical Framework', in R. W. Jones and A. O. Krueger (eds), *The Political Economy of International Trade* (Oxford: Basil Blackwell, 1990) pp. 31–48.

Jones, R. W., and Kierzkowski, H., 'Globalization and the Consequences of International Fragmentation', in R. Dornbusch, M. Obstfeld and E. A. Calvo (eds), *Money, Capital Mobility and Trade: Essays in Honor of Robert Mundell* (Cambridge, MA: MIT Press, 2001).

Krueger, A. O., 'Growth, Distortions, and Patterns of Trade among Many Countries', *Princeton Studies in International Finance*, 40 (Princeton University, International Finance Section, 1977).

Krugman, P., *Development, Geography and Economic Theory* (Cambridge, MA: MIT Press, 1995).

Kuznets, S., *Modern Economic Growth* (New Haven: Yale University Press, 1966).

Lewis, W. A., *The Theory of Economic Growth* (London: Allen & Unwin, 1955).

Murphy, K., Shleifer, A., and Vishny, R., 'Industrialization and the Big Push', *Journal of Political Economy*, 97 (1989) 1003–26.

Myint, H., 'The Classical Theory of International Trade and the Underdeveloped Countries', *Economic Journal*, 68 (1958) 317–37.

Myint, H., 'The Inward and Outward-Looking Countries of Southeast Asia', *Malayan Economic Review*, 12 (1967) 1–13.

Nelson, R., and Phelps, E. S., 'Investment in Humans, Technological Diffusion and Economic Growth', *American Economic Review* (May 1966) 69–75.

Nurkse, R., *Problems of Capital Formation in Underdeveloped Countries* (Oxford: Basil Blackwell, 1953).

Ohyama, M., and Jones, R. W., 'Technology Choice, Overtaking and Comparative Advantage', *Review of International Economics*, 3 (1995) 224–34.

Prebisch, R., *The Economic Development of Latin America and its Principal Problems* (New York: United Nations, 1958).

Rosenstein-Rodan, P. N., 'Problems of Industrialization of Eastern and South-Eastern Europe', *Economic Journal*, 53 (1943) 202–11.

Rostow, W. W., *The Stages of Economic Growth: a Non-Communist Manifesto* (Cambridge University Press, 1960).

Singer, H. W., 'The Distribution of Gains between Borrowing and Investing Countries', *American Economic Review*, 40 (1950) 473–85.

Veblen, T., *Imperial Germany and the Industrial Revolution* (London and New York: Macmillan, 1915).

Viner, J., *International Trade and Economic Development* (Oxford: Clarendon Press, 1953).

10
War, Peace and Growth[1]

Sebastian Edwards

Introduction

An important part of Anne Krueger's research has dealt with the relationship between economic policy and growth in developing countries. Her numerous articles on commercial policy and growth, including her detailed studies on Turkey and Korea, have been an inspiration for a generation of scholars (Krueger, 1978, 1988). In much of this work Anne Krueger has tried to identify the factors behind a rapidly growing economy, at the same time as trying to explain why some nations grow slowly over long periods of time.

Slow growth can be the result of a number of interrelated factors, including low capital accumulation, slow productivity gains, and inappropriate national policies. Another cause of slow growth, and one that has received relatively little attention in the literature, is prolonged war and/or, more specifically, a long civil armed conflict. In this chapter I analyze the growth record and growth prospects of El Salvador, a small Central American country that for almost a decade (the 1980s) was engulfed in a civil war. In 1989 a peace agreement was reached between rebel and government forces, and El Salvador faced the challenging task of rebuilding its economy and attaining sustained growth. During the period 1991–98 El Salvador amassed an impressive record, with real GDP growing on average at 5.1 per cent, the second highest rate in Latin America. Moreover, in 1999 El Salvador went through a peaceful and contested presidential election that showed that, ten years after the signing of the peace agreement, democracy is being consolidated. The future of El Salvador's peace process will largely depend on the country's ability to sustain rapid GDP growth. Only to the extent that this is the case will it be possible to expand employment opportunities, and to satisfy the many social demands of the population at large. In many ways, El Salvador is an example of the challenges faced by countries that end a prolonged civil conflict. Its experience is worth studying by those interested in nation rebuilding at the end of a civil war.

The rest of the chapter is organized as follows: In the following section I provide some background information, and I discuss the historical sources of growth in El Salvador. In this section I use a new data set to estimate the evolution of total factor productivity from 1950 through 1997. In order to put El Salvador's case in perspective, I compare the estimated TFP growth figures with those obtained for other Latin American countries. In the third section I deal with the relationship between capital accumulation, savings and growth. I argue that, since domestic savings tend to increase slowly, foreign savings tend to play a crucial role in countries that go through a major acceleration in GDP growth. In order to investigate this issue in detail, I develop a *current account sustainability* framework to analyze El Salvador's ability to rely on foreign savings.[2] Finally, in the last section I offer some concluding remarks.

The sources of growth in El Salvador since the peace agreement

Between 1965 and 1980, El Salvador's growth record was mediocre. According to the World Bank's *World Development Report*, during this period El Salvador's GDP grew at an average rate of 4.4 per cent, significantly slower than Costa Rica (6.3 per cent) and Guatemala (5.9 per cent); slightly faster than Honduras (4.1 per cent), and faster than Nicaragua (2.6 per cent). During the period 1981–90, things turned sour when, due to a number of factors, including the war and the debt crisis, GDP growth was barely positive – at 0.9 per cent. This situation changed drastically in the 1990s when, as a result of the peace agreement and the implementation of a first round of reforms, the Salvadoran economy experienced accelerated growth. According to the United Nations Economic Commission for Latin America (CEPAL), during the period 1991–97 average GDP growth rose to 5.3 per cent, the highest rate in Central America and one of the highest in all Latin America. During this period El Salvador not only experienced a growth recovery, but it was also able to re-establish macroeconomic equilibrium. Inflation was reduced, the exchange rate stabilized, and the external sector accounts were under control. However, throughout the period 1991–97 growth was uneven (Figure 10.1).

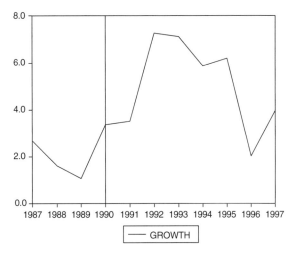

Figure 10.1   GDP growth in El Salvador, 1987–97 (per cent per annum)

Total factor productivity growth in El Salvador: a historical perspective

Modern economic theory emphasizes the role of four fundamental determinants of growth: (1) the accumulation of physical capital; (2) the increase in the size of the labour force; (3) the accumulation of human capital, through an expansion and an improvement of the educational system; and (4) total factor productivity (TFP) growth. This latter factor captures improvements in the production process aimed at increasing the efficiency level and reducing costs.[3]

Numerous multi-country studies have suggested that during the last few decades TFP growth has been a fundamentally important source of aggregate growth in successful economies – including in the so-called 'tigers'. Some studies have even found that TFP growth accounts for almost one half of average aggregate growth in some developing countries.[4] In Latin America, however, average TFP growth over long periods of time has tended to be rather low. In a comprehensive study, Elias (1990) estimated that for the 1940–90 period TFP growth averaged less than one percentage point in every large Latin American nation (Argentina, Brazil, Chile, Colombia, Mexico, Peru and Venezuela). Most experts agree that, for a particular country, a 'take-off' into high rates of GDP of growth will generally require that TFP growth accelerates significantly.[5]

In this section I provide estimates of TFP productivity growth in El Salvador, both from a historical perspective and for the more recent periods. The analysis proceeds as follows: As a first step I use a new panel data set, put together by the World Bank for the period 1950–90, to compute TFP growth for 93 countries (including El Salvador). These calculations provide evidence on the behaviour of TFP growth in El Salvador during the war years, and allow us to place El Salvador's performance in comparative perspective. Moreover, these calculations provide evidence on the behaviour of TFP growth during the war years of 1980–89. The second step consists of updating the main data – fixed capital stock, labour force, and stock of human capital – for El Salvador for the period 1991–97. In the third step these data are used to compute two alternative measures of TFP growth in El Salvador in the period 1991–97. The fourth, and final step consists of analyzing these estimates in order to build the groundwork required to analyze El Salvador's growth prospects.

TFP growth, 1950–90: cross-country-based estimates

Ten-year averages of TFP growth were constructed for 93 advanced and developing countries – see Edwards (1998) the list of countries. The starting point is the estimation of a random effect growth equation using panel data for 1950–90. The raw data on total physical capital, human capital and real GDP were taken from Nehru and Dhareshwar (1993). The following equation was estimated using a 3555 observations panel data set:

$$\text{Growth}_{jt} = \alpha \, d\log K_{jt} + \beta \, d\log L_{jt} + \gamma + \varphi_j + \mu_t + \varepsilon_{jt} \qquad (10.1)$$

As customary, K and L stand for the stock of fixed capital and the labour force. φ_j, μ_t and ε_{jt}, are country-specific, time-specific and common i.i.d error terms, and γ is a common fixed effect term. $\alpha + \beta$ was restricted to add to one. The estimated factor shares were then used to construct yearly estimates of TFP growth. Finally, these were averaged to construct decade-long estimates of TFP growth. A 1950–90 average was also constructed. The estimated parameters from equation (10.1) were also the bases for calculating the updated TFP growth figures for El Salvador for the 1991–97 period that are reported below.

In addition to equation (10.1), a growth equation that included human capital as an additional regressor was estimated.

$$\text{Growth}_{jt} = \alpha \, d\log K_{jt} + \beta \, d\log L_{jt} + \theta \, d\log H_{jt} + \gamma + \varphi_j + \mu_t + \varepsilon_{jt} \qquad (10.2)$$

H stands for the 'stock' of human capital, also obtained from Nehru and Dhareshwar (1993). In this case $\alpha + \beta + \theta$ was restricted to add to one. These estimates were used to construct a second set of TFP growth series, called TFPH. These two TFP growth variables behave very similarly – a regression of TFP on TFPH for the complete 1960–90 period yielded a slope coefficient of 0.93 with a standard error of 0.04. Two batteries of consistency checks suggest that these new estimates of TFP growth are 'reasonable'. First, correlation coefficients between these new indexes and those calculated by Nehru and Dhareshwar (1993) and Fischer (1993) were high (between 0.77 and 0.91). And second, the orders of magnitude of the new TFP growth estimates for a number of randomly selected countries correspond approximately to those calculated by other authors. Cook's distance statistic, however, indicated that Iraq was a gross outlier, with an estimated average rate of TFP growth of -13 per cent in the period 1981–90. After removing Iraq from the sample, the number of observations was 92 countries. Table 10.1 contains the estimated coefficients from the estimation of equations (10.1) and (10.2).

In Table 10.2, I provide summary statistics on the TFP growth estimates calculated using the procedure described above. Data are presented for the complete 92 country sample, for a subgroup of 19 Latin American countries (that includes El Salvador), and for El Salvador. For the complete sample, as well as for the Latin American countries, I have provided data on the first quartile, the median, the third quartile, the ninth decile, the 95th percentile, as well as on the mean.

The following important information emerges from Table 10.2. First, for the 1950–90 period as a whole, Latin America's performance in terms of TFP growth was slightly below that of the complete sample. Second, during some of the subperiods, Latin America as a group outperformed the broader sample of developed and developing countries.

Table 10.1   Estimated coefficients from panel growth equations for 92 countries, 1950–90

Coefficient	Equation (10.1)	Equation (10.2)
α	0.566	0.563
	(19.740)	(14.621)
β	0.433	0.263
	(11.674)	(7.105)
θ	—	0.174
		(2.015)

Note: Numbers in parentheses are *t*-statistics.

Table 10.2   TFP growth estimates for full sample, Latin America and El Salvador: ten-year averages, 1950–90

	1950–90	1950–60	1960–70	1970–80	1980–90
The world:					
1st Quartile	0.4	0.3	0.8	0.2	−0.7
Median	1.1	1.2	1.8	1.1	0.8
3rd Quartile	1.8	2.2	2.5	2.0	1.6
9th Decile	2.2	4.4	2.9	3.2	2.8
95th Percentile	2.6	5.3	3.7	3.9	3.3
Average	1.0	1.3	1.5	1.0	0.3
Latin American countries:					
1st Quartile	0.2	0.3	1.2	0.2	−1.4
Median	0.8	1.1	1.8	1.3	−0.3
3rd Quartile	1.7	2.1	2.2	2.0	0.2
9th Decile	1.9	2.6	2.3	3.0	1.0
95th Percentile	2.1	4.1	2.9	5.4	2.4
Average	0.8	1.1	1.7	1.2	−0.5
El Salvador	0.5	0.9	1.2	1.7	−1.7

Source: Estimated by the author. See text for details.

Third, and more important for the purpose of this analysis, the data show that, even prior to the war, El Salvador's performance in terms of TFP growth was quite modest. As may be seen, the country's TFP growth was never among the top 25 per cent of performers in Latin America, and in a number of subperiods it was even in the bottom half of the sample. Not surprisingly, the country did particularly poorly during the 1980s, when, as a result of the war, productive capacity suffered significantly. An important consequence of this poor record during the 1980s is that, once a peace agreement was achieved, the country was able to experience a rapid recovery in TFP and overall aggregate growth.

The estimates on TFP growth reported above are roughly in line with those of other authors. Harberger (1990), for example, reports a median for TFP growth in 'rapid growth' middle-income countries during 1965–80 in the range of 1.6 to 2.9 per cent. These figures are not very different from the ninth-decile figures obtained in this chapter, as reported in Table 10.2. In a more recent paper, Harberger (1998) reports TFP growth for a large group of countries for the period 1971–91. The median for the ten fastest-growing countries was 1.83 per cent, while that for the ten slowest growing countries was 0.83 per cent.[6] Hsieh (1998) used a novel methodology to compute TFP growth in the rapid-growing East Asian nations, and found that it ranged from 1.5 per cent in Korea to 3.7 per cent in Taiwan. Barro and Sala-I-Martin (1995) report TFP growth estimates for 11 developing countries, ranging from 0 to 2.3 per cent. The New York investment bank Goldman-Sachs recently provided new estimates of TFP growth for a group of 22 emerging economies, including seven Latin American nations, not including El Salvador, for the period 1960–98. The range of Goldman-Sachs estimated TFP growth goes from a maximum of 5.9 per cent for China in 1990–98 to a minimum of −3.3 per cent in Peru in 1980–90.

Peace and TFP growth in El Salvador, 1990–97

The next step in the analysis is to update the TFP growth for El Salvador for the 'peace period' of the 1990s. The point of departure is the Nehru and Dhareshwar (1993) data on capital stock, labour force and human capital discussed above. Information on fixed capital formation for each year is used to update the country's capital stock. In doing this I used an 'infinite inventory' approach, maintaining Nehru and Dhareshwar's (1993) assumption of a 4 per cent rate of aggregate depreciation.[7] The data on the labour force were updated using the census, El Salvador's Ministerio de Economía, and World Bank sources. The increase in the labour force was assumed to average between 2 and 3 per cent over the relevant period, while the rate of growth of human capital is assumed to increase at 1 per cent per year.

The estimated coefficients for the aggregate production functions (10.1) and (10.2), reported in Table 10.1, were used to calculate each factor's contribution to growth. Two basic estimates of TFP growth for every year were thus constructed. The first one, called TFP, includes only physical capital and labour while the second one, called TFPH, in addition includes human capital. Figure 10.2 presents the estimated evolution of both TFP measures for 1990–97.

As Figure 10.2 shows, both TFP and TFPH show a similar pattern of productivity growth in El Salvador during the 1990s. Productivity growth was positive, but lower than 2 per cent, during 1990–91; it increased substantially in 1992 and was very high until 1995. In 1996, however, it declined significantly, becoming slightly negative, only to recover somewhat during 1997. For the complete 1990–97 period, the average rate of growth of TFP is 2.1 per cent, while the average for TFPH is 2.4 per cent. The very rapid growth of TFP and TFPH in 1992–95 can be attributed to two factors: first, the end of the war normalized production in large parts of the country; and second, the initiation of the reform process by the administration of President Alfredo Cristiani gave a tremendous initial boost to efficiency and productivity. The fact that

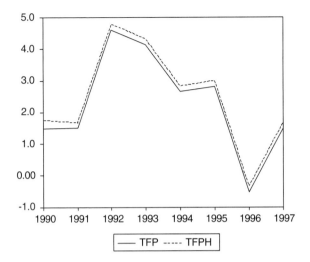

Figure 10.2 Estimated TFP growth series, 1990–97 (per cent per annum)

Note: TFP is estimated total factor productivity; TFPH is estimated total factor productivity, including human capital. See the text for details.

the starting conditions were characterized by such low productivity allowed for very significant gains to be achieved in a relatively short period of time. Both of these factors are unique, however, and it is highly unlikely that the type of TFP growth achieved during these early years will be repeated in the future.

To put these estimates in perspective, it is interesting to compare them to those recently computed by Goldman-Sachs (1998) for a group of Latin American countries. The Goldman-Sachs estimates have two very attractive features: first, they were obtained using the same basic data set as that used in this chapter; and second, they provide the only source of up-to-date estimates of TFP growth for a relatively large number of Latin American countries. Table 10.3 contains Goldman-Sachs' estimates of TFP growth for the eight Latin American countries in their sample. As may be seen, El Salvador's estimated rate of TFP growth during the 1990s is very high when compared to that of the Latin American countries included in the Goldman-Sachs sample. With a range of 2.3–2.5 per cent, during this decade El Salvador is ranked as the Latin country with the second fastest rate of TFP growth; only Peru, another country that moved from a quasi-civil war situation to a more tranquil political environment, experienced a higher rate of growth of total factor productivity. The estimates presented in Table 10.3, as well as those by Harberger and other authors, suggest that achieving a sustained average TFP

Table 10.3   Total factor productivity growth in
selected Latin American countries during the
1980s and 1990s

	Estimated TFP growth (per cent per annum)	
	1980–90	*1990–97*
Argentina	−2.4	1.5
Brazil	−1.5	0.9
Chile	1.0	2.1
Colombia	0	−1.3
Ecuador	−1.3	−0.1
Mexico	−2.4	−1.8
Panama	−2.9	−1.0
Peru	−3.3	5.4
Mean	−1.6	0.7
Median	−2.0	0.4

Source: Goldman-Sachs (1998).

growth rate in the neighbourhood of 2.0–2.2 per cent for long periods of
time represents a challenge for most countries, including El Salvador.

Foreign savings, current account sustainability and growth

Existing historical evidence indicates that an increase in long-term sustained growth requires rapid TFP growth as well as a higher rate of capital accumulation (both physical and human). In many developing
countries the potential for increasing investment, and thus the stock of
fixed capital, is often limited by a low level of domestic savings. What
makes this situation particularly difficult is that domestic savings change
slowly through time. This means that, in many cases, development
strategies aimed at accelerating growth tend to rely (at least during their
early phases) on higher foreign savings. The extent of foreign savings,
however, is limited by the current account deficit the country in question can run. The issue of a 'sustainable capital account' has recently
moved to the centre of analyses of crisis prediction and prevention in
emerging countries (Milesi-Ferretti and Razin, 1996). In this section I
deal with this problem from El Salvador's perspective. The section is
organized as follows. First, I provide a brief discussion of the behaviour
of savings and investment in El Salvador. Next I develop a simple model
of current account sustainability. Finally, the model is applied to the case
of El Salvador, where 'sustainable' paths of foreign savings are estimated.

Savings and investment in El Salvador

Figure 10.3 presents the evolution of the gross fixed capital investment ratio in El Salvador for 1975–97. As may be seen, although this ratio has been significantly below 20 per cent during the last few years, it reached 23 per cent in the mid-1970s. Figure 10.4 contains data on the recent behaviour of the domestic saving to GDP ratio in El Salvador. The figure also includes information on public and private saving ratios. According to these data, in 1997 the domestic savings to GDP ratio was 15.3 per cent; during the same year the private savings ratio was 13.5 per cent and the public savings ratio was 1.9 per cent. Figure 10.5 displays the recent evolution of external savings in El Salvador during the same period.[8] As may be seen from Figure 10.5, external savings have exhibited a declining trend since 1990. In 1997, they were even *negative* – that is, during that year the current account was in *surplus* – a situation that is rather unusual for a developing country. In the rest of this section I analyze the sustainable level of the current account (and, thus, foreign savings) in El Salvador, including some dynamic aspects of current account behaviour.

Current account sustainability: a basic framework

During the last few decades there has been a considerable evolution in economists' views regarding the current account. In an important contribution entitled *Does the Current Account Matter?*, Corden (1994) makes a distinction between the 'old' and 'new' views on the current

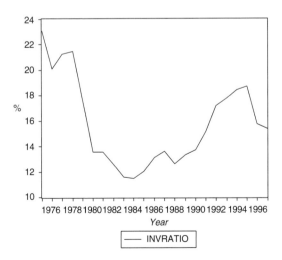

Figure 10.3   Investment ratio in El Salvador, 1975–97 (per cent per annum)
Note: INVRATIO is the ratio of gross investment to GDP. See text for details.

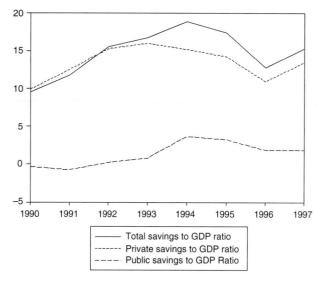

Figure 10.4   Domestic, private and public saving ratios in El Salvador, 1990–97 (per cent per annum)

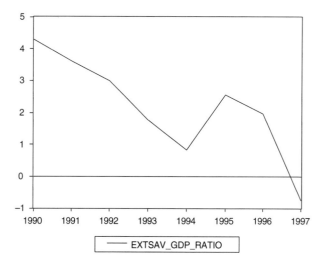

Figure 10.5   External savings to GDP ratio, El Salvador, 1990–97 (per cent per annum)

Note: Ratio of foreign savings to GDP. See text for details

account. According to the former, 'a country can run a current account deficit for a limited period. But no positive deficit is sustainable indefinitely.' (Corden, 1994, p. 88). The 'new' view, on the other hand, makes a distinction between deficits that are the result of fiscal imbalances and those that respond to private sector decisions. According to Corden (1994, p. 92) the extreme version of this new view states that 'an increase in the current account deficit that results from a shift in private sector behaviour – a rise in investment or a fall in savings – should not be a matter of concern at all'.

In the aftermath of the Mexican crisis many analysts argued that the 'new' view was seriously flawed. While some, such as Bruno (1995), argued that large deficits stemming from higher investment were not particularly dangerous, others maintained that any deficit in excess of a certain threshold – say, 4 per cent of GDP – was a cause for concern. Partially motivated by this debate, Milesi-Ferretti and Razin (1996) developed a framework to analyze current account sustainability. Their main point is that the 'sustainable' level of the current account is that level consistent with solvency. This, in turn, means the level at which 'the ratio of external debt to GDP is stabilized' (Milesi-Ferretti and Razin, 1998).

The basic idea behind this type of sustainability analysis is captured by the following. Under standard portfolio theory, the net international demand for country j's liabilities can be written as a proportion of the country's GDP:

$$\delta_j = \gamma_j^* Y_j \tag{10.3}$$

Equation (10.3) simply states that, in long-run equilibrium, the net international demand for country j assets, can be expressed as a proportion γ_j^* of the country's (potential or sustainable) GDP. The determinants of the factor of proportionality include relative returns and perceived risk of country j and other countries (see Edwards, 1999).

In this framework, and under the simplifying assumption that international reserves do not change, the 'sustainable' current account – that is, the current account deficit consistent with a stable ratio of the country's (net) liabilities in hands of foreigners – is given by

$$(C/Y)_j = \{g_j + \pi_j^*\}[\{\alpha_j\theta_j - (1-\alpha_{jj})\}\lambda_{jj}] \tag{10.4}$$

where g_j is the country's sustainable rate of growth, g is the long-term rate of growth of real GDP, α_{jj} is country j's asset allocation of its own assets, and π_j^* is a valuation factor (approximately) equal to international inflation. It is also assumed that country j's wealth is a multiple λ of its (potential or full employment) GDP, and that country j's wealth is a fraction β_j of world wealth (W). Finally, Y_j is (potential) GDP, and $\theta_j = (1 - \beta_j)/\beta_j$. Notice that if $\{\alpha_j\theta_j - (1 - \alpha_{jj})\} < 0$, domestic residents' demand for foreign liabilities exceeds foreigners' demand for the country's liabilities. Under these circumstances the country will have to run a current account surplus in order to maintain a stable (net external) liabilities to GDP ratio. Notice that according to equation (10.4) there is no reason for the 'sustainable' current account deficit to be the same across countries. In fact, that would only happen by sheer coincidence. The main message of equation (10.4) is that 'sustainable' current account balances vary across countries and depend on whatever variables affect portfolio decisions, and economic growth. Portfolio decisions, in turn, depend on the perceived degree of country risk and interest rate differentials, among other variables. These determinants of country risk tend to change through time and, in particular, as a result of changing political conditions, such as the end of a civil conflict.

Using a very similar framework to the one developed above, Goldman-Sachs has made a serious effort to actually estimate long-run sustainable current account deficits for a number of countries (Ades and Kaune, 1997). Using a 25-country data set, Goldman-Sachs estimated the ratio of external liabilities foreigners are willing to hold – γ_j^* in the model sketched above – as well as each country's potential rate of growth. According to the Goldman-Sachs model the sustainable level of the current account deficit for the Latin American countries in their sample – a sample that does *not* include El Salvador – is in the range of 1.3 per cent of GDP (Ecuador) to 2.9 per cent of GDP (Argentina, Chile and Peru).

The analysis presented above concentrates on the long-run sustainable level of the current account. Equally (if not more) important, however, are transitional issues arising from changes in portfolio allocations. These, however, can have a fundamental effect on the way in which the economy adjusts to changes in the external environment. For example, the speed at which a country absorbs surges in foreigners' demand for its liabilities will have an effect on the sustainable path of the current account (Bacchetta and van Wincoop, 1998). The key point is that small changes in foreigners' net demand for the country's liabilities may generate complex equilibrium adjustment paths for the current account. These current account movements will be necessary for the new portfolio allocation to materialize, and will not generate a disequilibrium – or unsustainable – balance. However, when this equilibrium path of the current account is contrasted with threshold levels obtained from models such as the one sketched above, analysts could (incorrectly) conclude that the country is facing a serious disequilibrium.

Dynamic issues can be explicitly added to the analysis presented above. This would allow one to move beyond the long-run equilibrium level of the current account deficit, and compute its *sustainable path* through time. Equation (10.5) provides a plausible representation for the way in which the current account responds to change in portfolio allocations. In this equation γ_t^* is the new desired level (relative to GDP) of foreigners' (net) desired holdings of the country's liabilities; γ_{t-1}^*, on the other hand, is the old desired level.

$$(C/Y)_t = (g + \pi^*)\gamma_t^* + \beta(\gamma_t^* - \gamma_{t-1}^*) - \eta((C/Y)_{t-1} - (g + \pi^*)\gamma_t^*) \qquad (10.5)$$

where, as before, $\gamma^* = [\{\alpha_j\theta_j - (1-\alpha_{jj})\}\lambda_{jj}]$. According to this equation, short-term deviations of the current account from its long-run level can result from two forces. The first is a traditional stock adjustment term $(\gamma_t^* - \gamma_{t-1}^*)$, that captures deviations between the demanded and the actual stock of assets. If $(\gamma_t^* > \gamma_{t-1}^*)$, then the current account deficit will exceed its long-run value. β is the speed of adjustment, which will depend on a number of factors, including the degree of capital mobility in the country in question, and the maturity of foreign debt. The second force in equation (10.5) which is captured by $-\eta((C/Y)_{t-1} - (g + \pi^*)\gamma_t^*)$, is a self-correcting term. This term plays the role of making sure that in this economy there is, at least, some form of 'consumption smoothing'. The importance of this self-correcting term will depend on the value of η. If $\eta = 0$, the self-correcting term will play no role, and the dynamics of the current account will be given by a more traditional stock adjustment equation. In the more general case, however, when both β and η are different from zero, the dynamics of the current account will be richer, and discrepancies between γ_t^* and γ_{t-1}^* will be resolved gradually through time. As may be seen from equation (10.5), in the long-run steady-state, when $(\gamma_t^* = \gamma_{t-1}^*)$ and $(C/Y)_{t-1} = (C/Y)_{\hat{t}}$, the current account will be at its sustainable level, $(g + \pi^*)[\{\alpha_j\theta_j - (1-\alpha_{jj})\}\lambda_{jj}]$.

In the rest of this section, I use the framework developed here to analyze the dynamics of current account behaviour in El Salvador. This analysis, in turn, provides information on the dynamics and sustainable level of foreign savings in El Salvador.

Current account sustainability in El Salvador: estimates and simulations

In the simulation exercise reported below, the following assumptions were made.

Asset holdings by foreigners

Cross-border asset allocations by foreigners – including multilateral institutions – is at the heart of the current account sustainability approach developed in this paper. Table 10.4 contains estimates of total claims on El Salvador held by foreigners in 1997–98. While the data on public sector debt are quite reliable, those on private sector holdings of Salvadoran assets are more tentative. Two things emerge clearly from this table. First, asset holdings by foreigners as a proportion of GDP have increased very rapidly between 1997 and 1998, and second, their level in 1998 does not appear to be on the excessive side. In fact, this figure (30 per cent) appears to be on the low side, especially when compared to some countries' foreign debt (a much narrower measure that excludes holdings of equities, as well as the stock of foreign direct investment). For example, in many Central European countries the external debt ratio is around 50 per cent of GDP. In Argentina, on the other hand, total foreign debt over GDP is 25 per cent of GDP, while total Argentine assets held by foreigners have been estimated to be at 44 per cent of GDP. This then suggests that if El Salvador continues to pursue the right type of policies, there is possible room for this ratio to increase further in the future. For this reason, in the simulations performed here I assume a range of values for $(\alpha_j \theta_j \lambda_{jj})$ from 27 to 35 per cent of GDP. More specifically, in the main simulation I assume that foreign holdings of Salvadoran assets are in

Table 10.4 Estimated claims on El Salvador held by foreigners, 1997–98 (US$ billion)

	1997	1998
1. Public Sector Debt	2702	2617
Multilaterals	1695	1785
Other	1007	832
2. Claims on Private Sector[a]	200	1030
Total (1 + 2)	2902	3667
Total as percentage of GDP	25.8	30.2

Note: [a] Rough estimate based on Central Bank and IMF data.
Source: IMF, Central Bank of El Salvador. This is gross debt.

the process of increasing from 27 to 35 per cent of GDP. I further assume that this process is spread through a four-year period.

Holdings of foreign assets by domestic (El Salvador) residents

In most countries it is rather difficult to estimate the stock of assets held by domestic residents in the rest of the world. El Salvador is not an exception. In the absence of reliable data, and on the bases of data for other countries, in the current simulations I have considered four alternative values: 3, 5, 7 and 10 per cent of GDP.

Sustainable rate of growth of GDP

On the basis of an analysis developed by the Salvadoran Foundation for Economic and Social Development (FUSADES), I assume an average rate of growth of *potential* GDP of 6 per cent per annum.

Basic estimates of the 'long-run sustainable' current account in El Salvador

In Table 10.5 I present some basic estimates of El Salvador's long-run sustainable current account based on the methodology sketched above, and for alternative combinations of foreigners' and Salvadorans' demands for assets. As may be seen, these numbers range from 1.4 to 2.6 per cent. The lower part of this range, however, corresponds to extremely conservative assumptions that imply that foreigners' demand would decline from its current level. For this reason, the more realistic numbers are in the 2.2 to 2.6 per cent range.

These numbers, however, assume a static situation and do not take into account possible changes in asset allocations by international

Table 10.5 Estimated long-term sustainable current account deficit in El Salvador under alternative asset demand scenarios: current account deficit as percentage of GDP*

El Salvador's demand for international assets $((1-\alpha_{jj})\lambda_{jj})$	Foreigner's demand for El Salvador's assets $((\alpha_j\theta_j)\lambda_{jj})$		
	0.27	0.30	0.35
0.03	1.9%	2.2%	2.6%
0.05	1.8%	2.0%	2.4%
0.07	1.6%	1.8%	2.2%
0.10	1.4%	1.6%	2.0%

Note: *These computations assume a long-run growth rate compatible with our 6 per cent target, and world inflation equal to 2 per cent per year.

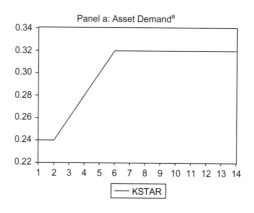

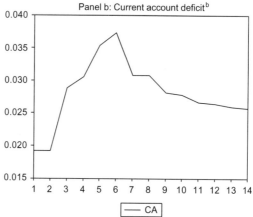

Figure 10.6   Simulation of current account balance

Notes: [a] KSTAR is the assumed ratio of Salvadoran liabilities demanded by foreigners, relative to GDP. The units in the horizontal axis are assumed to be years.
[b] CA refers to the ratio of the current account deficit to GDP. The units in the horizontal axis are assumed to be years. See text for details.

and/or domestic investors. The recent evaluation of the Salvadoran economy by international rating agencies, as well as by other observers, and the successful privatization of key infrastructure companies in the midst of a hostile international environment suggest El Salvador is facing a (small) increase in the (net) international demand for its assets. More specifically, in estimating the dynamics of the sustainable current account in El Salvador I assume, as a *Base Case Scenario* (BCS), that the country is experiencing a gradual increase in the international net demand for its assets from 24 to 32 per cent of GDP. This assumption is compatible with an increase in foreigners' demand for El Salvador's issued liabilities from 27 to 35 per cent of GDP, with Salvadoran demand for foreign assets remaining at 3 per cent of GDP. Moreover, in the BCS I assume that this process takes, overall, four years to be completed. Equation (10.5) was used to simulate the sustainable dynamic path of the current account in El Salvador: the results appear in Figure 10.6. *Panel a* captures the assumed evolution of the net stock demand for Salvadoran-issued liabilities, while *panel b* displays the simulated path of the current account deficit. These figures show clearly that the current account overshoots as a consequence of the increased stock demand for Salvadoran assets. As may be seen, according to this simulation the country starts with a steady-state current account deficit of 1.9 per cent of GDP, a level compatible with 6 per cent growth, 2 per cent international inflation and a stock demand for assets of 0.27; the final steady-state current account is 2.6 per cent of GDP, corresponding to the figures computed in Table 10.5. What is particularly interesting for the purpose of this chapter is that, according to this simulation, the average current account deficit, along the sustainable path, is around 3 per cent of GDP for the first five years of this transition – that is, for years 3 through 7 in Figure 10.6 *panel b*. This represents a substantial contribution to the total savings effort of the country, and is likely to help it move further away from the stagnation of the war years.

Concluding remarks

This chapter has dealt with the recovery of growth in El Salvador, during the post-civil war period. This subject is closely related to one of Anne Krueger's intellectual interests: the determinants of growth in emerging countries. The analysis presented here has focused on two issues: the evolution of total factor productivity in El Salvador in the period 1950–97, and the determination of the sustainable path of the current account and, thus, of foreign savings. The computation of TFP growth shows that in the postwar period El Salvador experienced a major jump in productivity growth. However, to the extent that productivity gains eventually slow down – a process that already appears to have begun – the country will have to rely more heavily on capital accumulation as a source of growth. The analysis on the dynamics of current account sustainability presented in the third section of this chapter indicates that El Salvador will likely have room for increasing its reliance on foreign savings in the years to come. This will, in turn, allow the country to finance a higher rate of investment. In the longer run, however, the challenge will be to generate substantial increases in domestic savings.

Notes

1. This is a revised version of a paper prepared for the project on 'Economic Prospects for El Salvador at the Turn of the Century' sponsored by FUSADES. I am indebted to Jaime Acosta, Juan Andrés Fontaine, Richard Snape and Alejandra Cox Edwards for very helpful discussions. I thank Alejandro Jara and Rajesh Chakrabarti for their assistance.
2. On current account sustainability analysis see Milesi-Ferretti and Razin (1996).
3. See Barro and Sala-I-Martin (1995) and Harberger (1998).
4. Some authors, including Allwyn Young (1995), have recently argued, however, that once the correct data on inputs are used, the role of TFP in the 'tiger countries' declines significantly.
5. See Edwards (1998).
6. These estimates were by Harald Beyer.
7. This figure is not very different from the implied depreciation rate used by Al Harberger in his detailed and disaggregated analysis of TFP growth in El Salvador.
8. All of these ratios – including the data on the investment/GDP ratio in Figure 10.2 – were constructed using central bank data and are based on savings, investment and GDP *at current prices*.

References

Ades, A., and Kaune, F., 'A New Measure of Current Account Sustainability for Developing Countries', *Emerging Markets Economic Research* (New York: Goldman-Sachs, 1997).

Bacchetta, P., and van Wincoop, E., 'Capital Flows to Emerging Markets: Liberalization, Overshooting, and Volatility', NBER working paper no. 6530 (April 1998).

Barro, R., 'Notes on Growth Accounting', NBER working paper no. 6654 (1998).

Barro, R., and Sala-I-Martin, X., *Economic Growth* (New York, London and Montreal: McGraw-Hill, 1995).

Bruno, M., 'Currency Crises and Collapses: Comment', *Brookings Papers on Economic Activity*, 2 (1995) 278–85.

Corden, W. M., *Economic Policy, Exchange Rates, and the International System* (Oxford and Chicago: Oxford University Press and The University of Chicago Press, 1994).

Edwards, S., 'Openness, Productivity and Growth: What do we Really Know?', *Economic Journal*, 108 (447) (March 1998) 383–98.

Edwards, S., 'On Crisis Prevention: Lessons from Mexico and East Asia', NBER working paper no. 7233 (1999).

Elias, V., *Sources of Growth: A Study of Seven Latin American Countries* (San Francisco: ICS Press, 1990).

Fischer, S., 'The Role of Macroeconomics Factors in Growth', *Journal of Monetary Economics*, 33 (3) (December 1993) 485–512.

Goldman-Sachs, 'GSDEEMER – New Estimates on Revised Measures of Relative Productivity', *Emerging Markets Biweekly*, 98/17 (1998).

Goldman-Sachs, *Emerging Markets Economic Research*, various.

Harberger, A. C., 'Reflections on the Growth Process', working paper (UCLA, 1990).

Harberger, A. C., 'A Vision of the Growth Process', *American Economic Review* (March 1998) 1–32.

Hsieh, C. T., 'What Explains the Industrial Revolution in East Asia', working paper (Berkeley: Department of Economics, University of California, 1998).

Krueger, A. O., *Liberalization Attempts and Consequences* (Cambridge, MA: Ballinger Publishing Co. for the National Bureau of Economic Research, 1978).

Krueger, A. O., *Development with Trade* (Oakland, CA: ICS Press, 1988).

Milesi-Ferretti, G. M., and Razin, A., 'Sustainability of Persistent Current Account Deficits', NBER working paper no. 5467 (1996).

Milesi-Ferretti, G. M., and Razin, A., 'Sharp Reduction in Current Account Deficits: an Empirical Analysis', *European Economic Review*, 42 (1998) 897–908.

Nehru, V., and Dhareshwar, A., 'A New Database on Physical Capital Stock: Sources, Methodology and Results', *Revista de Analisis Economico* (Chile, 1993).

Young, A., 'The Tyranny of Numbers', *Quarterly Journal of Economics*, 110 (3) (August 1995) 641–80.

11
Space and Growth: a Thünen–Schumpeter Perspective

Herbert Giersch

An IOU for Anne

Competition among economists is presently generating an abundant supply of books and articles which display a high level of professional quality. We are free to choose but must select from too large a heap of reading material. A rational choice is quite time-consuming. One way out is to concentrate on authors who have given us rich food for thought in the past. High up on my own reading list is Anne Krueger. I owe her a great intellectual debt and hence a contribution to the Festschrift in her honour. Moreover, I learned a great deal from her in private discussions when she visited Kiel before and after her successful service in the World Bank. Even a phone call from her is a memorable event.

A contribution to the Krueger Festschrift gives me the opportunity to explain the system of thought which comes up in my mind whenever I try to understand the growth of the global economy. It is a vision rooted in the German tradition of Johann Heinrich von Thünen (1783–1850), Walter Christaller (1893–1969) and Alfred Weber (1876–1963). It has inspired August Lösch (1906–1945) and Andreas Predöhl (1893–1974) who were among my teachers when – as a soldier – I privatized some spare time to study at the University of Kiel (1941–42). The location of this early professional 'indoctrination' happened to be the Institute of World Economics for which I later received responsibility (1969–1989); and which continues to keep me well as an emeritus president under an Advisory Board of which Anne Krueger is a member.

The conceptual framework[1]

A Thünen perspective

Assume that the globe we mean by globalization is a plane rather than a ball and that the plane is a circle, with economic limits we call frontiers. Moreover, the plane is homogeneous in the sense that no location offers any particular physical advantage, neither on the ground (soil) nor in the sky (weather). Hence, the density of population is equal everywhere, except that family members and workers live under one roof to cultivate the land around it. All land is private property; and holdings take the form of hexagons because hexagons come closest to circles and fit together without overlapping.

Every farm uses the soil for the same product. Land and labour can be combined in variable proportions. Let me call the product the 'Thünen good', in honour of Johann-Heinrich von Thünen who discovered the influence of space – by observation and calculation – on his own farm in Northern Germany and happens to be the originator of marginal productivity theory. The Thünen good, this is the inference, will be produced with different factor combinations: less labour per unit of land at the periphery, more labour near the centre of the farm where people live and sleep. Labour intensity of land use thus declines with increasing distance from the centre. The allocation and factor combination is such that it minimizes the (total) loss of workers' time needed for going to and returning from the fields. With given working time, this allocation promises maximum output and maximum labour productivity over the whole area. Average costs are a minimum. The value of the marginal product of labour is the same everywhere.

A 'Thünen farm' is limited by a frontier and, therefore, has a centre. The centre attracts activity, and the frontier pushes activity towards the centre. The same holds for the re-allocation of labour which occurs when we allow for product differentiation with fixed coefficients. Goods which require much labour input – using land intensively – will be produced close to the centre. This will push the optimum locus of production of labour-saving (land-intensive) Thünen goods towards the periphery. And the same type of good, if it can be produced with variable input combinations, will use up more labour per unit of land closer to the centre and less labour closer to the periphery.

The periphery, if taken as given, determines the centre; and the centre, if given, determines the periphery. This holds not only for the Thünen farm. It also holds for a 'Thünen plane' which is a large homogeneous area covered by numerous Thünen farms and by other units of production (breweries, factories) which use ubiquities (water) and sell the output (beer, city goods) to widely scattered consumers (again in markets shaped as hexagons). The size of the market areas for city goods will depend upon scale economies and transportation costs. Large economies of scale will make for large (hexagonal) market areas; high transportation costs tend to make the market area smaller. A city good produced under conditions of a natural monopoly on the Thünen plane will find its optimum in the centre. It may be called a 'national good'. An example is defence. If weapons become cheaper the optimum defence area will expand (ceteris paribus); as if transportation costs for (the public good) 'defence' declined, as if the bullets had a wider reach. Several Thünen planes may form a defence union.

We also deduce from Thünen that goods which are more expensive to transport will find their optimum locus of production closer to the centre. They will, at this (more) central location (a ring in Thünen's exposition), be produced with more labour per unit of land. Labour-intensive forestry close to the central city serves as an example. The reason is simple: labour, being mobile, will bear no transportation costs. High transportation costs at the periphery will push mobile labour towards the centre until its marginal product is the same everywhere. The population density, therefore, declines towards the periphery. More important: land, being completely immobile, will have prices declining strongly from the centre towards the periphery; and the more expensive land – closer to the centre – will be used in combination with more labour. Labour is a substitute for land. The immobile factor land has to bear all the disadvantages of the location; and it cashes all locational advantages in the form of a rent. A couple of decades ago, the Thünen approach led me to the proposition: (i) that tariff frontiers had raised the attraction of national centres; and (ii) that forming a customs union in Europe – the removal of internal frontiers – would strengthen the European centre (Brussels) at the expense of national centres (Giersch, [1949] 1991). The subsequent history of European integration, however, turned out to be less dramatic. In actual fact, several counteracting forces were at work: a secular decline of transportation costs, a geographic expansion of the European Union, and a liberalization of Europe's external trade. Finally, internal labour mobility was less than anticipated – particularly after unemployment had gone up in central areas in the 1970s.

Apart from scale economies in the production of private and public goods, including defence, there are centripetal forces arising from the advantages of agglomeration. Transportation costs have already been mentioned. The higher they are, the more advantageous is a more central location. In addition, transaction costs can be a minimum in central market places where people repeatedly meet face to face. Rules of honesty and fairness then emerge, similar to language. They are particularly important for the exchange of information. Truth will eventually emerge from competition among rumours. All the advantages of the centre, and of proximity to the centre, show up in the price of land. They make land values decline sharply from the centre to the periphery. Immigration – that is an increase in population on the Thünen plane – will raise land values everywhere.

If we consider output per unit of land and portray it in the vertical dimension, we make the plane transform into a cone-like figure (Giersch, 1979, 1993). The cone symbolizes the centre – periphery paradigm, logically based on transportation costs and other impediments (frontiers). It amounts to a 'pattern prediction' in Hayek's sense. In the author's opinion it can be useful as a tool for a better understanding of world economic growth. Take capital formation. An increase of the capital stock lifts output per unit of land and per unit of labour. The cone becomes higher. At the same time, the cone will, if it can, expand into new lands at the periphery where the price of land is low. With more capital per unit of land, the marginal product of capital goes down everywhere, and the rent of land rises. Moreover, the cone becomes steeper if savings are channelled into investment through a central capital market (say New York) and if it is more costly to monitor the investment over larger distances from the centre. The interest rates to be paid will then rise from the centre towards the periphery, and the use of capital will decline per unit of labour and even more so per unit of land – sky scrapers in the centre, huts at the periphery. A decline in communication costs – notably transportation costs – will benefit the periphery. It will lower the rent of land near the financial centre.

Such capital-intensive growth will go along with diminishing returns of investment, and will drive the real rate of interest down.

Heckscher–Ohlin–Samuelson

The widely known Heckscher–Ohlin theorem (HO) allows for the distance between countries. It does not allow for internal transportation costs. Also, in contrast to the Thünen model, HO consider that factors of production, though completely mobile within countries, are completely immobile between them. The HO focus is on trade as a substitute for factor movements. Labour from an overpopulated country will emigrate, but can only do so in the form of relatively labour-intensive goods; and an underpopulated country will export land in the form of land-intensive products. The potential for gainful trade is exhausted when factor prices have become equal (Samuelson, 1949). This potential will not be completely exhausted if it is too large for the trade that can take place. There may be: (i) too large discrepancies in factor endowment; (ii) too great differences in the size of the (two) countries; (iii) too many factors in relation to the number of goods that can be traded; (iv) too large economies of scale that quickly lead to full specialization in one of the countries; and (v) important non-pecuniary externalities that reject or lock-in factors in certain uses.

The process of factor price equalization through trade is braked by transaction costs, including transportation costs for the goods shipped from one country to the other. Transportation costs thus protect the scarce factor from competitive pressures and prevent the abundant factor from reaping the full gains of exporting to foreign markets.

The Thünen model is focused on factor price equalization through factor movements. Hence, labour is assumed to be completely mobile. It could make land values equal all over the plane but is stopped by transportation costs for goods.

Goods affording relatively high transportation costs (like wood) compared to their value will find their optimum location rather close to the central market place, where land has a higher value and calls for a more intense cultivation. However, saving land by using more labour is subject to diminishing returns. It, therefore, cannot bring about full equalization of land prices in the face of transportation costs for goods. These costs are not fictitious; they represent resources that have alternative uses. Only if they were zero in real terms could land values be the same everywhere, would the centre lose its locational advantage. Only in this utopian case, would the plane shrink to become a point – as it is in the HO world.

The Heckscher–Ohlin–Samuelson (HOS) proposition nevertheless has its place in the Thünen model. It then predicts that trade is mainly centre–periphery trade, that is, trade between countries (Thünen rings) with different factor endowments. Trade emerges to make differences in factor endowments economically less relevant. In contrast, trade among locations with the same factor endowment is tantamount to the division of labour between persons who have the same talents, the same comparative advantages (like identical twins). They cannot exploit the advantages of trade – unless they have different tastes (Leontief, [1933] 1949). Trade among locations on the same Thünen ring will, therefore, be intra-industry trade; that is, trade in sophisticated products that compete with each other but serve somewhat different tastes. It is here, where genuine competition works – despite the specialization that the division of labour brings about. Not being 'perfect', this monopolistic competition is an open system – in contrast to the centre–periphery trade (with perfect competition) that is fully determined.[2]

If we want to draw interesting conclusions from the HOS theory of international factor price equalization through trade, we had better ask why the theory's straightforward prediction fails to be observable in the real world. The reasons have partly been mentioned indirectly; they may be made more explicit and summarized as follows:

(i) land is not a homogeneous plane but shows important differences in quality and situation (site, geographic diversity, natural resources, mineral deposits);

(ii) there are transaction costs and transportation costs; they depend on distance and weight, on natural obstacles, on government interventions, on differences in laws and regulations, on difficulties in communication (language);

(iii) frontiers reject economic activities as do deserts and mountains or rivers without bridges;

(iv) scale economies give rise to the formation of market areas for goods, particularly for goods that are heavy and standardized;

(v) complementarities between inputs (for example, coke and ore) and between inputs and outputs (ore and steel) give rise to agglomeration tendencies in the choice of industrial location (raw material orientation);

(vi) a multitude of activities in central places promises cross-fertilization and attracts sophisticated consumers who pay for city advantages in terms of higher rents or costs of congestion;

(vii) monopolistic competition flourishes in central places and among similar locations; it gives rise to discoveries and innovations;

(viii) centres of knowledge production – with their supply of knowledgeable personnel – attract innovative firms.

What this amounts to is that the real world is bound to be diverse and that there are economic and geographic reasons to expect that, even in the long run, there will remain differences in population density, despite migration, and differences in real wages, despite trade and capital mobility.

Thünen and Stolper–Samuelson

We can easily incorporate the HOS theory of factor price equalization through trade into the Thünen paradigm if we consider that the full equalization of factor prices is prevented, for example, by the costs of transporting goods (to and from central places). At least land values will not become equal, not even with full mobility of labour and capital. What applies to land, may similarly hold for labour if labour is immobile between countries (as HOS assume). Labour, for example, may not become equally scarce through trade if transportation costs are high or if the two countries greatly differ in their capital endowment. Nevertheless, it is imaginable that labour (as a class), in a small country where it is the scarce factor, will suffer absolute welfare losses from the mass import of labour-intensive products from a large country with abundant labour. Labour may fear that its real wages decline, as the Stolper–Samuelson theorem (StS) shows (Stolper and Samuelson, [1941] 1949). But by focusing on an eccentric case, a mere possibility, this theorem is not of great help in the public policy debate.

In the Thünen framework we can investigate a parallel case. Just assume that on the Thünen plane a distorting tax on transport has existed and is now removed. Transportation costs everywhere will decline. The decline is more important for the periphery which gains relatively and absolutely. The gain is smallest for the centre; landowners there may even lose absolutely.

Now take the StS case and assume that the initial allocation of resources between the countries is not an efficient equilibrium but severely distorted: a small labour-scarce country (America) is facing a labour-abundant country that is much larger (the rest of the world). Underpopulated America, rich in land and capital per unit of labour, starts trade with an overpopulated and capital-poor world.

Where then is America in the Thünen model? With regard to labour and land, it is positioned at the periphery (underpopulated); with regard to capital, it is to be identified with the centre. With three factors of production, it will be necessary to study various cases. But in a quick intuitive judgment, it appears plausible to place America at the centre where land is expensive and the value of land per head of population is high, similarly high as the stock of capital. Land values are excessively high if we account for the agglomeration effect of the transportation tax. More centre–periphery trade – after the removal of the transportation tax – will alleviate the labour shortage in the centre, thus reducing the scarcity element in the centre's wages. Moreover, there will be migration from the centre towards the periphery, a conclusion that needs to be discussed more intensely. Another side-effect is the change in factor proportions towards more labour-saving methods in the centre and towards more labour intensity at the periphery. As a whole, the picture looks less alarming in the Thünen framework for the following reasons:

- The viewer is not led to focus on what happens in the country where workers initially earn a scarcity rent and are, therefore, bound to lose by opening up trade – in contrast to the rest of the world, where workers must gain.

- Factor movements gain attention as a substitute for trade, including migration by people who are dispersed in space and are, therefore, affected to a different degree.

- The losers, being geographically dispersed, cannot be easily thought of as forming a social class of protesters.

- The losers will include workers and consumers who could move closer to the periphery where land and local goods are cheaper.

- Compensating these reluctant losers may be left to local communities and their redistribution policies. Such decentralization may be easier than overcoming the resistance of vocal labour organizations.

- Landowners in the centre, who lose from the deglomeration effects, include speculators who readily adjust their expectations, instead of raising their voice. Apart from this, we recognize the problem of agricultural protection in advanced countries.

- The Thünen plane, though homogeneous, makes us aware of the real world's geographic diversity. Less inclined to abstract from distance and dispersion, we adopt a more individualistic outlook.

- StS, in dealing with point-economies, get around the problem of aggregation in an elegant manner, whereas the Thünen approach starts from individual values and sticks to methodological individualism by suggesting a pattern prediction, instead of treating countries and populations as if they were centrally administered entities (called 'economies').

All in all, spatial economics is closer to methodological individualism than the neoclassical analysis. By taking the 'rest of the world' into consideration, the Thünen approach is less partial, more cosmopolitan, more optimistic. If working people are prepared to move, it is only land values that will be negatively affected. In the Thünen framework we can imitate the StS case of more trade between an underpopulated area and an overpopulated area by assuming that migration is forbidden.

Labour then has to move in the form of labour input used for the production of goods to be exported. On the Thünen plane, lower transportation costs make (some) labour move from the centre towards the periphery while land, becoming (virtually) more mobile in the form of land-intensive products, is 'shipped' to the centre. Easier trade, thanks to lifting a tax on transportation, makes the price of pure land (sites) more equal – reducing it for central land, and raising it in the peripheral rest of the world. Trade includes, of course, tourism – the export of climatic advantages, geographic diversity, and historic memories.

As to globalization, the two approaches offer different perspectives:

(i) The Thünen approach predicts that the periphery gains at the partial expense of the centre. This appeals to our sympathy for the needy, whom we expect to live in remote places. Yet we easily lose sight of the urban poor. In the StS model, all workers who are visibly on the scene – in the labour-scarce country – can lose from more trade. The gains accruing in the rest of the world are not in the limelight.

(ii) In the Thünen model, the gainers and losers are dispersed; they are differentiated according to distance. This gives the impression that only few workers will actually lose. Therefore, the question of compensating the losers on a large scale does not arise as a serious problem of political economy. In the StS framework, an extreme case is considered to show that Labour as a whole could lose absolutely. Labour would then forcefully demand compensation.

(iii) In the Thünen model, compensation can be forcefully claimed only by landowners in the centre. Those who might be addressed to finance it would be landowners closer to the periphery. The compensation issue, therefore, does not arise as a class conflict.

(iv) In the Thünen framework, the critical issue is not the question of free trade versus protection but the access of a labour-abundant country to an economic union (such as the European Union). The entrant will certainly improve the attractiveness of its locations. Part of the adjustment will take the form of migration – straight to the places that cease to suffer from the repulsive effects of a frontier and, indirectly, towards the periphery of the enlarged market system.[3] Those afraid of too much migration towards the centre should consider that there will be an outflow of capital from the centre towards the periphery. If deglomeration is not sufficiently pushed by migration, the outflow of capital is a (partial) substitute. In other words, too much agglomeration of labour may be due to an insufficient out migration of capital.

(v) Freer trade alone – without factor movements – and freer trade with a labour-abundant country (as in the StS model) places all the adjustment costs on labour. In the Thünen case – with factor movements – people have two additional options: migration and investment abroad.

(vi) The issue of free trade versus protection in the StS model reflects the problems of the 1930s as seen from an Anglo-American perspective, though it also applies to present relations between Mexico and the United States. The StS perspective is bilateral and limited to trade. The Thünen approach is wider in scope by including factor movements as forms of adjustment. Peripheral land is benefiting, and owners of mobile factors can relocate the use of their specific skills and their mobile capital. As indicated, there is scope for intra-personal or intra-group compensation.

(vii) The Thünen model invites one to think about small steps on a wide front (globalization) as opposed to one large step on a small front (free trade versus autarchy). It then appears that the former case is more in line with human nature and less of a shock; that is, more gradualist in time, more general in scope. Broadly speaking, a partial change – with other things being equal – may turn out to be more objectionable on 'second best' grounds than a general move towards freedom that takes full account of what is to be done 'mutatis mutandis'.

Different models can be taken to represent different policy paradigms: HOS stands for free trade; StS stands for freer trade, but with compensation of losers; and Thünen stands for free trade plus free capital mobility plus free migration. The objective they have in common is an increase in the scope of opportunities: freer choice. The Thünen perspective is most comprehensive. It covers the classical paradigm of specialization in a market of virtually unlimited extent and the case of neighbouring countries forming an economic union with a common market for capital and business investments as well as for physical and human capital. The compensation issue is less likely to arise in this wider context and in present circumstances because workers can now be seen as owners of human capital, who are more capable of adjusting than the miners or manual workers of the past who had few professional alternatives. There is one exception: farmers in central areas, if exposed to competition from the periphery, tend to claim and obtain compensation in form of special arrangements (such as EU's Common Agricultural Policy).[4]

Growth in the Thünen perspective

Let us now take human capital explicitly into consideration. If two countries integrate their goods markets and their factor markets (unification, globalization), with one country (the richer one in the West or the North) having a more skilled labour force, there is reason to suspect that wage spreads will widen in most – perhaps all – places. The larger the number of participants, the greater will be the diversity of talents and skills. This has relevance for unification (as in Germany) and for globalization in the sense of more trade and capital mobility between North and South or between centre and periphery.

- The gainers will presumably include (i) those skilled people in the skill (rich) country who find new outlets in the larger market (the South or the periphery); and (ii) the unskilled workers in the unskilled (poor) country who feel an easing of their abundance.
- The losers are likely to include the unskilled people in the skill (rich) country and the skilled people in the poor country. Both lose the scarcity rents they captured under autarchy.
- In other words: by merging, both countries become more similar in factor scarcities, while income dispersion between top and bottom – over an area that has become larger – is greater. The (few) poor in the neighbourhood of the rich in the rich country lose under the competitive pressure of the (many) poor in the poor country. And the rich in the rich country gain from the new opportunities arising for them in the enlarged market. As demagogues say: the rich become richer, the poor become poorer.
- In the poor country, income differentials are likely to become smaller in two respects: (i) income opportunities at the bottom improve, thanks to greater proximity to the rich who demand personal services or make grants; and (ii) there is a decline of the scarcity rent for skill at the top. Will this help the poor country to catch up? Perhaps yes, if opportunities motivate people to acquire skills as can be expected in a liberal democratic society.

We must also take into account that the rich country integrating with the poor neighbour is likely to be rich not only in skills, but also in capital resources. This leads us to expect a capital flow to the poor country bolstering a process of catching up. As the gap in the level of development and income narrows between the two areas, the income dispersion is likely to become less pronounced.[5]

Exploiting trade opportunities does not necessarily generate long-term growth. For this we need a source of technical and institutional improvements. Product innovations help to overcome Gossen's saturation law for household consumption; and in production, the decline of marginal productivity is to be checked by process innovations. Wherever the new knowledge comes from, its application mostly happens under the pressure of genuine competition. This is where entrepreneurs enter the scene. They are the prime movers; they detect profit opportunities from 'new combinations' (Schumpeter) and turn them into innovations, thereby engaging in a process of 'creative destruction'.

Where should we expect the new combinations to emerge on the Thünen plane or – measuring output per unit of land in the vertical dimension – on the Thünen cone? Where do we find the driving force? The answer is: presumably close to the centre or top; that is, close to the central market. The centre has some dynamic contributions to make, in the following way:

(i) it is the place most likely to generate information about market saturation;
(ii) it offers itself as a test market for new products;
(iii) it is the financial centre attracting affluent savers and courageous investors;
(iv) it is most likely the best place for the market in ideas and information;
(v) it thus attracts people who are curious and future-oriented;
(vi) it stimulates rivalry in the use of knowledge for economic advance;
(vii) it makes use of low transaction costs to transform the market for ideas into a sort of fountain;
(viii) it allows exploitation of economies of agglomeration, here to be understood as the gains from complementarity in research and development;
(ix) it attracts institutions of higher education and research to nearby places;
(x) it facilitates interdisciplinary brainstorming and promotes open-mindedness.

What we are trying to conceptualize are the locational conditions for the meeting of creative minds in the market of ideas. The ghost we are hunting can be listed as: (i) cooperation without the costs of formal transactions; (ii) cross-fertilization and mutual stimulation of minds; (iii) intellectual reciprocity without bureaucracy; (iv) enthusiasm without euphoria; (v) spontaneous cooperation without dirigism; and (vi) competitive team spirit.[6]

What matters are basic differences in talent (personal factor endowments), low transaction costs for the division of labour among minds (agglomeration) and outside competition for prestige or profit.[7]

At this stage, we must consider that the Thünen interpretation of the world economy suggests the hypothesis that transportation costs and agglomeration advantages lead to a hierarchical system of centers as it was described by Christaller (1933) for Southern Germany. We recognize world centres, continental centres, national centres, regional centres, and local centres down to the village level. The height and architecture of church towers, library towers or community buildings tells us about the relative importance of a centre in former times and in space. All these centres offer possibilities for knowledge creation.[8]

The Schumpeter volcano

Schumpeter spoke of 'creative destruction'. My preferred metaphor is that of a volcano which is ejecting the lava of new knowledge from the top of a Thünen cone to destroy old structures and to fertilize the area for the emergence of new ventures and new cones (Giersch, 1979, 1993). Yet this way of looking at the world did not become a successful innovation in academic parlance. Even the notion of a Thünen–Schumpeter model found little resonance. The lesson fits to my assertion: the world of progress is oriented towards the volcano; it does not care so much for what is going on at the periphery.

The metaphor of a volcano cone which grows under the impulses of creative destruction, is apt to illuminate the modern (Promethean) growth process in several respects:

(i) Growth goes along with 'competition from elsewhere' – mostly 'from above'. It amounts to the devaluation of consumer and producer goods, ahead of their wear and tear, by product innovations. New products offer utility or save resources, including time, in households as well as in firms.

(ii) New goods incorporating product innovations may be called 'Schumpeter goods'. Their optimum locus of production is, as indicated, close to the top of the Thünen cone. When these goods lose their uniqueness in the course of time they find their optimum location further down the Thünen cone where they become part of the trade that is governed by monopolistic competition. Then we may recognize them as 'Thünen goods' – goods which are subject to small improvements in response to the pressures of 'competition from below' – that is, from poorer countries.

(iii) Poor countries have a catching-up potential to the extent that they import capital, do not fail to invest in education and skill, and gain export markets for Thünen goods. The exportables also include goods that are heavily dependent on the local supply of natural resources (climate, shores and mountains, raw material deposits). We call these goods 'resources-based goods' or 'Ricardo goods' (see Hirsch, 1974).

(iv) Countries on the move from the Ricardo periphery towards the more central Thünen rings – catching-up countries – will import capital and, therefore, run a deficit on their balance of payments current account. The deficit is healthy to the extent that it promises an increase of the country's export potential. The speed of export growth should match world economic growth so as to demonstrate that the country's world market shares are not declining.[9]

(v) Countries in a catching-up process do surely benefit from the inflow of investment capital – just as savers, lenders and share-holders in the more advanced lending countries gain from the movement of capital towards the periphery.

(vi) The same holds for technical knowledge. Knowledge may be available free of charge but it still has to be actively acquired at the receiving end. What counts for the knowledge transfer is the bottleneck between give and take. Widening it may promise high returns for subsequent investment flows.

(vii) Such returns are one of the explanations for the reconstruction miracles in postwar Europe to the extent that the miracle countries had suffered bottleneck losses: a partial destruction of their physical capital stock during the Second World War. In this respect, they had experienced 'destruction prior to creation'; and as the population was eager to regain prewar standards of living, the postwar growth was really 're-creation after prior destruction'.

(viii) A Martian observer with a Thünen perspective might have discovered a hole in the world's Thünen cone at the end of the Second World War and could – now in retrospect – describe Europe's postwar growth as a 'reconstruction with overshooting'. This overshooting gave rise to the emergence – or re-emergence – of the Western world's second growth pole. In the past, the top of the European income cone could be suspected to lie somewhere between the estuaries of the Thames and the Rhine. It is now looking more like an income ridge stretching along the Rhine or like a cone shifting its top towards the South (Giersch, 1979, 1993).

(ix) Leaving aside the influence of pure distance, we notice the influence of diversity; geographic and cultural. It is one of the characteristics of Europe. Geographic diversity is a plausible explanation for the cultural and political heterogeneity that characterizes Western and Central Europe, in contrast to Eastern Europe and Continental Asia (Weede, 1990). This heterogeneity gave rise to polypolistic and oligopolistic rivalry among cities and among states (jurisdictions). Sometimes it led to war; but normally it appears to have been what we now call 'locational competition' for mobile capital. Max Weber identified this competition as part of the process that led to the birth of capitalism and to what has been described as the 'European Miracle' (Eric Jones, 1981).

(x) The Thünen approach suits the present age of globalization since its focus is on factor mobility. In the HOS world, trade is in the limelight – trade as a substitute for factor movements. In the Thünen world, factor movements assume priority as prime movers. Migration of human capital affects the regional pattern of growth. Capital movements are taken to be autonomous, guided by differences in profit expectations (the marginal efficiency of capital); they are not induced – as in the Bretton Woods world – to close gaps in the balance of payments on current account. 'Imbalances' in the current account are, therefore, normal and not necessarily a reason for concern.

While the HOS approach is static and deterministic, the Thünen approach ends up in the indeterminacy of the open society. Free trade is not enough. The gains from trade include contacts with people who happen to have different capabilities and objectives, different ambitions and experiences, different tastes and backgrounds. In this respect, globalization is strongly driven by horizontal communication, which includes trade as a special case. But the main characteristic of globalization is foreign direct investment by firms which are becoming more multinational. They invest in foreign locations to substitute capital movements for trade, quite in line with the perspective of the Thünen model, promoting simultaneously the flow of knowledge from the centre to the periphery which serves as a substitute for centrifugal migration.

The deglomeration gap

Migration turns out to be a puzzle for the Thünen approach to globalization. From Samuelson's theorem we indirectly learn that in the real world factor price equalization through trade is limited by the existence of transportation costs for goods; and from the Thünen model we deduce that a lowering of transportation costs in general should have a deglomeration effect benefiting the periphery at the expense of the centre. The puzzle is that we do not observe a general tendency of people moving away from the centre, though there are interesting cases such as the return of Spanish and Portuguese guest-workers to their home countries (after Spain and Portugal had joined the European Common Market and started to catch up with the centre) which seem to confirm the Thünen model's prediction.

Why do we not observe the deglomeration effect of declining transportation costs? Here is a list of ten possible answers that should give rise to further reflections:

(i) The deglomeration effect may be subject to a long behavioral or statistical time-lag; it will be observable only in the longer run.

(ii) The deglomeration effect is perhaps counterbalanced by differential population growth due to high birth rates and improving health conditions in poor peripheral areas. This exerts pressure to migrate towards the centre.

(iii) People in rich urban agglomerations enjoy an increasing life expectancy and tend to stay where they are.

(iv) People becoming poor in the neighbourhood of the rich benefit from local transfers in wealthy central areas instead of moving to low-cost locations at the periphery.

(v) Centres become more attractive due to environmental improvements.

(vi) Centres are growth poles which offer prospects of upward mobility which add to a high level of current incomes. They depend on technological progress which seems to be accelerating, particularly in urban agglomerations.

(vii) There is part-time migration to the periphery in periods of dissaving for consumption – for example on weekends and during vacation periods. We lose sight of this in a model which assumes production and consumption to take place in the same locations.

(viii) There is a high-income elasticity of demand for goods to be consumed and enjoyed in common (cultural and social events, professional gatherings, sports games, exhibitions, and casual conversation); and disposable incomes do rise when transportation costs go down.

(ix) Telecommunication is an imperfect substitute for travelling, which in turn is still not cheap and comfortable enough to be a perfect substitute for living in the centre.

(x) Agglomeration is a residual likely to prevail as long as centres offer unexploited advantages of agglomeration, be it in production or consumption or just in human life.

If all of this – taken together – should come close to a tautology it cannot be too far from the truth. It surely is a preliminary truth because it calls for empirical investigations. Exceptions often confirm a rule by revealing its tacit assumptions.

Notes

1. I greatly value critical comments by Richard Snape and Robert M. Solow on an earlier version. The usual disclaimer applies.
2. Open competition in this sense includes competition in finding out what the preferences are (Hayek's 'competition as a discovery procedure') and what tastes could be developed (cultivated) or even created by new products (product innovation). At this stage, 'understanding' comes in to complement explanation. The observer from Mars – like the central planner in a socialist system – will neither predict nor find it rational that seemingly the same goods are being shipped from A to B and from B to A. Objectively, and in the Ricardian tradition of economic thought, this appears to be pure waste. But persons who are participants in the game of imperfect (monopolistic) competition can make sense of it. The 'imperfection' prevents the determination and the anticipation of the outcome; it thus allows competition to be like an open race in which participants engage with high hopes and unintentionally stimulate each other. The unplanned outcomes are product innovations or cost reductions (process innovations). Competitive efforts may appear as a waste to those observers who take circumstances and outcomes as given: for example, the auctioneers in a Walrasian world or the pricing authority in a Lange–Lerner model of competitive socialism; the same holds for observers who interpret technical progress as an exogenous factor of economic growth. Yet, in our context, competitive efforts are to be understood as an investment, as a real cost factor for the gains (profits) to be expected from successful ventures into the unknown, from heroic jumps through the fog of uncertainty. It is here where competition can be visualized as a 'procedure of discovery' (Von Hayek, 1968) and where an observer with intuition can get closer to the truth than a backward-leaning scientist who is confined to information that happens to be measurable – and has correctly been measured in actual fact.
3. It is as if the guest-workers from the Iberian Peninsula that had been attracted by the industrial centres of the Rhine Valley suddenly felt homesick when the European Common Market expanded to include Spain and Portugal. Similarly, there is a strong presumption for East Germany to gain from the eastward extension of the EU and for Berlin to become more attractive in anticipation of the EU entry of the Baltic States and of Poland and the Czech Republic.

4. To complete the comparison, it is pertinent to refer to two fundamental statements concerning trade theory. One is Ohlin's dictum that the theory of international trade is merely a special case of a more general location theory. The other is a formulation from August Lösch (1939, 1941). He insisted that the classical theory of international trade tacitly assumes that countries are points (representing islands like Britain) rather than two-dimensional planes (like continental countries bordering each other) and that the theory of comparative advantage applies to persons rather than countries. Both statements are almost self-evident in the Thünen context. The Thünen model not only takes account of space and dispersion, it also indicates what we can – or have to – expect from globalization and international factor mobility. The Lösch quote also reminds us that the world economy is not simply a conglomerate of nation states but a system of rules and (spatial) jurisdictions allowing individuals to engage in an extended division of labour permitting them to develop and exploit their talents. The Thünen perspective thus fits the individualistic and universal view of globalization better than does a Ricardian vision focused on nation-states.

5. Yet there is a further presumption to be taken into consideration: a population of any sort which starts to run or move ahead in competition is bound to show more inequality than a group taking a rest. Differences in talent do not become visible when talents are underutilized – for example, in periods of stagnation. This is why acceleration goes along with greater inequality and why regulation and taxation for greater equality or justice are likely to slow down economic development. The 'big trade-off' (Arthur Okun) is perhaps more closely related to speed or growth than to static efficiency.

6. This factor of production can be supposed to emerge from the belief (fiction) that the group – by frictionless interaction – can be more than the sum of its members and that, therefore, the individual as a group member can earn an enhanced reward – in the form of salary, profit participation, dividend, prestige. Whatever the forms of coordination – hierarchical or horizontal – their costs will have to be lower than they are within firms or in common markets. Top people, cooperating with each other without coercion, are likely to produce 'Promethean' growth. How could we capture and measure this growth spirit? If we fail as economists we will have to trespass into neighbouring academic territory.

7. In one sense it is the exact opposite of what Marx meant by the 'idiotism of country life' – a phenomenon of the periphery. Hence, our attention is attracted by the centre. Our focus here is the cheap and easy access to the market for new ideas, the fun or excitement of the campus. Local research groups will be made more coherent – and will be stimulated in their internal productivity – by competition with research groups that are located in similar places not too far away. Such monopolistic competition among groups, characterized by efficient internal cooperation, seems to be an essential ingredient of a progressive order. (I once denoted this interaction, among and within teams and groups, with a synthetic word: 'coopetition' (Giersch, [1992] 1993), not realizing that it would also be used in a different sense (Nalebuff and Brandenburger, 1996).) The ideal place for such a mixture of spontaneous cooperation and competition is probably somewhere close to the centre's university towns.

8. The central places for specializing in the creation of knowledge must enjoy academic freedom and financial independence; that is, essentially freedom and time for the pursuit of curiosity. The knowledge that is useful for industry is often a by-product of basic research – an unintended, though highly valuable, side-effect. From this effect we expect mutual attraction: Firms may move closer to research laboratories, and laboratories are becoming part of modern factories.

9. Participants in the public policy discussion often ignore both growth and the cross-border flow of resources. They tend to imply that trade deficits are always a symptom of excessive consumption and decline. These considerations may have relevance for some of the 'tigers' and their role in the Asian crisis of 1997–98.

References

Christaller, W., *Die zentralen Orte in Süddeutschland* (Jena: Fischer, 1933).

Giersch, H., 'Economic Union between Nations and the Location of Industries', *Review of Economic Studies*, 17 (21) ([1949] 1991) 87–97.

Giersch, H., 'Aspects of Growth, Structural Change, and Employment: a Schumpeterian Perspective', *Weltwirtschaftliches Archiv*, 115(4) (1979) 629–52, and in H. Giersch (ed.), *Openness for Prosperity: Essays in World Economics* (Cambridge, MA: MIT Press, 1993) pp. 15–35.

Hirsch, S., 'Hypotheses Regarding Trade Between Developing and Industrial Countries', in H. Giersch (ed.), *The International Division of Labour Problems and Perspectives* (Tübingen: Mohr (Paul Siebeck), 1974) pp. 65–82.

Jones, E. L., *The European Miracle: Environments, Economics and Geopolitics in the History of Europe and Asia* (Cambridge: Cambridge University Press, 1981).

Leontief, W., 'The Use of Indifference Curves in the Analysis of Foreign Trade', in H. S. Ellis and L. A. Metzler (eds), *Readings in the Theory of International Trade* (Philadelphia: Blakiston Comp, 1949) pp. 229–38.

Lösch, A., *Die räumliche Ordnung der Wirtschaft* (Jena: Fischer, 1940).

Lösch, A., 'Eine neue Theorie des internationalenHandels', *Weltwirtschaftliches Archiv*, 50 (1) (1939) 308–28.

Nalebuff, B. J. and Brandenburger, A. M., *Co-opetition* (New York: Doubleday Books, 1996). German edition: *Coopetition – kooperativ konkurrieren: Mit der Spieltheorie zum Unternehmenserfolg* (Frankfurt/Main: Campus, 1996).

Samuelson, P. A., 'International Factor-Price Equalization, Once Again', *Economic Journal*, 234 (1949) 181–97.

Stolper, W. F., and Samuelson, P. A., 'Protection and Real Wages', in S. Ellis and L. A. Metzler (eds), *Readings in the Theory of International Trade* (Philadelphia: Blakiston Company, [1941] 1949) pp. 333–57.

von Hayek, F. A., 'Der Wettbewerb als Entdeckungsverfahren' (Kiel: Institut für Weltwirtschaft, Kieler Vorträge N. F. no. 56, 1968).

von Thünen, J. H., *Der isolierte Staat in Beziehung auf Landwirtschaft und Nationalökonomie* (Hamburg: Perthes, 1826).

Weber, A., 'Industrielle Standortslehre' (Allgemeine und kapitalistische Theorie des Standortes) in *Grundriss der Sozialökonomik*, VI Abteilung, III. Buch, B I. (Tübingen: Mohr (Paul Siebeck), 1914) pp. 54–82.

Weede, E., *Wirtschaft, Staat und Gesellschaft* (Tübingen: Mohr, 1990).

12

The Virtuous Circle
Savings, Distribution and Growth Interactions in India

Deepak Lal and I. Natarajan

Introduction

One of the landmarks of Anne Krueger's tenure at the World Bank was the initiation of five large-scale comparative studies of various issues in development. Deepak Lal co-directed the study of the political economy of poverty, equity and growth. This unsurprisingly found that the proximate causes of growth and of differences in growth performance were differences in the rate and efficiency of investment. The synthesis volume (Lal-Myint, 1996) was largely concerned with explaining the latter. The purpose of the present contribution in honour of Anne is to try and provide some explanations for the differences in investment and hence savings rates. We do this by developing a very simple framework for charting the virtuous circle between growth and savings in India – in particular, the effects of growth on the shifts of households from low to higher savings income brackets, thereby raising aggregate savings, which in turn feeds back into higher growth.

The empirical basis of our exercise is the annual Market Information Survey of Households (MISH) conducted by the National Council of Applied Economic Research (NCAER) between 1985–86 and 1995–96. These surveys collect information on household income for the sample households and provide disaggregated information on income distribution. The chapter is in three parts. The first part provides a highly condensed account of how the savings–growth interactions charted in this chapter differ from those conventionally derived from the permanent income/life cycle hypothesis. The second part estimates a simple simultaneous equation model of the savings–growth interactions for the 1951–95 Indian time-series data. The third part provides our projections for growth and the distribution of income until 2007, based on a simple model which combines the distributional effects of growth on the aggregate savings–investment rate, which in turn determines the future growth rate.

Savings–growth interactions

The dominant theoretical models of the determinants of savings and growth are the permanent income/life cycle (PI–LC) explanations for savings and the Solow–Swan model of economic growth. Within these twin frameworks the steady-state growth rate is determined by the exogenous variables of population growth and technological progress, while the savings rate is independent of the level of permanent income and is affected by the growth rate purely through the changing age-dependency ratio (which depends on the rate of population growth) and productivity growth.[1] In the LC framework, saving is done by the young, dissaving by the old. If population and productivity are stationary, the PI–LC incomes of the young are the same as the old, savings and dissavings are equal, so net savings will be zero. With productivity growth, the young are richer than their parents had been at the same age and so their saving is greater than their parents; hence net savings is positive.[2] But this framework eschews the interactions between savings and growth mediated through changes in income distribution which are our concern.

Both frameworks have been questioned. Thus, the Solow–Swan framework, making the determinants of steady-state growth exogenous, with savings affecting the level but not the growth rate of steady-state income, has been sought to be repaired by 'endogenous' growth models, by making the savings–investment rate an endogenous determinant of steady-state growth rates. They have not been found persuasive by either theorists (see Solow, 1994) or practitioners (see Pack, 1994). Scott's (1989) 'endogenous' growth model, departing in major ways from the Solow–Swan framework, is more persuasive.

For Scott, there is no independent technical progress explaining growth, which is determined by only two variables: total savings and labour force growth.[3] Scott finds his model provides a better 'fit' than the neoclassical model for the growth record of OECD countries. In Lal–Myint (1996) the growth experience of 25 developing countries is also found to be in consonance with the Scott rather than the Solow–Swan model. Accepting Scott, there would be a direct relationship between per capita income growth and the rate of investment and its efficiency.[4] This is the first building block for our savings–growth interactions.

The dominant PI–LC hypothesis of the determinants of savings finds a relationship between savings and the rate of growth in terms of life cycle 'hump savings'.[5,6] But savings is independent of the level of permanent income and also of the distribution of income (see Modigliani, 1970).

But, as Summers and Carroll (1989) note, the positive empirical relationship found between savings and growth should show up in differences in age-consumption profiles of countries with differing growth rates, if it is due to the life cycle. This is not so for comparisons of Japan, Canada and the United States. Deaton (1990) also finds this for comparisons of the Ivory Coast, Hong Kong, rural Indonesia, Korean cities and Thailand.

The dynamic version of the PI–LC model is provided by Hall (1978) who showed that if consumers have rational expectations (RE), tomorrow's $(t+1)$ new information will have no relation to what is already known today (t). So changes in consumption between t and $t+1$ should not be correlated with any current information, for example about current income (y) or expected (E) income changes. So, $E(C_{t+1}) = C_t$ (assuming a quadratic utility function and a constant rate of interest (r) equal to the rate of time preference (i)).

As Hayashi (1997) shows, this is essentially a model of self-insurance and assumes: (i) households have no insurance opportunities available through markets or private transfers; and (ii) parents and children form independent and unrelated households in LC (with a finite time horizon for the consumer) or else a dynasty in PI (with an infinite time horizon for consumers). The purely dynastic PI model is fairly strongly rejected by the evidence. But the LC model, if expanded to allow for the exchange of non-market services provided by children and for gifts and bequests from parents, does have some validity. The crucial difference between the PI and LC models lies in whether consumption is influenced by expectations about offspring's income. We have no data to asses this for India. But the studies summarized in Lal-Myint (1996) on private transfers show that these are substantial in many developing countries and are based on a mixture of the exchange (LC) and altruistic (dynastic PI) motives.

For Japan, Hayashi (1997) shows that the evidence is consistent with the dynastic PI model. Typically, Japanese households have extended families and intergenerational bequests are significant (as would also be true of India). The infinite horizon PI assumption therefore seems better than the finite horizon LC assumption. But the existence of large bequests would not in itself lead to high savings rates. For example, Hayashi (ibid., p. 374) notes that in a stationary economy, each generation passes on its assets to the next, but each generation consumes all its income, and hence there is a zero savings rate.

But if the infinite time horizon PI model is combined with the neo-classical growth model (which implicitly assumes a representative immortal dynastic family), then, as Christiano (1989) has shown, a theoretical explanation of Japanese savings behaviour can be provided. Thus, assume that initially the country starts off with a low capital stock, so the marginal productivity of capital (and hence return on savings) is high. But the low capital stock also implies a low level of income, say not much above subsistence, which implies that the marginal utility of consumption is very high. This suggests that the dynastic family will then not save much, even given the high return to savings. But suppose there is some exogenous change in the economic environment (for example, that associated with the recent economic liberalization in India) which improves the efficiency of investment and gives a major boost to the level of income. As income rises, the marginal utility of consumption (*i*) falls below the productivity of capital (*r*) and savings becomes positive as the dynastic family starts accumulating wealth. This then leads to a virtuous circle between savings and growth on the 'traverse' as income levels rise and converge to the steady-state 'target' income of the country's peers in Barro's (1991) 'conditional convergence' framework. Also in this process, as Christiano's simulations for Japan show, the increase in the growth rate *precedes* the rise in savings. This extended PI framework seems the most appropriate to understand savings behaviour in India and the other high savings economies of East Asia.

Furthermore, for individual developing countries, as Deaton (1990) notes, the key prediction of the life cycle hypothesis of a unitary elasticity of consumption with respect to 'permanent income' has been uniformly rejected. Studies for Latin America (Musgrove, 1979), Sri Lanka (Muellbauer, 1982), Thailand (Paxson, 1989), and India (Bhalla, 1979, 1980) find it is less than unity – so savings is not independent of the level of income. This was the assumption underlying the Keynesian consumption function where average savings rates increased with income.[7] Moreover, in its Kaldorian version (Kaldor, 1955–56), the distribution of income between capitalists and workers with differing propensities to save is an important determinant of the overall savings rate.

Bhalla (1980) provides the most robust study of savings behaviour in rural India based on NCAER's three-year longitudinal sample survey data for 1968–70. He finds that a non-linear savings function provides the best 'fit' to the data. This savings function behaves in Keynesian fashion during the middle-income range and then at higher-income levels asymptotically approaches a savings rate which is constant and independent of permanent income in line with the life cycle hypothesis.

Such a savings function can be rationalized in terms of a model which combines the 'hump savings' underlying the life cycle model with a model of 'precautionary savings' recently developed by Deaton (1990). He argues that in poor agrarian economies subject to pervasive climatic risk, savings is motivated not by the intergenerational 'hump savings' motive where savings made in relatively productive youth are used to finance consumption in an unproductive old age. Rather, facing pervasive liquidity constraints and stochastic shocks to their income, the motive is precautionary: using savings as a buffer stock to smooth consumption between good and bad years. 'Consumption is not a function of any simple concept of wealth such as permanent income, but a non-linear function of cash on hand [which includes income as well as liquid assets accumulated from past savings]' (ibid., p. 70). The propensity to consume out of assets will be lower the higher the asset level of the household. The savings function will be non-linear.

This provides a link between the distribution of households by different income levels and aggregate savings. With savings rising with 'assets, and thus with conventionally measured permanent income' (ibid.), the effects of growth on savings will now be mediated through its effects on the income-asset levels of different households. One robust finding of Lal-Myint (1996) is that growth does 'trickle down'. The more rapid the growth, the greater the reduction in the head count of the poor below an intertemporally constant but nationally variant real poverty line. As the savings propensity increases with the household income level, growth shifts households of the low (or zero and negative) income-savings classes into higher (and positive) income-savings classes, thereby raising the aggregate savings level. This 'distributionally' mediated effect of growth on savings is different from that postulated by the permanent income/life cycle theories which rely on the effects of growth on the dependency ratio – an effect not supported by the evidence from age-consumption profiles. It provides a more plausible explanation of the virtuous circle whereby rapid growth, by moving low income-savings households into higher income-savings brackets, raises the aggregate savings rate which in turn fuels rapid growth. This would provide one explanation for the explosive rise in savings and growth rates in the Asian miracle economies, including, most recently, that of China. Can India get into this virtuous circle? We attempt an answer in the third section.

Savings and growth: India 1951–95

In this section we briefly examine the question of causality between savings and growth from the Indian time-series data.[8] An examination of the autocorrelations and partial autocorrelations of the savings series suggested an AR(1) process. To capture the non-linearity of the savings function we estimated a quadratic function with per capita income.[9] Granger causality tests showed that the null hypothesis that 'savings is not Granger caused by per capita income' could be rejected at both lags 1 and 2 at the 1–5 per cent level. The estimated savings function was:

$$s = a + b \cdot y(-2) + c \cdot [y(-2)]^2 + u \qquad (12.1)$$

where s is the savings–income ratio, y is per capita income and u is an error term assumed to follow an AR(1) process.

Table 12.1 (A) provides the estimates, based on two stage least squares (TSLS), and also lists the instruments used. The per capita income growth rate $dy/y = g$, is in turn assumed to be determined by savings/investment.[10] In the absence of 'foreign savings', domestic savings and investment would be the same. But clearly they are not and g will be determined by the ratio of investment to income (I/Y). Again, an AR(1) process was warranted for the per capita income growth series, while the Granger causality test showed that the null hypothesis that 'per capita income growth is not caused by the investment ratio' could be rejected only at the fourth lag at the 7 per cent probability level. As agricultural income in India is dependent on the variability of

Table 12.1 Savings growth regressions, 1954–95

	Savings growth regressions		
(A)	$s = -19.79^*$	$+0.03\ y\ (-2)^{**}$	$-5.81\text{E-}06\ y(-2)^2$
	(1.76)	(2.30)	(1.56)
Instruments: time, population growth			
$R^2 = 0.88$			
DWS = 1.89			
(B)	$g = -2.05^*$	$+0.13\ [(I/Y)-4]^*$	$+0.63\ ga\ ^{***}$
	(1.84)	(1.92)	(2.93)
Instruments: time, modgln = difference between investment–income and savings–income ratios			
$R^2 = 0.84$			
DWS = 1.77			

Note: Figures in brackets are t statistics; significant * at 10%; ** at 5%; *** at 1% levels.

the weather, we tried both a climatic index and the rate of growth of agricultural output (*ga*) as dependent variables in explaining per capita income growth rate along with the investment ratio lagged four periods. The agricultural growth rate gave the better 'fit' so the results from that TSLS regression are reported in Table 12.1 (B). The estimated regression is of the form:

$$g = a1 + b1 \cdot [(I/Y) - 4] + c1 \cdot ga + v \qquad (12.2)$$

where *v* is an AR(1) error term.

The simultaneous equation model formed by these two equations is then closed with two identities:

$$I/Y = s + \text{modgln} \qquad (12.3)$$

where modgln is the difference between the savings and investment ratios, labelled after Modigliani (1970) who used this variable to identify his simultaneous equation model of savings and growth.

The second identity links per capita income with its growth rate:

$$g = 100(\log y - \log y(-1)) \qquad (12.4)$$

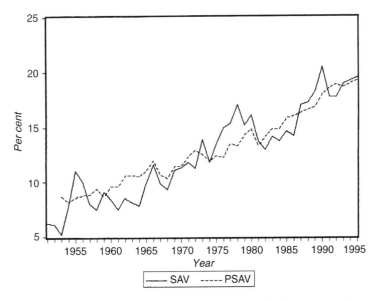

Figure 12.1 Actual and estimated savings, India, 1950–95 (percentage of income)

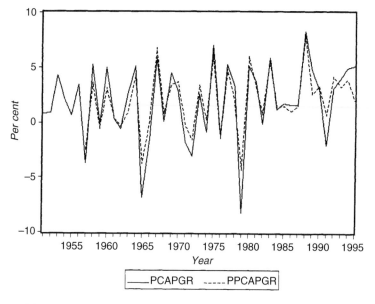

Figure 12.2   Actual and estimated per capita growth rates, India, 1950–95

The solutions of this model with the estimated and actual savings and per capita income growth rates are shown in Figures 12.1 and 12.2 respectively. Despite the various measurement and other errors involved, the model works reasonably well.

Savings, distribution and growth in India

Using the data available from the NCAER MISH surveys, we next make projections within an extension of this simple simultaneous equation model by including the effects of growth on the changing distribution of households in different income classes and hence with differing savings propensities.

The NCAER data on savings rate by household income, from the last available survey of 1975, provide these different propensities as set out in Table 12.2. The changing distribution of households by income level as a result of growth is based on the NCAER MISH surveys, using the projection methods of Natarajan (1997).

The projections of the interactions between growth, distribution and savings are made from the following model. Suppose household savings is the only source of savings, which equals investment. From the

Table 12.2 Savings–income ratios

Income class	Household's average income (1994–95 prices) (Rs. p.a.)	Rural	Urban
Low	16 000	0.0625	0.0516
Lower middle	34 000	0.1773	0.1403
Middle	58 000	0.2894	0.2257
Upper middle	83 000	0.4126	0.3337
High	120 000	0.4033	0.4422

Source: derived from NCAER data (1975).

simple Harrod–Domar (HD) identity we have:

$$g = s/c \qquad (12.5)$$

where g is the growth rate of output, s is the savings/investment ratio, and c is the incremental capital output ratio.

The savings rate as a function of the changing distribution of income is derived as follows. Suppose there are j income classes, with constant average real income in each income class $y(h)'$ $[h = 1 \ldots j]$. Growth changes the percentage of the population in each income class $w(h)$. If y is per capita income, the ratio of the average income in each income class to per capita income is: $v(h) = y(h)'/y$ $[h = 1 \ldots j]$, and the propensity to save in each income class is $s(h)$ $[h = 1 \ldots j]$, then the aggregate savings ratio s is given by:

$$s = s(1) + \sum_{h=2}^{j} [s(h) - s(1)]w(h) \cdot v(h) \qquad (12.6)$$

Assuming that the savings propensity rises with each income class, so that $s(1) < s(2) \ll s(j)$, the expression in square brackets will be positive. With growth, the $w(h)$ changes, with the higher order w rising at the expense of the lower order w as more of the population moves into the higher (fixed) real-income classes. As per capita income y rises, v (the ratio of the average to per capita income in an income class) will fall for all income groups. In the limit, the whole population will be in the highest-income class $y(j)'$, and each w except $w(j)$ will be zero. The per capita income will converge to the average income $y(j)'$, and hence $v(j)' = 1$. Then substituting (12.6) in the HD growth equation (12.5):

$$g = [s(1) + (s(j) - s(1))]/c = s(j)/c \qquad (12.7)$$

The savings rate, and thus the growth rate, will converge to that given by the savings propensity of the highest income class with which we started. The data on w for our projections is from NCAER MISH (Natarajan, 1997). As investment differs from the household savings determined by the above method, an adjustment based on the historical ratio of investment to household savings in the 1980s of 1.2 times was used to develop the investment figures used in the HD equation (12.5).

We also need estimates of the incremental capital output ratio c. The historical series on this represents the realized values of c, reflecting not only the efficiency of investment but also fluctuations in output caused by the weather and differential capacity utilization as a result of variations in the control regime. Ceteris paribus we would expect the value of c to have declined as a result of the 1991 reforms which removed many foreign trade and price controls and industrial licensing. From the time path of incremental capital–output ratios (ICORs) as estimated by Drabu (1997), from the time series of gross domestic capital formation and gross domestic product (charted in Figure 12.3), the ICORs declined from their 1970s levels in the 1980s and then fell further in 1994–95. Similarly the *India Development Report 1997* (Indira Gandhi Institute of Development Research, 1997) notes that

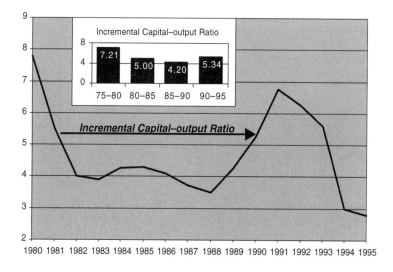

Figure 12.3   ICORs
Source: Drabu (1997).

the three-year average investment rate in the post-reform period does not seem to have exceeded that in the pre-reform period, while there has been a marked improvement in the growth rate: 'One might thus conclude that the improvement in growth rate noticed in recent years has taken place without a corresponding improvement in investment rate. This implies a fall in ICOR in recent years as compared to pre-reform period' (p. 38).

Finally, if we compare Indian ICORs with those from China (derived from the data in the *World Development Report*, 1991), in its pre-reform period the Chinese ICOR was 4.5, close to India's historical ratio. In the post-reform period the Chinese ICOR (until 1990) fell to 3.5. This compares with our estimate of 3.8 for the post-reform ICOR in India.[11]

We base one of our projections on the assumption that as the current reforms work their way through, the Indian ICOR will also decline to 3.5. The second projection assumes that the current ICOR of 3.8 continues unchanged. But as the reform process is still incomplete, we also need some estimate of what the ICOR could be on the optimistic assumption that the reforms are completed and the Indian economy's productivity then matches that of the East Asian 'tigers'. As the ICOR for Korea appears to be about 3.1, we assume this for the third and most optimistic projections.

Table 12.3 summarizes the projected savings and growth rates on these assumptions from our model of the interactions between growth, income distribution and savings. The first alternative assumes that the

Table 12.3 Projections, 1995–96 to 2006–07

		Alternatives for *c*			
	Years	*Alt 1*	*Alt 2*	*Alt 3*	*Alt 4*
Savings rate	1995–96	19.71	19.71	19.71	19.71
	2001–02	24.50	24.50	24.87	24.66
	2006–07	29.79	28.99	30.62	29.65
Growth Rate	1995–96	6.43	6.43	6.43	6.43
	2001–02	8.19	8.19	9.20	8.61
	2006–07	12.26	9.73	12.56	10.85
Poverty ratio	1995–96	31.16	31.16	31.60	31.60
	2001–02	16.51	16.51	15.58	16.12
	2006–07	5.08	6.30	4.07	5.34

Alt 1: *c* interpolated between 3.8 and 3.1 for 2002–03 to 2006–07.
Alt 2: *c* = 3.8 from 1997–98 to 2006–07.
Alt 3: *c* interpolated between 3.8 and 3.1 for 1997–98 to 2006–07.
Alt 4: *c* interpolated between 3.8 and 3.5 for 1997–98 to 2006–07.

reforms will remain stalled until another fiscal crisis (say) at the end of the millennium forces their completion, leading to a fall in the ICOR to the Korean level of 3.1 by 2006–07. This leads to an increase of household savings from 19.7 per cent in 1995–96 to 24.5 per cent in 2001–02 and to 30 per cent in 2006–07. The growth rate rises to 8.19 per cent in 2001–02 and to 12.26 per cent in 2006–07.

The second alternative assumes that there are no further reforms so that the value of c remains at 3.8, the growth-induced rise in savings again boosts the growth rate to 8.19 per cent per annum in 2000–01, with the household savings rate rising from 19.7 per cent in 1995–96 to 24.5 per cent, and by 2006–07 to 29 per cent, which yields a growth rate of 9.73 per cent per annum.

On the most optimistic assumption (alternative 3) that the reform process will be completed speedily so that the ICOR declines to 3.1 from 1998–2007, the household savings rate rises to 24 per cent in 2000–01 and 31 per cent in 2006–07, with the growth rate accelerating to 9.2 per cent per annum in 2000–01 and 12.56 per cent per annum in 2006–07.

An intermediate and perhaps more realistic assumption (alternative 4) is that there will be some continued reforms but they will be drawn out, so that the ICOR will decline to the Chinese level in the 1980s of 3.5 from 1998–2007. This boosts the growth rate to 8.6 per cent per annum in 2000–01, and 10.9 per cent in 2006–07, and the savings rate to 24.7 per cent and 30 per cent in these respective years.

The model also allows projections of the percentage of households in the different income classes given the alternative growth scenarios. The average income in the lowest-income class in the MISH is above the poverty line usually used to determine the head count index of poverty in India. We adjusted the cut-off point of this income class to correspond to the Planning Commission's poverty line, so that the head count index from MISH corresponds to that from the Planning Commission's estimates for 1987–88 and 1993–94. The proportion of the population in this income class will provide an indication of the extent of poverty alleviation flowing from the alternative savings–growth scenarios. The aggregate poverty figures on the different growth–savings interaction scenarios are reported in the second part of Table 12.3.[12] The dramatic reduction in poverty is obvious, even with the current unfinished reforms (alternative 2). If this process can be completed and India can achieve ICORs comparable to the East Asian miracle economies (alternative 3), structural poverty can be virtually eliminated by 2007.

Conclusion

This essay has charted and calibrated an important and hitherto neglected dimension of the savings–growth interaction, whereby the distributional effects of growth boost savings and thereby growth. Removing the controls which have repressed the Indian economy for nearly half a century provides a boost to growth which, through the distributionally mediated rise in savings, leads to a virtuous circle. The 1991 reforms have already put India on this path, and if the reforms can be completed, it can achieve savings and growth rates comparable to the Asian miracle economies. Moreover, as in these economies, if this happened, abject low-end structural poverty would be virtually eliminated. This is the prize on offer, and it is within reach.

Notes

1. Changes in the savings rate affect the level but not the rate of growth of steady-state income. However, with rising savings rates as the economy moves from one steady-state equilibrium to the next, on the 'traverse', the rate of growth of income would be higher than the natural rate of growth in the steady state given by the sum of population growth and labour augmenting technical progress.
2. Thus in the one good model with overlapping generations living for two periods – working in the first and retiring during the second, with Cobb–Douglas production and utility functions with population growing at the rate n, labour augmenting technical progress at the rate z, with $s = S/Y$ the savings/income ratio, Y national income, r – the marginal product of capital and i – the rate of time preference, s at date t will be determined by:

$$s(t) = (1-r)(1-i)[dY(t)/Y(t)] \tag{i}$$

   With steady-state growth, the rate of growth will be the natural rate of growth equal to $n+z$, and equilibrium savings will depend purely upon r, i, z and n. The age-dependency ratio (the ratio of the old to the young) is defined as $1/(1+n)$. A rise in the population growth rate raises the average propensity to save as it increases the number of young savers relative to old dissavers.
3. Strictly this should be the growth in the quality adjusted labour force, for one of Scott's key points is that depreciation as it is usually measured is not an economic concept, and that it effectively represents the transfer of income (in the form of higher wages) with growth to labour. It is these rising wage costs that reduce the quasi-rents on 'old' machines and hence to their economic redundancy rather than any physical depreciation as is assumed in the national income accountants' estimates of depreciation.

4. Scott's model leads to a simple linear relation explaining the growth rate of output g, where s is the savings/investment rate, and the growth rate of the (quality-adjusted) labour force (which we proxy by the rate of growth of population), n:

$$g = a \cdot s + b \cdot n \qquad \text{(ii)}$$

The Solow–Swan growth equation by contrast is:

$$g = a + b \cdot n \qquad \text{(iii)}$$

where a is to be interpreted as the exogenous rate of technical progress, z. In per capita terms, in the Scott model, per capita income growth $(g - n)$ would be a function of the savings/investment rate, while in the Solow–Swan framework it would be a function of the exogenously given rate of technical progress.

5. Excellent surveys of the literature on savings and development are to be found in Gersovitz (1987), Deaton (1990) and Besley (1995).

6. This concept is due to Harrod (1948).

7. The savings function from the permanent income/life cycle hypothesis can be expressed as:

$$S = a + b \cdot Yp + c \cdot Yf + u \qquad \text{(iv)}$$

where Y_p is permanent income Y_f transitory income and u an error term. The permanent income/life cycle hypothesis maintains that $a = 0$, and $c = 1$. The Keynesian hypothesis is that $a < 0$, and that as there is no difference between Y_p and Y_f, that $b = c$.

8. These series are provided in Lal–Natarajan (1999).

9. We have made no attempt to decompose measured income into its permanent and transitory elements. This may be justified by Lahiri's (1989) analysis of the time-series data on savings, in which he did decompose current income into anticipated (permanent) and unanticipated (transitory) elements and found this was not of any importance.

10. This can be thought of as either the result of a simple Harrod–Domar type model of the warranted rate of growth where $g = s/c$, where c is the incremental capital–output ratio, or if one believes in them, from the AK type of endogenous growth model, or else flowing from Scott's model linear relationship in per capita terms set out in equation (12.7).

11. The WDR 1991 statistical appendix yields the following estimates of ICORs:
    China: 1965–80 $g = 6.9$; $I/Y = 31\%$; so $c = 4.5$; 1980–89 $g = 9.7$; $I/Y = 34.9\%$; so $c = 3.5$
    India: 1980–89 $g = 5.3$; $I/Y = 23.9\%$; so $c = 4.5$.
    Korea: 1980–89 $g = 9.7$; $I/Y = 29.8\%$; so $c = 3.1$.

12. The appendix tables in Lal–Natarajan (1999) give these proportions for the rural, urban and all-India levels for different years for the alternative projections.

References

Barro, R. J., 'Economic Growth in a Cross-Section of Countries', *Quarterly Journal of Economics*, 106 (May 1991) 407–43.

Besley, T., 'Savings, Credit and Insurance', in J. Behrman and T. N. Srinivasan (eds), *Handbook of Development Economics*, vol. 3a (Amsterdam: North-Holland, 1995), pp. 2123–207.

Bhalla S., 'Measurement Errors and the Permanent Income Hypothesis: Evidence from Rural India', *American Economic Review*, 69 (1979) 295–307.

Bhalla, S., 'The Measurement of Permanent Income and its Application to Saving Behavior', *Journal of Political Economy*, 88 (1980) 722–43.

Christiano, L., 'Understanding Japan's Saving Rate: the Reconstruction Hypothesis', *Federal Reserve Bank of Minneapolis Quarterly Review* (Spring 1989) 10–25.

Drabu, H. A., 'The IMF Can Do Better', *Business Standard* (9 April 1997) 11.

Deaton, A., 'Saving in Developing Countries: Theory and Review', *World Bank Annual Conference on Development Economics* (1990) 61–96.

Gersovitz, M., 'Saving and Development', in H. Chenery, and T. N. Srinivasan, (eds), *Handbook of Development Economics*, vol. 1 (Amsterdam: North-Holland, 1988) pp. 381–424.

Hall, R. E., 'Stochastic Implications of the Life Cycle–Permanent Income Hypothesis: Theory and Evidence', *Journal of Political Economy*, 96 (1978) 339–57.

Harrod, R., *Towards a Dynamic Economics* (London: Macmillan, 1948).

Hayashi, F., *Understanding Saving* (Cambridge, MA: MIT Press, 1997).

Indira Gandhi Institute, *India Development Report 1997* (New Delhi: Oxford University Press, 1997).

Kaldor, N., 'Alternative Theories of Distribution', *Review of Economic Studies*, 23 (1955–56) 83–100.

Lahiri, A., 'Dynamics of Asian savings – the Role of Growth and Age Structure', *IMF Staff Papers*, 36 (1989) 228–61.

Lal, D., and Myint, H., *The Political Economy of Poverty, Equity and Growth* (Oxford: Clarendon Press, 1996).

Lal, D., and Natarajan, I., 'The Virtuous Circle – Savings, Distribution and Growth: India 1951–2007', mimeo, UCLA and NCAER (July 1999).

Modigliani, F., 'The Life Cycle Hypothesis of Saving and Intercountry Differences in the Saving Ratio', in W. A. Eltis, M. Scott and J. N. Wolfe (eds), *Induction, Trade and Growth* (Oxford: Oxford University Press, 1970) pp. 197–225.

Muellbauer, J., 'The Measurement of Long Run Living Standards: an Application and Evaluation of the Permanent Income Hypothesis', *World Bank Living Standards Measurement* Study (Washington, DC: World Bank, 1982).

Musgrove, P., 'Permanent Household Income and Consumption in Urban South America', *American Economic Review*, 69 (1979) 355–68.

Natarajan, I., 'Forecast of Income Distribution and Emerging Market Structure in India', NCAER (New Delhi: mimeo, 1997).

NCAER, *Survey of Income and Its Disposition* (New Delhi, 1975).

Pack, H., 'Endogenous Growth Theory: Intellectual Appeal and Empirical Shortcomings', *Journal of Economic Perspectives*, 8 (1) (1994) 55–72.

Paxson, C. H., 'Household Savings in Thailand: Responses to Income Shocks', *Princeton University Research Program in Development Studies* (Princeton, NJ, 1989).

Scott, M., *A New View of Economic Growth* (Oxford: Clarendon Press, 1989).

Solow, R., 'Perspectives on Growth Theory', *Journal of Economic Perspectives* 8 (1) (1994) 45–54.

Summers, L. H., and Carroll, C., 'The Growth–Saving Nexus', *NBER Conference on Savings* (Maui, Hawaii, January 1989).

Part III
Political Economy

13
Congressional Voting on International Economic Bills in the 1990s

Robert E. Baldwin and Meredith Crowley

Introduction

Because the United States is the world's traditional leader in promoting globalization, US international economic policies have important implications for other countries as well as for US citizens. Consequently, an understanding of the political, economic and social forces shaping congressional voting behaviour on trade and foreign assistance bills is important for both public- and private-sector leaders in the United States and other countries. The change in the voting behaviour of the US Congress (specifically, the House of Representatives) between the early and late 1990s from supporting trade-liberalizing measures such as NAFTA and the GATT Uruguay Round, to rejecting efforts to renew fast-track authority for the president and approving import quotas for the steel industry, makes an analysis of congressional voting patterns especially relevant as we approach the next century.

In this study we investigate the relative importance of various political and economic factors shaping voting behaviour on a number of international economic bills that came before the US House of Representatives in the 103rd Congress (1993–94) and 105th Congress (1997–98). We also analyze the votes on the steel quota bill in the early part of the 106th Congress by those individuals who were members of the House in the latter part of the 105th Congress. A summary of the bills and the roll-call votes on these measures is presented in Table 13.1. These bills include legislation that approved NAFTA, the GATT Uruguay Round, the renewal of the authority of the president to submit trade agreements to Congress for an up or down vote without amendments – so-called fast-track authority – and disapproved the extension of most-favoured-nation status (MFN) for China. In addition, we include in our analysis several

Table 13.1 Description of bills and voting records

Bill	Bill description	Votes		Date
		Yes	No	
103rd Congress				
GATT FT	to grant a fast-track authority for the GATT Uruguay Round	295	126	22 June 1993
NAFTA	to approve the North American Free Trade Agreement	234	200	17 November 1993
GATT UR	to implement the GATT Uruguay Round Agreement	288	146	29 November 1994
Disapp. China MFN 93	to deny most-favoured-nation status for China 1993	105	318	21 July 1993
Disapp. China MFN 94	to deny most-favoured-nation status for China 1994	75	356	9 August 1994
Foreign Oper. 93	to authorize Foreign Operations FY 94 Appropriations	309	111	17 June 1993
Foreign Oper. 94	to authorize Foreign Operations FY 95 Appropriations	337	87	25 May 1994
For. Op. Conf. Rep. 94	to agree to the For. Op. FY 95 Approp. Conference Report	341	85	4 August 1994
State Dept. Auth. 93	to approve State Dept and Foreign Assistance FY 94–95	273	144	22 June 1993
State Dpt Conf Rep 93	to recommit the St Dpt and For. Assist FY 94–95 Conf. Rep.	195	209	28 April 1994
Expt Admin Reauth	to authorize Export Admin Appropriations FY 93–94	330	54	16 February 1993
Subsidize US cargo shipping	to subsidize US cargo shipping in Marine Security Act	347	65	4 November 1993
Increase tonnage fees on shipping	to increase tonnage duties on certain entries into the US	294	122	2 August 1994
105th Congress				
FT98	to extend fast-track authority in 1998	180	243	25 September 1998
Disapp. China MFN 98	to deny most-favoured-nation status for China 1998	166	264	22 July 1998
Disapp. Vietnam MFN 98	to deny most-favoured-nation status for Vietnam 1998	163	260	30 July 1998
CBI Parity	to extend NAFTA benefits to Caribbean countries	182	234	4 November 1997
African Growth	to support measures that promote trade with Africa	233	186	11 March 1998
Ex-Im Bank & OPIC Funds	to cut funding for the Overseas Private Investment Corporation and the Export–Import Bank	40	387	30 July 1997
Steel Quotas	to impose quotas on steel imports	289	141	17 March 1999

non-trade bills dealing with issues such as funding for the Export–Import Bank and various US foreign assistance programmes.

Econometric model and data

A single equation probit model is used to analyze the voting behaviour of members of Congress.[1] A vote in favour of a bill (yes) is assigned a value of one and a vote against the measure (no) is assigned a zero. We draw on the theoretical and empirical work of both economists and political scientists to include three sets of explanatory variables in the voting equations: variables measuring ideology, economic conditions and campaign contributions.[2] The description and mean of each variable are given in Table 13.2.

The ideological variables indicate if a member of Congress tends to be pro-business or pro-labour, an internationalist versus domestically-oriented, concerned about environmental issues, a fiscal conservative, and so on. Political scientists have long emphasized the importance of ideology in shaping voting behaviour (see Bender and Lott, 1996, for a review of this literature). Some economists have also stressed the significance of ideology in influencing governmental behaviour. Corden (1974), for example, develops the notion of a conservative welfare function in which governments seek to prevent any important economic group from incurring significant economic losses. Researchers generally use the ratings by various interest groups – for example, the US Chamber of Commerce – to measure the ideological views of legislators. The ratings indicate the percentage of votes on which a legislator supported the position of the interest group on legislation of particular concern to the group. A rating of 100 indicates complete agreement with the interest group's views.

In our probit regressions, we include ratings of House members by four interest groups – the American Conservative Union (ACU), the American Federation of Labor-Congress of Industrial Organizations (AFL), the Chamber of Commerce (COC), and the League of Conservation Voters (LCV). These ratings were obtained from the web sites of the various organizations. For the bills considered by the 103rd Congress, the ratings used are an average of the 1993 and 1994 ratings by the groups (excluding the ratings on any bill being analyzed). For the bills voted upon by the 105th Congress, the ratings are those for 1997. We generally expect that the higher a member's rating by the ACU, AFL or LVC, the more likely the legislator voted against measures promoting

Table 13.2   Means and descriptions of variables

Dependent variables	Description	Mean
103rd Congress		
GATT FT	1 if member voted for GATT Fast-Track Authority for the Uruguay Round	0.703
NAFTA	1 if member voted for the North American Free Trade Agreement	0.539
GATT UR	1 if member voted for the GATT Uruguay Round	0.664
Disapp. China MFN 93	1 if member voted to deny most-favoured-nation status for China 1993	0.249
Disapp. China MFN 94	1 if member voted to deny most-favoured-nation status for China 1994	0.172
Foreign Oper. 93	1 if member voted for Foreign Operations FY 94 Appropriations	0.779
Foreign Oper. 94	1 if member voted for Foreign Operations FY 95 Appropriations	0.796
For. Op. Conf Rep 94	1 if member voted for For. Op. FY 95 Approp. Conference Report	0.802
State Dept Auth 93	1 if member voted for State Dept and Foreign Assistance FY 94–95	0.710
State Dpt Conf. Rep 93	1 if member voted for St. Dpt & For. Assist FY 94–95 Conf. Rep.	0.484
Expt Admin Reauth	1 if member voted for Export Administration FY 94 Authorization	0.984
Subsidize US cargo shipping	1 if member voted to subsidize US cargo shipping in Marine Security Act	0.901
Increase tonnage fees on shipping	1 if member voted to increase tonnage duties on certain entries into the US	0.702
105th Congress		
FT 98	1 if member voted to extend Fast-Track Authority in 1998	0.426
Disapp. China MFN 98	1 if member voted to deny most-favoured-nation status for China 1998	0.385
Disapp. Vietnam MFN 98	1 if member voted to deny most-favoured-nation status for Vietnam 1998	0.386
CBI Parity	1 if member voted to extend NAFTA benefits to Caribbean countries	0.436
African Growth	1 if member voted to support measures that promote trade with Africa	0.556
Ex-Im Bank & OPIC Funds	1 if member voted to cut funding for the Overseas Private Investment Corporation and the Export–Import Bank	0.094
Steel Quotas	1 if member voted to impose quotas on steel imports	0.674

Table 13.2 Contd.

Dependent variables	Description	Mean
Explanatory variables		
ACU	1993–94 Rating by the American Conservative Union (out of 100)	46.7
ACU97	1997 Rating by the American Conservative Union (out of 100)	53.1
AFL	1993–94 Rating by the AFL-CIO (out of 100)	58.7
AFL97	1997 Rating by the AFL-CIO (out of 100)	51.5
COC	1993–94 Rating by the US Chamber of Commerce (out of 100)	59.5
COC97	1997 Rating by the US Chamber of Commerce (out of 100)	66.4
LCV	1993–94 Rating by the League of Conservation Voters (out of 100)	51.4
LCV97	1997 Rating by the League of Conservation Voters (out of 100)	47.0
Democrat 93–94	1 if member is a Democrat	0.590
Democrat 98	1 if member is a Democrat	0.475
Union	1991–92 Private sector district unionization rate	0.121
X/M employment	Employment in net export industries/ employment in net import industries	1.37
1–11 yr edu.	1990 Fraction of population (25+) without a high school degree	0.25
12 yr edu.	1990 Fraction of population (25+) with a HS degree, without college degree	0.49
Unemployment	1990 District unemployment rate (per cent)	6.4
Unemployment 98	1998 District unemployment rate (per cent)	4.3
Per capita Income	1990 District per capita income, thousands of $s	14.4
Labour contributions	Labour group contributions, 1991–92, thousands of $s	53.5
Labour contributions 96	Labour group contributions, 1996, thousands of $s	63.9
Business contributions	Business group contributions, 1991–92, thousands of $s	152.2
Business contributions 96	Business group contributions, 1996, thousands of $s	175.3
Food	1993 Employment in SIC 20/total district employment	0.017
Tobacco	1993 Employment in SIC 21/total district employment	0.000
Textiles	1993 Employment in SIC 22/total district employment	0.007
Apparel	1993 Employment in SIC 23/total district employment	0.011

Table 13.2   Contd.

Dependent variables	Description	Mean
Lumber	1993 Employment in SIC 24 total district employment	0.008
Furniture	1993 Employment in SIC 25/total district employment	0.005
Paper	1993 Employment in SIC 26/total district employment	0.007
Printing	1993 Employment in SIC 27/total district employment	0.015
Chemicals	1993 Employment in SIC 28/total district employment	0.009
Petroleum	1993 Employment in SIC 29/total district employment	0.001
Rubber prods.	1993 Employment in SIC 30/total district employment	0.001
Leather	1993 Employment in SIC 31/total district employment	0.001
Stone, clay, glass	1993 Employment in SIC 32/total district employment	0.005
Primary metals	1993 Employment in SIC 33/total district employment	0.007
Fabr. Metals	1993 Employment in SIC 34/total district employment	0.015
Mach. ex Elec.	1993 Employment in SIC 35/total district employment	0.018
Elec. Equip	1993 Employment in SIC 36/total district employment	0.015
Transp. Equip	1993 Employment in SIC 37/total district employment	0.017
Instruments	1993 Employment in SIC 38/total district employment	0.009
Misc. Mfrs.	1993 Employment in SIC 39/total district employment	0.004

trade liberalization and increased US government assistance to foreign countries. In contrast, we expect COC ratings to be positively correlated with affirmative votes for these policies. We also include a dummy variable (Democrat) indicating Democrat or Republican party membership, with a one signifying the former and a zero the latter. We expect most Democrats to oppose and most Republicans to support trade liberalization and foreign economic assistance.

The second group of independent variables measures general economic characteristics of a member's district. Both economists and political scientists stress the importance of economic factors in influencing legislative voting behaviour. Among the economic variables we include are the proportion of individuals over 25 with no high school degree, the fraction of individuals with a high school diploma but no college degree, the level of per capita income, and the unemployment rate. These are taken from the Census publication *Population and Housing Characteristics for Congressional Districts of the 103rd Congress.* However, we update the unemployment rate to 1998 using data from the Bureau of Labor Statistics to analyze bills of the 105th Congress. The proportion of unionized private sector workers in each district as of 1991–92 is from Box-Steffenmeier, Arnold and Zorn (1997) and was provided by the authors. We hypothesize that legislators with districts characterized by higher proportions of individuals with little (1–11 or 12 years) education, lower per capita incomes, higher unemployment rates and higher proportions of unionized workers will be more likely to vote against trade liberalization and foreign aid.

Hypothesizing that legislators from districts where the ratio of jobs in net export industries to jobs in net import industries is high will be more likely to support freer trade, we construct a variable that measures the relative importance of export-sector jobs to import-competing sector jobs. We divide industries (at the four-digit SIC level) into those for which the United States is a net importer and those for which it is a net exporter. Then, we sum up the total employment in these net exporting and net importing industries for each congressional district. Finally, we calculate the ratio of net exporting to net importing sector employment (X/M employment) for each district (see Baldwin and Magee, 2000).

Another set of economic variables included in the regressions is the percentage of total employment in congressional districts in particular two-digit manufacturing industries (see Table 13.2). This information is estimated from data collected at the county level in the 1993 *County Business Patterns.* If a county contains more than one congressional district within its borders, we estimate the number of workers in an industry for each district by using the fraction of the county's population (in 1990) residing in each district. Data on population size by congressional district and county are reported in *Congressional Districts in the 1990s* (1993). We expect that the higher the percentage of a legislator's constituents employed in such import-sensitive industries as textiles and apparel the more likely the legislator will vote against trade liberalization, while the higher the employment percentage in export-oriented sectors such as electronic equipment the more likely he or she will support market-opening international policies.

The final set of variables included in the regressions measures campaign contributions from various interest groups. Both political scientists and economists have developed theoretical models in which campaign contributions influence voting behaviour. Political scientists believe that such contributions enable interest groups to gain access to legislators and that by lobbying these legislators interest groups may be able to influence their votes. Economists take a more direct approach in their models by assuming that politicians implicitly exchange votes favourable to interest groups for campaign contributions. Data on the campaign contributions used in analyzing the bills of the 103rd Congress are taken from Makinson and Goldstein (1994). The labour and business contributions variables consist of the total contributions received by each representative in the 1992 election from political action committees (PACs) that Makinson and Goldstein identify as representing labour or business interests, respectively. In analyzing the bills of the 105th Congress we update this information to 1996 from the web site of the Center for Responsive Politics, where Makinson is the executive director. We generally expect that labour PAC contributions will be negatively related to approval of trade-liberalizing measures and business PAC contributions positively related to these measures.

Findings

What variables matter?

Tables 13.3 and 13.4 present the results of our statistical analysis of twenty international economic measures that were voted on by members of the 103rd and 105th Congresses. The first column of Table 13.3 lists these bills, while the first row lists the explanatory ideological, general economic, and contributions variables included in the regression equations. The industry-specific economic variables, the percentages of total employment in particular two-digit SIC industries, are shown in Table 13.4. The estimates presented for each bill (row-wise) indicate the effect of a unit increase in each of the independent variables (above their mean values) on the probability of a favourable vote for the measure. In the GATT Fast-Track vote, for example, a unit increase in the ACU's rating from its mean of 46.7 reduces the probability of a favourable vote by seven-tenths of one per cent. We indicate whether the coefficients are statistically significant at less than (or equal to) the 1, 5 or 10 per cent level.

The coefficients of the ideological ratings of House members have the predicted signs and are statistically significant for most of the international economic measures analyzed. As expected, legislators rated highly by the COC favour liberal trade policies whereas those highly rated by the AFL tend to oppose such measures. For example, pro-business members strongly supported such measures as NAFTA, the GATT Uruguay Round, MFN for China and Fast-Track 1998, whereas pro-labour legislators opposed these policies. Both groups tended to support the non-trade international economic measures, although the marginal coefficients for a number of these measures are low and not statistically significant. One understandable exception to this latter point was the strong support by members highly rated by the AFL for a bill that increased subsidies to US shipping. Similarly, members highly rated by the COC supported bills that provided funding for foreign assistance operations and the export administration programme.

Members highly rated by the American Conservative Union consistently opposed trade-liberalizing and foreign assistance bills. Their fiscal conservatism easily explains their opposition to legislation that provides funds for assisting other economies, but one usually presupposes that conservatives favour freer trade. If ACU is the only interest group rating variable used in the regressions, its coefficient is insignificant (though indicating opposition to trade liberalization) for such measures as NAFTA, the GATT Uruguay Round and Fast-Track 1998 (but not for MFN). But once a measure of the pro-business, open-market orientation of some conservatives is introduced, namely, their rating by the COC, the coefficient of the ACU variable enters with a statistically significant sign indicating opposition to liberal trade and foreign aid policies.

In the 103rd Congress, the coefficient of the ratings variable of the League of Conservation Voters did not enter in a statistically significant manner in the GATT Fast-Track, NAFTA or GATT Uruguay Round votes. However, it was statistically significant in the votes on MFN for China with a sign indicating opposition to granting China this status. In contrast, in the 105th Congress the coefficient of this variable is statistically significant in a manner indicating support for MFN for China and for extending quota-free rights for textiles to both the Caribbean nations and the countries of Sub-Saharan Africa. However, it is not statistically significant in the Fast-Track 1998 vote.

Whether a member was a Democrat or Republican generally does not matter in voting on the various bills, once the other ideological and various economic variables are included. An interesting exception, however, concerns the votes on MFN for China, where the coefficient

Table 13.3 Marginal voting effects of explanatory variables

	Ideological variables					Economic characteristics						Campaign funding	
	ACU	AFL	COC	LCV	Dem.	Union	X/M employ.	1–11 yr educ.	12 yr educ.	Unemp.	Per cap income	Labour contrib.	Business contrib.
103rd Congress													
GATT FT	-0.007[b]	-0.004[c]	0.004[c]	-0.002	-0.052	-0.532	0.082[c]	-1.427[b]	-0.835	-0.002	0.0000	-0.0011[b]	0.0009[a]
NAFTA	-0.016[a]	-0.011[a]	0.009[a]	0.000	-0.087	-2.038[a]	0.167[a]	-1.544[b]	-1.133	0.022	0.0000	-0.0029[a]	0.0010[a]
GATT UR	-0.019[a]	-0.008[a]	0.012[a]	-0.001	0.042	-0.159	0.079[c]	1.027	-0.103	-0.056[a]	0.0000	-0.0015[a]	0.0009[a]
Disapp. China MFN 93	0.012[a]	0.007[a]	-0.003	0.005[b]	-0.374[a]	-0.383	-0.068[c]	-0.295	-0.487	-0.023	0.0000	0.0008	-0.0005[c]
Disapp. China MFN 94	0.009[a]	0.005[a]	-0.006[a]	0.004[b]	-0.419[a]	-0.536	-0.101[a]	-0.561	-0.280	0.008	0.0000	0.0000	-0.0002
Foreign Oper. 93	-0.003	0.002	0.005[b]	0.006[b]	-0.085	0.335	0.037	-0.806	-1.138	-0.017	0.0000	-0.0002	0.0004[c]
Foreign Oper. 94	-0.008[a]	0.001	0.006[a]	0.001	-0.048	0.515	0.023	-0.546	-1.071	0.004	0.0000	-0.0003	0.0003[c]
For. Op. Conf Rep 94	-0.008[a]	0.002	0.007[a]	0.001	-0.061	0.489	0.014	-0.577	-0.959	0.007	0.0000	-0.0002	0.0003[c]
State Dept Auth 93	-0.014[a]	0.002	0.004	-0.002	0.146	-0.827	0.115[b]	-0.113	-0.279	-0.006	0.0000	-0.0016[b]	0.0004
State Dpt Conf Rep 93	-0.008[a]	0.002[a]	0.007	0.001	-0.061[a]	0.489	0.014	-0.577	-0.959	0.007	0.0000	-0.0002[b]	0.0003[c]
Expt Admin Reauth	-0.001[a]	0.001[b]	0.001[a]	0.000	0.024	-0.010	-0.001	0.103	0.020	-0.002	0.0000	0.0000	0.0001[c]

Subsidize US cargo shipping	0.000	0.002[a]	0.000	0.000	−0.079[a]	−0.098	−0.002	0.198[c]	0.201	0.006	0.0000c	0.0001	0.0001[c]
Increase tonnage fees on shipping	0.008[b]	0.014[a]	0.004	0.003	−0.046	−0.145	−0.003	−0.328	0.665	0.015	0.0000	0.0007	−0.0001

105th Congress

FT98	−0.013[a]	−0.007[b]	0.014[a]	0.000	−0.162	−2.193[b]	0.148[b]	−2.584[a]	−1.706	0.015	0.0000	−0.0023[a]	0.0005[b]
Disapp. China MFN 98	0.005	−0.008[a]	−0.028[a]	−0.004[c]	−0.196	0.340	0.016	1.690[b]	1.807[c]	−0.063[b]	0.0000[a]	0.0014[b]	−0.0005[b]
Disapp. Vietnam MFN 98	0.012[a]	0.000	−0.012[a]	−0.002	−0.404[a]	0.283	0.053	1.589[b]	−0.466	−0.050[b]	0.0000	0.0016[a]	−0.0004[c]
CBI Preference	−0.010[a]	−0.003	0.011[a]	0.004	−0.237	−0.418	0.109[b]	−1.784[b]	−1.290	0.014	0.0000[c]	−0.0023[a]	0.0008[a]
African Preferences	−0.011[a]	−0.001	0.012[a]	0.006[b]	−0.373[b]	−0.598	0.182[a]	−2.674[a]	−2.708[b]	0.093[a]	0.0000[b]	−0.0009	0.0006[b]
Cut Export Finance & OPIC Funds	0.000[a]	0.000[c]	0.000[a]	0.000	0.007	0.008	−0.001	0.015	0.029	0.000	0.0000	0.0000	0.0000
Steel Quotas	0.000	0.003[c]	−0.008[a]	−0.005[a]	−0.025	−0.083	−0.098[b]	1.341[b]	1.919[b]	−0.010	0.0000	0.0012[c]	−0.0002

Note: a, b, c indicate significance at the 1 per cent, 5 per cent or 10 per cent level, respectively.

242 Trade, Development and Political Economy

Table 13.4 Significant industry coefficients in voting analysis

	Food	Tobacco	Textiles	Apparel	Lumber	Furniture	Paper	Printing	Chemicals	Petroleum	Rubber products	Leather	Stone,clay,glass	Primary metals	Fabr. metals	Mach. ex elec.	Elec. equip.	Trasp. equip.	Instruments	Misc. mfrs
103rd Congress																				
GATT FT			−						+											
NAFTA										−						−	+			
GATT UR	−		−			−														
Disapp. China MFN 93	−	+																		−
Disapp. China MFN 94									+	+										−
Foreign z Oper. 93	−							−	−	−	+			−						
Foreign Oper. 94	−	−						−		−	+							−		
For. Op Conf Rep 94	−							−		−								−		
State Dept Auth 93						+														
State Dpt Conf Rep 93			−											−						
Expt Admin Reauth			−																	
Subsidize US cargo shipping	−				+	−	−								−					
Increase tonnage fees on shipping	−		+	+							−								+	
105th Congress																				
FT98		+	−						−	+							+			−
Disapp. China MFN 98			+	+		−	+				−					−				
Disapp. Vietnam MFN 98				+	−		+													
CBI Parity					+		−												−	
African Growth		−																	−	
Exp–Imp Bank Funds	−				+				+	−					+					
Steel Quotas								+					+	+	−				+	+
Pro liberal trade & for. assist votes	3	1	0	0	0	5	2	0	1	3	4	0	0	1	1	2	2	0	0	2
Anti liberal trade & for. assist votes	4	2	7	4	2	0	2	4	5	4	1	0	3	1	0	1	0	2	5	1

of the variable indicates strong support by Democrats for continuing this status for China. Apparently, this is an issue where party membership makes a unique difference for members' votes.

Various economic conditions have the expected effect on voting patterns on international economic issues and are statistically significant. For example, the higher the ratio of workers employed in export-oriented industries to workers employed in import-competing sectors in a member's district the more likely the legislator was to vote in favour of such trade measures as GATT Fast-Track, NAFTA, GATT Uruguay Round, MFN for China, and extending quota-free rights for textiles to the Caribbean and parts of Africa and to vote against import quotas for the steel industry.[3] As might be expected, the coefficient of this variable is usually not associated with voting on general foreign assistance legislation in a statistically significant manner.

The coefficients of variables reflecting the relative importance in a congressional district of individuals especially concerned about the job-displacing and wage-decreasing effects of globalization – namely, the proportions of unionized workers and of individuals with only 1–11 years of education have the expected signs in all the votes for which the estimates are statistically significant. The coefficient of the unionization variable is statistically significant (in a protectionist direction) in the NAFTA and Fast-Track 1998 votes, suggesting that the labour unions are successful in mobilizing their members to exert political pressure on members of Congress only in such high – priority trade measures. Members in districts with a relatively high proportion of individuals with less than a high school education tended not only to oppose NAFTA and Fast-Track 1998 but also the GATT Fast-Track legislation, the 1998 extension of MFN to China, the extension of MFN to Vietnam, and the granting of a quota-free status for textile imports from developing countries of both the Caribbean and Sub-Saharan Africa. In addition, they supported the 1999 steel quota bill. The sign of the coefficient of the high school education variable (12 years of education) also generally indicates opposition to trade liberalization and foreign economic assistance, but the coefficient is statistically significant in only a few votes.

As one would expect, the higher the district unemployment rate the more likely the district's representative was to vote against the GATT Uruguay Round, but the coefficients of this variable for the other trade bills in the decade are either statistically insignificant or opposite in sign to what would be expected. Contrary to our expectations, the sign of the coefficient of per capita income usually indicates greater opposition to trade liberalization and foreign aid programmes the higher per capita income, although the coefficient is statistically significant in only a few cases. The coefficients of the proportions of workers employed in particular two-digit SIC industries in members' districts are statistically significant in the various voting regressions in a relatively small number of cases. These relationships are presented in Table 13.4, where the various bills are listed in the first column and the industries in the first row. Rather than listing the magnitude of the marginal coefficients and their significance levels, we only indicate the signs of those coefficients that are statistically significant at the 10 per cent level or less.

The signs of the coefficients for some industries are what would be expected from various studies about the employment impact of trade liberalization on different industries, but the reasons for the signs of others are not at all obvious. Furthermore, the liberal trade versus protectionist influence of some industries switches among the various bills. This is the case for the food and petroleum industries, for example. Industries that tend to have a protectionist impact on voting behaviour are textiles, apparel, lumber, printing, chemicals, transportation equipment and instruments. Those industries with a liberal trade and foreign aid influence are furniture and electronic equipment.

Returning to Table 13.3, the coefficients of the final set of explanatory variables included in the regression equations – namely, campaign contributions by labour and business PACs – have the predicted sign and are statistically significant in most of the votes. The pro-trade, pro-foreign-assistance influence of contributions by business PACs is especially pervasive, with the coefficient of this variable being statistically significant in 15 of the 20 votes analyzed. The protectionist influence of labour PAC contributions is most important for trade votes.

The marginal coefficients of business PAC contributions indicate that, in those cases where the coefficient was statistically significant, a $1000 increase in a member's contribution from business PACs increased the probability of a vote promoting trade liberalization and foreign aid by between 0.10 percentage points (NAFTA) and 0.01 percentage points (subsidization of US cargo ships). The marginal coefficients of the labour PAC contributions are not only of the opposite of but tend to be absolutely larger than those for business PACs. Where significant, a $1000 increase in contributions from labour PACs decreased the probability of a pro-freer trade or pro-foreign aid vote from 0.29 percentage points (NAFTA) to 0.02 percentage points (1993 Conference Report on State Department funding).

Sources of the voting shift in the late 1990s

As noted in the introductory section and detailed in Table 13.1, members of the House became reluctant in the late 1990s to support new trade-liberalizing legislation and actually voted for the imposition of quotas on steel imports in early 1999. More specifically, the House vote in 1993 on NAFTA was 234 in favour and 200 against passage of the bill, and in 1994 the vote on implementing the GATT Uruguay Round was 288 in favour and 146 in opposition. In contrast, in the fall of 1998 only 180 members voted to provide fast-track authority to the president while 243 voted against doing so, and in March 1999 289 members voted for the imposition of steel import quotas while 141 members opposed this action. The purpose of this section is to try to determine if this shift in voting patterns is attributable to changes in the relative importance of particular subsets of the variables included in our probit regressions or to other factors not included in our econometric model.

To gain insights into why House members changed their voting behaviour between the time they approved NAFTA and when they rejected the 1998 bill to renew fast-track authority, we successively replace each probit coefficient (not the marginal coefficient) in the Fast-Track 1998 regression with the comparable coefficient in the NAFTA regression, keeping the other coefficients unchanged, and then calculate how this changes the predicted proportion of favourable Fast-Track 1998 votes. Table 13.5 presents the basic probit regressions for NAFTA and Fast-Track 1998, while Table 13.6 shows how inserting the NAFTA coefficients into the Fast-Track 1998 probit equation changes the estimated proportion of members approving the Fast-Track 1998 bill.

As Table 13.6 indicates, the probit regression model of the Fast-Track 1998 vote predicts that 42.5 per cent of House members vote in favour of the bill (the actual percentage was 42.6). However, if the coefficient on the ACU variable in the NAFTA probit model, for example, replaces the ACU coefficient in the Fast-Track 1998 probit model, the predicted proportion of favourable votes on Fast-Track 1998 drops to 37.1 per cent, since the ACU coefficient in the NAFTA regression is an absolutely larger negative number than the Fast-Track 1998 coefficient, namely, -0.041 vs -0.038. If the coefficient for the AFL variable in the NAFTA model is substituted into the Fast-Track 1998 model (all other variables keeping their Fast-Track 1998 values), the predicted proportion of favourable votes drops to 37.9 per cent. Again this occurs because the absolutely larger negative AFL coefficient in the NAFTA equation indicates stronger opposition to NAFTA than to Fast-Track 1998 on the part of members whose ideological leanings are being

Table 13.5   NAFTA and Fast-Track 1998

	NAFTA		Fast-Track 1998	
	Probit Coef.	*Std Error*	*Probit Coef.*	*Std Error*
ACU	−0.041	0.011	−0.038	0.011
AFL	−0.028	0.008	−0.019	0.008
COC	0.023	0.008	0.042	0.008
LCV	−0.001	0.007	0.001	0.006
Democrat	−0.221	0.377	−0.470	0.464
Union	−5.147	1.831	−6.392	2.609
X/M employ	0.421	0.141	0.419	0.184
1–11 yr. edu.	−3.900	2.220	−7.636	2.769
12 yr. edu	−2.862	2.656	−4.981	3.346
Unemp.	0.054	0.057	0.046	0.079
Per capita income	0.000	0.000	0.000	0.000
Labour contributions	−0.007	0.002	−0.007	0.002
Business contributions	0.002	0.001	0.002	0.001
Food	1.776	6.036	5.525	7.245
Tobacco	19.659	46.730	91.626	42.485
Textiles	−2.302	4.353	−18.709	8.037
Apparel	7.742	7.789	2.598	9.853
Lumber	−2.473	7.231	7.893	9.182
Furniture	24.675	15.343	10.349	10.440
Paper	−7.003	10.851	−7.514	13.030
Printing	9.999	14.262	17.052	18.417
Chemicals	−16.655	7.730	−25.605	11.979
Petroleum	−11.255	26.274	64.226	31.243
Rubber products.	17.243	13.779	12.682	15.797
Leather	17.795	29.910	31.014	32.089
Stone, clay, glass	12.046	21.334	−32.949	25.642
Primary metals	−16.767	14.904	−13.562	16.854
Fabr. metals	15.175	12.155	2.832	14.125
Mach. ex elec.	−20.095	8.723	14.790	9.976
Elec. equip	20.194	7.833	21.693	8.720
Transp. equip	2.792	4.664	2.637	5.590
Instruments	−17.020	11.296	−43.943	14.279
Misc. mfrs.	3.471	17.613	−21.115	37.554
Constant	4.661	2.460	4.775	2.754

measured by their AFL ratings. In contrast, those rated highly by the Chamber of Commerce supported Fast-Track 1998 more strongly than NAFTA, as the higher Fast-Track 1998 COC coefficient indicates. This means that if the support by this group for Fast-Track 1998 had been

Table 13.6   Predicted outcomes of the Fast-Track 1998 vote

Model	Predicted percentage of Aye votes for Fast-Track 1998
Fast-Track 1998 probit model	42.5
Fast-Track 1998 model using the following NAFTA probit coefficients:	
ACU	37.1
AFL	37.9
COC	16.5
LCV	41.0
ACU, AFL, COC, and LCV	9.5
Democrat	44.2
1–11 years of education	60.6
12 years of education	59.6
1–11 and 12 years of education	74.3
Per capita income	50.4
Unionization rate	44.9
Unemployment rate	43.0
Export–import employment rate	43.3
All industries (two-digit SIC)	44.0
Labour contributions	41.8
Business contributions	45.5
Constant term	41.7
All variables	53.8
Actual percentage of Aye votes for Fast-Track 1998 vote	42.6

the same as in the NAFTA vote, everything else remaining unchanged, the predicted percentage of those voting for Fast-Track 1998 would have only been 16.5 per cent.

If the NAFTA coefficients for all four ideological variables – namely, ACU, AFL, COC and LCV – are used in the Fast-Track 1998 equation, the percentage of favourable votes is only 9.5 per cent. Thus, despite the defeat of Fast-Track 1998, on balance, the support of those assumed to be ideologically in favour of a liberal trade policy was stronger for Fast-Track 1998 than for NAFTA, and the ideological opposition of those opposing freer trade was weaker for Fast-Track than for NAFTA. In view of the shift in the composition of the House from a Democrat to Republican majority, this result is not surprising.

The results of similar calculations for the general economic factors affecting voting behaviour indicate the main source of the decline in support for continued trade liberalization. When the NAFTA coefficients for the proportions of individuals with 1–11 years of education and 12 years of education are substituted in the Fast-Track 1998 equation, the predicted percentage of favourable votes rises to 60.6 per cent and 59.6 per cent, respectively. The predicted percentage of favourable votes rises to 74.3 per cent if the NAFTA values for both are used simultaneously. Using the NAFTA coefficient for the per capita income variable also works in this direction, raising the predicted percentage of favourable votes to 50.4. It appears that either because of direct political pressure from these groups or because legislators became convinced that trade liberalization was unfairly hurting less-educated individuals, legislators became reluctant in the late 1990s to move forward with further liberalization by approving fast-track authority for the president.

Other economic factors do not seem to have played a major role in changing the voting pattern of House members. The substitution of the NAFTA coefficient for the unionization variable increases the proportion of favourable votes on Fast-Track 1998 only to 44.9 per cent while the use of the NAFTA coefficient for the ratio of employment in industries with a net export surplus to employment in industries with a net import surplus increases the predicted proportion of yes votes on Fast-Track 1998 to 43.3 per cent. Similarly, substituting the NAFTA coefficients for employment shares of all the individual industries raises the predicted proportion to only 44.0.

Another possible reason for the failure of the Fast-Track 1998 bill could have been a relative shift in the pro-protectionist versus pro-freer trade impact of PAC campaign contributions. However, using the NAFTA coefficient for the campaign contributions by labour groups lowers the predicted proportion only slightly, to 41.8 per cent, and introducing the NAFTA business contributions coefficient raises the predicted per cent only moderately, to 45.5 per cent.

Conclusions

The econometric results of this chapter are broadly consistent with the political economy models of economists and political scientists who have hypothesized that voting by members of Congress on international economic issues is influenced mainly by the ideology of the legislators, the nature of economic conditions in their districts, and the magnitude of the campaign contributions they receive. More specifically, we have found that when international economic bills are perceived to affect only a small part of the economy in an important manner, such as the funding of the foreign assistance programmes of the US government or the subsidization of US shipping, the general ideological views of legislators seem to play the most important role in shaping their decisions. The coefficients of the campaign contribution variables, especially business PAC contributions, generally have the expected sign and are sometimes statistically significant in the votes on these bills. The coefficients of such general economic characteristics of districts as the proportion of workers with a high school education or less, the ratio of employment in export-oriented industries to import-competing industries and the proportions of unionized workers are generally not statistically significant in the votes on these measures. In contrast, when the bills being considered are viewed as having important economic implications for an appreciable part of the economy, as in the case of NAFTA or Fast-Track 1998, the coefficients of the variables measuring ideology, general economic conditions, and PAC contributions from business and labour are all often statistically significant. Membership in the Democrat or Republican party generally did not influence voting behaviour once other factors were taken into account, except in the case of granting MFN status for China or Vietnam.

The shift in voting behaviour in the House of Representatives from endorsing NAFTA in the early 1990s to refusing to grant fast-track authority to the president in the late 1990s seems to be mainly due to a change in attitude by legislators in districts with high proportions of less-educated individuals. The ideological ratings actually indicate stronger support for Fast-Track 1998 than for NAFTA, while the voting impact of the contributions variables is roughly the same in both voting equations. These findings suggest that significant efforts on the part of the US government to provide better positive domestic adjustment programmes and safeguard mechanisms for less-educated workers may be necessary to alleviate the concerns of legislators about the adverse impact of increased globalization on these workers and to regain a legislative majority for further trade liberalization.

Notes

1. In a previous paper co-authored by one the authors of this chapter, Baldwin and Magee (1998) addressed the possible endogeneity of campaign contributions by estimating a simultaneous-equation, full-information maximum-likelihood model of voting behaviour and campaign contributions. They found mixed evidence on the endogeneity issue, with single-equation probit regressions generally yielding the same set of statistically significant variables.

2. For a recent review of political-economy models developed by economists, see Rodrik (1995). See Morton and Cameron (1992) and Smith (1995) for recent surveys of the work of political scientists in this field.
3. It should be noted that the marginal coefficients reported in Table 12.3 for the steel quota bill are based only on those members of the 105th Congress (1997–98) who were in the House of Representatives at the time of the vote in March 1999 as members of the 106th Congress.

References

Baldwin, R. E., and Magee, C. S., 'Is Trade Policy for Sale? Congressional Voting on Recent Trade Bills', *Public Choice*, 105 (2000) 79–101.

Bender, B., and Lott, J., 'Legislator Voting and Shirking: a Critical Review of the Literature', *Public Choice*, 87 (1996) 67–100.

Box-Steffenmeier, J., Arnold, L., and Zorn, J., 'The Strategic Timing of Position Taking in Congress: a Study of the North American Free Trade Agreement', *American Political Science Review*, 91 (1997) 324–38.

Congressional Districts in the 1990s: a Portrait of America (Washington, DC: Congressional Quarterly Inc., 1993).

Corden, W. M., *Trade Policy and Economic Welfare* (London: Oxford University Press, 1974).

Makinson, L., and Goldstein, J., *Open Secrets: the Encyclopedia of Congressional Money and Politics* (Washington, DC: Congressional Quarterly Inc., 1994).

Morton, R., and Cameron, C., 'Elections and the Theory of Campaign Contributions: a Survey and Critical Analysis', *Economics and Politics*, 4 (1992) 79–108.

Rodrik, D., 'Political Economy of Trade Policy', in G. M. Grossman and K. Rogoff (eds), *Handbook of International Economics* (Amsterdam: North-Holland, 1995) pp. 1457–94.

Smith, R., 'Interest Group Influence in the US Congress', *Legislative Studies Quarterly*, 20 (1995) 89–139.

14
Financial Crisis in East Asia: Underlying and Precipitating Factors

Malcolm Gillis

Introduction

Anne Krueger is best known around the world for her contributions to international economics – including economic development. But much of her work transcends these fields. Nowhere is this more evident than in her highly influential article published more than a quarter of a century ago: 'The Political Economy of the Rent-Seeking Society' (Krueger, 1974). This insightful contribution integrated elements of the economic theory of bureaucracy with the systematic study of economic policy making. This theory, in the hands of Professor Krueger and later writers, reveals how efforts of entrepreneurs, traders and managers to gain favourable treatment from government diverts energies and resources from productive activities, thereby curbing economic growth and also skewing the rewards from economic activity.

The corrosive effects of rent-seeking behaviour were very much in evidence in the East Asian economic crisis of 1997–99 in Thailand, Korea and Malaysia, and especially in Indonesia. This chapter seeks to show how rent-seeking behaviour interacted with underlying structural problems as well as transient economic events to yield disastrous outcomes in four East Asian nations in 1997–99.

This contribution identifies significant antecedents and precipitating factors for the financial meltdown in East Asia in 1997–98 following a quarter century of very strong economic performance of the emerging nations of the region. There those who argue that the crisis stemmed largely from beyond the borders of the afflicted countries, including malevolent foreign *dei ex machina*. Others claim that the downturn in Malaysia, the virtual collapse of financial markets in Thailand and Korea and the free fall of the Indonesian economy in

1997–98 were primarily the consequences of self-inflicted policy wounds, many traceable to unusually intense rent-seeking behaviour.

The evidence shows that endogenous as well as exogenous factors were both important. The tap roots of the crisis were put down decades ago, when virtually all East Asian societies adopted the Japanese model of finance, thereby embedding very bad banking practices in highly vulnerable financial sectors. Other factors, economic and social, contributing to the crisis are also discussed. The chapter ends with a reminder that, in peering into the future, we should take care not to rely much upon extrapolations based upon the very recent, anomalous experience. The affected economies and societies are notably resilient; still, some will recover much later than others. In any case, virtually all of the basic attributes that fueled enviably high economic performance in emerging East Asian nations from 1970 to 1996 remain: strong national stress upon access to primary and secondary education, widespread habits of thrift and continued, if somewhat diminished reliance upon market forces instead of interventionist policies. Finally, there are also favourable demographics (Bloom and Williamson, 1998), including a declining dependency ratio, thereby increasing per capita productive capacity, and rising female participation in the labour force. Just as the almost unbridled euphoria about East Asian economic prospects in the early 1990s was misplaced, subsequent pronouncements of doom and gloom are also inappropriate, except perhaps for Indonesia, the nation most severely afflicted by the crisis.

As late as October 1997, the international press, indeed, articles in some economic journals, were still touting the 'Asian Miracle'. In November 1997, the *World Paper* maintained that 'Indonesia has no real problem'. Also in November, President Clinton dismissed Asian financial turmoil as 'a few glitches in the road' (*Economist*, 10 January 1998). It should not be surprising that it took months for impressions of 'glitches' to turn into cruel realities. Perceptions were clouded by three decades of experience with virtually unprecedented economic success recorded by the original 'gang of four' – Korea, Hong Kong, Taiwan and Singapore, the Asian economic tigers, and the later-emerging so-called tiger cubs: Thailand, Malaysia and Indonesia.

This chapter focuses upon the experiences of the recent ailments of one of the tigers, Korea, and the infirmities of three cubs: Indonesia, Malaysia and Thailand. All four experienced very strong performance through the 1980s and well into the 1990s. Acceleration of economic growth was especially notable in the ten years prior to the crisis for the three cubs, Thailand, Indonesia and Malaysia. By the 1980s all four countries were experiencing GDP growth rates at least three times as high as other middle-income developing nations, and at least twice as great as high income developed nations in Europe, Japan and North America. By the first half of the 1990s, annual rates of economic growth in the emerging East Asian nations were nearly four times those of high-income nations, and at least ten times higher than other middle-income countries (Gillis, 1998).

Moreover, all four countries reviewed herein posted remarkable export growth; all had brought inflation under control. Finally, all four experienced relative exchange rate stability up to mid-1997.

For two decades before 1996, the economic policy prowess of all four nations had been repeatedly and roundly praised by the World Bank and International Monetary Fund (IMF) as exemplars for poorer emerging nations. Their credit ratings were glittering: for example, as recently as 1996, Thailand raised global money at just eighty basis points above US Treasury notes. Notwithstanding these seemingly unassailable strengths, only a few short months were required to bring three of these economies very close to the brink of collapse while applying a severe brake to the economic growth of a fourth, Malaysia.

Onset of acute crisis

The East Asian financial meltdown is best viewed against the backdrop of major changes in the structure of the international financial system. These changes have, by increasing competition and expanding international trade, helped to fuel large improvements in living standards, especially in East Asia. Under these circumstances, the meltdown was especially wrenching. Crises earlier in the decade wrought havoc in Mexico and several other Latin American nations, but nothing approaching the severity and scale of East Asia in 1997–99. Alan Greenspan has suggested that the recent turbulence is best seen as stemming from the same sources that have brought such marked increases in the efficiency of the international financial structure: while that structure induces potentially beneficial flows of productive capital to emerging nations, it has significantly increased capacities for creating chain reactions of losses by transmitting effects of ill-advised investments (Greenspan, 1998). Moreover, owing to greater and more readily accessible information, market discipline now is far more draconian and unforgiving than ever before.

These far-reaching changes provided an economic environment well suited for magnifying the effects of ongoing structural weaknesses, unbridled rent-seeking and policy missteps in four nations.

The factors triggering the 1997–98 East Asian financial calamity differ notably from the underlying factors. The latter account for the severity of the crash, once the house of cards had been shaken. We first examine the precipitating, then the underlying factors.

By 1997 the financial sectors of all four nations were saturated with a volatile mixture awaiting a spark that was not long in coming. The first spark stemmed from a little noticed event in May in Tokyo, which had its first important reverberations in Thailand within days, three months before the then-surprising devaluation of the Thai baht.

In early May, rumours spread from Tokyo that Japanese officials, concerned over the slippage of the yen, were about to raise interest rates. This was especially worrisome because it threatened the 'carry trade' – a financial technique allowing investment houses and insurers to borrow yen and dollars at low interest rates from lenders in Japan and the United States, then placing the proceeds in much higher-interest-bearing short-term loans in Southeast Asia, generally to finance longer-term projects. Incredibly, offshore lenders seemed to wholly ignore exchange-rate risks, not only because their loans were denominated in dollars or yen, but because exchange rates in the region had been stable for years. In the Thai case the government had repeatedly and solemnly promised that the baht dollar exchange rate would remain fixed (Feldstein, 1999, p. 6). The rumours from Tokyo, while unsubstantiated, were sufficient to induce an initial mild sell-off of Thai securities. In the very highly levered, feverishly speculative economic environment that was Thailand in May 1997, initially modest capital outflows became, in short order, a virtual avalanche of flight from Thai markets and the Thai baht. Business failures mounted steadily; by the end of June, there were reports of a 'hollowing out' of the Thai banking system and 16 of the largest finance companies had been closed. Before the end of July, the baht fell by 25 per cent. Shortly thereafter, what Paul Krugman (1998) has dubbed financial 'bahtulism' began to spread to other parts of Asia, as some jittery bankers and investors with more access to money than sense came to realize that Malaysia and Indonesia were – like Thailand – also in Asia. A contagion of panic clearly fuelled the crises for several months (Radelet and Sachs, August 1998; Feldstein, 1999; Dornbusch, 1998; Phelps, 1999). A major crisis had appeared almost out of nowhere.

Reaction within the distressed economies and in leading world financial centres was one of near disbelief. On the eve of the meltdown, none of the four East Asian governments had resorted to excessive credit creation. In no case were exchange rates crassly overvalued

(Dornbusch, 1998). Large fiscal deficits, the source of dozens of currency crises in this century, were not in evidence in any of the four countries, although *prospective* fiscal deficits likely did play a role.[1]

The cascade of bad news continued unabated from June to January. Skittish investors found new grounds for pessimism in the unwillingness of the United States to consider measures to help soften the financial blow to Thailand. Other conditions in the region then came into play, creating a potent witches' brew. Had these other factors been absent, the crash might have been delayed by many months and, in any case, the region-wide consequences might have been less devastating. Indonesia was in an especially vulnerable condition, having accumulated as much as $65 billion in private sector dollar- and yen-denominated external debts, with an economy already severely hamstrung by deep-seated corruption arising from rent-seeking activities and governmental responses to them. Indonesia also had the misfortune of being in the middle of a disastrous drought in 1997, just as the health and the political supremacy of longtime President Suharto began to be publicly questioned and just as oil export prices began a slide toward $10 a barrel.

Malaysia was neither as vulnerable nor nearly as heavily mortgaged. Regrettably though, a relatively mild weakening of the Malaysian ringgit in the aftermath of the Thai devaluation called forth from the prime minister a series of epithets and incendiary pronouncements well suited to confirm all the worst fears of footloose global investors, who began in September 1997 to desert what had long been viewed as one of the most stable financial havens in the region.[2]

The unbroken flow of distressing news was not long in inciting herd instincts among foreign banks and foreign as well as local investors. A surge in outflows of capital pounded the financial markets and currencies of the whole of Southeast Asia, including largely innocent bystanders such as Singapore and the Philippines. Lenders discovered, to their acute dismay, that having loans denominated in dollars or yen is no insulation from exchange-rate risk when currencies plunge by 20, 30, or 80 per cent, for then foreign exchange loans tend not to be repaid, however they are denominated (Radelet and Sachs, 1998, p. 29). Hong Kong and Taiwan, armed with large reserves, and with sounder domestic financial institutions, received repeated shocks over the next six months, but emerged solvent if not unbowed. Korea stayed the course until late October, when the won also began a precipitous slide as offshore lenders began to realize that their assumptions about government guarantees on loans to private firms might have been misplaced. By late December 1997, seven of Korea's largest conglomerates (*chaebols*) had collapsed; more were to follow in 1998.

By January 1998 the frightful dimensions of the financial meltdown were starkly evident. Between stock market slides and currency depreciation, a $1 investment in the Singapore stock market in June 1997 was only worth $0.49 on 15 January 1998. One dollar invested in the Kuala Lumpur market was valued at $0.25 in mid-January. And one dollar sunk into the Jakarta stock exchange in June was worth about a dime in mid-January and only a nickel a week later. By way of contrast, a dollar invested in the Taiwan stock market still had a value of $0.75 in mid-January 1998.

Although the details varied from country to country, by early 1997 several financial commonalities were notable across the four afflicted nations.

1. Financial institutions only recently released from long-standing shackles, typical under directed-credit systems, were totally unprepared to function in a newly globalized world economy. Deeply embedded banking practices in concert with the worst forms of rent-seeking behaviour flourished.
2. There was an abundance of short-term external borrowing by financial institutions (bank and non-bank) and by politically connected private entities, who in turn lent heavily for long-term projects (Dornbusch, 1998).
3. Much of the credit made possible by heavy short-term offshore borrowing had been channelled toward very highly levered local clients (Krugman, 1998; Dornbusch, 1998).
4. Strong inflation had been much in evidence in local asset markets – especially for land and buildings (Krugman, 1998). In turn, this provided a basis for further borrowing through inflated values for collateral.

To these factors must be added the lemming-like tendencies of faraway as well as local investors, and specifically local conditions such as severe drought and political uncertainty in Indonesia, a sharp decline in oil export prices, affecting primarily Indonesia, egregiously inappropriate policy responses in Malaysia, and uncertainties stemming from elections in Korea in December 1998.

In all four of the afflicted nations, weakening currencies began to transform merely marginal loans into non-performing ones. By November, bad loans of East Asian banks, according to the *Economist*, accounted for over 15 per cent of total loans in Thailand, Indonesia, Korea and Malaysia.

Inflated asset prices, especially in the overinvested land and property sectors, began to spiral downward soon after the initial shocks in May–June, adding mightily to financial stress for the already very heavily indebted firms that had benefited from the pre-crash loan bubble and who had posted grossly inflated asset values as collateral. In the pre-crisis year 1996, private flows from commercial banks to the most severely affected Asian nations reached $56 billion. Very little time was required for ample capital inflows to turn into frenetic capital flight from the four countries. By 1998, there was a net negative flow of nearly $20 billion back to foreign banks. Growing downward pressure on the baht, rupiah, ringgit and won made it progressively more difficult to imagine repayment *ever*, of debts that had financed acquisitions of what became steadily deteriorating asset values.

The economy of the entire region edged closer to free fall in November and December. By early January 1998, debt ratings for all the troubled economies save Malaysia had been downgraded to junk status. By late January, Korea and Malaysia began to arrest the process of economic decline. Still, Korea suffered only after major bankruptcies in carmaking, steel, shipbuilding, and construction. By January, Korea's problem was one not of insolvency, but of illiquidity: Korean foreign debt in late December was but $150 billion, but somewhat more than half of that was short term. By April 1999, Korea's debt rating was restored to pre-crisis level. Thailand suffered a contraction of nearly 7 per cent in GDP in 1998 amidst growing insolvency of financial institutions, but also has begun to claw its way back to growth. Still, tens of thousands of jobs were lost all across the Asian arc of crisis.

In the end, Indonesia may end up paying the heaviest price of all. The cumulative effects of decades of cupidity and duplicity in finance and government threatened to wreck the economy throughout 1998 and well into 1999.

Antecedents to crisis

The crash was not *caused* by the threat of movements in Japanese interest rates, or by the poor health of Suharto, or the severe drought in Indonesia, or by the intemperate, inflammatory remarks by Prime Minister Mahathir of Malaysia. Nor was the crisis caused by speculators, or by the panicked behaviour of other investors including European and American banks as well as Asians themselves.[3] Such transient factors merely provided the sparks to light a financial bonfire that had been decades in the making.

Sociopolitical factors

The financial meltdown was traceable to multiple underlying factors both sociopolitical and economic, most of which were of relatively long standing. All were present to greater or lesser degree in all four countries, although the relative roles played by each varies greatly as between them. Some were exogenous in origin, well beyond the control of the afflicted countries. It is nevertheless true, however, that in all four nations there were an ample number of largely self-inflicted wounds. Among the several roots of the East Asian financial crisis one stout, well-nourished, and deep tap root stands out: the prevalence of the Japanese model for banking and finance throughout the nations of the region. In the financial field, as in almost no others, East Asian nations have generally sought to emulate the Japanese. Unfortunately, they succeeded.

The postwar Japanese model for banking and finance is perhaps best characterized as a cumbersome, bank-centred command and control system for channelling financial resources from small and medium-sized savers to much larger borrowers, at subsidized rates. The Japanese model of finance was at least consistent with Japanese efforts to pioneer the industrial order of the past. The basic idea was to squeeze consumption in order to supply Japanese industry with very cheap subsidized capital. (By early 1999 the discount rate in Japan had been pushed down to 0.25 per cent in the hopes of averting a deflationary spiral.) And where financial processes in North America tend to be transparent, in Japan they strongly tend toward opacity. In the Japanese model, banks are intimately involved in the operations of borrowing firms, to an extent unthinkable in North America. Also typical in the Japanese model are relationships between bank regulators and regulatees that are rather tighter and cosier than is usually thought consistent with financial probity.[4] The system is further complicated by the existence of intricate cross-shareholding arrangements between large firms. Traditional Japanese-style finance also allows very ample scope for exercise of central government discretion in directing loans to favoured sectors, to specific enterprises, and even individual cronies. Where the banking system is also dominated by government-owned banks, as in Indonesia, the influence of government officials can be quite direct, as in so-called 'command' loans to particular firms.[5] In other East Asian nations, including Korea as well as Japan, the role of governments in directing loans tends to be more subtle, and indirect: over the years banks in both nations have been well conditioned by the government to lend money to firms and industries.

This kind of 'hand-in-glove' relationship between governments and financial institutions easily degenerates into 'hand-in-the-till' arrangements. Accordingly, Dornbusch has succinctly labelled the Asian financial crisis as a 'crisis of corrupt governments' (Dornbusch, 1998; see also Phelps, 1999, and Barth et al., 1999). Examples of deep-seated financial corruption in a network of crony capitalism are plentiful from Jakarta to Tokyo.[6] Moreover, partly because of the absence of arm's-length lending, and partly because of the ability of banks to exert ongoing direct control over enterprise management, finance on the Japanese model has typically involved acceptance of degrees of enterprise leverage that would be unimaginable in North American practice, often resulting in debt–equity ratios in excess of ten-to-one or even twenty-to-one (Dornbusch, 1998; Gillis and Wells, 1980) and typically involving misallocation of resources to projects that cannot generate income to cover debt service.

Deep involvement of bankers in the operations of borrowing firms might have been less damaging had loan proposals from client firms been systematically evaluated using modern banking methods. However, systematic loan analysis as it is known, but perhaps not always practiced in Canada and the United States is still not all that common in Japan, and is almost absent in the East Asian nations that adhere to patterns of banking developed in Japan.[7] Rather, even when political connections do not intrude, reliance in lending is placed, loosely, on the availability of collateral rather than on projected or even past rates of return.

With little or no systematic analysis of borrowers' requests, it should not be surprising that such a large proportion of recent loans in East Asia ended up in the hands of property developers to finance acquisition and construction of land and buildings, relentlessly driving up the prices of these assets (Krugman, 1998; Phelps, 1999). Seen against the unusually high lender tolerances for debt-financed projects, one is tempted to look no further for a fairly plausible explanation for the severity of the crash. But there was much more.

If these considerations were not enough, other very serious deficiencies of the institutional framework for banking and finance in Korea and the three other nations predisposed their systems to a very high degree of vulnerability. Disclosure requirements for firms, both private and government owned, remain grossly defective, where they are even present. Especially in Indonesia and Thailand, and to a significant extent Malaysia and Korea, lenders as well as outside stockholders have little notion of the accuracy of financial data supplied to banks, much less published by firms. In addition core accounting conventions and standards date mainly from colonial times, and bear little resemblance to modern internal information systems of larger North American enterprises. To be sure, the murky accounting rules prevailing in East Asia do generate large quantities of information, but much of it is essentially useless to the uninitiated outsider, if not the owners. There are, therefore, many serious issues of non-transparency in borrowing and lending, a condition well suited for flourishing rent-seeking activity. The combination of very weak disclosure requirements and defective accounting systems means that lenders typically have had only the faintest idea of the financial state of health of borrowers. Under such circumstances it is understandable that banks rely heavily upon the borrower's government and/or family or political connections as indicators of creditworthiness.

The East Asian crisis also reflects failures in financial regulation.[8] Financial rules and regulations are rudimentary in all four countries. In Indonesia, private banks habitually breached rules prohibiting lending of more than 20 per cent of a bank's capital to related parties. And as in Japan, financial regulation throughout the region is not infrequently hamstrung by corruption. Severe regulatory failure has extended well beyond Japan, to what passes as the region's paragon of financial correctness: Hong Kong. There, a large, aggressive, allegedly dynamic, and now extinct investment bank (Peregrine) had, by 1996, managed to bestow loans equal to almost 40 per cent of its capital on a single debtor in Indonesia, simply because of her family connections.

Cultural factors helped, in some afflicted East Asian nations, to exacerbate the problems just noted. Particularly in Indonesia and Malaysia, and to an extent in Thailand, subordinates tend strongly to avoid bringing bad news to superiors, both in the public and private sector. There is an oft-repeated phrase in Indonesia that encapsulates this tendency: 'Sedang bapak senang'. That is, as long as the boss (or father) is happy, do not ruin his day (with bad news). This attitude accounts for the fact that news of a major failure of the all-important rice crop in May 1972 reached the Indonesian cabinet only in August of that year. It helps us understand why in 1982 the cabinet and the president remained unaware – for seven months – that on the Indonesian Island of Kalimantan a forest area the size of Belgium had burned. It helps to explain why in 1997 distressing financial news out of Jakarta, Bangkok and Kuala Lumpur tended to dribble out over a period of months, not days.

In addition, the legal infrastructures of many, but not all, East Asian nations contain notable obstacles to bankruptcy.[9] As a result, managers, workers, lenders and investors face diminished incentives, relative to North American firms, to act prudently. In the United States, when bankruptcy threatens, the creditors can force a firm into bankruptcy. Whereas in East Asia, insolvent companies can continue to act with impunity, delaying interminably the needed restructuring of over-leveraged firms.

The example of Taiwan, which succeeded in avoiding through 1998 the worst of the East Asian meltdown, may be instructive. There, legal obstacles to bankruptcy have virtually vanished, and bankruptcy when it occurs is not a particularly unusual or disruptive event. By contrast, it is not even clear that the thousands of Thai, Indonesian and Malaysian enterprises that stopped servicing their debts in 1996 can be forced into bankruptcy under prevailing law or under so-called reforms enacted in 1998 and 1999. In all three nations so-called extrajudicial procedures will likely be necessary to close them.

Economic factors

Internal vulnerabilities would in any case have rendered the financial sectors of East Asian nations highly susceptible to very serious financial distress – even without disruptive pressures from the external sector. Unfortunately, such pressures were present; their effects were greatly magnified by the dramatic increases in international capital flows over the past decade. But the benefits of financial globalization have been accompanied by an ever more harsh market discipline.

Virtually all East Asian nations had, prior to 1997, liberalized domestic financial policies so as to better partake of the benefits of financial globalization – cheaper capital and readier access to the accompanying technology.

As long as new capital inflows, especially debt, find their way to good projects capable of generating sufficient returns to keep lenders and investors happy, the combination of globalization and domestic financial liberalization, in East Asia as elsewhere, is good for all concerned: banks, borrowers, investors and workers. Nevertheless, there are additional risks – in borrowing or lending – in a currency not your own, especially when borrowers are financial institutions who turn around and extend uncovered loans denominated in local currency. This practice involves risks even in the most serene market circumstances. But the risks are especially large when, as in much of East Asia in recent years, there is growing mismatch between maturities: borrowing short-term to finance longer-term projects (Dornbusch, 1998; Krugman, 1998). Moreover, growing globalization of finance has, inevitably, been accompanied by growing volatility in financial markets. Perturbations in these markets may leave nations with large financial systems such as the United States or Japan relatively unscathed, but can easily swamp more vulnerable nations, even large ones who nevertheless have relatively small financial markets. It is worth remembering that although Thailand has nearly 60 million inhabitants, her financial system is, in terms of assets, like that of Malaysia, far smaller than that of the state of Texas.

The problem, however, is more than just one of size. In Korea, Indonesia and Thailand, the banking sector is much larger than either the bond or equity sectors (Barth et al., Summer/Fall 1998, p. 38). This contrasts sharply to the United States, where the banking sector is less than half the size of the bond and equity sectors. Where the banking sector is large relative to the total financial system, it stands to reason that such a financial system will be greatly affected by difficulties arising from the banking sector. Where banking has a relatively small share of total finance, vulnerability to banking shocks is less severe, as in the S&L crisis in the United States in the 1980s.

The foregoing elements made up a truly infernal mixture, made even more unstable by one additional consideration: 'moral hazard'. Moral hazard stems from the undervaluation of risks associated with one's actions, where the consequences of this undervaluation are shifted to others. In finance, moral hazard arises when, in the presence of insured risk (de facto or de jure) there is little or no pay-off to the insured for taking measures to reduce risk of loss. Clearly, when the liabilities of financial institutions are perceived as explicitly *or* implicitly guaranteed by the government, moral hazard is present.[10] Moral hazard has an international dimension when foreign money centre banks have the expectations that they will be bailed out, especially when they overlend to firms or governments abroad.

In Indonesia, Korea and Thailand, to a lesser extent Malaysia, and perhaps in the operations of the IMF in East Asia, moral hazard has been much in evidence in national and international financial transactions. Even though creditors of financial institutions rarely had explicit guarantees of repayment backed by governments, American, Japanese and European banks (and other financial institutions and private investors) nevertheless tended strongly to view their loans as wholly or partially guaranteed by the governments of the borrowers or, indirectly, by the International Monetary Fund.[11] Offshore lenders then had little incentive to exercise due diligence – or indeed any diligence – in vetting loans to East Asian borrowers, since they perceived little of their own money to be at risk. In the words of one French banker in 1998, later deeply mired in Korean private sector debt problems, 'We thought we were making a loan to Korea Inc.'

What is to be done?

The Asian financial meltdown has brought forth several proposals to reduce the scope of future crises. Many of these schemes focus upon reforms seeking a 'new global financial architecture'. Virtually all of these call for radical restructuring of the International Monetary Fund or the World Bank, or both. While some changes in the mission or the structure of the Fund and Bank might help ameliorate some future crises, emerging nations are well advised to also devise measures to protect themselves. Some have stressed the need to control risk at the international level. Dornbusch (1998) offers a fairly ambitious proposal that would provide timely assistance to countries who comply with a tightly written and audited scheme requiring greater attention to balance sheets, with assistance conditional upon compliance with strict capital standards for banks. Greenspan (1998) has suggested a similar approach. Some argue that greater liquidity is the key to such self-protection (Feldstein, 1999).[12] Others stress the need for adequate hedging of bank borrowing dominated in foreign currency (Lal, 1998).

International reforms could help, but most of what has to be done to allow resumption of sustained economic progress in East Asia will need to be accomplished internally, because the roots of the problem are mostly internal. The process has been and will be painful. It goes without saying that thoroughgoing, fundamental reform of financial legislation is in order, sooner not later. The help of outsiders, however, remains essential. Moral hazard is, nevertheless, a problem for those who would render assistance. Those who argue that 'bail-outs' only encourage future outbreaks of irresponsible financial behaviour in the future do have a legitimate point. The trick will be to find ways of reducing moral hazard to tolerable levels. At the same time, there is some plausibility to the claim that the refusal of the United States to take an active role in stabilizing Thailand in the summer of 1997 caused the crisis to spread unduly rapidly to other countries in the region.

Now is not the most propitious time to place new limits upon the ability of the IMF to respond in timely fashion to such crises. However, once a modicum of stability is restored, the IMF and, to an extent, the World Bank will need to begin rethinking their missions and policies. The Fund in particular needs to consider well the meaning of 'Procrustean'; one size does not fit all in programmes of economic rescue. The Fund also needs to reflect at length on how its operations may contribute to international moral hazard in bank lending. There are, after all, cases in which applications of IMF orthodoxy may have hastened economic collapse (Dornbusch, 1998; Barth et al., 1998; Radelet and Sachs, 1998; Lal, 1998).

In the end, the restoration of prospects for economic progress in the afflicted nations requires internal corrective measures that will bear full fruit only over many years. Measures to narrow the scope for the most corrosive forms of rent-seeking are clearly in order. A good beginning would be the adoption of fundamental reforms in accounting conventions and standards – along with legislation allowing for greater transparency in financial markets (financial disclosure, arms'-length lending practices) adoption of workable bankruptcy laws as well as relatively rudimentary regulations regarding capital requirements for financial institutions, systematic analysis of loan requests, measures to narrow the scope for conflicts of interest (especially those related to self-dealing), and penalties for irresponsible financial practices. It is also supremely important that governments in the region henceforth go to great lengths to avoid anything resembling implicit – much less explicit – government guarantees of loans made to local financial institutions by making it abundantly clear that anything that might be perceived as implicit guarantees will be honoured only with implicit repayments.

Above all, banking and other financial practices suitable for the next century will need to be developed and embedded in financial systems throughout East Asia. The Japanese bank-centred financial model so widely utilized in East Asia may have been appropriate for Japan at one point, but it is clearly unsuited to the needs of the smaller nations in the region – and most likely is no longer suited for Japan.

A decade of unwarranted euphoria over East Asian economic prospects turned into equally ill-founded myopia within a few short weeks in 1997. Virtually all of the afflicted economies began recovering within a year, save Indonesia. Real growth for Korea in 1999 was just above 10 per cent, and is projected at 11 per cent for 2000. In mid-April 1999 Korea was able to sell $1 billion of five-year notes, the first offering to win investment grade since end-1997. Indeed, by the end of 1999 interest rates have fallen below pre-crisis levels. Thailand seemed to have turned the corner in 1998, while Malaysia's political troubles seem to overshadow any strictly economic ills. But even optimists forecast zero growth for Indonesia in 1999. Real growth for that year was, however, positive. The rest of the world should take care that it does not learn too much from this debacle, while bearing in mind that most of the very strengths that carried East Asian economies to such commendable heights, until suddenly in the summer of 1997, are still very much in evidence.

Notes

1. A recent paper by Burnside, Eichenbaum and Rebelo argues that the crisis was caused by large prospective deficits associated with implicit bail-out guarantees to failing banking systems: investors realized that large losses in the banking system were associated with large increases in government deficits in the near term, and that the public knew that the banks were in trouble before the currency crisis. There seems to be little doubt that expectations of government bail-outs of banking enterprises was one of many factors exacerbating the crisis once it had been set in motion (see Burnside, Eichenbaum and Rebelo, 1998). For a contrary view, see Radelet and Sachs (1998, pp. 52–3).
2. The recent policies of the Mahathir government seem well characterized by the philosophy 'ready, fire, aim'. One example was the hastily announced measure imposing capital controls, which remained in effect from September 1998 to February 1999, giving temporary relief to the economy but even greater succor to influential domestic private sector actors.
3. Two recent papers, one focusing upon currency markets of Southeast Asia, the other focused on the Korean equities market, find little or no evidence that foreign investors were behind the severe market meltdowns in 1997 (see Brown, Park and Goetzmann, 1998; and Choe, Kho and Stulz, 1998).
4. The system is deeply imbedded, so much so that through 1998 it proved remarkably resistant even to the determined reform efforts of chief regulator Hakuo Yanagisawa, facing in 1999 financial bail-out costs of between $300 and $600 billion.
5. The role of state-owned banks in the collapse was especially important in Indonesia, where 48 per cent of bank assets resided in state-owned institutions. In 1997 comparable figures for Korea, Malaysia and Thailand were 13 per cent, 8 per cent, and 7 per cent, respectively (Barth et al., 1999, p. 38).
6. Former Federal Reserve Chair Paul Volcker visited Indonesia in January 1998 at the request of decision-makers there, to provide his perspectives on the region-wide meltdown. At the end of the discussion, Indonesian President Suharto asked, in clear puzzlement, 'But we are doing little today that is much different from what we have been doing all along. Why now are we in such distress?' Mr Volcker had no ready answer, but upon his return to the United States in mid-January asked the author his views on the matter, from

his perspective of 25 years of involvement in East Asian economic policy issues. The author's answer was that President Suharto's general impression was correct. They were doing little different than before. What the president failed to acknowledge were the pernicious cumulative effects of three decades of rampant corruption in undermining the bases of virtually all institutions in the economy, financial, fiscal, social and cultural.

7. In the United States, the loan approval process ordinarily involves, at a minimum, close scrutiny of *recent* financial performance and – according to the Federal Reserve System – in about 30 per cent of cases formal projections of borrowers' future performance (Federal Reserve Bank of Dallas, 1998). Evidently, for loans to Korean and Indonesian borrowers, US banks neglected to apply the same standards as in loans to US firms.

8. Not everyone agrees that inadequate bank supervision and legislation were major reasons for the recent severe *banking* problem in East Asia. Dissenters argue that the problem was not one of regulatory failure, but rather was a predictable outcome under the economic theory of regulation when state ownership of banks is widespread (see Barth et al., 1999). There is merit in this view, so far as it goes. But denial of any role for regulatory failure in East Asia reflects a certain lack of institutional knowledge of Asian financing.

9. Until 1999 it was virtually impossible to force a debtor into bankruptcy in Indonesia. One may easily file bankruptcy papers in Korea, but with little or no concrete results. In both Thailand and Philippines the problem is similar to Korea's. According to the *Economist* (24 January 1998), 14 000 Korean firms did go bankrupt in 1997, but very few cases were settled.

10. For a lucid, rigorous discussion of moral hazard in the recent East Asian context, see Krugman (1998).

11. For a discussion of international moral hazard implicit in recent IMF operations in East Asia, especially Indonesia, see Lal (1998).

12. The experiences of Taiwan, Hong Kong and Singapore in the recent crisis support the view that countries with large foreign exchange reserves can more easily ward off currency attacks.

References

Barth, J. R., Brumbaugh, R. D., Ramesh, L., and Yago, G., 'The East Asian Banking Crisis: Government vs. Markets', *Jobs and Capital* (Winter, 1998; 1999).

Bloom, D. E., and Williamson, J. G., 'Demographic Transitions and Economic Miracles in Emerging Asia', *World Bank Economic Review*, 12(3) (September 1998) 419–55.

Brown, S., Park, J., and Goetzmann, W., 'Hedge Funds and the Asian Currency Crisis', NBER working paper, no. 6427 (Cambridge, MA, 1998).

Burnside, C., Eichenbaum, M., and Rebelo, S., 'Prospective Deficits and the Asian Currency Crisis', NBER working paper, no. 6758 (Cambridge, MA, 1998).

Choe, H., Kho, B-C., and Stulz, R., 'Do Foreign Investors Destabilize Stock Markets?: The Korean Experience in 1997', NBER working paper, no. 6661 (Cambridge, MA, 1998).

Dornbusch, R., 'Meltdown Post-Mortem', *International Economy* (November–December 1998) 20–7.

Dornbusch, R., 'Finance and Economics: Can One Size Fit All?', *The Economist* (28 March 1998) 8.

Feldstein, M., 'Self Protection for Emerging Market Economies', NBER working paper, no. 6907 (Cambridge, MA, 1999).

Gillis, M., *Turbulence in Emerging Markets: Antecedents in East Asia* (presented at Federal Reserve Bank of Dallas, 30 January 1998).

Gillis, M., and Wells, L. T., 'Negotiating and Implementing Minerals Agreements with Multinationals' (1980), in M. Gillis and R. Beals (eds), *Tax and Investment Policies for Hard Minerals* (Cambridge, MA: Ballinger Press, 1998) pp. 140–6.

Greenspan, A., Remarks at the Annual Meeting of the Securities Industry Association, Boca Raton, Florida (Washington: The Federal Reserve System, 5 November 1998).

Krueger, A. O., 'The Political Economy of the Rent-Seeking Society', *American Economic Review*, 64 (1974) 291–303.

Krugman, P., *What Happened to Asia?*, http://web.mit.edu/krugman/www/DISIN-TER.html (January 1998).

Lal, D., 'Don't Bank On It, Mr. Blair', *The Spectator* (26 September 1998) 17–19.

Phelps, E., 'The Global Crisis of Corporatism', *New York Times* (20 March 1999).

Radelet, S., and Sachs, J., 'The Onset of the East Asian Financial Crisis', NBER working paper, no. 6680 (Cambridge, MA, 1998).

15
The Evolution of Dual Economies in East Asia

Helen Hughes

Introduction

With a resurgence of export-led economic growth, the underlying causes of the East Asian 'crisis' are being ignored. Much of the investment undertaken within East Asia in recent years was channelled into unproductive enterprises and projects. Much was stolen. A significant proportion of the 1990s private capital flow to East Asia was egregiously risky. Many flows were not supported by the sort of project and sovereign risk analysis that shareholders and depositors have a right to expect from international financial institutions. It is deeply mystifying that these flows were not perceived as contributing to the weakness of the East Asian economies by the International Monetary Fund (IMF), the World Bank and the Asian Development Bank which had responsibility for monitoring the East Asian economies. The World Bank set the analytical tone of denying emerging structural problems in its widely promoted *Asian Miracle* (1993). It claimed that the East Asian countries were '... better able than most to allocate physical and human resources to highly productive investment and to acquire and master technology' (pp. v–vi).

A few perceptive observers (for example, Lingle, 1997) provided clearly argued early warnings of the damaging effects of the rise of cronyism. They were ignored. In close contact with senior East Asian government officials, the multilateral institutions were unwilling to embarrass their member governments by pointing out the cost of cronyism. Following the IMF's half-century of persistently bailing-out any country that ran into balance-of-payments difficulties, a number of private lenders suspended risk assessment. 'Moral hazard' prevailed in international capital operations.

Most analysts have focused on the collapses of financial institutions and devaluations of exchange rates that became necessary once the hollowness of much of the unproductive investment was exposed (McLeod and Garnaut, 1998; Radelet and Sachs, 1998; Hill and Arndt, 1999; Montes and Popov, 1999). They have ignored the growing evidence of the rise of damaging crony capitalism in East Asia that has been exposed in the discussion of entrepreneurship (Hewison, 1989; McVey, 1992; MacIntyre, 1994; Robison and Goodman, 1996; Searle, 1999). They have not explained why countries known for their prudent macroeconomic policies for some thirty years abandoned them in the mid-1990s. The East Asian economies had for so many years been known for their outward orientation and their rapid export-led growth, that the destructive roles of industrial and associated fiscal and financial policies in encouraging crony capitalism were not given attention. Fiscal stability was allowed to draw attention away from the other fiscal, industry and financial policies that were superseding business criteria in allocating loans and were hence the primary causes of the collapses of 1997 (Moreno, Pasadilla and Remolona, 1998).

The partial adoption of outward-oriented models of development in much of East Asia in the 1960s and 1970s lulled observers. China's 'open door' policy in 1979 seemed the crowning achievement. The 'development economics' (Lal, 1983) that had swamped the thinking of most developing countries had been partially rejected in East Asia in favour of an early recognition that outward orientation and openness was more likely to bring growth than protectionism and *dirigisme*. Liberalization made considerable progress. Competing in international markets encouraged liberal reforms. Except in Hong Kong, Singapore, and later in Taiwan, however, privileged local entrepreneurs in protected domestic industries were able to prevent the completion of liberal reforms that would have led to competitiveness in domestic markets. Industrial and financial policies, often under the guise of nationalism, encouraged the strengthening of crony capitalists. Dual economies emerged in most East Asian countries, with high costs resulting from distorted micro- and macroeconomic policies tailored to suit highly influential cronies. The viability of exports was threatened.

By the middle of the 1990s, crony interests in Thailand, the Republic of Korea (Korea), Malaysia and Indonesia, desiring to protect the dollar values of their assets, were exerting pressure on ministries of finance and central banks to overvalue exchange rates. Current account deficits expanded. Short-term loans were sought abroad to shore up financial systems collapsing under non-performing loans. When acute foreign investors realized the weakness of the investments they had funded, they began to withdraw as much capital as they could. Local investors fled to 'safe' currencies. Exporters could not access inputs, grossly inefficient, highly leveraged producers were exposed, and real estate 'bubbles' burst. Workers in the formal sectors were thrown out into the street. Incomes declined sharply in the informal sectors that supplied medium-sized and large-scale enterprises. After some thirty years of poverty reduction, the tide turned.

The evolution of dual economies

The East Asian economies cover a wide spectrum of countries. Each country's development path has been distinct within a common outward-oriented framework that has made East Asia's growth more rapid and more egalitarian than that of other developing countries (Hughes, 1995). The rise of cronyism (except in Hong Kong, Singapore and Taiwan) also had different characteristics in each economy, but common effects in undermining competitiveness and growth.

In the early postwar years, Hong Kong, under a British colonial regime, was trade-oriented, creating strong employment and economic growth. When Singapore left the Malaysian Federation, it turned sharply toward export-led growth. As city states, both were too small for protectionist illusions.

Postcolonial land reforms had given Taiwan and Korea a healthy economic start but highly protectionist policies led to severe budget, balance-of-payments and inflationary problems. United States civilian aid kept both economies afloat, but by the mid-1950s, the United States was dismayed by economic stagnation, dependence on aid and corruption in Taiwan. It persuaded Taiwan's rulers to allow liberal technocrats to stabilize and partially to liberalize the economy by threatening to withdraw civilian aid. Authoritarian political ties to leading entrepreneurs made it impossible to reduce tariffs, so a barrage of export incentives was used to offset protection for the domestic market. These introduced new distortions. Similar reforms were encouraged by the United States in Korea, but the *chaebol* group of crony conglomerates was closely enough linked to the highly authoritarian governments to ensure that trade and other liberal reforms were limited. The *chaebols* continued to benefit from *dirigiste* industry and financial policies. In particular, they continued to receive privileged access to the repressed financial system at the cost of small and medium-sized entrepreneurs.

Despite these shortcomings in Taiwan and Korea, opening up to trade almost immediately solved balance-of-payments problems and led to accelerated growth. Together with Hong Kong and Singapore, Taiwan and Korea became the economic 'tigers' of East Asia. Employment grew so rapidly that poverty was reduced to negligible proportions within a generation. But although Taiwan and Korea started from similar positions in the early 1960s, by the 1970s they had begun to differ in economic structure.

In Taiwan a continuing, albeit slow, process of liberal reforms, notably in freeing up the financial sector, reducing trade barriers and limiting *dirigiste* industrial policies, encouraged the growth of medium- and small-scale enterprises. By the 1990s, internal economic competitiveness had increased markedly, contributing to political liberalization. Taiwan was catching up to the industrial democracies in more respects than per capita income.

Studies of the transformation of the 'tiger' economies through export orientation (Krueger, 1981; Krueger, Lary, Monson and Akrasanee, 1981) contributed to the encouragement of Malaysia, Thailand and Indonesia to follow. But in these latter countries, as in Taiwan and Korea, limits on the extent of reform were obtained by monopolistic groups that had their start in the protectionist years. Production for domestic markets remained regulated and protected. Large, inefficient public sectors remained. Some liberalization of trade and other markets had to be pursued to make the rapid expansion of exports possible but export incentives were also necessary. Petroleum rents were utilized in Malaysia and Indonesia, at least to some extent, to offset protectionism and further social objectives. Rapid economic growth led to a substantial reduction of poverty, to less than 5 per cent of the population in Malaysia and from some 60 per cent to some 15 per cent in Thailand and Indonesia. Industry and *dirigiste* financial policies, and distorted fiscal policies, however, allowed favoured interests – cronies – to obtain many monopolistic privileges. In Indonesia and Malaysia, nationalist, anti-Chinese, political support for industry and distorted financial measures encouraged the evolution of entrepreneurs closely linked with, and dependent on, government favouritism.

The Philippines was an exception to East Asian growth. The economy was strongly import-substitution-oriented from the 1950s, with accompanying other micro- and macroeconomic policy distortions. Cronyism became as entrenched as in the many Latin American corporatist economies, with concomitant micro- and macroeconomic difficulties resulting in periodic economic crises. Economic reform was not possible until the collapse of the Marcos regime. The return of exiled entrepreneurs then helped to loosen, but not to radically transform, crony structures. Lifting financial repression in the 1990s has been the principal achievement, limiting the impact of the East Asian crisis. The Philippine economy is, however, still far from competitive. A strong export sector has not emerged and the economic outlook is not encouraging (Yap, 1999). The Philippine economy remains more akin to the Latin American corporatist economies than to the dual economies of East Asia.

Although the introduction of some market measures to rural production and the encouragement of exports led to a marked change of economic pace in China and Vietnam, neither country has moved far along the transition road to markets. Overseas Chinese owned and managed export industries have provided China with booming economies along the Eastern seaboard and comfortable external reserves. Some 'cooperative' (private) township and village enterprises have followed the example of the Overseas Chinese firms, but provincially- and nationally-owned state enterprises are in dire straits. Both economies remain stifled by regulation. Private entrepreneurship is penalized. Even rudimentary financial sectors are lacking. Both economies are extreme examples of distorted development, with Communist Party cadres dominating domestic and foreign joint-venture investment, either directly or through state enterprises. Investment in inappropriately capital- and technology-intensive processes and industries is leading to low levels of urban employment formation and hence to poverty, notably in rural areas. Rural–urban migration is not only thwarted by location regulations, but also by the lack of job growth. The beneficiaries are the Communist Party civilian and military cadres who have been the main recipients of industrial and financial policy privileges. Close regulation has enabled exchange-rate devaluation to be avoided, albeit at the cost of employment and living standards. The government of Vietnam is still repressing all attempts at private enterprise. More than 300 million people – some 25 per cent of the population – are estimated to be living in poverty in China. These are similar orders of magnitude to the incidence of poverty in India. In Vietnam the majority of people are still living in poverty.

Policies and institutions that created crony capitalism

The wide-ranging international development debates have greatly influenced policies and institutions in developing countries. Several trends came together to create an outward, liberal orientation in East

Asian countries from the late 1950s to the 1980s. Hong Kong's colonial administration, struggling with an influx of immigrants from China, saw no option but trade. When Singapore had to leave Malaysia in 1965 and at the same time had to face the withdrawal of British armed forces and *confrontasi* from Indonesia, it also had no other option. The reduction of aid from the United States transformed policy responses in Taiwan and Korea. Indonesia's economic failure under Sukarno's socialist policies was a strong factor. The defeat of communist forces in Malaysia and Indonesia cleared the way for liberal economic ideas. The Cold War was a factor, with Communist China looming over Asia until the end of the 1970s, providing United States support for economic reform.

Liberal views were strongly supported by, mostly US, academic institutions, both in teaching graduate students from East Asia and providing continuing intellectual inputs when they returned home. German, other European and Australian academics also contributed. These scholars also began the tradition of empirical studies that demonstrated the high economic and social returns to liberal, compared to *dirigiste*, policies. IMF and World Bank lending included surveillance reporting and dialogues that reinforced the liberal economic messages. The Economic Commission for Asia and the Far East (later the Economic and Social Commission for Asia) and other United Nations agencies continued to favour 'development economics' *dirigisme*, but, lacking theoretical and factual foundations, their influence was limited. Developing countries following the 'development economics' paradigms were lagging East Asian growth worldwide.

The four 'tigers', Malaysia, Thailand and Indonesia thus built up groups of liberally oriented technocrats who were able to influence policy debates and introduce micro- and macroeconomic reforms. In contrast, several liberal economists were forced to leave the Philippines during the Marcos years.

The liberal technocrats were, however, far from dominant, particularly in the larger East Asian countries. Hundreds, and in some cases thousands, of traditional bureaucrats, who manned the majority of the policy and administrative posts in most ministries, had limited educational backgrounds and outlooks. They were highly susceptible to protectionist and other *dirigiste* views. Most were very poorly paid and did not have the opportunities to supplement their earnings by spells of well-paid international positions. They had the support of those local academics who also did not have the opportunity to study abroad. Accepting the necessity to break balance-of-payments constraints through exports, they were, nevertheless, profoundly protectionist and *dirigiste*, particularly if they were accustomed to supplementing their incomes from the opportunities that *dirigiste* policies created. The Japan Inc. model of development became appealing to these bureaucrats in the 1980s by combining subsidies to exports with industrial policies for the domestic market. Such policies received strong backing from the media. Until the late 1990s influential media world-wide, and particularly in the United States, saw Japan surging ahead of all other countries into the 'Asian century' because of its non-market orientation (Lindsey and Lukas, 1998). Critical components of policy in all East Asian countries except Hong Kong, Singapore and Taiwan, therefore remained essentially *dirigiste* during the swing toward liberal economic policies, enabling cronyism to develop until by the 1990s it dominated the dual East Asian economies.

Bureaucratic decision-making involved the granting of privileges, providing opportunities for 'favoured' applicants to 'buy' permission and for bureaucrats to 'sell' it (Tanzi, 1998; Bardhan, 1997). Cronies were able to acquire permission to engage in monopolistic activities. In a crony environment, projects that had low socio-economic returns and often failed in the long run despite the privileges they received, earned considerable benefits in the form of high management incomes, superprofits and income in kind, such as the use of cars and housing. *Dirigiste* policies institutionalized corruption. The economic, social and political structures and institutions created severely distorted East Asian economies (including Japan's), and had negative effects on political life. As monopolistic practices become entrenched, reform, as the Japan Inc. model has underlined in its homeland during the 1990s decade-long recession, became extremely difficult.

Industry policies

Industry policies seek to 'pick winners' to improve on market outcomes. However, the overwhelming evidence from centrally planned and market economies where intervention to improve on 'market failure' has been rife, indicates that 'government failure' has even higher costs. The East Asian experience suggests that industry policies, by encouraging cronyism in the place of competitive markets, spread the power of large entrepreneurs from manufacturing to construction, real estate and banking. Enterprises in all fields became tightly linked into family-held empires, with strong linkages to those that were politically powerful, held key military positions and managed economic policies and state-owned sectors. Small numbers of entrepreneurial families thus accumulated vast holdings of wealth, invested it in an array of businesses and assets bolstered by government support and formed cross-empire holdings. They established substantial financial holdings abroad that gave them preferential access to international capital markets with implicit, and in many cases, explicit government guarantees for borrowing. A tight grouping of landed Philippine families reaches back to the 1920s. Industrial policies in Korea in the 1950s led to the creation of the *chaebols* that internalized the conflicts between competitive production for export and monopolistic production for the domestic markets. In Indonesia, military investments, sometimes with Chinese partners but sometimes directed against them, began to flourish after 1965, peaking in the 1980s and 1990s (McVey, 1992). In Malaysia, the New Economic Policy that sought to promote ethnic Malays (Bumiputras) was able to use petroleum rents to foster new business groups (Searle, 1999). In Thailand, the growth of crony companies appeared to be less ostentatious, but no less powerful (Hewison, 1989).

Import-substitution (IS) policies built bureaucratic support for selective incentives for manufacturing enterprises. The principal function of ministries of industry was to structure monopolistic industrial development. Numbers of producers of each group of products were limited to avoid 'excessive' competition. Ministry bureaucrats, working with business, became the judges of appropriate levels of industrial capacity. In countries committed to protection – that is, to closed markets – there seemed to be a choice between one producer able to exploit economies of scale, and several firms producing on inefficiently low levels of output. Bureaucrats believed that they had to choose either economies of scale or internal competition. Inevitably they licensed several oligopolistic producers and thus achieved neither competitiveness nor economies of scale. Production licensing began in industries such as steel and chemicals, but came to be applied to all manufacturing and many service industries.

'Basic' and 'pioneer' industries to which privileges were to flow were defined by legislation. Ministry of Industry officials were judged too slow in evaluating industrial investment proposals. The corruption associated with IS licensing was known to be widespread. New boards of investment (BoI), economic planning boards and economic planning units were established throughout East Asia to administer industry subsidy protocols, mainly for foreign, but also for local investors. Efforts were made to link proposed subsidies to the capital to be invested, the proposed size of the workforce and types of new technology to be introduced to 'pick' foreign and local 'winners'. Concepts of value-added at international prices were ignored in favor of subjective points systems notorious for their double counting and arbitrariness. The outcomes inevitably and invariably fostered cronyism rather than productivity and competition.

The BoI were to be 'one-stop shops' where foreign and local entrepreneurs could complete their negotiations quickly and efficiently. Several common features emerged. The proposals placed before BoI bore little resemblance to the actual investment, employment and technological inputs that could be discerned three, five or ten years after the starting date. Except in Singapore, reliable records were not kept, so that ex-post evaluations could not be undertaken even in the few cases where it was thought desirable to do so. Only Singapore's Economic Development Board became a real 'one-stop shop'. Elsewhere investors not only had to negotiate with BoI, but also with Ministries of Industry, with Customs, with public utilities and with local governments.

Except in Singapore, negotiations typically took months. Sometimes years elapsed before a satisfactory arrangement was made. In Thailand the initial negotiations with foreign investors took place over lunch in air-conditioned, candle-lit nightclubs, with Philippine bands making eavesdropping impossible. High-level representatives of foreign firms and their local partners negotiated with senior officials of the Board of Investment. Once the main outlines of an arrangement were settled, further negotiations could take place in the Board's offices. Well-connected entrepreneurs, and those wishing to be well connected, were able to scoop the pool of monopolistic business opportunities.

Incentives to exports

Protection of domestic industry raised costs above international costs of production. Hence, incentives (subsidies) to exports to offset the high costs of protectionism so that producers could earn as much in manufacturing for export as for domestic markets, seemed to be a clever policy. Incentives to exports took the form of direct subsidies, tariff exemptions and drawbacks, 'wastage' allowances, monopoly shares of domestic markets, credit subsidies and tax holidays. The bureaucrats who allocated such incentives earned 'rents' and so did the entrepreneurs who benefited from them. These rents did not add to national output (Krueger, 1974), but dead-weight rent-seeking became a way of life. Protection offsets were particularly important in Korea where they made substantial contributions to *chaebol* profits while discriminating against other producers. In practice, only tariff exemptions and drawbacks seemed to be effective (Herderschee, 1990). Incentives to exports, and the regulatory regimes that necessitated them, were highly praised by *dirigiste* economists (Amsden, 1989, 1991; Wade, 1988, 1991a, b, 1992) and accepted by the World Bank (1993). The structural damage that they imposed on East Asian economies was thus widely condoned.

Tax holidays

The International Chamber of Commerce in the 1960s argued that to attract foreign investment to developing countries – predominantly for IS – multinational firms should be courted by special incentives. Tax holidays were the most frequent form of subsidy for foreign investors, but the Chamber also suggested privileged access to land and subsidies for utilities such as energy and water. On equity grounds, such subsidies had to be extended to domestic investors. They were adopted widely, even though it quickly became evident that they were not effective (United Nations, 1968). As well as creating dead-weight rents and opportunities for corruption, they undermined countries' fiscal bases and the ability to finance social and physical infrastructures. Competition for tax holiday privileges has been an important component of industry policy with large cash benefits to cronies. Tax holidays did not benefit investors from countries that did not allow tax deduction for taxes 'forgiven' by tax holidays. Tax revenues were thus shifted from poor recipient countries to rich investing countries. Tax holidays, however, produced generous rents for other entrepreneurs and for bureaucrats. East Asian countries still bid against each other in extending tax holidays and other subsidies, particularly to foreign investors, despite the financial costs and corruption they engender.

Foreign investment flows into protected industries

The rule of law, a liberal, open-policy regime, the absence of arbitrary regulations and associated corruption, and competitive public utility services are known to be the effective incentives to domestic and foreign investment. An intensive debate in the 1960s and 1970s highlighted research findings that clearly indicated that the costs and benefits accruing from foreign investment flows were determined by recipient countries' domestic policies. Incentives undermined the economic settings that determine cost–benefit outcomes.

A considerable, though not known (Athukorala and Hill, 1998), proportion of private foreign investment flows to East Asia has in recent years gone into protected and monopolistic enterprises. Their profits went into other uneconomic projects such as real estate speculation that dissipated the benefits of foreign as well as local investment. Foreign investment, stimulated by subsidies and protective tariffs, led to high levels of oligopolistic excess capacity. East Asian countries have at least five and perhaps ten times the capacity of likely motor vehicle demand for decades to come. Inadequate scales of production make exports only possible with subsidies. While the local associates benefit, the chief beneficiaries are the shareholders, mainly in the United States and Japan, of the parent motor vehicle firms that earn highly protected monopolistic profits. Foreign motor vehicle oligopolists, including Ford-Mazda and BMW, invested $10.2 billion in Thai motor vehicle production in 1998–99 (*The Australian Financial Review*, 5 July 1999). Mercedes and Volkswagen are adding to their investment in Thailand. Volvo and Citrôen are in place and Renault and Jaguar are investigating new investment possibilities. Korea, Indonesia, Malaysia and the Philippines are also fostering major motor vehicle investments. Of these countries, only Korea is producing motor vehicles at internationally competitive prices. The other producers will be relying on high domestic protection and export subsidies for positive returns to their shareholders. To *The Australian Financial Review*, the Thai investment is 'a case study in economic recovery' (5 July 1999). The losers are the consumers who pay excessive prices for motor vehicles, the taxpayers who pay for the subsidies and those denied jobs in competitive industries. Bureaucrats provide the chief support for incentive handouts even when they do not benefit from under-the-counter payments. When the issue of replacing tax holidays for exports by an across-the-board tax reduction was proposed in Singapore in the early 1990s, the reform was strongly opposed by Economic Development Board officials. They argued that without 'tax holidays' as talking points, new firms coming to Singapore, or old firms expanding production, would have no reason to talk to them! Their jobs were at stake. The reform was defeated.

Financial repression

The suppression of interest rates below market levels for favoured borrowers, notoriously practiced in Japan and in most East Asian economies, prevented the emergence of sophisticated, competitive financial sectors in East Asian economies. Financial liberalization was too slow, too late and rarely accompanied by adequate prudential financial regulation. Indonesia was a notable example (Suwandi, 1995).

Financial repression was a key concomitant of industry policies, magnifying the distortions they created. Credit rationing to favoured recipients by nationalized banks played a key role in building up the *chaebol* in Korea. State-owned banks also made a major contribution to the emergence of crony capitalism in Indonesia. When, belatedly,

Indonesian and Korean banks were denationalized, industry policies had created the family groupings that could dominate banking. The reasonably open financial sectors in Hong Kong, Singapore and Taiwan were exceptions. The management of most East Asian banks did not adopt appropriate transparency and accountability measures. Internal financial transactions within crony groups led to a high proportion of non-performing loans. Foolish international firms were seduced by promises of high returns into lending on the basis of flimsy information about the banking institutions and the projects for which they were lending. These practices continue. Daewoo, the leading Korean *chaebol* succeeded in raising $60 billion from other Korean firms in September 1999 to avoid bankruptcy (*The Australian Financial Review*, 7 September 1999). Bankruptcy was postponed, but only by a year. Bankruptcy has been held at bay for other *chaebols* by continuing cross-financial flows. Government directives to reduce debt are being ignored. Similar practices are keeping cronies afloat in Thailand, Malaysia and Indonesia.

Paradoxically, growing democratization of political processes played a counterproductive role in the events that led up to the collapses of 1997. Before the rise of crony capitalism, liberal bureaucrats in ministries of finance and central banks succeeded in using the strength of export-orientation in the economy to maintain budget and balance-of-payments stability. In Korea, Indonesia and Malaysia, there were inflationary and balance-of-payments blips, but macroeconomic management had been in the national, not sectional, interest for some 30 years. By the middle of the 1990s, however, crony lobbyists and parliamentarians were able to ensure that prudent policies were overruled, leading to the overvaluation of exchange rates and hence to the 1997 'crises'.

Fiscal policies

Because inflation was generally kept under control, the multilateral financial institutions claimed that fiscal and monetary policies were in good shape in the years leading up to 1997. But fiscal policy is not merely a question of budget surpluses or deficits. Fiscal policies cannot be regarded as prudent merely because budget deficits were contained until the mid-1990s. With the exception of Hong Kong, Singapore and Taiwan, taxation was highly regressive, inefficient and arbitrary. Tax avoidance and evasion by crony capitalists was rampant and others followed suit wherever they could.

Public services, swollen by armies of regulators, ate up a disproportionate share of revenues, leaving inadequate resources for infrastructure.

These resources were further reduced by government intervention, often on national grounds, in allocating contracts in infrastructural sectors and projects. Without transparent and competitive tendering, accountability declined, allowing privileged companies to make large monopolistic profits at the cost of taxpayers and consumers. The expansion of infrastructural facilities slowed. By the mid-1990s it was becoming evident that high savings rates did not mean adequate private or public infrastructural investment. The crony firms stole, wasted or siphoned abroad a significant proportion of national savings.

Infrastructure was lagging a long way behind the needs of most East Asian economies. The World Bank saw this as an inherent rather than as a policy- and institution-created problem. Vast sums have been projected to indicate a need for unprecedentedly large new inflows of foreign capital into East Asia (World Bank, 1996). Infrastructure privatization and foreign capital inflows, far from overcoming current shortages, are frequently making them worse. In the absence of appropriate policies and prudential regulation of utility sectors, many inappropriate oligopolistic joint ventures are being formed between selected cronies and foreign investors in telecommunications, energy and toll roads. Transparency and accountability are totally absent. Multinational institutions are encouraging a climate of renewed reckless lending similar to that underwriting the flow of private capital to East Asia in the 1990s.

The public ownership and management of utilities is often highly inefficient, but it does not follow that private oligopolies will provide cost-effective alternatives. Evidence of the high costs of ill-conceived 'build, own, operate and transfer' projects is already pressing for attention (Soonthonsipirong, 1999). Before the last 'crisis' has been paid for, the next one is in the making.

The international dimension

Prior to the 1940s, most economists argued that disequilibrium had international origins. IMF economists in the late 1940s, 1950s and 1960s were influential in converting the economics profession to the thesis that most international disequilibria had domestic origins. The IMF, as the guardian of fixed exchange rates until the early 1970s, introduced country surveillance reports to urge policy changes that would enable countries to avoid undue exchange-rate changes. Domestic policy reforms were the principal requirements for the granting of credits and loans. When the world moved to flexible exchange rates, the IMF lost its prime raison d'être but continued its macroeconomic surveillance, funding countries with balance-of-payments difficulties, often repeatedly, because the reforms contained in conditionality agreements were not implemented. Such funding, usually supported by World Bank loans, introduced substantial 'moral hazard' into international capital markets. Private lenders and developing-country public and private borrowers became convinced that the IMF, backed by the World Bank, other regional banks and bilateral governments, would provide perpetual credit to developing (and transitional countries) no matter how counterproductive their economic policies. Eventually, developing-country taxpayers would pay off such loans.

The World Bank management has for long been more concerned to achieve a high flow of lending than to ensure that its resources were efficiently allocated. Recipient governments have been as well aware of this imperative as World Bank staff. As the perceived shortage of international capital that prompted the World Bank's establishment turned into high levels – and at times floods – of liquidity, the World Bank's conditionality became totally ineffective. Like the IMF, it poured resources into countries that had no intention of following prudent economic policies.

Serious economic analysis was thus neglected, if not abandoned, and is still not being undertaken. There is little sense of urgency in seeking trade reforms that would put pressure on monopolistic producers. Industry policy, with its invitation to corruption, continues to be implemented. No changes are being made in the motor vehicle industry and other attention-grabbing joint-venture investments. Progress in bankruptcy procedures has been minimal. The $117.7 billion package put together by July 1998 by the IMF, the World Bank and the Asian Development Bank, and bilateral donors for Indonesia, Korea and Thailand (International Monetary Fund, 1999, p. 24) has rescued the cronies that were responsible for the 1997 crises. The loans will have to be repaid by the, mostly low-income, taxpayers.

Because efficient export sectors continue to operate in dual East Asian economies, exchange rates have appreciated and confidence is returning – except, perhaps in Indonesia and Japan. Security prices are reviving with new inflows of foreign speculative and returning domestic funds. Foreign investment in inefficient motor vehicle production is being supported by large subsidies. National and international cronies are alive and well in East Asia.

Conclusions

Once *dirigiste* policies entrenched crony capitalists in East Asian economies, liberal reforms become increasingly difficult to initiate and carry through. It is extremely naïve to consider that efficient corporate governance, transparency in government–business relations, and competition policy can be achieved if the *dirigiste* policies, and the institutional structures to which they have given rise, are not changed. Crony corporates are hiring more and better accountants and lawyers to give an appearance of transparency and accountability while their transactions are becoming increasingly devious. Dismantling protectionist policies and offsets to protection, radically reforming fiscal and financial policies, and, above all, putting an end to all industry (including public utility) policies that 'pick winners' is the only way that efficiency and competitiveness can return to East Asia. The BoI have to go. At present there is no evidence that a start is being made to reform these key policies that support crony capitalism. Some recovery may be expected because the economies remain dual. Without an attack on crony sectors, a return to long-term rapid growth rates is unlikely.

The revelation of the depth of East Asia's financial problems took an unduly long time. Mindless support of capital flows, regardless of project or sovereign risk, exacerbated the depth of domestic economic and financial collapses. The multilateral financial institutions' creation of moral hazard in international capital markets was also a factor. But, finally, the competitiveness of international capital markets found the cronies out. Unfortunately, the rescue packages put together under IMF and World Bank leadership are enabling reforms to be avoided. Putting an end to the multilateral institutions' underwriting of careless lending and borrowing is at least as urgent as policy reforms in East Asian countries.

References

Amsden, A., *Asia's Next Giant: Korea and Late Industrialization* (Oxford University Press, 1989).

Amsden, A., 'Diffusion of Development: the Late Industrializing Model and Greater Asia', *American Economic Review: Papers and Proceedings*, 81 (2) (1991) 282–6.

Athukorala, P., and Hill, H., 'Foreign Investment in East Asia: a Survey', *Asian Pacific Economic Literature*, 12 (2) (1998) 23–50.

Bardhan P., 'Corruption and Development: a Review of Issues', *Journal of Economic Literature*, 35 (1997) 1320–46.

Commonwealth of Australia, *Asia's Infrastructure in the Crisis: Harnessing Private Enterprise* (Canberra: Department of Foreign Affairs and Trade, East Asia Analytical Unit, 1998).

Herderschee, J., *Incentives for Exports: a Case Study of Taiwan and Thailand*, unpublished PhD thesis (Canberra: National Centre for Development Studies, 1990) (mimeo).

Hewison, K., *Bankers and Bureaucrats: Capital and the Role of the State in Thailand*, Monograph 34 (New Haven: Yale University, Southeast Asian Studies, 1989).

Hill, H., and Arndt, W. (eds), 'Southeast Asia's Economic Crisis: Origins, Lessons and the Way Forward', *ASEAN Economic Bulletin*, 15 (3) (1999).

Hughes, H., 'Why have East Asian Countries Led Economic Development?', *Economic Record*, 71 (212) (1995) 88–104.

IMF, *Annual Report 1998* (Washington, DC, 1999).

Krueger, A. O., 'The Political Economy of the Rent-Seeking Society', *American Economic Review*, 64 (1) (June 1974) 291–303.

Krueger, A. O., 'Export-led Industrial Growth Reconsidered', in W. Hong, and L. B. Krause (eds), *Trade and Growth of the Advanced Developing Countries in the Pacific Basin*, Papers and Proceedings of the Eleventh Pacific Trade and Development Conference (Seoul: Korea Development Institute, 1981) 3–34.

Krueger, A. O., Lary, H. B., Monson, T., and Akrasanee, N., *Trade and Employment in Developing Countries*, (Chicago and London: The University of Chicago Press for NBER, 1981).

Lal, D., The *Poverty of Development Economics*, Hobart Paperback, no. 16 (London: Institute of Economic Affairs, 1983).

Lindsey, B., and Lukas, A., 'Revisiting the "Revisionists": the Rise and Fall of the Japanese Economic Model', *Trade Policy Analysis* no.3 (Washington, DC: CATO Institute, Center for Trade Policy Studies, 1998).

Lingle, C., *The Rise and Decline of the Asian Century: False Starts on the Path to the Global Millennium* (Barcelona: Sirocco, 1997).

MacIntyre, A. (ed.) *Business and Government in Industrialising Asia* (Sydney: Allen & Unwin, 1994).

McLeod, R. H., and Garnaut, R. (eds) *East Asia in Crisis: From Being a Miracle to Needing One?* (Sydney: Routledge, 1998).

McVey, R. (ed.) *Southeast Asian Entrepreneurs* (Ithaca: Cornell University Press, 1992).

Montes, M. F., and Popov, V. V., *The Asian Crisis Turns Global* (Singapore: Institute of Southeast Asian Studies, 1999).

Moreno, R., Pasadilla, G., and Remolona, E., 'Asia's Financial Crisis: Lessons and Policy Responses', in R. Moreno and G. Pasadilla (eds), *Asia: Responding to Crisis* (Tokyo: Asian Development Bank Institute, 1998).

Radelet, S., and Sachs, J., 'The East Asian Financial Crisis: Diagnosis, Remedies, Prospects', in W. C. Brainard and G. L. Perry (eds), *Brookings Papers on Economic Activity*, 1 (1998) pp. 1–90.

Robison, R., and Goodman, S. G., *The New Rich in Asia: Mobile Phones, McDonald's and Middle Class Revolution* (London and New York: Routledge, 1996).

Searle, P., *The Riddle of Malaysian Capitalism: Rent Seekers or Real Capitalists?* St Leonards and Honolulu: Allen & Unwin and University of Hawaii Press, 1999).

Soonthonsipirong, N., 'Are Build Transfer Operate Regimes Justified?', *Policy Discussion Paper* 99/05 (Adelaide: Centre for International Economic Studies, Adelaide University, 1999).

Suwandi, T., *Financial Deregulation in Indonesia and the Continuing Policy Issues*, PhD dissertation (Canberra: Australian National University, 1995).

Tanzi, V., 'Corruption Around the World', *Staff Papers*, 45 (4) (1998) 559–94.

United Nations, *Foreign Investment in Developing Countries* (New York, 1968).

Wade, R., 'The Role of Government in Overcoming Market Failure: Taiwan, Republic of Korea and Japan', in H. Hughes (ed.), *Achieving Industrialization in East Asia* (Sydney: Cambridge University Press, 1988) pp. 129–63.

Wade, R., *Governing the Market: Economic Theory and the Role of the Government in East Asian Industrialization* (Princeton: Princeton University Press, 1991a).

Wade, R., 'How to Protect Exports from Protection: Taiwan's Duty Drawback Scheme', *The World Economy*, 14 (3) (1991b) 299–310.

Wade, R., 'East Asia's Economic Success: Conflicting Perspectives, Partial Insights, Shaky Evidence', *World Politics*, 44 (1992) 270–320.

World Bank, *The East Asian Miracle: Economic Growth and Public Policy* (Oxford: Oxford University Press, 1993).

World Bank, *Infrastructure Development in East Asia and Pacific: towards a New Public–Private Partnership* (Washington, DC, 1996).

Yap, J. T., 'The Philippine Economy in 1999: Prospects and Key Issues', *Development Research News*, Philippine Institute for Development Studies, 17 (1) (1999) 1, 4–7, 16.

16
Does the US Foreign Economic Assistance Program Have a Future?[1]

Vernon W. Ruttan

Since the mid-1990s, the US foreign economic assistance program has enjoyed a period of benign neglect. This is in sharp contrast to the late 1980s and early 1990s when the US Agency for International Development was the subject of vigorous criticism from both the right and the left. Reform proposals included the extensive reorganization or even the elimination of the agency. Changes in both the domestic and international political environment suggest that the US economic assistance program as it has been conceived and managed since the early 1950s is no longer viable. Some critics view this as a cause for celebration. But I come to this conclusion reluctantly.

In this chapter I first identify the series of visions that have guided US development assistance in the past and review some of the lessons that have been, or should have been, learned from development assistance experience. Finally, I suggest some elements of a new vision that should guide US development assistance policy in the future.

Six visions

US development assistance policy, following the post-Second World War relief and recovery efforts in Western Europe and East Asia, has been guided by a series of six successive strategic visions:

The *first* was a vision of a post-Second World War liberal political and economic order. This vision was articulated by the architects of the new postwar institutions – the World Bank, the International Monetary Fund, the General Agreement on Tariffs and Trade, and the United Nations and its specialized agencies and voluntary programmes. The vision was induced by a perception that economic autarchy and political repression in the interwar period were major sources of the Great Depression and the Second World War.

The *second* vision was outlined as the fourth point in President Harry S. Truman's inaugural address of 20 January 1949. In that speech, Truman proposed 'a bold new program for making the benefits of scientific advances and industrial progress available for the improvement and growth of underdeveloped areas'. This was the technical assistance vision.

The *third* vision was articulated by John F. Kennedy in his presidential campaign: 'A more prosperous world would also be a more secure world.' This articulation held out the promise of refocusing the security concerns of the Eisenhower administration from containment to development. The assistance policy that emerged emphasized the transfer of large financial resources by both bilateral and multilateral institutions.

The *fourth* was the vision advanced by members of the House Foreign Affairs Committee in the late 1960s and early 1970s – a 'New Direction' in foreign assistance that would focus on basic human rights and human needs. Aid should be directed to achieve greater equity among peoples, both within and among countries – to achieve political empowerment and improvement of the economic well-being of the poor majority in the poorest countries.

The *fifth* was the doctrine of closer linkage between economic and security assistance articulated in the Report of the Commission on Security and Economic Assistance (the Carlucci Report) and in speeches by Secretary of State Alexander Haig and UN Ambassador Jeanne Kirkpatrick during the first Reagan administration. Translation of the doctrine into policy was, however, confronted by an AID administrator whose emotional commitments were closer to the New Direction themes than to the right wing of the Reagan administration.

A *sixth* vision, sustainable development, emerged during the closing years of the Bush administration. Its central theme was intergenerational equity – 'sustainable development is development that meets the needs of the present without compromising the ability of future generations to meet their own needs' (World Commission on Environment and Development, 1987, p. 43). Unlike earlier visions, the vision of sustainable development did not emerge from official levels – from either the administration or the Congress. It was advanced first by the international environmental community and later by a broad coalition of NGOs. It was initially greeted with cautious scepticism at official levels. Its momentum was enhanced when environmental crisis became a central issue in the vice presidential campaign of Senator Al Gore. It was embraced as a unifying foreign assistance theme during the early years of the Clinton administration.

Throughout the almost five decades, from the 1940s to the mid-1990s, there have been two overarching constraints on the pursuit of the several visions or strategies outlined above. The *first* is that United States development assistance policy has largely been derivative of Cold War containment strategy. The growth and decline in the magnitude of assistance flows have been dominated by the intensity of the Cold War (Moledina, Qayyum, and Ruttan, 1997). The decline in economic resources for development and strategic assistance since the end of the Cold War is only the most recent manifestation of this relationship. When effectiveness in the use of aid resources for development purposes has appeared to be in conflict with short-run strategic objectives, the strategic objectives have generally dominated assistance policy.

A *second* is the continuing gap between the articulated objectives of assistance policy and the limited resources that have been made available to realize those objectives. The commitment to global poverty reduction in the 1970s, to debt restructuring in the 1980s and to transition in the formerly centrally planned economies in the 1990s are among the more egregious examples of the gap between rhetoric and resources (Zeuli and Ruttan, 1996). In the last Bush administration budget the fiscal 1993 budget authority for US bilateral economic assistance, including both development (DA) and strategic or supporting (ESF) assistance, amounted to less than $8 billion; by 1999, it had fallen to almost $5 billion (both in current dollars). The gap between America's pretensions and its willingness to support them has lead to inevitable disillusionment concerning both the US and multilateral assistance efforts. Both the Bush and the Clinton administrations responded to the opportunity to support the dramatic political and economic transformations underway in the former Soviet Union by offering advice rather than aid (Maynes, 1999).

In spite of the constraints of doctrine, resources and vision under which US assistance policy has laboured, there are important lessons from past experience. Let me turn first to some of the lessons from assistance for sector development and then to the lessons from assistance for policy reform.

Lessons from sector development assistance

Assistance to physical infrastructure development

During the 1950s and 1960s, large-scale investment in transport facilities (roads, railroads, ports, airports) and multi-purpose resource development projects (power, flood control, irrigation) occupied a very prominent place in both bilateral and multilateral development assistance portfolios. Many of these projects made substantial contributions to the development of recipient countries. Others became a burden. During the 1970s, infrastructure projects were severely criticized on technical grounds. Cost overruns were often substantial; the technology was often incompatible with the level of country development; failure to consider exchange-rate distortions often led to inappropriate investments. During the 1980s, infrastructure investments became the subject of intense scrutiny and severe criticism by the environmental community. Some of this criticism was valid. Much of it was overblown. It is again possible, however, to take a much more positive view of lending for infrastructure development.

Development of transportation infrastructure such as roads and ports enabled economic activity to expand more rapidly than without foreign assistance. Experience gained in these projects enabled construction firms in Korea and Turkey to compete in international markets (Krueger, 1993, p. 53). The technical, environmental and economic aspects of project evaluation and design have become more sophisticated. And the services provided by infrastructure are essential for economic growth. But the decline in bilateral assistance resources has meant that the United States no longer plays a significant role in assistance for large infrastructure development.

Agricultural and rural development

Sustained growth in agricultural production requires a close articulation of public and private sector support for research, development and technology transfer. The private sector has generally been relatively efficient in the development and transfer of mechanical and chemical technology and in the distribution of technical inputs. The public sector has been more effective in the development of biological technology. Public sector agricultural research and extension have achieved rates of return that are among the highest available to either national governments or development assistance agencies (Hayami and Ruttan, 1985, pp. 63–72). The underinvestment in agricultural research and related activities in agricultural production, processing and distribution development reflects a continuing failure on the part of both donor agencies and national governments to understand the role of agricultural development in generating economic growth and in contributing to more equitable income distribution.

Efforts by bilateral and multilateral donors to assist in community and rural development programmes have met with much less apparent success than have attempts to enhance agricultural production. One of the major sources of disillusionment has been the lack of consistency between the dynamics of rural development and the imperatives of donor assistance. Successful rural development programmes tend to be small in geographic scope and slow to implement, impose intensive demands on professional and administration capacity, are difficult to assess within the framework of conventional cost–benefit analysis, and are difficult to monitor. A second source of disillusionment has been the difficulty of achieving congruence between the local self-help and resource mobilization philosophy of rural development programmes and the objectives of donors to achieve measurable improvements on basic human need indicators within the space of the project cycle (Hayami and Ruttan, 1985, pp. 403–14).

Assistance for investment in human resource development

Both development theorists and assistance agencies were slow to recognize that investment in education and other forms of human capital represented a high pay-off source of economic growth. As evidence began to accumulate indicating high rates of return to education, perspectives began to change. Assistance in health and family planning also came to be recognized as an investment in human capital. The initial transfer of health technology from Western society to developing countries has often been inappropriate. We have transferred illness recovery systems rather than health systems. There is an enormous challenge facing the development assistance community, as well as national health systems, to design systems that enable families to live healthy lives so they do not have to enter the illness recovery system. There is also an enormous need for the establishment of health research capacity in the tropics. Less than 10 per cent of global health research is directed to the major diseases and health problems of the developing world. The resurgence of malaria and tuberculosis, the high cost of dealing with infectious disease, the failure to make progress in dealing with parasitic disease, the emerging AIDS epidemic, and the health effects of environmental change suggest that over the next two decades the health dimension of human resource development should command a level of attention similar to that received by agriculture in the 1960s and 1970s (Bell, Clark and Ruttan, 1994; Lederberg, 1996).

Lessons from assistance for policy reform

The influence of domestic economic policy on the effectiveness of donor economic assistance

The effectiveness of economic assistance has been strongly conditioned by both the macroeconomic and the sectoral economic policies of the host country. The contrast between the effectiveness of assistance to Korea before and after 1961 and the effectiveness of assistance to Ghana and Ivory Coast during the 1960s and 1970s is among the more dramatic examples. In the early 1960s Korea was still regarded as an economic 'basket case'. The Syngman Rhee government managed economic policy to maximize foreign economic assistance rather than to enhance economic growth. It was only after more growth-oriented policies were adopted in the mid-1960s that investments in the physical and institutional infrastructure, funded by US economic assistance in the 1950s, began to pay off. At independence in 1957 Ghana had a well-established export sector, a reasonably well-developed physical infrastructure, a relatively high level of literacy, and the highest per capita income in Africa. The Ivory Coast lagged behind Ghana in practically every indicator of development. By the early 1980s, the economic situation in the two countries was essentially reversed. Ghana has pursued policies of import substitution and direct state intervention in almost every area of economic activity. In the Ivory Coast, government policy was directed toward guiding rather than controlling the private sector. Since the late 1980s, the situation in these two countries has again reversed with Ivory Coast lagging and Ghana advancing more rapidly as a result of a vigorous programme of policy reform.

Policy dialogue and policy-based lending

The effectiveness of economic assistance is influenced (i) by the degree of convergence in the views of the donors and recipient countries concerning the latter's economic policies; and (ii) by the importance of economic development objectives relative to other donor motivations in decisions concerning the volume and allocation of economic assistance. The dominance of donor-strategic interests relative to commitment to economic policy reform has been demonstrated repeatedly in the case of Turkey. The willingness of the United States to support Turkish policy in trading-off economic reform against short-term strategic concerns contributed to the severity of the series of growth cycles experienced by the Turkish economy (1950–58, 1959–69,

1970–79). For an even more extreme example, one can turn to the history of US economic assistance to Egypt.

Among the many factors that have influenced the effectiveness of policy dialogue between donors and recipients, two have been particularly important. One is the degree of convergence of the views of donors and recipients concerning the need for and importance of proposed reforms. A second, and closely related factor, is the ability of recipients to bring substantial professional capacity and experience to bear on issues of institutional reform, policy analysis and program implementation. When these factors are not present, reforms are often implemented both reluctantly and ineffectively.

The influence of the size of assistance flows on national economic growth

The effect of the size of development assistance flows on the rate of economic growth of recipient countries represents a continuing theoretical and empirical puzzle. The evidence to support a conclusion that differences in the level of development assistance have accounted for major inter-country growth differences is not available. There is substantial evidence that assistance resources have generated high marginal rates of return – rates of return that are high relative to what the same resources would have earned in the donor countries (Peterson, 1989). There is evidence, though somewhat inconclusive, that in the absence of effective macroeconomic policy there is a negative relationship between the size of foreign aid transfers and the rate of economic growth. But the evidence is not available to support a conclusion that differences in the level of development assistance have accounted for major differences in inter-country economic growth rates or other foreign development indicators.

Economic assistance and the achievement of noneconomic objectives

There is a consistent pattern of jeopardizing the achievement of the principal economic objectives when projects are burdened with divergent objectives. Divergent objectives sharply reduce the chances for achieving success even of the most immediate primary goals. In the Philippines, for example, linking economic assistance to the continuation of military base rights failed to generate economic development, contributed to political repression, and eventually failed to secure the continued access to base facilities. It is too much to ask a multiple-purpose water development project to be a catalyst for regional economic development. It is enough if it delivers power and water efficiently to users. It is too much to ask a legal training programme to become a catalyst for democratic development. It is enough if the competence of the legal system can be enhanced to render justice more effectively. The linkage between the two major components of basic human needs and rights – improvement in economic well-being and the strengthening of civil society – is not always as obvious as their advocates suggest.[2]

Political development

The strengthening of democratic institutions has traditionally ranked relatively high, at least at a rhetorical level, among the objectives of US foreign assistance policy. With the end of the Cold War, there have been renewed calls 'to promote freedom and democracy around the world'. Building democratic participation in development was among the four major initiatives listed in early pronouncements by Deputy Secretary of State Wharton and Aid Administrator Atwood at the beginning of the Clinton administration. But US commitment to political development has, like the commitment to economic development, often faltered when confronted with short-term strategic considerations.

In the case of economic development, both sector development and policy efforts have been able to draw on a powerful body of economic thought – primarily neoclassical economic theory – that provides the analytical tools with which to address issues of development practice and the design of economic reform. The application of these tools, even when used with skill and sensitivity, has not represented a guarantee against failure in project, programme, or policy design. There is no similar body of theory that can serve as a guide in the design of a programme to strengthen the institutions of governance or of a programme to achieve a liberal political order (Ruttan, 1991, pp. 269–91).

One of the few guides available is the empirical generalization that political liberalization is more sustainable when it is preceded by a successful programme of economic liberalization. The generalization is sufficiently strong to support a conclusion that a poor country is fortunate if economic liberalization runs sufficiently ahead of political liberalization to generate economic growth at the same time that political reforms are being put in place. This generalization is clearly consistent with recent East Asian experience. Korea, Taiwan and Singapore certainly cannot be classified as liberal democracies. Nevertheless, they, and several of the second echelon states in the region, have developed political systems capable of sustaining policies consistent with economic growth. And economic growth seems to be inducing effective demands for modest political liberalization.

One way of summing up is to insist that advising 'shock treatment', as we have often done in Eastern Europe and the former USSR, for countries with weak or missing market institutions or limited technical capacity that they go 'cold turkey' on policy reform has reflected a lack of willingness to invest the intellectual energy necessary to understand the institutional foundations for political order and economic growth in the economies and the societies for which reform prescriptions are being made. In the pursuit of reform, motivation has often outrun knowledge, capacity and humility.

What is the bottom line? What should we have learned from the past? At the risk of only slight overstatement, let me make two assertions. The first is that structural reform – the removal of distortions in monetary, fiscal, trade, commodity and consumer policy – is a prerequisite for effective economic performance. It raises the rate of return to growth-enhancing investment. But it is not a primary source of economic growth. At best, it can reduce the gap between the level of output that has already been achieved and the level of output that is potentially feasible.

The second is that the real sources of economic growth are investment in human and physical capital and in productivity-enhancing technical and institutional change. These more fundamental investments must draw on financial, political and intellectual resources that are not readily mobilized in the short run and often not by the public sector. They do not generate immediate increments in economic growth. They often require a generation or more to mature. The failure to make the investments needed to expand technical and institutional capacity in the 1970s is a major reason why the responses to the policy reforms of the 1980s were often disappointing.

Toward renewed commitment?

Now let me turn to the future of US development assistance. In this section, I lay out a programme that I view as consistent with US interests and capacities in a post-Cold War world. In the next, a more limited programme, the minimum that the United States should ask of itself, even in an environment of constrained assistance budgets and a growing weariness with the burdens of world leadership. Both scenarios will be conditioned by a search for a post-Cold War rationale for US development assistance. Is there anything that can, or will, replace the

Cold War as a rationale for the mobilization of US resources to assist in the development of poor countries? Both scenarios attempt to take into consideration the changes in the global economy over the last several decades and the changing role of the United States in the global economy and polity.

Changes in the international and the domestic economy and polity imply a much different mission for an US economic assistance programme than in the past. The US bilateral programme should be reformed to operate in a mode of economic cooperation rather than economic assistance. US assistance efforts should focus largely on the high pay-off areas of human capital development and of technical and institutional change. My own preference would be for an Economic Cooperation Administration (ECA) with much of its bilateral economic development and humanitarian assistance activity organized in two semi-autonomous institutes, along with the several public foundations, under an ECA umbrella. This model specifically rejects proposals to fully incorporate development assistance into the State Department. Neither the State Department, nor an assistance agency that operates under direct State Department administration, could be relied on to give substantial weight to the perspective suggested by this model or to defend the allocation of resources needed to support long-term development objectives in those countries of the world that fall outside short-term security interests, even though this would be in the long-term national interest of the United States.

An Institute for Scientific, Technical and Economic Cooperation

In today's world, the United States has as much to learn from as to teach by strengthening technical and intellectual interchange. The mandate of an Institute for Scientific, Technical and Economic Cooperation (ISTEC) should be to enhance the two-way exchange of knowledge and technology among all nations rather than simply to give technical assistance to poor countries. The ISTEC mandate should include the OECD and the formerly centrally planned economies, as well as the less developed countries. Emphasis should be strongest in areas such as agriculture, health, population and environment. It should also include cooperation in the areas of institutional reform, policy analysis, and program implementation. Programme operations should be largely subcontracted to universities, research institutes, and the sectoral departments and agencies such as Agriculture, Health, Education and Welfare, Environmental Protection, and the National Institute of Standards and Technology in which the scientific and technical capacity to implement the ISTEC programme resides. The funding necessary to maintain the capacity for the nation's major research universities to participate in ISTEC programs should be placed on a long-term institutional grant basis, somewhat similar to that provided by domestic agricultural research.

An Institute for Private Voluntary Cooperation

Humanitarian concerns for the poor in the poorest countries and for those displaced by international conflict and domestic repression will continue to represent a basic impulse for foreign assistance for a wide spectrum of the American public (Rielly, 1999).

Official assistance agencies do not have a strong record of performance in this area. Many private voluntary organizations (PVOs) have established a strong record of capacity to deliver emergency humanitarian assistance. Most have had much greater difficulty in establishing a credible record of effectiveness in the delivery of development assistance (Eicher and White, 1999). An Institute for Private Voluntary Cooperation (IPVC) should be organized to provide resources and oversight for programmes managed by PVOs. Resources should be made available on a competitive basis. Too much present funding has been treated as an entitlement. A major emphasis should be placed on strengthening indigenous PVOs. Much of food aid, except that allocated for so-called market development, should be channelled through the IPVC. The PVO community should be encouraged to become more effective in using food aid as an instrument of development than in the past.

The public foundations

In addition to the ISTEC and the IPVC, support should be expanded for the publicly supported development foundations. These include the Asia Foundation, the Inter-American Development Foundation and the African Development Foundation. The historical roots of the Asia Foundation were deep in Cold War doctrine. It has emerged, however, with substantial capacity to work on issues of democratization and privatization items that should be high on the foreign policy and foreign assistance agenda. The Inter-American Foundation and the African Development Foundation are products of the New Directions and basic human needs foreign assistance thrust of the 1970s. They have now emerged with substantial capacity to work directly with the poor and with the informal sectors in poor countries. A cautious expansion of support for the programmes of these public foundations and for the creation of several new public foundations such as the more recently established Eurasia Foundation and a public foundation to work in the area of sustainable energy systems would seem warranted. My caution stems from concern that rapid growth in support could outrun the capacity of the public foundations.

Security assistance

The component of the foreign economic assistance budget allocated to the support of strategically important countries under the Economic Support Fund has declined more rapidly than has development assistance since the mid-1980s. The overwhelming share of ESF resources is now allocated to the Middle East. As security assistance budgets declined, there was a frantic search in Washington to find new threats that might reverse the decline. It is now time for a complete reassessment of US policy, including assistance policy, toward the Middle East.

The Nixon Doctrine, first articulated on Guam in 1969, prepared the way for US military disengagement from Southeast Asia. It is now time for the United States to promulgate a new Middle East doctrine along the lines suggested in the mid-1970s by George Kennan (1977). The first element in that doctrine should be that the United States no longer has vital strategic or security interests in the Middle East. A second element should be that the United States does have an interest, short of direct military intervention, in the continued reduction of tensions between Israel and the Arab states in the region. A third element should be that the United States would welcome the emergence of representative governments in the region. As progress is made in reducing the flow of ESF resources to the region, the funds should be shifted to other bilateral and multilateral assistance activities.

Multilateral assistance

The United States should continue to look favourably on requests for modest expansion of the borrowing authority and replenishment of soft-loan lending facilities at the World Bank and the regional development banks. The relationship between the United States and several of the UN specialized agencies and voluntary programmes remains troubled. In the 1980s the ascendancy of the State Department Bureau for International Organizations, relative to the sectoral departments, in the formulation of US policy toward the UN specialized agencies, combined with personal antagonisms between bureau administrators and specialized agency directors-general and growing arrears in US budget contributions, resulted in a weakening of the US role in several of the specialized agencies that has continued through the 1990s.

In spite of this troubled history, it is now in the US interest to provide stronger US support for the work of the United Nations Development Program and the specialized agencies and voluntary programmes in the 1990s. The easing of US–USSR tensions has removed some of the ideological tensions that have frequently spilled over into US relationships with the specialized agencies. Multilateral assistance should be viewed by the US government as a less expensive, and often less frustrating, approach to assisting some of the economically and politically least developed countries. The United States should move immediately to paying its arrears to the UN and to its specialized agencies.

Building on United States capacity

The plethora of development assistance reform proposals advanced during the closing years of the Reagan and Bush administrations and during the Clinton administration has lacked the sense of vision that would be necessary to unlock the fiscal and policy constraints on assistance to poor countries. In the immediate future, more than half of bilateral economic assistance will continue to be allocated to advancing the peace process and related political objectives in the Balkans and the Middle East. A significant portion of the remaining economic assistance will be allocated to support the economic and political transition process in Eastern Europe, Russia and the other successor states to the USSR. A much smaller but still substantial flow will likely be directed to facilitating democratic reform in Southern Africa. As these priorities are met it appears that substantially less than $1.0 billion will be available for US bilateral economic assistance to the poorest countries in Asia, Africa and Latin America.

As the US development assistance effort has atrophied in the post-Cold War era, a number of contrarian observers, ranging from Peter Bauer (1972) to Deepak Lal (1996), have raised the question of why aid? One argument is that aid has been ineffective in generating growth and eliminating poverty. A second is that rapid development of international financial institutions has relieved the need for official financial transfers. I have responded to these and related arguments elsewhere in greater detail than would be appropriate in this essay (Ruttan, 1989). I have argued that the economic and political policies pursued by both the developed and developing countries have bound the modern world into an implicit social contract. Increased interdependence among nations has extended the moral basis for social and economic justice from the domestic to the international spheres (Arrow, 1983, p. 188). The growth of global and political interdependence implies a decline in the significance of national boundaries. Since national boundaries are no longer coextensive with the scope of economic and political interdependence, they do not mark the limits of social obligation in the sharing of the benefits and borders associated with interdependence.

My recommendation is to refocus the limited resources the United States seems willing to make available around the programme areas identified below that have historically generated high rates of return and which remain particularly relevant to the poorest countries of the world.

Agriculture and food security

Agricultural commodities have been available on relatively favourable terms in world markets since the early 1980s. But the fifty or so poorest countries in the developing world have not yet succeeded in developing and sustaining the agricultural research, extension and infrastructure investment that will enable them to meet the demands that will be placed on agricultural producers during the early decades of the next century (Ruttan, 1998). Few have been able to design and put in place the institutions needed to assure the poor equitable entitlements to basic subsistence. The food situation in much of Africa has become increasingly precarious. The continuing decline in support for agricultural development by US/AID and by the multilateral institutions since the 1980s, particularly the decline in support for agricultural research, should be reversed.

Natural resources, energy use and environmental protection

The closing decades of the twentieth century have seen a major transition in concern about capacity to achieve sustainable economic growth. It is now clear that technical change is capable of releasing the most serious threats to growth arising out of resource constraints. But the environmental effects of agricultural and industrial intensification are posing new threats to the sustainability of economic growth. These threats range from unwise exploitation of forest and fisheries resources, failure to deal with local and regional groundwater pollution and soil degradation, and to the broader issues of how to respond to the demands by the developed countries that they confront the issue posed by global environmental change. Only a few developed countries, and even fewer developing countries, have begun to put the technologies and institutions in place needed to respond to these threats (Ruttan, 1998).

Health and population

The design of health systems to meet the needs of the poor majority in the least developed countries continues to evade the efforts of assistance programmes. A series of health threats – malaria and tuberculosis resurgence, failure to make significant progress in parasitic disease, the high cost of responding to infectious disease, the health effects of environmental change and the debilitating impact of the AIDS epidemic on working-age populations – point toward the emergence of a global health crisis in the early decades of the twenty-first century. Capacity for essential national health research needs to be strengthened. Health delivery and maintenance systems need to be designed and implemented which give the family and the community a central role in the health system. Continued support for the demographic transition represents an important component of efforts to achieve food security and sustainable improvements in other dimensions of human development (Bell, Clark and Ruttan, 1994).

Education and human capital

It has been clear since the mid-twentieth century that broad-based economic growth can be sustained only if all people have the opportunity to acquire the basic skills and knowledge that facilitate effective participation in the economic development of their country. Advances in science and technology have raised both public and private returns to improvements in education. Yet access to even the most basic levels of education remains strongly biased against rural areas, against girls and against the urban poor in too many countries.

These priorities imply a far less adequate assistance effort than is consistent with either US capacities or responsibilities. They are, however, consistent with the limited resources that are likely to be available for economic assistance by the United States to the poorest countries in the immediate future. They are consistent with, but do not exhaust, the elements usually included in the sustainability agenda. Each draws on scientific, professional and technical capacity in which the United States has much to offer. There is no presumption that all programme areas should be operative in all countries. The programme initiative should draw on the capacities of universities, private voluntary organizations, and the public foundations in a way that assures sustainability in the development of programme capacity.

Self-containment

The willingness of the United States to play a hegemonic role in global economic and political affairs has been severely eroded (Rielly, 1999). Henry Kissinger insisted that in the emerging world order 'the United States can neither withdraw from the world nor dominate it' (Kissinger, 1994, p. 19). But the declining willingness of the US economy to sustain a first-class global posture in economic affairs cannot fully account for the constraints under which US foreign economic assistance will be forced to operate in the first decade of the twenty-first century. It cannot account, for example, for the failure of the United States to settle its debts with the United Nations and its specialized agencies.

Even as the Clinton administration has realized substantial success in efforts to repair the performance of the domestic economy that became increasingly apparent during the closing decades of the Cold War, US capacity and inclination to aggressively pursue foreign policy goals, particularly foreign economic assistance, has become increasingly tentative. Thomas L. Friedman, of the *New York Times,* has noted that while continuing to project a vision and commitment to a more peaceful, democratic and prosperous world, the Clinton administration has, in practice, defined a policy of 'self-containment' (Friedman, 1993).

Are there any forces at work which might reverse the further decline in assistance resources? One could be the emergence of one or more common threats to the well-being of both developed and developing countries. There was a good deal of rhetoric in the early and mid-1990s about sustainable development and environmental security.

There is little doubt that the transnational nature of a number of environmental threats – global climate change, ozone depletion, acid rain and others – will require the strengthening of international institutions. There is also the possibility of global health and food crises emerging as we move into the first decades of the next century. Either could result in an international resource mobilization effort to resolve the crisis. But I do not visualize, at least in the short run, any of these common concerns generating the political support that will be needed to prevent the continued erosion of US assistance resources. The most likely prospect is for each assistance constituency, within the government and outside, to continue to attempt to carve out for its favoured programme area (population, environment, agriculture, Eastern Europe, the Middle East, Southern Africa) a larger share of a declining assistance budget.

The continuing fatigue and disorientation in the US bilateral effort will not be resolved by the typical Washington remedy by reorganizing AID.

Moving organizational boxes around (as in the 1979 reorganization that created IDCA), attempts to rationalize interagency conflict and cooperation (as in the 1990 food aid reforms), or proposals to incorporate AID more fully into the State Department will not resolve the problem.

A new world order?

The problem of lack of focus will not be resolved until a new post-Cold War vision of the kind of world that the United States wants to live in during early decades of the twenty-first century captures the political and popular imagination. Such a vision can only be perceived dimly at this time. It is tempting to embrace the rhetoric of 'sustainable development' in an attempt to capture a vision for the future. I have resisted, however, because the concept of sustainability has become so elastic that it can be stretched to cover almost any reform agenda. It has become an umbrella under which constituencies with widely diverse and often inconsistent agendas can march without confronting their disagreements.

The international environment in which assistance efforts will be conducted in the early decades of the twenty-first century will be vastly different from the bipolar world of the Cold War era. We will continue to be confronted with what Harlan Cleveland has termed 'a New World disorder'(1993). Many centralized nation-states are perceived by large numbers of their peoples as increasingly less relevant to their economic and political needs. This trend is most apparent in large multinational states. It also includes many small multinational states: states that incorporate geographically based national minorities, whether Amer-Indian nationals in Guatemala, ethnic minorities in the former Yugoslavia and the USSR, or ethnic minorities in Rwanda and Burundi.

Governments will be forced to deal more creatively with their constituent nationalities than in the past. The constitutional design challenge of the next several decades will be how to simultaneously achieve political autonomy and economic viability. On the political side this means a pragmatic search for constitutional arrangements that will assure ethnic and other political communities sufficient autonomy to satisfy their civic needs. Economic viability requires that political autonomy be achieved within a constitutional framework that will permit financial resources, commodities, services and people to move freely across political borders.

What should be the role of US economic assistance in an environment of pervasive economic and political disorder? US national security will rarely be threatened by the small conflicts of natural liberation or ethnic cleansing. Nor will conventional military responses be particularly effective in restoring order. But idealism will continue to represent a compelling source of American foreign policy. The liberal impulse that inspired US leadership in the design of the post-Second World War international system and the US bilateral aid program, will insist that the United States play a constructive role in responding to the new international disorder.

But the implications for US development assistance policy are far from clear. The capacity and motivation of the US bilateral development assistance programme, as we have known it throughout most of the postwar period, has been largely eroded. It is doubtful, in the absence of a new vision and a new consensus, that the US assistance agency can survive in its present form.

Notes

1. In this essay, I draw heavily on my earlier work on the evolution of the US development assistance program. See Krueger, Michalopoulos, and Ruttan (1989) and Ruttan (1996). I also draw on Kapur, Lewis and Webb (1997), and Krueger (1993, 1998).
2. This point is made with respect to the World Bank assistance by Kapur, Lewis and Webb (I, 1997, p. 48).

References

Arrow, K. J., *Social Choice and Justice* (Cambridge, MA: Harvard University Press, 1983) pp. 175–89.

Bauer, P. T., *Dissent on Development* (London: Weidenfeld & Nicolson, 1972).

Bell, D. E., Clark W. C., and Ruttan, V. W., 'Global Research Systems for Sustainable Development: Agriculture, Health and the Environment', in V. W. Ruttan (ed.), *Agriculture, Health and Environment: Sustainable Development in the 21st Century* (Minneapolis, MN: University of Minnesota Press, 1994) pp. 358–79.

Cleveland, H., *Birth of a New World: An Open Moment for International Leadership* (San Francisco, CA: Jossey-Bass, 1993) pp. 77–104.

Eicher, C. K., and White, R., *NGOs and the African Farmer: a Skeptical Perspective* (East Lansing, MI: Michigan State University Department of Agricultural Economics, January 1999) pp. 99–101.

Friedman, T. I., 'A New Kind of Foreign Policy', *Star Tribune* (Minneapolis, 3 October 1993) 26A.

Hayami, Y., and Ruttan, V. W., *Agricultural Development: an International Perspective* (Baltimore, MD: The Johns Hopkins University Press, 1985).

Kapur, D., Lewis, J. P., and Webb, R., *The World Bank: Its First Half Century*, vols I and II (Washington, DC: The Brookings Institute, 1997).

Kennan, G. F., *The Cloud of Danger: Current Realities in American Foreign Policy* (Boston, MA: Little Brown, 1977).

Kissinger, H. A., *Diplomacy* (New York: Simon & Schuster, 1994).

Krueger, A. O., 'Whither the World Bank and the IMF?', *Journal of Economic Literature*, 36 (1998) 1983–2020.

Krueger, A. O., *Economic Policies at Cross Purposes: the United States and the Developing Countries* (Washington, DC: The Brookings Institution, 1993).

Krueger, A. O., Michalopoulos, C., and Ruttan, V. W., *Aid and Development* (Baltimore, MD: The Johns Hopkins University Press, 1989).

Lal, D., 'Foreign Aid: An Idea Whose Time Has Gone', *Economic Affairs* (Autumn, 1996) 9–13.

Lederberg, J., 'Infectious Disease – a Threat to Global Health Security' *Journal of the American Medical Association*, 276 (1996) 412–19.

Maynes, C. W., 'Squandering Triumph', *Foreign Affairs*, 78 (January–February 1999) 15–23.

Moledina, A. A., Qayyum, A., and Ruttan V. W., 'Did Cold War Tensions Influence US Foreign Aid Allocations? An Empirical Study' (St Paul, MN: University of Minnesota, Dept. of Applied Economics, 18 June 1997) (mimeo).

Peterson, W. L., 'Rates of Return to Assistance Capital: an International Comparison', *Kyklos*, 42, fasc. 2 (1989) 139–85.

Rielly, J. E., *American Public Opinion and US Foreign Policy, 1999* (Chicago, IL: Chicago Council on Foreign Relations, 1999).

Ruttan, V. W., 'The Transition to Agricultural Sustainability', *Proceedings of the National Academy of Sciences*, 96 (May 1999) 5960–7.

Ruttan, V. W., *United States Development Assistance Policy: The Domestic Politics of Foreign Economic Aid* (Baltimore, MD: The Johns Hopkins University Press, 1996).

Ruttan, V. W., 'Why Foreign Economic Assistance?', *Economic Development and Cultural Change*, 37 (January 1989) 412–24.

Ruttan, V. W., 'What Happened to Political Development?', *Economic Development and Cultural Change*, 39 (1991) 265–91.

World Commission on Environment and Development, *'Our Common Future': the Brundtland Report* (Oxford: Oxford University Press, 1987).

Zeuli, K. A., and Ruttan, V. W., 'US Assistance to the Former Soviet Empire: Toward a Rationale for Foreign Aid', *The Journal of Developing Areas*, 30 (1996) 493–524.

Index

ITALIAN ACTORS
of the
RENAISSANCE

ISABELLA ANDREINI
(From her *Lettere*, 1607)

ITALIAN ACTORS
OF THE
RENAISSANCE

By Winifred Smith
AUTHOR OF *The Commedia dell' Arte*

BENJAMIN BLOM New York/London 1968

First Published New York, 1930
Revised 1968
by Benjamin Blom, Inc., Bronx, New York 10452
and 56 Doughty Street, London W.C. 1

Library of Congress Catalog Card Number 68-20249

Printed in the United States of America

TO
MY BROTHER
PRESERVED SMITH
AND
THE DEAR MEMORY
OF OUR PARENTS

CONTENTS

[ix]

ILLUSTRATIONS

PREFACE

This little book is the outgrowth of studies
undertaken a number of years ago in connection with my volume, *The Commedia dell'
Arte,* published in New York in 1912. It
makes no great claim to originality or even to
completeness of scholarly record, but only attempts to present accurately to English readers
a few of the outstanding and picturesque figures in the Italian theater during and shortly
after Shakespeare's lifetime, some of whom
the Elizabethan dramatists may possibly have
seen and of most of whom they certainly had
heard. The lives of these men and women,
vivid in themselves, are somewhat important
also in the history of their profession, since
their trials and triumphs show clearly the un-

certainties of artistic careers bound in complete dependence to aristocratic patrons.

My debts to the Italian and French historians who have printed most of the original letters and documents here translated and arranged, are fully recognized in my notes. In further acknowledgment I should like to thank many Italian friends who have generously opened their libraries to me or helped me with letters of introduction, among them chiefly Signor Emilio Rè of the Archivio di Stato in Rome, Dr. G. M. Monti of Bari, Professor Torelli of the Archivio at Mantua, and the very kind directors of the Archivio at Modena. My thanks are also due to the editors of the *Modern Language Review* for permission to reprint the chapter on "G. B. Andreini as a theatrical innovator."

W. S.

ITALIAN ACTORS
of the
RENAISSANCE

Winifred Smith

A TRAVELING COMPANY OF ITALIAN ACTORS,
16TH CENTURY

(Frescoes from Schloss Trausnitz)

CHAPTER I

ACTORS are notoriously interesting but unaccountable people, uncertain in their temperaments, given to wandering about in a most unsettled way, subject to extraordinary ups and downs of fortune. They themselves are probably no different essentially to-day from what they were three hundred years ago, but the conditions of their lives have changed somewhat; they still have alternate moments of glory and depression, they still wander, they still are somewhat unaccountable, yet on the whole they have won their fight in civilized countries for the recognition of their art as art and as a socially important one. In general they no longer apologize for it at great length, assuring the public that it is justified by being actually a sermon in disguise. Dramatists do

[3]

that sometimes,—Mr. Bernard Shaw in speaking of plays does little else but assert that they are to be endured and even enjoyed as sugared pills are swallowed, wholesome doses of agreeably disguised medicine,—but actors are on the whole theory free, accepted for their own worth and, within the limits of their talents, allowed to live their own lives. Moreover, they very seldom now, as in the past, depend absolutely on one patron. The public, the managers' associations, the dramatists' leagues, do of course to-day limit the actor's freedom, but he can now counter in his own interest with his own Equity Association, his own managers, even his own organized subscription theaters.

In the sixteenth century conditions were quite different. Before 1560 actors had hardly emerged in southern Europe from a state of serfdom and vagabondage; they could not actually be sold, like the company Stanislavsky describes in early nineteenth-century Russia, but they might be kidnaped, tortured, imprisoned without trial, even assassinated, by their superiors; they had almost no independence of movement, and lived from hand to mouth practicing their art under many vexatious restrictions from church and state, taxed for the benefit of the poor, the clergy and the prince, and unable to regulate their affairs save in the narrowest limits.

In all the countries of Europe actors suffered from the tyranny or oppressive favor of their patrons; everywhere the leaders of troupes had similar difficulties in forming and in keeping together their companies and in pleasing their capricious masters; universally the humbler members of the organizations made trouble, both for their leaders and for their employers, through jealous plots and insubordination; in almost no recorded instance was it possible for players to gain real and perma-

nent independence and certainty of subsistence, no matter how hard and constant
their toil. The limitation of their opportunities and the galling restraints of their dependence may easily be read here and there in the
works of the dramatists of all countries, but
may perhaps be most plainly seen in the mass
of documents which still survive to record the
lives of certain Italians who, in the terms of
their contemporaries, "made the stage illustrious" between 1560 and 1700. It is from
these records that I have selected some facts
and some letters that are interesting in themselves and significant in the history of the actor's profession.

In one particular the Italians' experience
differed from that of their foreign rivals; in
all their companies they included a number,
always three and often several, regularly
trained women, who added enormously to the
success of their plays and who also occasioned

endless complications in their troupes' and scandals to the more puritanical among their spectators and critics.[1] To Nashe and to Thomas Heywood, and they must have seen the best as well as the worst, all these women were no more than a kind of "squirting, baudie comedians" who could not have led decent lives or have showed forth the "honest ensamples" which it was the function of playing to exhibit; to many of the Roman priests of their own country they were equally anathema; in Spain the warfare waged against them was particularly continuous and bitter;[2] yet they persevered in their careers, added literary laurels to their crowns, became at least as famous as their husbands and brothers, and assuredly were the chief cause for that superiority of their country's plays so generally recognized by their audiences if not by their envious rivals.

[1] See Notes, p. 189.

The presence of women and their prominence in these troupes is undoubtedly to be accounted for in two ways: in part through a recognition of the close connection that existed in Italy from the fifteenth to the seventeenth century between wandering charlatan showmen and actors of the regular drama, and in part through a study of the important place assigned women in all Italian courtly theories of life. When among the *cantimbanchi* called in to enliven a princely wedding, female dancers and singers were found to be of no less talent and beauty than youths performing with them, the great ladies before whom they exhibited their tricks and sang their songs naturally interested themselves in rewarding and encouraging such feminine genius, and where princesses like Isabella d'Este were fairly numerous and powerful, their generosity was influential in early establishing and long maintaining the fashion of including actresses

THE PALACE OF THE ESTE, FERRARA, ABOUT 1500

among the dramatic "servants" of aristocratic houses. In vain classicists pointed back to Terence, protesting that women should have no part or merely a silent one on the stage; in vain the church, recalling the Garden of Eden, thundered against the abuses and temptations fostered by the charms and wiles of Eve when exhibited in public spectacles,—the actresses continued to be sufficiently favored by their noble patronesses, and, incidentally, sufficiently welcome on more than one account to their noble patrons, to hold their positions and even to defend them by learned disquisitions of Platonic inspiration, upon the divinity of all beauty and genius, feminine as well as masculine. Their apologist, Niccolò Barbieri, in his little *Supplication* defending the theater as he knew it at first hand, says that it is far better for women than for boys to play female rôles, both for reasons of morality and of art; that women have to be met and their charms withstood everywhere, since they are "half the world," and that therefore the stage is as good a place as any for learning to admire them impersonally; finally that, since it must be admitted some actresses take advantage of their opportunities to tempt young men, they ought rather to be thanked as teachers of the ways and perils of vice than to be prevented from showing such useful warnings.[3]

While this theoretic battle raged over their heads the women generally took the best way to establish their right to self-expression and independent subsistence by making themselves indispensable through perfection in their art; they occupied themselves, together with the men in their companies, to quote again from Barbieri, in improving their talents and consolidating their position in every way, choosing to study and translate the classics of several languages, to learn beautiful passages from them, to imitate great poets by their own original compositions, and to acquire all that was to be known of the science and philosophy of the time, as, he adds, is easy of proof from the list of their many published works.[4] They were so skilled in memorizing that a certain Celia is commended for learning new rôles "at sight"; they were so eager to practice all the arts that many of them went in for sculpture and painting as well as for the various kinds of music, vocal and instrumental, considered absolutely essential to their equipment; [5] moreover many of them were so pious that they gave alms of their earnings, dedicated their children to the church, wore hair shirts under their gay costumes and died at last in religious retirement, fasting and praying for the forgiveness of their sins of worldliness or worse.[6]

Among them, men and women alike, were of course many mean scoundrels, many hypocrites, some murderers, more thieves, and not a few slovenly artists and commonplace souls whose virtues and talents were insufficient to meet the demands of their profession or the great vicissitudes of their fortunes; these last have for the most part passed into oblivion, leaving to the historian a sense of their presence that is like a dark mist around the bright light shining from the memory of their leaders. All together, geniuses and nonentities, worked to create a beautifully expressive art, to diffuse the culture of their country abroad and to add to it at home; all together suffered opprobrium and honor, lavish reward and unjust punishment; all strove more or less unconsciously, more or less successfully, to better their social position, to put the actor's career on a par with the poet's and painter's, and to bring the professional actor class into a better repute than during the middle ages the church had allowed it to hold.

CHAPTER II

EARLY COMPANIES, DEPENDENT AND INDEPENDENT

AS early as the last quarter of the fifteenth century the great houses of Este and Gonzaga began to cultivate their passion for the theater. Isabella d'Este has left many letters indicating the extravagant love she and her father, her sister the Duchess of Milan, and her husband the Duke of Mantua, cherished for the stage of their time as well as the way they built and shaped that stage for future generations. Isabella writes of her father's private theater at Ferrara on the occasion of her brother's marriage to Lucrezia Borgia (1502),[1] as an immense square hall, holding full five thousand persons, with a great dais at one end, the ceiling, floor and steps to

[15]

which were covered with green, red and white carpets,—perhaps, though this she does not hint, intended to symbolize the theological virtues of faith, hope and charity, cryingly needed in greeting so dubious an honor as alliance with the tainted Borgia bride. In the middle of the hall the women were seated, at its sides the men, guests being admitted first and the Ferrarese themselves later. Five comedies were given during the festivities, all classical and all gorgeously costumed with special sets of garments, one hundred and ten of them, made for the occasion and exhibited beforehand to the public in order that the Duke might not be accused of meanly using the same outfit in more than one play. The comedies were given in Latin and might possibly have been a trifle tedious had each play not been enlivened by most elaborate interludes of spectacle, music and dancing, all allegorical in theme, of course, and far more palatable to that princely-childish audience than mere Plautus and Terence unadorned.

For more than a hundred years after this brilliant fête the houses of Mantua and Ferrara were patrons in chief of the Italian theater. Isabella's brother, Alfonso I, built a pleasure ground on an island in the Po (1520), which became in time the most famous of outdoor delights, as its owner and his heirs kept up the practice of entertaining their guests there by plays and pastorals performed in the open. "All imaginable pleasures, such as gardens, fountains, woods, fields, vineyards, and divers kinds of tame and wild animals" existed on Belvedere, as the isle was called, and each detail was made to contribute toward a wonderful setting for poetic drama.[2] The lovely background, indeed, could not always quite reconcile the spectators to the tedium of over-ambitious attempts at long classical representations, such as a comedy which lasted five

[17]

hours and a tragedy that began at ten in the evening and droned on till long after dawn, of which a hearer writes that it was perfect in scenic setting and "bore out what I remember to have read, that tragedies should move to wrath and pity, for this one moved us to wrath against the poet and to pity for the spectators, since it lasted six hours in a cold place, most tediously." [3] Another play dragged out its "harsh prose, very ill-pronounced" for seven long hours,[4] till it was marvel that any one endured to listen to the end.

Yet as the professional actors improved in knowledge and common sense such awkward experiments gradually gave place to a better order of dramas. Tasso seems himself to have directed the rehearsals of his short and beautiful pastoral, *Aminta,* at least for its first performance in simple form, on the Island of Belvedere, June, 1573, collaborating for the occasion with the Gelosi, an already famous

ALFONSO D'ESTE I, THIRD DUKE OF FERRARA, 1505-34

troupe of traveling players, referred to at this time as "the actors who every year, summoned by His Highness, come at the end of autumn and go with him to the seashore, where for one whole carnival season, to their great gain and to the pleasure of the entire city, they serve him by playing comedies; they are very ready in imitating all kinds of persons and all human actions, especially those which are apt to rouse laughter, in the which they are so excelling that they would move to mirth even Heraclitus himself." [5]

Here is an important early reference to a troupe already solidly organized under patronage of a noble house. Yet there exist still earlier documents proving that groups of entertainers were attempting to organize themselves independently. What became of these rash men is not altogether clear; perhaps they did not succeed in their gesture toward freedom,—certainly they had no such long history as some of the companies attached to princely houses. They probably disbanded soon, for although their rules, like those for other groups, were not dissimilar to the regulations binding medieval gilds, there was actually in the sixteenth century no recognized Italian gild of actors and consequently no strong organization to which companies aspiring to independence from patrons might attach themselves.

The attempt to copy gild models may be clearly seen from a set of curious provisos found in the archives of Padua, under date of February 15, 1545.[6] The eight men involved—there are no women mentioned here—are headed by Ser Maphio, "called Zannino da Padova," and agree to form "a fraternal company," and to observe "without hate or rancor,—but with love," the following laws, from Easter, 1545, to Carnival, 1546:

1. The object is to play comedies "from place to place," obeying Ser Maphio.
2. In case of illness the sick man is to be supported by the common funds.
3. The company is to go all together to play under Zannino's rule.
4. The money gained is to be kept in a small chest with three keys held by three different members of the group; this chest is to contain all moneys taken in and is never to be opened nor cash removed from it except by consent of all. In case any member of the troupe should take it into his head to run away and abandon the others, "to his great dishonor and shame," he shall lose all rights and privileges and all use of the money, which is to be kept for division among the whole company, "fraternally united."
5. A fine is to be levied on those who run away, 100 lire, one third of which is to go to the "governors (rettori) of the place where we are," one third to the poor, and one third to the company.
6. A horse is to be bought from the common funds, "to carry the luggage."

7. Money in the chest is to be divided in Padua in June.
8. In September the company is to travel.
9. Members are not to gamble with each other at cards or in other ways, except for food.

The history of this Venetian and Paduan troupe can be followed only a little way; it is known to have played in Rome in 1549, after being reformed in 1546 with nine new members; there its leader died, as the result of a bloody feud with a horse-tamer, who, however, as is recorded in a Latin document, recognized his culpability, made peace with Maphio before his death, and promised to help support the comedian's young daughter.

Thirty years later, in 1575, another group of men drew up a somewhat similar agreement in Naples, "as to the making and playing comedies in this city and other lands and territories of this kingdom and any other kingdoms, provinces, duchies and places whatsoever in the world." As in the case just cited, these companions are to forfeit money if they fail to play their parts and the fines "are to be paid in whatsoever part of the world justice reigns"; but illness or imprisonment may be pled in excuse for absence, and the fine in these cases remitted. The pay is to be divided equally among all, and a servant is to be paid jointly by all, the money to be counted and distributed every Sunday night. This troupe, more religious in profession than Maphio's, insists that each member confess three times a year, that any member hearing another swear must denounce him (to the Inquisition, says Croce) and that no gambling be allowed in their hall.[7] Pious and well-intentioned though they were, they left no other trace in history than this expression of their ideals. They may have merged into another company with a strong patron or have scattered after a season's wandering because of the competition or the hostility of rivals or of moralists.

Certainly mere professions of piety were not alone sufficient to keep traveling players out of trouble. The church, not easily lulled by well-sounding words, was never friendly to the stage. In 1568 the ecclesiastical authorities in Bologna listed a formidable number of reasons, typical of many urged against actors generally, why "Zani's comedies" (probably the improvised plays later called *commedie dell' arte*) should not be encouraged.[8] "They play for the most part lascivious and dishonest pieces which corrupt good morals," "they are generally vagabonds of evil repute, who carry about with them women of bad life," they bear away from the city a great deal of money and give cause to youths and boys to rob their fathers in order to pay for a play, and to run away from school and shop; "to the performances crowd courtesans, young men and boys, whence arise occasions for a thousand sins;" moreover, the year being one of scarcity, it is unwise to throw away money, and in these heretical times, when "religion is so infested by the infidels," the number of performances must be cut down to three a week, after the harvest, and only those pieces are to be allowed from which censors have removed all "immoral words," allusions to Holy Writ or "blame of the priesthood" and no characters are to take part in clerical dress; "women, boys, priests and friars" are to be shut out entirely from performances, and no processions of actors through the streets "with drums or other instruments or dressed for the play," are to be tolerated in the city.

Such decrees against the *comici,* frequent in the annals of the time, and doubtless immensely irritating to the actors, were, nevertheless, not strictly observed in most cities.[9] Sometimes, as in Rome, January, 1574, there was scandal because cardinals and priests attended a "dishonest" play and the Holy Father forbade the comedians all performances in private houses, schools and seminaries, "as very dangerous and of great distraction to youth." [10] Sometimes, as in Paris in 1571, the secular powers refused permission to a troupe to act in the city, for their comedies "teach only folly and adultery and serve as a school of debauchery to the youth of both sexes." In this case the actors, the famous company of the Gelosi, not masterless men, but firmly supported by the king, their patron, were able to flourish a royal license in the faces of the city fathers and to continue to play, to their great gain, in the Salle de Bourbon. [11]

The church and state, indeed, rarely saw eye to eye in the matter of licensing actors, for priests of the type of Archbishop Carlo Borromeo of Milan were shocked by the obscenities and indecencies in "these abominable and

LUCREZIA BORGIA, WIFE OF ALFONSO D'ESTE

most rascally plays," while the aristocracy thoroughly enjoyed them.[12] Occasionally Heaven seemed to be visibly encouraging churchly severity, as in 1576, when the plague broke out in Milan during the festivities for Don Juan of Austria, but more often clerics bowed to the superior force of the secular arm and contented themselves by prescribing the times and places of performances or going through the motion of censoring plays before presentation. There was certainly no interference of either religious or lay inspiration based on moral grounds that was effective enough to prevent the *Intermedii* given in private houses from being much like the modern Follies in their exploitation of beautiful actresses, posing as Venus or Spring or the Graces, and adorned only by a few roses or their own long locks.[13] As to the "teaching delightfulness and delightful teaching," which Philip Sidney, in imitation of Italian critics, declared to be the aim of dramatic writing, all the *comici* claimed to be interested in just that and based their defenses of their profession on that high ground and no other.[14] Perhaps Machiavelli's solemn enunciation of the moral aim of comedy, whether or not spoken with his tongue in his cheek, is the neatest voicing of the prevalent theoretic point of view:

It is certainly of great value to men, and especially to youths, to know the avarice of an old man, the fury of a lover, the tricks of a servant, the greediness of a parasite, the misery of a poor man, the ambition of a rich one, the deceits of a courtesan, the little faith there is in every man; these examples fill comedies and all these things may with greatest usefulness be represented. (*La Clizia.*)

Yet the princes of the Renaissance, like the leisured classes to-day, however much they profess morality, cared little enough for "examples" so long as they were amused by the plays given before them, nor, as Barbieri observes, did the actors, "who serve princes for their entertainment," really attempt to offer moral counsels. What aristocratic audiences could not endure was boredom, still less impertinence or denial of their wishes. They recompensed largely those who pleased them and punished severely those who did not, as various records make quite plain. Doubtless their wish to bind firmly to themselves the best of the wandering mimes accounts for the small success of such troupes as Maphio's, which attempted an organization free of patronage. A few instances will show the favors and powers of patrons, pleased or displeased.

The Ferrarese agent in Paris in 1572 writes his master of the king's delight in the Zanni, the only good actor in a company of Italians then at court, "who are really, to give them their proper name, beasts"; yet the clown is given forty-five scudi a week by royal command in order to keep him.[15] The accomplished Gelosi, whom some historians identify with this "bestial" company, were notable for their many changes of fortune, from favor to disfavor, although on the whole they were more fortunate than most. In a letter to the Governor of Genoa, 1572, they say a great deal about their "honest and exemplary comedies," which are universally desired by the nobility and have been approved by the Archbishop of Milan, "the Most Reverend Carlo Borremeo, mirror of Christian life"; they say nothing of their long struggle to obtain his grudging consent to their playing in his diocese, but add that they have never been exiled from any city.[16]

The final boast they could not long make, however. In May, 1579, a ducal decree exiled the Gelosi from the city and state of Mantua, apparently for reasons explained in a letter preserved in the Archives of Modena: [17]

The Duke of Mantua wanted a comedy which the Gelosi played with especial success, in which all the characters were hunchbacked. His Highness laughed constantly and took the greatest pleasure in the piece. When it was over, he called the principal actors and asked which one was the author of the piece. Zanni said he was, but Pantalone and Graziano each claimed the honor, expecting a good recompense. So the Duke, furious, had them all imprisoned and condemned them to the gallows. The poor unfortunates were put to the torture and had all the difficulty in the world to obtain their lives from the Duke, who kept repeating that he wanted pieces composed by good actors, not by this band of rascals.

In such cases as these the actors were entirely in the power of their patrons; they had surrendered such rights of free citizenship as they had had, in return for liveries, high pay and more or less regular employment on the terms of upper servants. Consequently they occasionally had to suffer from the whims and passions of their "natural lords." The more intelligent of the *comici* seem to have been persuaded that their best good in the long run was to be found in service, and on the whole history justifies them; they were more often protected and rewarded than punished. Princes therefore were able to attach to themselves, from the latter third of the sixteenth century, the best of the professional players in effective and somewhat stable troupes.

CHAPTER III

TO the year 1580 belongs a series of letters and records which throw some light on the methods taken by princely patrons in the formation of acting companies and their gradual attachment to certain aristocratic families. In 1580 the young Prince, afterward Duke Vincenzo I of Mantua, seems to have set about the foundation of a troupe by high-handedly ordering a few members, the most accomplished, apparently, of one company to be transferred into another, at which act of tyranny the leader of the band threatened with decimation, a woman named Vittoria Piissimi, complained to a secretary of the Duke in terms which he reported as follows: [1]

She says she doesn't know why His Highness the Prince tries to injure her by dismembering her company in this way, for she has never failed in duty to His Highness, neither by day nor by night nor at any hour, and now for all reward she has to swallow this affront.

The secretary ventures to recommend that the order be rescinded, as Vittoria has in fact always been ready to serve at any minute.

Her sincere eagerness to please and her need for protection are sufficiently indicated by her letter of apology for not having been able to play at Mantua the past carnival season and of hope that she and Pedrolino, one of her fellows, have not lost favor by their failure to come. That they had not, but that on the contrary the Prince was attempting to make these two players the nucleus of his chief company, joining others of fame to them, appears in a rather confused letter from a well-known clown, the Arlecchino, Drusiano Martinelli, the same who is shown by an English record to have acted with his troupe in London, before

THE CASTLE OF ST. GEORGE, MANTUA

Lent, 1577-8.[2] Drusiano writes to the Prince Vincenzo of Mantua:

I have heard that Your Highness would like me and my wife to enter the troupe of Pedrolino, a thing which I would willingly have done for the love of Your Highness and because I've given the affair so much of my heart's blood, and just to obey my lord and master, for I could do nothing in the world that would be so dear to me. However Pedrolino's people have made an arrangement with Vittoria's and I have a good company—for I manage mine better now—so that we shall make the 3d troupe. [Probably meaning the third attached to the Duke of Mantua.] Now if Your Highness wishes plays in Mantua this carnival time, there is no better company than mine, since the Gelosi and the Confidenti [Vittoria's] are to be in Venice; wherefore if Your Highness wants us for this carnival, say "yes" or "no" to the bearer of this—who is my father—either on paper or by word of mouth so that he can bring it me, but it would be better to write if we are to come, because my companions would obey more readily. If we do not hear within a month we will go to Naples for the Carnival.

No more! Humbly embracing Your Highness' knees, Your Highness'

Most Humble Servant,

DRUSIANO MARTINELLI,

Husband of Madonna Angelica.

From Florence, 17 Sept., 1580.

The troublesome couple, Angelica and Drusiano, who will later reappear in this history, seem at the moment not to have taken so prominent a place as several other players in the Prince's negotiations "for a most excellent company," for instance a popular actress, Giulia Beolco, to whom Vincenzo during his search writes in a wheedling tone of entreaty requesting that she join his favorites, the Confidenti:

CARISSIMA MIA: The Company of the Confidenti, by whom I am now served, wishes to have you as one of their number, a thing which would also be well pleasing to me, for I have heard of your excellence; wherefore it would give me no small satisfaction if you, putting aside every other engagement, would come here to serve me, obliging them who love you much.

Yours to do you pleasure,
THE PRINCE OF MANTUA.

Giulia seems to have resisted this plea, though flattering and from a nobleman young, handsome, rich and freehanded with his wealth; she doubtless thought twice over a proposition that made her no definite offer and that would if accepted bring her into subordination to Vittoria Piissimi, the *prima donna* of the Confidenti. That popular actors did resist even to the point of refusing similar enticements is clear enough from a letter of Francesco Andreini to Vincenzo on the subject of the same negotiations, dragged out at the time of writing (1583) to the third year:

. . . Since I am so greatly obliged by the most noble grace of Your Serene Highness, I can do nothing, to my great grief, except thank your most courteous thought for having considered me and my wife fit to be enrolled in so worthy a company. But being bound and tied to the Gelosi and more particularly to the well-known Alvise Michiele, director of the public theater in Venice, I am constrained not to accept the proposal and the wish of Your Highness; to form this one company for you [this is bold] three would have to be broken up, which is a difficult thing, even though to Your Highness every most difficult thing is very easy to do. Further, finding myself alone in Ferrara I could not without asking leave of my companions fail to offer you the company of the whole Gelosi for your service. With which, praying you to hold me and my wife among the number of your least servants. . . .

FRANCESCO ANDREINI,
Comico Geloso.[3]

But alas for youthful ambitions! The Duke, Vincenzo's father, like the feudal tyrant he was beneath his layer of classical culture, grew jealous of his son's enterprise in engaging players for the court and forbade the Prince's license any validity. Vincenzo had usurped one of his father's privileges by sending out a permit to the Duke's servants in May, 1585, as follows:

By virtue of this present, we grant the actors called the Uniti [apparently the band brought together from the other companies] license to play in this city after to-day for all the time they shall remain and in guarantee we give them this paper signed by our notary and sealed with our chief seal.[4]

The Duke's reply, through one of his secretaries, is loud with the fury he must have felt on learning of his heir's interference with court matters, an interference expressed too in such a good imitation of his own lordly manner; his proclamation says plainly that no actor may play in the city without the *Ducal* permission, and further, in another note:

His Highness commands that the actors now playing here [in Mantua] shall immediately be given order to depart without stopping at all; they merit still more severe punishment for having said they had *His Highness'* permission to remain in Mantua and act when that was not true. This order you are requested to convey to them with a question as to whom they obeyed in making for themselves so falsely a shield of His Highness' person.[5]

Notwithstanding this rebuke, Vincenzo finally, after a long struggle not ended till he himself became Duke, assembled his company. In 1589 Vittoria Piissimi, former head of the Confidenti, and Isabella Andreini, leading lady of the Gelosi, the two most famous actresses of the age, were playing side by side, alternately as *prima* and *seconda donna,* in the troupe of the Gelosi, "the Duke of Mantua's servants." A contemporary and a severe judge of the stage, Tommaso Garzoni, praises the two women equally; Vittoria is "a beautiful witch of love . . . with harmonious and pleasing speech, accomplished and graceful actions, affable and sweet style, enticing and charming

FRANCESCO ANDREINI

(From his *Bravure del Cap. Spavento*, 1615)

sight, savorsome and sugared smiles, a carriage haughty and noble." Isabella he calls the "ornament of the stage, a proud spectacle of virtue no less than of beauty, who has so adorned her profession that while the world lasts, while the centuries endure, while times and seasons have life, every tongue, every voice will echo her famous name." Both ladies must have been of comparatively virtuous life as well as of professional excellence or Garzoni would not have spoken so enthusiastically, for he vituperates actors who shame human nature with their vices, and only praises those whose careers show "most moral habits of living."

Isabella, to whom was due most of the fame of the Gelosi, lived her forty-two years in an unusual brilliance of glory. Of Venetian family, born at Padua in 1562, educated classically with all the thoroughness of a great lady or a mime of the Cinquecento, a member of the Pavian Academy of the Intenti, poet and dramatist, she devoted herself from the day of her marriage at the age of sixteen principally to her husband's profession, the stage. Her bent seems to have been strongly intellectual from her youth, for she says in one of her dedications,—and it is possible to feel her sincerity under the vicious windings of a fashionable style,—

Anaxagoras, when he was asked why he was born, said, "To contemplate the stars," which thing since it could only be done through the medium of knowledge, shows us that every one who is born awakes with the desire for wisdom; now I, sent by the Creator of this world to be its citizen, and having had born in me by chance a desire for knowledge far more ardent than it is in many women of our age, who, though by study several of them have become noted, wish only (may this be said with exception of those who to the highest and most glorious thoughts have entirely devoted themselves) to labor with their needle, their distaff, and their embroidery; since then, I say, this desire for knowledge was born in me

most ardently, I wished with all my strength to
nourish it. And although at my birth Fortune
was niggardly of the gift which is essential to
this enterprise [a roundabout way of saying
modestly that she had small intellect!] and
although I have always been very far from a
state of leisure . . . nevertheless in order not
to wrong the talent which God and Nature gave
me and in order that my life might not be
called a continuous slumber, and because I
know that every good citizen is bound to his
utmost to benefit his fatherland, I could, so to
speak, hardly read before I devoted myself to
the composition of my *Mirtilla,* a pastoral
poem, which has since been printed. . . .
After this I struggled with the fatigue of writing my poems, and not content with these
efforts, managed to steal from time and the
demands of my exhausting profession, a few
hours to devote to the composition of these
letters.[6]

So well received were Isabella's efforts to
improve her mind and her countrymen's
morals through the "delightful teaching" in
her literary works, that, as a contemporary

records, "she was accepted and crowned with laurel by the members of the Academy of the Intenti of Padua," [7] and again in Rome "she was crowned in effigy between the pictures of Tasso and Petrarch, after a banquet offered her by the Most Eminent Cardinal Cintio Aldobrandini, the great Mecænas of the virtuosi, where at table there were six learned cardinals, Tasso . . . and other very famous poets, among whom in lovely rivalry writing and composing sonnets, the Andreina most wittily, next after the great Torquato, carried away the finest praise of all." [8]

Her *Lettere,* now so tediously unreadable in their stilted expression of idealistic commonplace, were printed six times in fairly large editions, between 1607 and 1647; her other works also sold well. Medals were struck with her head on the obverse side and Fame blowing the trumpet of her glory on the reverse. Poets wrote innumerable sonnets punning on her name, and recounting her accomplishments in music and poetry and acting. Her husband, the first and most fervent of her admirers, devoted his life after her death to preserving her literary remains and her fame, dedicating his own works to her memory,—"Isabella, fair in name, fair in body and most fair in soul." [9]

Finally at her premature death in Lyons the municipality granted her a public and magnificent funeral, with a bronze tablet in the church where she was buried. The epitaph written by her husband commemorates "a Woman preëminent for virtue, The ornament of morality, Faithful to her marital relations, Religious, pious, a friend to the Muses, The chief of theatrical artists, who here awaits the Resurrection." [10]

Seven children were left to mourn her and to praise her as an excellent mother,—four daughters, all hidden safely away from the world's temptations in Mantuan convents, one son a monk, one a soldier under the Gonzaga, and one the inheritor of her talents, the actor-poet, Giambattista Andreini.[11] Tasso, Chiabrera, Marino and many other poets in Italy and France saluted Isabella's memory as they had her triumphs in life, with sonnets and songs: "the modern Sappho," "the loveliest Siren of the Stage," "an unconquerable Clio," "the Phœnix of the Italian Theater," "one of the Gods disguised as a mortal," a woman "who had no little knowledge of the problems of philosophy," [12] such were the terms in which they celebrated a genius all the more striking for its appearance in a woman's form. One questions only whether these mostly academic poets may not have been deceived into worship of their own shadows as they acclaimed in her a dexterity of handling which carried to its extreme an ingenuity of tenuous statement, a thin spinning-out of abstractions, which they would themselves have been glad to equal could they as systematically have substituted concepts for the more direct actualities of experience in their poetry.

The trick, for trick it easily became, of putting commonplace into tortured complexities of phrase, appears to have been second nature to Isabella; her not very numerous extant letters to the Duke of Mantua reek of the same style as her printed works. For instance at the time Vincenzo was favoring two companies other than the Gelosi, she writes: [13]

The ill that comes upon us by our own fault is most easy to bear, but that which falls without our sin, is intolerable; intolerable therefore is that evil and a most grave displeasure, Most Excellent my Lord, in finding myself little in favor with Your Highness,— favor which I very reasonably esteem as my life, disgrace which seems to have befallen me by the crime of others. But granting that my ungracious fate may have made me blamable in some manner toward Your Highness, I pray you, my kind Lord, to remember that Princes are merely Gods on earth, and as it is not fitting that Gods should cherish wrath or contempt toward mortals, so it is not right for you, my God on earth, to be angry or scornful toward me, your meanest servant; rather as it suits great souls to forget offenses, if I have committed through my folly any wrong, or if I have been injured by another's lie, I rejoice to think that Your Highness cannot but forget the offense and pardon it entirely; of which I and all the world will be assured when it shall please Your Highness to recall me to your most desired service, as I pray with all affection you may do. Begging God to give Your Highness and Your Most Serene Wife and Children all his greatest blessings,

From Bologna, 27 November, 1596,

Your Highness' Most Humble Servant,

ISABELLA ANDREINI.

But it was not lack of favor that the Andreini had ever long to complain of; rather they and their company were often embarrassed by too much wrangling among the great for the honor of their services. After 1571 the royal house of France frequently made it impossible for them to play before their natural lords and protectors in Mantua for months and even for years together. The royal and noble protectors of the artists were stronger than their enemies, at least for a long period of years, and the Italians benefited by their close bond with the royal house through Marie de' Medici, a bond of traditional service on their part and of patronage on their superiors'. No writ of prohibition from Parlement, no thunderous sermons from the pulpit, affected their popularity; in fact, for all their piety, they took a malicious pleasure in drawing audiences away from the representations given by the Confrèrie de la Passion and in forcing comparisons between the crowds at their own performances and the meager attendance at the sermons and Moralities of their enemies,[14] all

[57]

the while protesting vehemently that their only aim was to teach morality most effectively by presenting good and evil examples of life in exact models of dramatic art.[15]

It was on the third trip to France, in the winter and spring of 1603-4, that Isabella Andreini received the most marked favor from the French court, especially from Henri IV and his wife, Marie de' Medici. Henri commanded one of his secretaries to facilitate the return of the Andreini and their company to Italy, and his letter leaves no doubt of their having pleased him signally:

MONSIEUR DE VILLEROY, I write you this word to tell you that I have given permission to the actress, Isabelle, and her company to return to Italy: of which I notify you in order that you may make no difficulty about the passport which they need for their journey; let it be inclusive enough for them to take with them their baggage, their arms, rings, jewels and the money which they will declare to you.

HENRI II AND CATHERINE DE' MEDICI
(From Clouet's portrait)

May God have you in his holy keeping!
This XIII April, at Fontainebleau.

HENRY.[16]

Marie de' Medici adds her tribute in a note
to the Duchess of Mantua:

MY SISTER: Isabella Andreini, the actress,
is returning to Italy, so I write you a word in
her behalf to beg you to help her and honor her
with your good graces and kindness in whatsoever she may need, assuring yourself that while
she was here she gave the greatest satisfaction
both by her own and her troupe's performances
and both to the king, my lord, and to me.
Therefore I recommend her to you with affection. . . .[17]

A more definite impression of the "satisfaction" given by the actress and her companions
is to be found on a page in the contemporary
history by Pierre Mathieu, recounting among
the famous events of the year 1604, how "The
troupe of Isabelle Andreini played before the
king and queen. She is an Italian woman,

learned in poetry, whose equal has not yet been found for elegance, readiness and ease in all sorts of styles suited to the stage. If she had lived in Greece when comedy was in vogue statues would have been raised to her and she would have been crowned with flowers in the theater. . . . She was seen and listened to with great applause, and her comedies, serviceable to morality and often useful to princes in their diversion of the people,—as the clown said to Emperor Augustus,—charmed away vain thoughts and took the place of useless pursuits in Paris." [18]

The Andreini were, of course, not the only actor family who were richly favored by princes and employed by them during these years to divert their subjects and to silence critical murmurs. The Martinelli were almost equally distinguished though they were far from equally trustworthy, at least in their private characters. The first note of Drusiano's and his brother

Tristano's attachment to the Mantuan house is that already given under date of September 17, 1580; the summer of the same year saw them both at Ferrara, whence a court official wrote rather slightingly of them to the Duke, saying that none of the company was of importance except "the woman, who is of good presence . . . and sings to the lute quite charmingly; there are also [he adds] some youngsters who dance decently." [19] Whether or not the "woman" were Angelica, the later notorious wife of Drusiano, is not clear, but that the reference is probably to her seems strengthened by the fact that she was with the same company, the so-called Nuovi, at Mantua in January, 1582, where the Duke seems to have made a fool of himself for her sake; says the Florentine ambassador to Ferrara:

The Duke is so much carried away with this actress that he continually takes part in masquerades. [20]

Of Drusiano's visit to London unfortunately nothing is known beyond the reference to him in the Lord Mayor's order that he may play in the city from January 13, 1577, till Lent, nor, although in 1588 Drusiano tells his mother in a note from Madrid, "We shall be all this year in Spain," does he add any details as to their doings there.[21]   Indeed it is not until 1591 [22] that anything is clearly known about him and his wife.

On October 27, 1591, Drusiano writes from Milan to the Captain Alessandro Catrani, a "protector" of Angelica at the Mantuan court, the following startling account of a stage feud in which his wife played the part of injured heroine:

This will give you to know that Gasparo Inpriale here in Milan has been plotting to disfigure Angelica's face by the orders of the actress, Margarita,[23] without any regard to the promise given to His Highness, and it has hap-

pened in this way. Margarita prostituted herself to Gasparo in return for his promise to disfigure Angelica; he having heard that His
Highness was sending us to Milan suddenly,
as Your Excellency knows, came to Mantua to
arrange with her how it was to be done and at
our departure he followed us but without joining us; nevertheless he came to Milan and remains to carry out the business. But Heaven
has ruled that the plot be laid open, for God
inspired a chief gentleman of this place . . .
to inquire of Leandro, who in the past had been
an intimate friend of his, what kind of a
woman Angelica is and what kind of life she
leads. Leandro told him she was a married
woman who honestly practices the art of acting
and that she had been sent hither by His Highness [of Mantua] who had always favored her
with his grace, and he told him further the
favors, the compliments and the gifts that His
Highness had showered upon her. These
words affected the gentleman so much that he
told how Gasparo, through the medium of a
great friend of his, had asked his help in slash-
ing Angelica's face, and how he had thought

this enterprise unworthy of one of his station, and, in parting, particularly that for love of His Highness he had not wished to keep the affair secret but quietly to discover it, and, in order to convince Leandro how true it was, he advised letting it go a little farther, because Gasparo was attempting to make Angelica feel secure by politeness and by giving her presents of eatables so that she would be less wary of him; he added advice that he should not speak of this to any one until told to do so by a priest whom he would send; all this advice Leandro followed and as had been predicted, he found the truth; Gasparo made her presents and attended her and still attends her with the greatest politeness and offers of service. Now the gentleman, being besought by Gasparo to put an end to the affair, yesterday summoned Leandro to him and wished him to warn Angelica (without mentioning *him*), whereupon Leandro begged him to take the matter on himself since he as a gentleman could keep the affair secret. So to-day the gentleman came alone, secretly, to Angelica's room and told her what had passed, affirming that what he had told Leandro was all true and that what

HENRI IV AND MARIE DE' MEDICI

Gasparo had done was by commission of Margarita and that they had let the affair go so
far in order to prove it; and he advised her to
write His Highness, begging for letters to the
Count Piro Visconti here, who has favored
Angelica in a matter which she will describe
to you herself, so that he may give orders that
the business may come to nothing; he said if
she revealed his name he would have her
beaten to pieces though she were at the ends
of the earth; nevertheless if His Highness
wishes to know who the gentleman is and who
favors Gasparo, we will tell him by word of
mouth, and if His Highness has doubts of the
truth of all this and fears it may rise from
malignity, the way for him to clear it up is by
ordering the post secretly to give into his hands
all the letters that may come for Margarita and
Signor Massimigliano, and those that are put
into the post at Mantua for Gasparo Inpriale
and Carlo, who plays *Franceschina* [the
servetta], in comedy and when he has read
them and taken copies, let him reseal them
and send them out again so that they may be
received; thus in one way or the other will
the truth be discovered. Not that I suspect

[69]

Signor Massimigliano or Carlo to be involved in such an affair, but because many of Margarita's letters come enclosed in Sig. Massimigliano's and Gasparo's in Carlo's and the sign is this: if Margarita writes Gasparo recommending her affairs to his care, or bids him remember her or the like, . . . the "remembering" her means the injury to Angelica. . . . Wherefore Your Excellency will do me the favor of letting His Highness know all this and showing him this of mine, begging him on our account to take precautions since we do not know how to defend ourselves from Gasparo, not being sure whether His Highness would be pleased or not, for he bade Angelica to be good and not an enemy to Margarita, these were his words to her. May it please His Highness for the love of God to write the Count Piro in favor of Angelica, or may he allow us to leave Milan and come to Mantua, so that during this carnival we may serve him there. It seems ignoble of me to flee this way, being under His Highness' protection, . . . nevertheless I will do what His Highness commands, advising him that it be secret; all this saddens Angelica, the more that Gasparo comes this carnival to Mantua, so that His Highness having found this to be true can make known what he pleases of it or give me permission to make known that I am a worthy man who always do honor to my fatherland, for we are no brigands.

From Milan, 27 Oct. 1591.

His Highness' most devoted servant,

DRUSIANO MARTINELLI.

Other letters follow protesting that the thing is "most true" and begging the Duke to steal as many letters of Margarita's as he can, in order to send them on to Drusiano and Angelica by "a very private and trusty messenger!" Apparently Vincenzo took the part of the Martinelli in the affair, for a little later (July, 1592) he is told by Captain Catrani that the house commanded for Drusiano in Mantua is quite ready, though it is at the moment occupied by a certain Claudio, "who will leave with a very ill grace." Such an attention on the part of the Duke as providing a home for his "servants" must have been preceded by a definite agreement between him and the Martinelli, binding these distinguished actors to the service of Mantua. Indeed Drusiano writes from Florence, June 10, 1592, that he is exceedingly dissatisfied with the way the Grand Duke of Tuscany rewards him for playing and that he intends immediately placing himself and his wife under the protection of the House of Mantua:

Once in your employ, I can easily find some legitimate excuse to continue serving Your Highness honorably without losing the favor of the Grand Duke entirely. . . . I hope too to be able to show Your Highness some secrets which will be pleasing to you and at the same time useful in great measure.[24]

The arrangement is confirmed by documents of the following year, 1593, recording payments to Drusiano of various sums by the ducal treasurer, e.g. in March, 43 crowns for his

expenses, later other small and large amounts.
But prosperity did not improve Drusiano's
temper; he appears in a very ugly light in a
long letter from his former friend, Captain
Catrani, to a Ducal Councilor, dated 29 April,
1598. The Captain after recounting various
machinations by which he thinks Drusiano—
"a wretch"—has tried to undermine his credit
with the Duke, proceeds to particular griev-
ances: [25]

. . . While Drusiano was last in this city,
about five months in all, he lived chiefly at
my cost, on the money and food which I sent his
wife; he used to wait cheerfully for it though
he knew where it came from, and he himself
arranged for his wife to be with me and to
come to my house while he attempted to do
nothing but sleep, cat and let the world slip
by,—as I have made Your Excellency to know
before this, by several witnesses worthy of
credit. But since about a week ago I sent him
word by the maid that he'd have to find another way of living because I didn't choose to

support him longer, he is furious and talks of resorting to His Highness, especially when I tell him this house is mine because I pay for it . . . and he is treating his wife abominably, as His Highness may easily learn; further because I told him that most of the furniture in the said house is mine, and that I shall need it when I return. These are the real reasons for his having taken flight and for having talked of recourse to His Highness,—not zeal for his honor as he has said, because while I maintained him he consented to everything, like the infamous creature he is. When I discovered that I had a son by his wife, I caused the child to be properly brought up and have kept it near me or the Signora Hippolita Aldegatta for about six years. Drusiano has always known that I regarded the boy as mine and he has never said anything about it, but now, out of spite, knowing how much I love the child, he says he is going to ask His Highness to have it given back to him; I am certain His Highness will have regard to general opinion in this matter. Your Excellency should know that when I was liberated from prison . . . I gave all the furniture I had to the said woman so that she could have something to live on, for her husband had abandoned her; now she asserts that he sold it with some other small affairs of hers to Signor Lodovico Bagno for 200 crowns' credit, the which I have recently abandoned claim to and have contented myself that the said woman should have the money placed to her name, but this wretch seeing that I agree to this arrangement of something in which he had thought to have a part, treats his wife unbelievably ill, vituperating her every minute with curses greater than one would use to an outcast creature. . . . He has left her with no resources so that I had to give her a bed to sleep in, as well as other necessaries for the house . . . while I was out of Italy . . . with which she has maintained herself; otherwise she would have had to beg or to go into business publicly. . . .

That there were two sides to the trouble over Angelica is suggested in a letter from Tristano to the Duke, dated May, 1598, demanding that Drusiano be protected from Captain Catrani, who "has hired bravi to murder him"; "we ask no vengeance, however, [says the brother of the victim] nor even rightful justice; . . . as to the past, let it be no more talked of, so that we may all live justly as Christians." [26]

Notwithstanding the meanness and something more, shown by Drusiano in this affair and others, both he and his brother Tristano managed to keep well in the forefront of the Duke's favor. While Drusiano was playing with the Uniti in 1596, Tristano seems to have been with the Desiosi, who in 1595 had petitioned for permission to play their comedies "with modesty and decency and with good examples," that is, in order to teach virtue! And in 1595 the Duke speaks through his councilor as the assured protector of the Martinelli; in a letter to the Duke of Milan the official greets the friend of Mantua and adds:

The bearer of this to Your Highness will be Drusiano Martinelli, who in the comedies he plays takes the part of Arlecchino; or if not he, some other of the company of the Uniti, who are also called the Company of our Serene Lord, since they serve him privately, and also because they have been united and maintained by his authority. . . . His Highness hopes that they will be allowed to play their comedies in Milan and that they will be given the monopoly in order that all competition may be taken away and with it occasion for scandal.[27]

But by 1599 both brothers seem to have joined the Accesi, for they were called to France with this company by Henri IV in a letter of invitation to Tristano that was only the first of many equally flattering summons:

ARLEQUIN: Your fame having reached me, together with that of the good company of comedians you have in Italy, I have wished to make you cross the mountains and to draw you into my kingdom. So do not fail to make this journey with your troupe cheerfully for love of me; I shall have great pleasure in see-

ing you and in having you in my service and
I promise you shall be well treated to your
advantage and profit and that you shall not
regret the time you give to my service. . . .
Praying God, Arlequin, that he have you in
his holy keeping, from Paris, December 21,
1599.

HENRI.

Not, however, until after Easter was the
Duke of Mantua willing to let his protegés
leave him; on the nineteenth of April, 1600,
he writes to the son of the Duc de Maine, the
Duc d'Aiguillon:

MOST ILLUSTRIOUS AND EXCELLENT AND
VERY HONORABLE COUSIN: As the actors
called the Accesi are about to go to your country to play their comedies, the affection I have
for them on account of their constant situation
under my protection moves me to address myself to Your Excellency's kindness in asking
the support of your favor for them. I beg you
therefore to regard them as especially recom-
mended to you and to grace them as occasion
may offer. I shall be most grateful and shall

be ready to oblige you at all opportunities that may occur. . . .[28]

The recommendation was hardly needed, for these comedians, like the Gelosi, bore their welcome in their own skill. They were so pleasing to the Grand Duke of Savoy that they were detained by him at Turin for some time on their way to France, and again at Lyons they made so favorable an impression upon their audiences that they were obliged to remain there several months. During their sojourn, the king arrived in the city of Lyons to meet and marry his bride, Marie de' Medici, a grand-niece of the Duke of Mantua and therefore a well-inclined patroness of the duke's "Men." When the court took its way northward to Paris, in January, 1601, the Accesi followed in its train and prepared themselves for service at the Louvre.

This journey was marked by one of the violent quarrels which seem always to have been breaking out between members of these troupes, no matter how well treated and how equally paid they may have been. If the complaints of Fritellino (Piermaria Cecchini) are to be believed, Arlecchino (Tristano Martinelli) was planning to assassinate this rival of his, "for fear," says Fritellino, "I shall reveal to His Highness some of his bad tricks, once we are all back in Italy," [29] this accusation being made in a letter to the Duke of Mantua written from Paris, July 3, 1601. What was the occasion of Arlecchino's ill-temper and Fritellino's fear there is no means of knowing; possibly professional jealousy was at the bottom of the trouble, or perhaps one or other of the parties involved had cheated by claiming for himself more than his share of the rich gifts presented to the company by the king and queen.

Bickering was very frequently due to the distribution of the rewards which came to the

THE GELOSI IN A COMIC SCENE

(From a painting in the Carnavalet, Paris)

traveling actors with great irregularity but also
often with great lavishness. Since the custom
when they played in private houses was for
the master of the establishment to give one
large sum to be divided by the leader among
the members of his troupe, it is easy to see
how if the leader were ambitious and avari-
cious, as were both the Martinelli, there must
frequently have been ground for complaint
among his companions. How much, one would
like to know, of the "two or three hundred
ducats," which Tristano in one letter mentions
as an adequate "aid toward expenses" [30] was
he accustomed to give his right-hand man,
Cecchini, after their performances before the
Duke of Savoy or the King of France? When
the sums were smaller the difficulty of parting
with a portion of them would have been even
greater; there is no way of knowing how it was
met, in the case, for instance, of the purse of
fifty ducats paid to Tristano for one comedy

given in Chambéry, August 16, 1613. In
such moments as these, talented artists must
often have regretted the necessity that forced
them to organize into companies, for in the
older, freer days one skillful person who
pleased his patron would be likely to have all
to himself one hundred or more gold pieces,
witness the lucky rope-dancer, to whom Cos-
imo de' Medici paid this lavish sum in 1547.[31]
Yet a reduction in the possible sums of payment to one individual was accompanied by
greater regularity and assurance of reward, for
the members of the companies as well as for
the directors, and even in the later period
gratifications when in other than money form
were sometimes given to individuals who had
made especially brilliant hits; fine clothes and
chains of gold were then, like flowers now, sent
behind the scenes to the favorite.

Arlecchino never hesitated to beseech and

to flatter patrons if he saw the least chance of screwing them up to the pitch of generosity. Cecchini once said of him, "beyond his own interests he understands nothing." He was famed for the ingenuity of his begging methods.[32] Once during the months of his stay at the French court in 1600, he addressed Henri IV as though the king had been the clown and he himself the king, with these words: "Well, Arlequin, since you and your people have come here to amuse me, I promise to protect you, to give you a pension." The king did not contradict him, says the contemporary account, but interrupted him with, "There, there, you've taken my rôle on yourself long enough, now I'll take it back." [33]

And the royal rôle must have been that of a sufficiently generous patron, for the Accesi remained in Paris, quite satisfied, until at least the October of 1601, when they returned to their nearer duties in Italy, leaving the rich field of France to be gleaned after them, in 1603, by the Gelosi, of whom I have already spoken.

CHAPTER IV

GIAMBATTISTA ANDREINI AS A
THEATRICAL INNOVATOR

G IAMBATTISTA ANDREINI is slightly
known to English students because a few
eighteenth-century critics, beginning with Vol-
taire, decided that his mystery play, *L'Adamo,*
must have been the inspiring origin of Milton's
Paradise Lost.[1] That theory is now regarded
as an interesting supposition merely, and Andreini is ignored far more than he should be
by theatrical historians. The importance of
this once famous Capocomico and writer of
tragedies, comedies, histories, pastorals, lies
not so much in his creative power as a writer,
for that was not remarkable, as in his un-
wearied efforts to improve stage production,
efforts that influenced the French theater of

the seventeenth century quite as much as the Italian and that left a tradition carried over into England in 1660. Many of the devices which Pepys remarks in the plays he saw, the echo song, the machines, the changes of background, all new and wonderful in the London theater of his day, were a direct inheritance from the court spectacles that Andreini and his troupe, the Fedeli, invented and elaborated for their patrons, the ducal houses of Mantua and Ferrara and the royal house of France.

Early in the seventeenth century when Andreini began his independent work for the theater, after a rigorous training under his parents, there was the greatest irregularity in the manner of producing plays, although, contradictorily enough, there was much narrowness of critical dogma as to the way they should be produced. It was believed that scenic magnificence was only appropriate to pastoral dramas or to *intermedii;* tragedies and com-

edies were given in a less spectacular fashion
and usually with a fixed stage arrangement
which included painted scenery but not
changes of scene. Andreini, working with a
group of talented actors and under rich and
enlightened patrons, brought into the regular
drama much of the magnificence inherited
from the *Sacre Rappresentazioni* and the *intermedii*, published his plays with full stage directions which allowed their performance by companies other than his own, recognized and
encouraged the *melodramma*, paid close attention to costume and properties in their relation to the plays he gave, in short, contributed
in every way toward what his age and the next
regarded as realism and beauty in the drama.

He had of course a rich background to work
from. Since 1491, when Leonardo da Vinci
invented the apparatus for plays given before
the Sforza in Milan,[2] and 1519 when Raphael
painted the setting for Ariosto's *Suppositi*

[89]

given before Leo X in Rome,[3] great artists and princes had devoted their serious attention to the stage. The principle of realism had been partly recognized; Raphael, in the performance of the *Suppositi* just alluded to, made his background to represent Ferrara, the scene of the comedy, and other artists followed his example, reproducing well-known aspects of certain Italian cities such as were required by the plays they set.[4] Such realism was, however, confined to comedies, with their "imitation" of the everyday life of men. Tragedies, often closely following classical originals, had a more general and symbolic setting, as magnificent as the producer could afford, with palaces and towers built up on the stage sometimes to the number of ten, and with particular attention to the lighting, which was early recognized to have a definite relation to the mood of the spectator and to reflect the feeling of the tragedy.[5] For pastorals much license of fancy was allowed, with machinery moved about against an immovable background and with lights representing the heavenly bodies, turning in the ceiling.

In 1598 at Ferrara Angelo Ingegneri published his interesting little essay on dramatic poetry, *Della poesia rappresentativa,* and summed up toward the end of it his theories as to how plays should be presented in order to make them as true to life as possible. The pages on *L' Apparato* (pp. 62 ff.) contain such statements as:

The stage ought to resemble as closely as may be the place in which the story of the play is laid. For example, if the tragedy takes place in Rome, the Campidoglio should be shown with the chief palace, and the principal temples and other buildings. If the play is a comedy, the Pantheon should appear with the column of Antony or of Trajan, and the Tiber and some other points that would cause the city to be recognized. . . . But if a pastoral is to

[91]

be played, since the whole thing is rustic, any setting will serve . . . so that it contain woods, mountains, valleys, rivers, fountains, temples, huts and, especially, distant backgrounds. . . .

Ingegneri agrees in the main with de' Sommi in his emphasis on magnificence in the presentation of plays and still more on the importance of natural costumes and manners in actors. He insists again and again that the aim of dramatic art is the imitation of life, suggesting that the time has come to eliminate the ghost from tragedy, "for I have never seen a ghost on the stage that was not ridiculous," remarking that the chorus also often led the way to absurdities, as when it was brought in revering a king who had just been driven from his throne and who ought therefore to be shown as without a follower (p. 23) and discussing ways of producing naturalness of effect, such as the accounting logically for exits

Franca Trippa. Fritellino.

DUET AND DANCE IN AN ITALIAN COMEDY

(From Callot's *Balli*)

and entrances and the making occasions for choral odes and other music in the introduction of festivals, weddings, dances and other diversions (p. 17). Above all he urges, in true classic spirit, that tone should be preserved in dramatic art, as one way of bringing the spectator into touch with the story presented.

This essay by Ingegneri Andreini must surely have known, since he was in 1598 an eager young student of drama and an actor in his parents' troupe, the Gelosi, a company frequently engaged to play at Ferrara for the Don Cesare d'Este to whom the little book was dedicated. His own work reflects many of Ingegneri's ideas, though he never mentions this particular authority in any of his numerous acknowledgments of indebtedness to his predecessors in the prefaces to his published works, where he tells how he learned from them and how he ventured to improve upon their practices.

His first play, a tragedy, *La Florinda,* printed in Milan, 1606, and written for his wife, whose stage name was Florinda, is illustrated with a frontispiece showing how its author arranged his stage to represent the "forest of Scotland," where he set his play. In the midst is a large castle, not unlike the central structure on the Elizabethan stage, with a tower over it, a balcony and numerous windows as well as two doors for its two stories. At one side of the rather large stage is a small pseudo-classical circular temple, with pillars around it, on the other is a rustic hut with a waterfall behind it and a sunburst in the sky overhead; two paths bordered with trees lead to the temple and the hut, and in the center, before the castle, stands a group of four hunters, with a horse, a dog and three long lances. Obviously this set is of the composite kind used in the tragedies of the Cinquecento, demanding no change of scene, since all the three principal places mentioned in the text are on the stage at the same time. It is the point of departure for Andreini's theatrical experiments and shows how conventionally he began his career as actor-manager.

His next plays, *L'Adamo,* Milan, 1614, and *La Maddalena,* Venice, 1616, are almost as traditional in some respects as the tedious tragedy of *La Florinda,* though these two derive from the *Sacre Rappresentazioni* rather than from the classical imitations of learned playwrights in the sixteenth century. Yet both these plays show advance in knowledge of the stage and a great deal of daring in the use of scenic magnificence. All that their author had learned in years of experience with courtly spectacles he uses here, adding to his knowledge his own inventions. He says in the preface to *La Ferinda,* the comedy he printed in Paris, 1622, "for my happy fortune I saw in Florence and in Mantua many dramatic and musical works; I saw *Orfeo, Arianna, Silla, Dafne, Cerere* and *Psiche,* wonderful things, all of them," and goes on to speak enthusiastically of the "angelic" music which helped to give them charm. Accordingly he brought into his mystery plays as much music as he could arrange for, giving to *L'Adamo* a chorus of Cherubim and Seraphim and an answering chorus of "the spirits of fire, air, water and hell," with a ballet of the Seven Deadly Sins and other allegorical characters, and to *La Maddalena* a chorus of many angels, revealed when the "Gloria" opens to the sound of many trumpets.[6]

Perhaps Andreini was conscious that it would take a good deal of spectacular appeal to cover the tedium of his long poetic dialogues and the amount of moralizing that he managed to insert in the speeches of his principal characters; certainly it is hard for a modern reader to imagine these two long religious plays even as operas, unless he visualizes rather vividly the full stage directions the author supplies. The *Maddalena* is undoubtedly the more beautiful of the two; it opens with a description of the *"apparato,"* which "must be all sea and rocks; and in the distance on the sea a small bark, before the Prologue appears, with some fish frisking about; but after this the fish must never appear except when the symphony plays, and even then rarely. The sky should be all starry and in the midst of it the Moon, full; the Divine Grace (*Favor*) will appear as Prologue, on a car exceedingly bright, all adorned with stars and supported with clouds of both gold and silver, and the clouds shall be borne by two angels"; at the disappearance of the Prologue, "little by little the stars shall vanish and from the sea shall rise the dawn and after the dawn the sun, and as the Prologue has ended to the sound of melodious music, the setting, which was all

[99]

maritime, shall represent in part lofty palaces, in the midst of them the residence of Maddalena, the proudest possible."

It is hardly an exaggeration to call *La Maddalena,* as does Luigi Rasi, "The most beautiful mixture of comedy-drama-tragedy-melodrama-pantomime-dance ever seen on the stage," [7] though it is impossible to agree with him that it is "rich in original beauties." The text provides every opportunity for musicians, as Monteverde and Salomone de' Rossi discovered when they set it to music in 1618, and it is equally appealing to the stage carpenter and costumer. The thirty speaking characters outside the chorus are dressed with an eye to their parts in the fable, from the Magdalene herself, with her changes from worldly splendor to a penitential garb of hair shirt, rope girdle and sandals, "with a skull in her hand," to the Divine Grace in glory and the Archangel Michael in full shining armor.

L'Adamo is less free in its treatment of its theme than is *La Maddalena*. It contains some pageant-like features evidently imitated from the allegorical *intermedii* of Andreini's youth, such as the traditional procession of Pride drawn on her chariot by a giant, and the beautiful Serpent with the head, breast and arms of a man; mixed with these characters from religious history are several of classical inspiration, equally picturesque on the stage, such as Vulcan with his forge, constructing Hell, and infernal scenes that owe as much to Virgil as to the Biblical source of the story.

In the preface to *L'Adamo* (first edition, Milan, 1513),—a letter "to the benign Reader,"—the poet gives expression to the artistic conscience which was constantly alive in him and which drove him on from one experiment to another. Here he tells his difficulties with dramatic diction:

The dispute of Eve with the Serpent before she ate the apple was difficult. . . . Equally difficult was the debate of Eve with Adam, persuading him to eat (though she had then the gift of all knowledge). And this language was most difficult for my little strength, because the composition of it had to be naked of all the poetic ornaments so dear to the Muses and deprived of all reference to the things created in the years since then, for in the time of the first man there was nothing made. For instance I had to omit mentioning, when Adam spoke or when any one talked with him, bows, arrows, pennants, urns, knives, swords, lances, trumpets, drums, trophies, ensigns, harangues, hammers, torches, bellows, funeral pyres, theatres, treasuries and similar things . . . all introduced on account of original sin. . . . Moreover it was difficult to know in what way to make Adam speak, because so far as his knowledge was concerned he merited long, grand, full, sustained verses, but considering him as a shepherd and an inhabitant of the forest, he ought to be simple and sweet in his language; so I did the best I could with full verses, some broken and some completed. I have reason to think that the kindness of God, regarding my good intentions rather than my defects, . . . moving my hand, helped me to finish my work.

This nervous care for diction Andreini reveals again and again in the confidences to his patrons or to his "benign readers" which preface his various plays. He was among the first playwrights to meditate the Horatian laws for character decorum and to interpret them more liberally than the French academicians later in the century. He believed in the use of dialect as a method of characterization as well as for humorous appeal; in the description of *L'Apparato* prefixed to *Lelio bandito,* Milano, 1620, he says he hopes no one will object to the use of various languages and dialects in this play, for he has followed the rule of making each person speak "as he would do in real life." In *La Ferinda,* Paris, 1622, it is perhaps hardly realistic to bring on to the stage at once Frenchmen, Germans, Italians speaking the Venetian, Lombard, Genovan and Neapolitan dialects, a pedant using bad Latin, and a stutterer—here Giambattista was following the practice of the actors of the improvised plays who used dialect for comic effect—but he preserves the characteristics of each kind of speech with rather more care than would some of his contemporaries; that is, for all the personages except the German, in whose language no amount of good will can find much likeness to the speech of the Teutons.[8]

Costume, like speech, Andreini regarded as a means of characterization. He criticizes, in the preface to *La Centaura,* Paris, 1622, the practice of some of his contemporaries who write plays about twins, "a notable and improbable error," namely the dressing of these twins differently. "They should be dressed alike," says Andreini, since in life no two faces are alike, and their being twins must be em-

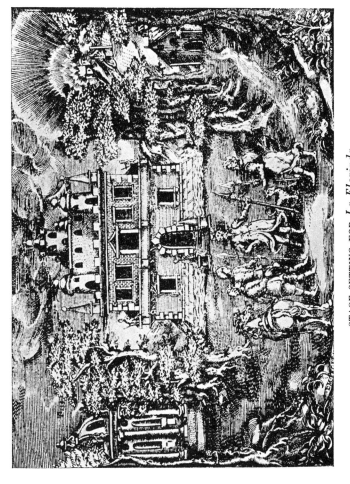

STAGE SETTING FOR *La Florinda*

phasized in such a way that the audience will understand their relationship, but "an invention must account for this likeness of costume: such as that used by my father and me in *I due Leli* [a play on which Giovan Battista and his father, Francesco, collaborated]; our twins had both heard of their father's death and so came on the stage dressed alike in black of the fashion of that city where the scene was laid."

In *La Centaura* he gives detailed directions for costumes, taking particular care that the two mad characters shall be dressed as wildly and as ridiculously as possible, that the nymphs shall present a "bizarre" appearance and that the family of four Centaurs, parents and two children, who give their names to the play, shall impress the eye with their strangeness. His symbolic characters in the same play and in others where such figures appear are given the usual conventional properties, such as a bellows and rope for Adulation, a bouquet of flowers with a serpent in the middle of it for Deceit, an enveloping black and white mantle for Falsehood. The medieval influence is strong here, as will be seen from the description of Divine Justice in the same play, *La Centaura:* "A woman of singular beauty, dressed in gold, with a crown of gold on her head, above it a dove in a halo of light, her hair spread on her shoulders, in her right hand a naked sword, in her left the scales."

Realism, the confessed aim of Andreini's art, it will be seen is here quite subordinated to scenic appeal and that is aided wherever possible by the use of elaborate symbolic figures. In fact he admits in his most important prefatory letter, that to *La Centaura,* that he could easily have done without allegorical figures such as Deceit, Adulation and their sisters, because the fable "is knit and unraveled without disguises or miracles," but that for the ornament of the stage, "to which one must pay great attention," and for "tragic pomp," which is equally important, he introduced such ornaments, as well as his unusual and splendid stage machinery.

It is to be feared that his wish to strike the eye of his spectators led the poet to forget himself in the stage carpenter at times. Certainly he devotes a great deal of careful attention to the magnificent bed on which his sick king is carried in (*La Centaura*) and justifies the use of it on the grounds of royal magnificence and of the improbability that an invalid monarch would stagger into the street to die. In *La Turca*, Venice, 1622, he uses "warlike maritime accidents," to great effect, in *Lelio bandito*, Milan, 1620, he describes an *Apparato* which represents "cavernous and woody mountains; at the right a castle, situated high and distant, from which one can descend into the middle of the stage; at the left a cottage on a hill, from which . . . one can descend by a stairway which is made to look like living rock." In the middle is a spacious cavern under which is a chest, covered with "a most beautiful carpet," the bed of Lelio, the bandit. The scene was supposed to be the Abruzzi mountains but there are no directions for peasant costumes.

The scene for *La Turca* was of a different sort and included a "painted background" (*prospettiva*) with a sea in the distance and around it "many high mountains, with huts of painted cardboard on them together with certain castles, showing that one could walk in these mountains and descend to the stage from them"; and in the last of the houses "there must be a window large enough to permit a woman to flee from it; and there must be two towers . . . one on the one side of three houses and the other on the other side of the other three."

Such painted scenery, it will be seen, An-

dreini used in his comedies, combining with
the traditional houses of the Italian comic
stage a landscape or seascape background to
give some of the beauty and variety which
similar sets contributed to the pastoral drama
of his day. He tells how he came to venture
upon his innovation, in the preface to *La
Ferinda,* Paris, 1622; he realized, he says, how
"poor and bare" his little comedy looked on
the stage, lacking the decorations to which his
audiences were accustomed in the gorgeous allegorical and pastoral entertainments to which
they were attached; "it lost much in the way
of variety of scenes, since into a comedy no
god comes nor is there any reason for violent
and rapid changes." Accordingly he set his
story in Venice, that picturesque city, half
land, half water, and tried to bring into his
commedietta some of the charm of those other
spectacular pieces, by having an allegorical
prologue recited by Thalia standing on a shell

in the midst of a sea, by introducing a ballet of fishermen and by giving lifelikeness to his Venetian scene through the incidental use of gondolas and gondoliers. In *La Turca* he repeated the Venetian theme but bettered his own invention by adding to his maritime scenery Turkish costumes for his chief characters, an enslaved brother and sister, and by concluding the comedy with a "trionfo," a "chariot, ornamented with many Turkish arms and banners with various lights painted on them."

"Commedia boschereccia et marittima" Andreini calls *La Turca,* in order, probably, to silence academic criticism of his mixing the genres of comedy and pastoral. He was always sensitive to such criticism, being himself a member of the Florentine academy of the Spensierati and well educated in Aristotelian theory, though not such a stickler for it as to permit his learning to stand in the light of his practical experience. He calls comedy "a mirror of human life, an image of virtue and an example to it," (Prologue to *Lo Schiavetto,* Venice, 1620), yet he is always willing to introduce romance and splendor and quaintness in order to vary his plot and his scene. He uses birds in *I due Baci,* another "commedia boschereccia," many roses in *La Rosa,* a group of dogs, "large and small," in *La Rosella* (1632). The scenery for *La Rosa* (1638) must have been particularly pretty, consisting as it did of a "prospettiva" painted with rows of cypresses, a lovely fountain in the middle, "arranged at the pleasure of the man who has charge of such things," houses on either side, hedged and almost covered by roses in flower, "so that the Villa where the comedy is to be laid, shall be called Bellarosa because of the abundance of roses there."

That he used devices for changing his scenery in the middle of some plays is abundantly evident. He remarks more than once that such changes "are now quite easy," though unfortunately he does not tell precisely how they were managed. We know that Leonardo invented a "Paradiso with seven planets which turned about" [9] and that he was followed by other mechanicians who helped actors with similar devices, as Inigo Jones helped Ben Jonson with his Masques. Sometimes it was the lights only which were made to revolve, sometimes the whole aspect of the stage changed, as in one of Andreini's most ambitious "opere reali," *L'Ismenia,* Bologna, 1639; the first stage direction reads: "Here appear many Cupids carrying a Temple, all gilded, putting it down at the right side of the stage, then, singing the following madrigal, they go." In the same play a Hypogriff "with a pleasant hiss," dances a ballet to the tune of his hissing (Act iii), and in Act iv another monster, not particularized, makes off with one of the maidens. The chief sensation comes in

G. B. ANDREINI
(From his *L'Adamo*, 1617)

the fifth act where "Thunder is heard, the stage shakes, the lights disappear, and, the theater being darkened for a moment, the lights come on again, showing that the iron Rock of Death has vanished and there remain only the two prostrate persons."

A still more ingenious device, not, however, involving a change of scene, was used for *La Rosa*, Andreini's reworking into pastoral romance of the Tancred and Gismunda story. He obligingly gives a detailed description of his management of the chief incident in his plot, so that other actors can easily produce the play if they wish. As for the device of Lelio's head in a basin, says the author, it may be well arranged as follows, so that the audience will be quite deceived: "A basin of brass or of silvered wood" must be filled with flowers, and it must have "an opening in the bottom like that in a lantern"; when it is brought in to Florinda by Cavaletta, he [the servant] must take care to keep his hands over it as he puts it on the floor; while it is there, "Lelio from a trap door underneath must put his head up through the bottom of the basin, so that when Florinda moves the flowers a little, she will at once see the head of Lelio. He withdraws instantly as she drops the flowers in horror and takes up the basin." Thus the company is saved the expense of having a stucco head made to resemble the hero of the play, and that hero himself, acted by the author of the tragicomedy, keeps in his own power the delicate management of his climax.

For the end of *La Maddalena* Andreini invented a machine similar to that used in modern representations of Berlioz' *Damnation of Faust,* if one can judge from the directions for the tableau of the Magdalene's salvation. "Suddenly Maddalena shall be raised somewhat from the earth by a subterranean device and at the same instant angels shall sustain her on either side, and at the same time the theater shall be made to look like the most barren desert." After the heroine looks "languidly" at the desert and laments her sins for a while, "the cavern opens, where an immensity of light shall be seen"; she recognizes the sepulcher of Christ, since "if it is desired a beautiful Crucifix, not too large, may appear there"; she kneels and prays, then "to the sound of a gentle Miserere" goes away, the Gloria with its chorus of chanting angels replacing all the desert and receiving the penitent to eternal happiness.

I forbear to quote others of Andreini's painstaking stage directions, which have a close likeness to those already given. His taste, it will be evident, was as much toward theatrical magnificence as it was toward emotional and burlesque acting. He of course wrote most of his plays for the use of the Fedeli, in which for many years his wife, the beautiful singer and actress, Virginia, "called Florinda," took the prima donna's rôles and he himself played the first lover. It is amusing to trace the way he "featured" his own and his wife's accomplishments and prepared here and there little opportunities for "hits" of different sorts. The tears and laments and fainting fits of Florinda in Andreini's first tragedy must have cost some pains in the performance of them, yet undoubtedly, as contemporaries witness, the fair-haired Virginia carried them off successfully and made the audience forget the interminable length of her speeches. Lelio, as Andreini invariably called himself on the stage, preferred comic effects to tragic and rarely missed a chance for burlesquing in his rôle or for introducing some of those dubious allusions or jests which most of his critics have found it so hard to reconcile with his bigoted piety.

As an actor Andreini was probably less original than as a stage manager. He was sur-

rounded by excellent players and had a good
deal of trouble at times to keep himself and
Virginia from being eclipsed by some of them.
Yet no one in the course of his career seems
to have challenged his supremacy in putting
on plays, either his own or those of his contemporaries. He was in constant demand at
the courts of France and Mantua and elsewhere during the fifty years of his active life.
Moreover he took a lively part in the contro-
versial literature of his day, defending with
unusual intelligence and persistence both his
profession and his own innovations in the theater. He pointed out in true Horatian fashion that the stage .was a great prophet of
righteousness, teaching the useful through the
beautiful, and that he himself never set aside
morality for mere amusement. "If there be
here or there some little licentious word," he
observes in the preface to *Lo Schiavetto,* "put
into the mouth of a low character, it is only

there like a thorn among roses," and can but call attention to the contrasting truths and beauties.

More important than these conventional declarations of intent are Andreini's actual practices and the use of his really formidable learning in the bringing the theater of his time to a sensible and intelligent recognition of its opportunities and its limitations. He never ceased to protest against the tactlessness of beginning plays with long uninteresting speeches which left the audience cold,[10] or, a proof that his thought had surpassed his teachers, against the academic rigidity which forbade the mixing of tears and laughter and of scenes "proper" to comedy with those associated with the melodrama or the pastoral. He never forgot that spectators like variety and brilliance, wit and movement and an image of their times. He sums up his own theory in a few words, and those might have been used

THE DUCAL PALACE, MANTUA

by Ingegneri or any other classicist: "The power of poetry, whether epic or dramatic, can be summed up as doing or pretending things true to life." (Preface to *La Centaura.*)

It was undoubtedly in large part his influence exercised on and through his company, the *Fedeli,* that helped actors and dramatists to adopt such aids toward realism as strict localization of action and definition of time, as it was his restless search for novelty that introduced and fixed stage improvements, so that at the end of the century Perrucci could say, "We do not know whether the ancients had as many changes of scene as the moderns, or of such a variety that thought cannot search for more, seeing that in a moment the stage is transformed from a palace into a city, from a hall into a wood, from a gallery into a garden, from a meadow into a heaven, from a heaven into a hell; into so many forms and with such swiftness and art that it seems rather an enchantment of the eyes than the work of machines." [11] Such magic was universal on the continental stage through the seventeenth century and, passing from Italy to France, from thence to London, transformed the English theater and called out the naïve raptures of the astonished Pepys and his friends, who found "the machines" used for the witches of *Macbeth* and the spirits of the *Tempest,* "beyond description."

CHAPTER V

GIAMBATTISTA ANDREINI AND HIS FELLOWS

AFTER the death of Isabella Andreini and the disbanding of the Gelosi which followed in 1604, Giambattista Andreini apparently continued in his hereditary duty to the Mantuan house by organizing a company of actors, among them some of his parents' fellows, and his own beautiful wife, Virginia, called Florinda in comedy. This band, the Fedeli, soon rivaled the memory of the Gelosi and became the first favorites of Duke Vincenzo, who spent upon them even more money than he and his father had given the older actors. Indeed the Duke's relations with his protégés seem to have been almost too intimate for his own comfort, so constantly was he called upon to mediate in their frequent disputes, to provide for their numerous children and to find them work at foreign courts.

Andreini's way to his patron's grace was considerably obstructed at first by the position of Piermaria Cecchini and his wife Flaminia, who had evidently had a great deal of authority, perhaps had headed one of the Duke's companies, in preceding years. Two letters from Cecchini to a ducal secretary written in September, 1606, complain bitterly of Lelio and Florinda as interlopers:

> They try to order us about, to bid us go and stay and do everything they please, but I, who am used to the society of the best actors of my time, cannot . . . endure such impertinences and will say of Lelio and Florinda . . . God preserve me and my like from being with them.[1]

The second note, dated September 20, 1606, gives a livelier account of the trouble:

MOST ILLUSTRIOUS LORD AND DEAREST
        PATRON:

My messenger is returned with the letter

from Your Excellency, which serves as an answer to the one I wrote you; I wished to read it to the company, and in order to have them all together, called them behind the scenes after the comedy and then we retired to the dressing-room; but Lelio, Florinda's husband, would not come, though I begged him to and even twice sent a servant to tell him that I spoke by order of His Highness; at all of which Lelio laughingly turned away and would not listen. The same servant, by name Francesco Lavagna, a Milanese, will witness this, also a jewel merchant called Od. Filippo, a friend to us all, who said he marveled at such contempt. . . . But now while I write comes a servant of Lelio's to speak to me about him; I will rise and listen and report faithfully to you. . . . The said Lelio wishes to know where the company will go after leaving Milan, and I told him that we will go to Bologna if we can manage to stay there and he sends me for reply to go where it best pleases him, so I am about to carry out the order of His Highness and send him away. . . .[2]

Apparently Andreini wished to winter in Milan or Bologna while the rest of the company preferred to travel; whatever the reason for the quarrel, it caused so much bitterness and disunion that the Duke finally authorized Cecchini to dismiss the Andreini on account of their rebellions. They immediately appealed to Mantua in plaintive letters describing their "stoning" by the company and followed up their notes by a journey to the court, where they were evidently so successful in representing themselves as the victims of jealousy that they were reinstated and from that time forth worked industriously for revenge on their defamers.

How completely they succeeded in turning the tables on the Cecchini within the next three years is almost ludicrously shown in Giambattista's words to the Duke: [3]

. . . The ways he [Cecchini] takes [of breaking up the company] are innumerable, but let these few facts serve as examples. First, he is the enemy and tyrant of all his fellows;

his wife never looks at nor speaks to any of us, and is not only thus discourteous to the Company but to the gentlemen of Turin . . . whence it has resulted that these despised lords have got the Cavalier Marino to write about her in such a way that when Your Highness sees the compositions you will understand the honor and glory she has left behind her in Turin! Moreover she speaks just as freely on the stage [i.e. in the improvised comedies] as in her own room against the honor of [our] actors, and on the stage too she has deigned to treat me very ill, but in this place I'll say no more of what she has done or said; Fritellino has managed to become I don't know just what with the Cardinal Aldobrandino, and he wishes Signor Cintio to be with him, and I assure you carries the whole matter very proudly. More, he has said to us openly, that Turin wants no more comedies, unless he's there, but in secret he has said that when we reach Mantua certain fine things will be discovered and that he will then take his way to Rome. . . .

The last of our difficulties was the assault on Messer Federico's son by one of the servants, particularly attached to Fritellino, one evening while we were returning from Millefonti; all the women were in the row and there was such a great storm altogether that I think Flaminia, who hates the boy like death, was at the bottom of the whole affair. So that on account of all these troubles I again, with all my people and my wife, beg Your Highness that when we leave Turin we may abandon these odious creatures, for I swear there is not a day you may not hear some displeasing news of them.

Your Highness is the shepherd of this flock, so pray take good care of it and drive out the infected sheep. All of us will be at Your Highness' service during the approaching Carnival, we all burn with this same desire, and I assure you I have found the troupe very different from what Fritellino painted them; God be my enemy if they are not all as virtuous as they are well-mannered. . . .

Turin, 14 August, 1609.

This letter had been prepared for by one from Florinda, Andreini's wife, to the Cardinal Gonzaga, written August fourth of the same year:

Flaminia [she writes], is hated by all Turin for her airs and for her mad love of

Cintio. . . . I have thrown down all her trophies here, however, and have pulled her nose
as far out of joint as she had turned it up in
pride. . . . The whole company complains of
her boldness and of Fritellino's.[4]

Florinda's temper over her rival's actions
was apparently a complex of professional and
personal jealousy, for Virginia Andreini was
a faithful wife to her giddy and unfaithful husband and must have despised Flaminia's weakness with all the bitterness of virtue. She herself was praised by Marino and other poetical
moralists for her "coldness," was pointed out
as one of the few great beauties who could come
into Duke Vincenzo's court without being
drawn into his "harem," in short was as celebrated as her famous mother-in-law, Isabella,
for her moral conduct,—"a flower of virtue
and of love," says one of the stanzas about her.
Marvelous indeed, when every one agreed that
her playing and singing "from a thousand

hearts drew a thousand sighs" each time she appeared on the scene! [5] When she sang Monteverde's lovely music to Rinuccini's *Arianna* at a Mantuan festival in 1608, and sang it perfectly after six days' study, she made a fame that lived as long as she did, a fame that no mere comic actress like Flaminia, however excellent, could hope to overcome.[6] So the two women continued in hatred of each other all their lives, making constant trouble for the leaders of their troupes and for their patrons. In 1612 the quarrel was still raging, as the Duke of Mantua tells his son, the Cardinal Gonzaga, *à propos* of negotiations for sending his "servants" to France:

Nothing that her Majesty, the Queen [i.e. Maria de' Medici] could command me or wish of me would I not undertake with all my heart, but the bringing together of a company of actors, a really good one, at this time of Florinda and Flaminia's being so at odds, seems to me

Cap Bonbardon.　　Cap. Grillo.

Cap: Esgangarato,　Cap: Cocodrillo.

QUARREL SCENES IN AN ITALIAN FARCE

(From Callot's *Balli*)

impossible, not merely difficult, for I've tried it,—all my efforts have not availed to unite them nor to persuade them to go together to play for the King of Hungary at his marriage as he desired, and this notwithstanding every favor offered them by his Majesty and myself.[7]

A fine show of haughtiness and independence that one wishes might illustrate a greater freedom than was actually attainable by these artists! In fact, however much they struggled to assert their rights, they had no chance to determine most of their movements for themselves; they were obliged, by their servile positions, to go where they were called and to play with or in rivalry to other servants of their masters. To be sure there were occasions, rare, like the one just cited, in which a stand was maintained in the face of their lords. In this case the Andreini were satisfied by the dismissal of Fritellino, who, evidently, from the following letter, lived with some of his companions through a period of enforced leisure and disfavor:

(To one of the Ducal secretaries.)
MOST ILLUSTRIOUS LORD AND PATRON:

I wrote many days, indeed many months, ago to Your Excellency begging you to intervene for me with His Serene Highness, to ask if he meant to give me that which he has many times promised, or in case he did not think me worthy, to ask that he would at least give me permission to dispose of my person as occasion offered; not having had any answer I fear His Highness has taken it ill that I went away on that occasion to form two companies, i.e. Arlecchino's for France and another for His Highness' service in Italy; should this last be true, I never mean that His Highness shall remain in displeasure with my work or my person, and as sign that I wish to keep myself free to answer the slightest beck from him, I have abandoned a great and certain prospective good which presented itself in Florence. . . . But I do not intend to live out of the service of His Highness, my lord; if I might believe my service is dear to him I should not apply myself to any other nor accept anything desirable or useful without his approval. All the actors I know will bear witness to the truth of what I say, and also to the signs of good will in the chains and medals which the Most Illustrious Grand Duke has given me and the magnificent clothes with which the Most Serene Grand Duchess has honored my wife,— all without our hoping or asking or even imagining such things. But I swear by my soul that I care more for the good words of my Most Illustrious Lord than for all the kindnesses and riches which all the other rulers of the world could give me, so I conclude begging His Highness to let me know if he will make use of me and of my, or rather *his*, company, or that he will tell me how he wishes me to act; I will do everything according to his wishes,—but let it be soon, for at the end of the Carnival I must pay the company; so I beseech Your Excellency to pardon my injuring your time by making you consume it in reading my tediousness,—but the subject required it. . . .

Modena, 30 January, 1612.[8]

No sooner were the Cecchini out of the way than the Andreini found a more serious cause for anxiety and grief than Fritellino and his wife had given them. They eyed in no friendly spirit the rapid advance to favor of Tristano Martinelli, who threatened to supplant them in what they were coming to regard as their own preserves, the Mantuan and French courts. Playing beside them in the rôle of first clown, and playing always with immense verve and originality, this famous Arlecchino soon began to draw the frivolous attention of his audiences away from the rather tedious lovers whom the Andreini usually impersonated, and to concentrate on himself the eyes,—and the gifts,—of all beholders. Florinda complains to the Cardinal in December, 1611, that she and Giambattista are having their authority undermined by this man:

I and my husband ought to have charge of forming the company so that we may not lose the fame we have gained here through it, for at present I have the very best company that is playing. That Arlecchino [Tristano Martinelli] has begged for permission to form a company pleases no one, indeed if license should be given him no actor would join him, they all know him to be too self-seeking. Therefore it is necessary if you please that every commission should be made out in the name of Lelio and Florinda as organizers of the troupe.[9]

Unfortunately for them their star was beginning to wane. Marie de' Medici favored Tristano more than his rivals, and in 1612 sent him the following unmistakable commission:

ARLEQUIN: Although I have been promising myself the choicest company of actors that Italy could provide, I have so far seen nothing but your letters full of excuses. I willingly accept them, knowing that the failure is not your fault; but you must really do your best to overcome the difficulties made by your company, and assure them that never has any troupe been so wished for in France as yours, since I hear it is very perfect. I am glad to know that Florinda and Flavia are content to come into my service, but I am annoyed that they are not at peace. [Florinda seems to have been jealous of every other actress!] Try to reconcile them; all who come with you shall return entirely satisfied. If possible bring Fritellino and Flaminia with you, I will favor them so that they will not regret coming,—let them understand,—and see that they come at once, with this promise that they shall find nothing to complain of, nor you either, at the Hotel de Bourgogne; a long time ago the order was given to the minister of finance at Lyons to pay you three thousand six hundred lire, the which will not fail to be paid you on arrival there to settle the expenses of the journey. I am writing to my cousin the Duke of Mantua and to the Cardinal Gonzaga, to see that your company is filled with talented persons and that it leaves at once for this city. I think that they will manage this and that through their aid all difficulties will cease,—knowing also that you on your part will do all you can. I will say no more except that I pray the Lord to keep you in his grace and that I will fulfill all that I have promised, by the faith of your Gossip.

Written in Paris, 4th September, 1612.

MARIE.[10]

Martinelli had boasted of the Queen's favor in a letter to the Duke of Mantua, dated August 1 of the same year, parodying the princely style:

MOST COUSINLY COUSIN AND MOST DEAR
    GOSSIP:

Having written in the past few days two letters and having had no reply, it seems to us that you care little for our person, nevertheless we shall not fail to repeat the letters until you are weary of them. . . . We give you news therefore that our most Christian Gossip, the Gallic Queen, makes more of us than of your own person, since she has invested us with two of her royal letters, one sent by the Signor Carlo de' Rossi, the which by his favor is not yet delivered, the other by our Ambassador, which was at once delivered, and which invites us into her beautiful kingdom of pounds and pence, making many offers which you will find in the copy of the said letter sent you herewith; examine it well and then give sentence as it may please you, and if you are willing that the company go in its own name, without costing you a sou, we will go, content with your favor and authority. . . . So do us the kindness to answer this at once that we may reply to our said Gossip according to your will, for without that we do not wish to go, since the whole desire of our person is only to please our dearest cousin and friendly Gossip; if it were not for your love, believe that no stage should ever see my Harlequinesque person, and this I say on the faith of Master Tristano; wherefore I beg Your Highness to do me the grace to let me know your intention on these matters of which I write, so that I may conform myself to your wish. I have no other desire than your favor; so ending I pray our Lord to keep you in his holy hands, together with your most serene little offspring. From Milan, 14th August, 1612.

Your Serene Highness' Most Affectionate Cousin and
    Most Christian Gossip,
            D. A. D. M.
[Dominus Arlechinus de Martinellis] [11]

In October of the same year the plans for a journey into France are not much farther advanced than in August; but Arlecchino is just as gay and just as familiar:

[Tristano Martinelli to the Duke]

MOST SERENE GOSSIP COUSIN, SALUTATION:

While we were getting into the coach to
come to Florence with the company, a post
arrived bringing a missive directed to our person from our Most Christian Gossip the Queen,
with three letters in it, one for us, one for you
and one for our Gossip with the red crest [the
Cardinal Gonzaga], wherefore at once we
send you yours and the said Gossip's, and ours
we had read to a Frenchman and copied, the
which copy we send your lordly gossipship, so
that you may decide what we can do to please
our dearest Gossip, the Queen, suitable to her
demand; as for uniting this blessed company,
there's more needed than the Harlequinesque
authority! Nevertheless you will be so good as
to begin by disposing Mistress Flavia to enter
your service, and if she object that it is un-
wholesome, tell her that she shall have sweet
medicine to cure her, and if she says she does
not like medicines to be sweet, tell her she
shall have bitter, since she prefers bitter to
sweet,—so she will have to be content; and
for pity's sake do not fail, dear our cousin, to
do your best in getting together a good com-

pany to go to France this Lent, for at this moment we are starting by foot post to Florence. . . .

Your oldest cousin,
ARLECCHINO, MOST CHRISTIAN GOSSIP.[12]

The writer repeats his commands at more length to the Cardinal Ferdinando Gonzaga later in the same month:

To my dearest Gossip, the Most Illustrious Tortellino, Rome:

DEAREST GOSSIP:

On the 25th of this present (but not of the present which we expected from you in our favor) I received from you a letter greatly, desired; . . . with much eagerness I opened your note, which with the fairest words and nevertheless with ill deeds gave me to understand that you love me and desire to please me, and other similar little expressions delicate to eat with mustard, so that reading them I had a kind of satisfaction from the words; but you would have given me much more if you had written me about my dear gallic Gossip who in the last of her royal letters consoles me by repeating several times "Come, Arlecchino, to us, for we wish to knit up our relationship," and the like fine words, and in all her letters to me she remembers to put this most beautiful clause, which so pleases and delights me, "you understand my letters but none too well or else you will not understand them, but to speak clearly why do you think I take such pains to write so many notes? . . . Now I wish to be consoled with deeds and not with words any more, wherefore be sure of a very handsome present from me to my Gossip Signor Arlecchino." So I write you, Oh, Sir Gossip, to put you in mind of the fact that love arises from utility and that if you had not several times sent me peacocks, capons, cheeses, roasts of veal, and what is more important, certain ducats and similar pretty little trifles, my friendship would not have gone out to you,—because of words and chatter I have no need, they being my stock in trade and I selling them so cheaply, for a sou every evening,—that is in three hours. However I have no doubt of your most courteous courtesy and being obliged to you for the generous liberality which induced me to accept you as my only Gossip, I am the more surprised that you have not answered my letters in the same

style, but I remembered this was probably not
your fault but your secretary's, who neither
understands nor means to understand my letters or else he is short of sight and of memory
or else he does himself credit in sparing you
the present you might make me, or else he
wishes me ill or else he envies Arlecchino's
fame, or else, what the devil else may it be that
prevents an answer? Therefore I pray you
if you wish me well, imitate my dearest Gossip
Maria de' Medici, queen of half the bridge at
Avignon, and in the reply to this give me the
sign which I await with so much eagerness, and
I beg do not let me die the death of Nero's
dog who died while looking at a certain
salmon; I send you the letter of Her Majesty
in which I see what she wishes, and that she
writes the same to Your Excellency and to my
Gossip the Duke, that is, namely, that you
both ought to form a good and perfect company of actors, with such persons in it as the
Lady Florinda, her husband, Flaminia, Fritellino, Cintio, Flavio, the Captain Rinocerente
and I and two other good people, i.e. a Grati-
ano and a good Pantaloon; these are the personages she desires to have in France. So you
and the Duke will have to make peace between

them all, for the strength of Arlecchino is not enough to do it; more I will not add except that I have promised Her Majesty to go to serve her for six months if the company she desires can be formed, and if the troupe is not such as she wishes I shall remain at home in order not to lose the little reputation I have acquired in France. So may your goodwill to see that the Queen is answered not fail, and because I am dying of sleep I conclude, begging your pardon for my brevity, Sir Gossip, and begging our Lord to give you a good memory of your Gossip, Arlecchino, who makes you a thousand bows as he speaks. From Florence, 26 October, 1612.

All yours, dearest Gossip,[13]

TRISTANO MARTINELLI.

Martinelli for all his self-interestedness seems to have had some conscience about fulfilling the duties imposed upon him as one of the ducal deputies. What he paid for his license is not known, but the sum may perhaps have been regulated in somewhat the same terms as those demanded of another actor-manager favored by Mantua in 1567, Leone de' Sommi, the Jewish leader of a company of Jews; in a petition to Francesco Gonzaga this man asks for the privilege of playing in a Mantuan "Hall" for ten years, offering cash to pay for his license and in addition to give to the poor of the city each year two sacks of barley or their cost.[14]

Whether the conditions governing his dramatic monopoly at this time were the same as those he agreed to in 1597 is not known. In that year the license issued to him declares T. Martinelli the chief of all charlatans and actors of every kind, none of whom may even set up a stage without permission from the monopolist in writing, "under pain of being stripped of all they have"; the prices he is to receive for his subletting privileges are set and only the Duke's special company is stated to be free from this tax.[15] Such a bargain would give to the petitioner the right of monopoly over his rivals, just as did the license of which Martinelli speaks in the above-quoted letter, but in neither case did the patent forbid all dramatic representations except those organized by the patentee; the latter was of course permitted to sublet his privileges to his less fortunate rivals, among whom must often have been some humble and doubtless despised charlatans like those mentioned here. Martinelli would be sure to drive a good bargain with his superiors and to see that he was not cheated by his inferiors in its observance. Perhaps his anxiety in 1613 that the rights of his subordinates should not be infringed indicates less conscience than a desire to keep all the emoluments of his position.

Certainly he was always looking out for the main chance; most of his letters at this time are nothing but thinly disguised requests for money or honors, or accounts of the reward he received from his patrons, for example the note from Fontainebleau, 1613, again to Alessandro Strighi:[16]

MOST ILLUSTRIOUS, MY LORD:

From Lyons I wrote you news of us and now because I know you like to hear good things of your servants I take the occasion of sending this by your agent. First, the company is acceptable beyond any reasonable belief! Because the people here are simply starved for comedies, everything seems good to them. Her Majesty had me paid in Lyons 1200 ducats and as soon as I arrived she gave me such welcome as you would hardly credit because it was quite beyond the custom of those in her rank, for after many fine words Her Majesty had me taken to her private rooms and herself put into my hands a chain worth two hundred doubloons with her medallion at the end of it; in the evening we gave a comedy and were immediately rewarded by 500 ducats and the promise of 200 ducats a month and all our expenses when we serve outside the city of Paris, and to me privately and secretly are to be given 15 ducats a month for the expenses of my wife, who will be confined in a few days; and the king has promised to be sponsor and his sister, the Queen of Spain, also, and they say they will with their own hands hold the child at the font; if a boy the king will have him, if a girl the queen, though my wife too will want her, so I am put to it to content all three, . . . for it seems Arlecchino's children are like kittens to give away. You see everything is being ordered by the Lord God for the best to my family. We shall be here till All Saints', then go into Paris where we shall play in public, which will be to our best gain. So far there have been given me six complete suits, with pockets lined with felt and money, so that I have now 1200 ducats. . . .

Your Excellency's Most Affectionate servant,

TRISTANO MARTINELLI,
called Arlecchino.

The reward of chain and medallion may have been the long-delayed recognition of a wittily invented petition published by Arlecchino when he was at the head of the Accesi in Paris in 1599-1600.[17] A unique copy of this petition exists in the Bibliothèque Nationale in

Paris and contains more pictures than words; first comes a dedication to Henri de Bourbon, followed by a sketch of the clown's grotesque parti-colored figure kneeling and praying for a medal and chain from the king and queen. A riddle, the answer to which is *Core* (heart), precedes another picture which has also the legend:

Quantunque la chaine et la medaglia
Pour la monstrer à ces Messieurs d'Itaglia.

The rest of the little volume contains alternately blank pages and pictures of Arlecchino and his fellows, with occasionally a repetition of the begging rimes, until toward the end a dream of Arlecchino's is recounted in which a "messenger of importance" solemnly announces to him in Latin, "You shall have a chain and medal." In one place it is hinted that he desires the medal particularly to preserve him from smallpox but there is no dis-

TRISTANO MARTINELLI AS HARLEQUIN, C. 1600

(From his *Rhétorique*)

guising the fact that his chief wish is to preserve himself from want in old age. He succeeded so admirably in this aim, thanks to his
skill in pleasing many rich lords and ladies,
that his will represents a very considerable
amount of wealth, and shows, like Shakespeare's will, how a clever and fortunate actor
even in those uncertain times was able to lay
up a fortune for his children. He leaves to his
wife "all his jewels, his clothes of silk and gold,
the chains given him by princes and queens,
his silverware, pictures, tapestries, and cover-
ings of gilded leather," though he wishes that
his pictures should be deposited eventually in
a chapel founded by him in the village of Dui
Castelli. He also left legacies to his legitimate
children and to an illegitimate son, and directed that money should be paid for a mass to
be sung every Tuesday morning at the high
altar of the SS. Annunziata in Florence "to
free his soul from purgatory!" [18]

CHAPTER VI

THE DECLINE AND FALL OF ARLECCHINO AND LELIO

NEGOTIATIONS for the trip to France were interrupted by confusions in the state of Mantua, first by the death of Vincenzo, then by that of his eldest son, Francesco, finally by the succession to the duchy of the Cardinal Ferdinand, the "Gossip with red crest," his resignation of his hat and his marriage. During these important events the Fedeli were forgotten by their patrons, or at least were allowed to wander about finding work as they could. In a letter from Lelio to the Duke, dated 13 December, 1612, Tristano and he appear as equally rewarded at a play in Pisa:

MOST ILLUSTRIOUS, MY LORD:
Many letters has Florinda written to Your

Highness in order to prove herself and me faithful servants of such a dear patron, and although we have had no answers, nevertheless we cannot believe that you have forgot your creatures. Now we should be glad to hear whether or no you wish comedies at Mantua this carnival, and if you do not, Arlecchino would like to know if the company may go to Rome. More, we must tell you that as soon as we arrived at Pisa the Highnesses there, that is to say Her Excellency the Archduchess, gave Florinda 2 yards of cloth worth five ducats the yard, oh, most beautiful! also 60 yards of trimming for it, in gold,—and all this quite spontaneously! 600 ducats His Highness the duke gave the company, and to me and Arlecchino, medals of gold worth 25 ducats. Now I have told Your Highness everything as Florinda bade me. . . .[1]

Other members of the troupe did not fare so well as Arlecchino in Paris. Lelio, with his wife Florinda, seems again to have passed momentarily into the shade, for when he is heard of it is in a sad way; Marie de' Medici writes in December of 1612 to the Duke of Mantua, asking him to interfere for Lelio, who was threatened with assassination by his fellows.[2] Yet he must have come out victoriously, for in one of his letters of the same period he speaks of Arlecchino's having deserted the company and run away to Italy, leaving the Andreini in full charge, and in July, 1614, the Queen again shows that she has taken Lelio under her special care, by notes of recommendation to the Duchess of Lorraine and to the Cardinal Gonzaga. The latter runs:

MY NEPHEW: . . . I take this occasion of telling you how much pleasure and contentment we have had from their acting [Lelio's and Florinda's company], and their respect and their obedience in all that was commanded them for our recreation and service, praying you to show them the same good will that we have shown them and to aid them in their private affairs and business both by your recommendation and by your kind care; I shall receive it [news of your favor] very thankfully, for I am sure that by their excellence in their profession they will be worthy. . . .

MARIE.[3]

Notwithstanding such support from the great, in fact partly because of it, all these dependent creatures lived through at best a stormy career. Artists, and therefore naturally restive under any restraint, these men and women were seldom free to do the simplest thing on their own initiative, much less to come and go, to work or rest as they chose. Of course their employers blamed them for insubordination, as does Don Giovanni de' Medici in a letter to Ercole Merliani, 1620:

The name of liberty is too sweet in their ears. . . . All these famous Lelios and Florindas and Flaminias and Fritellinos and Arlecchinos are more than eager and desirous of lordship and rule, so that these poor creatures, who are used to equality among themselves, can never be brought to a peaceful and quiet service. . . . They find it sweeter to command than to obey.

[161]

Equality among themselves meant constant intrigues and rivalry, with no real power in the leader to quell disturbances, although he was always held responsible for the troubles in his company; sometimes, like Pedrolino in 1576, a leader was thrown out of work because of his comrades' vanity or vices; sometimes his band was disrupted because a few of its members were too free with their tongues in the improvised comedies, as on the occasion in 1582 when the Gelosi played an offensive farce at the Mantuan court; three of its members were ordered to prison immediately unless they could walk across the room on a rope and when the rope broke and they fell, they were haled away to punishment, "half alive as they were." [4] Sometimes a whole company was out of work not only during Lent,—that was expected,—but for a long period before and after the penitential season, simply because their patron forgot them for new favorites. [5] An ac-

tress was occasionally snatched away from her
husband and her companions by the greedy
power of a noble admirer, like poor Beatrice
Adami, wife of the well-known Trappolino, in
1614; now and then an actor lost his life because he had imprudently offended one of his
patrons, as did the Leandro, whose real name
was Francesco Pilastri, murdered in the streets
of Genoa in 1594.[6] Again intrigues of rivals
discredited certain actors with their lords and
threw them into prison or drove them into
exile, where if they had no friends powerful
enough to help them they languished long or
quickly starved to death.[7] Is it any wonder
that beneath the jests and affectation of care-
lessness there lurks in their letters so much of
anxious servility? No amount of petting, no
money, no condescension at the baptismal font,
no protection afforded their children, could
make up to the actors for the fact that they
were absolutely in the power of capricious

nobles who cared in general far more for their own amusement than for anything else in the world.[8]

Tristano Martinelli, who boasts that he has among his "gossips" the King of France, the King of Spain, three queens, three dukes and two duchesses, fared, as I have shown, rather better than most of his fellows, thanks to his talents and to his foresight,[9] but even he had his ups and downs of fortune. And Piermaria Cecchini, although ennobled by the Emperor in 1616 and making the most of the honor on every occasion, and although he was extraordinarily persevering in consulting his master's interests, was disgraced almost as often as he was honored.[10] His first recorded misfortune seems to have followed the trouble with the Andreini recounted above. This crisis passed, again for three years Fritellino was in favor, but by 1619 the actor once more bitterly complained of neglect. To the Duke he writes:

MOST SERENE HIGHNESS:

For thirty-five years I have traveled about the world. I began my first comedies in the service of the most serene Guglielmo, your famous grandfather. I have always obeyed the orders of your illustrious house and never, never have I endured a wrong, an insult and a shame like that I am enduring at this moment. . . . The company declares me a rebel to Your Highness and curses me! And this is the end of all my service! I am going to Lodi with I know not how few companions, as though I were the most abandoned of men. But I shall know better how to conduct myself in future! Meanwhile may God preserve Your Highness, before whom I bow myself in devotion,

Your most unhappy servant,

PIERMARIA CECCHINI (Fritellino)[11]

The cutting blow to Cecchini was that he was forbidden to go to France with the troupe he had helped to form and train, and that in his place went the ever-successful and hated Tristano Martinelli, Dominus Arlecchinorum,[12] and with him the equally detested Andreini,—

Lelio and Florinda! But Fortune, whom all these poetical improvisers so frequently invoked in their stage speeches, was to turn her wheel again and again for those she favored at this time. Lelio indeed writes to Mantua, March 3, 1621,—the company had been in France for some months,—

I and Florinda, your servants, are very well and are much loved by their Christian Majesties, by the Most Christian Queen [Marie, the Queen-Mother] and by all the Princes of France, not merely of Paris; we are rewarded much more generously than formerly, so that we hope to be able to carry something good home to Italy.[13]

But Arlecchino was not so well satisfied. He complains jealously several times to his Italian patron of "the great discord in the company, especially between Lelio and Florinda," probably on account of the "Baldina" in whom Andreini was something more than interested.[14] And in April he begs the French

king to release him from his engagement and
to allow him to go home and redeem his vow
of leaving the stage forever:

Arlequin, very humble servant of Your
Majesty, knowing that you are about to start
on a long journey, begs that he may with the
King's leave, depart at the end of May to go
home to rest and to do his own business. He
will play no more comedies . . . he has resolved to appear no more on the stage in any
place whatsoever, first because of his advanced
age, secondly because of the promise he has
made to God to act no more, once this engagement was fulfilled. Wherefore the said Arlequin begs and beseeches Your Majesty not to
oppose his wish, and he will always pray Our
Lord for your happiness.
At Fontainebleau April 21, 1621.
Your Most Christian Majesty's
Very humble and very affectionate servant,
TRISTANO MARTINELLI, called Arlequin.[15]

The pious mask drops off in later documents; particularly in a long communication
from the other members of the troupe to their

Mantuan patron, Arlecchino stands revealed as the grasping tyrant he evidently appeared to his companions.[16] His fellows accuse him of having been from the very formation of the company the despot of them all, of having made secret arrangements for their performances and then of having kept to himself the rewards, of having himself spent twenty out of the fifty ducats received for one play, of having made a number of little portraits of himself for distribution in Paris, and of there having used the most shameless methods to acquire favor and to monopolize its fruits, finally of having left the company in the lurch by his hasty flight. The Duke is urged to punish Arlecchino for his insolent desertion of duty by sending him back post-haste to his companions, who all affix their names to the document.

Tristano, however, having been allowed by the king to go in June, remained in Italy for

NICCOLÒ BARBIERI AND HIS BOOK
(Title page of *La Supplica*, 1634)

some time, not at all in the devout retirement
his letter to Louis had suggested as his ambition, but in the heat of professional labors, first
in one then in another of the Italian courts,
until 1626, when he professes a desire again to
serve in France. But his accustomed protesta-
tions of devotion, his gift of three more portraits of himself and his thinly veiled avarice
were this time coldly received. What became
of the old comedian we can only guess from
his will, already quoted in proof of the financial success of his career.[17]

Andreini meanwhile, like Cecchini, pursued
his separate way, falling from high eminence
to misery in a comparatively few years. Yet
he had many more vicissitudes to endure before
he found himself entirely discarded from favor.
In 1620, when, as has been said, he and his
company were again summoned to France after
negotiations as tedious as had preceded their
former visit, Florinda complicated matters by

fits of mad jealousy of her husband's interest, alluded to by Cecchini, in the "Baldina," possibly the gay widow with seven children whom Andreini afterward married. Fritellino tried to have this firebrand removed from the troupe, writing to the Duke that "with secret arts she feeds such flames in this company that I cannot exist in their midst. . . . Three days ago Florinda ran away in tears to a church, pretending to be bewitched; she wished to order a coach to take her back to Mantua, when her father-in-law . . . made her stay . . . ; that little devil [the Baldina] only laughs at all this." [18] Just how the difficulty was met is not clear, but at least the actors were able to proceed to Paris, and when the king dismissed the Andreini in Lent, 1622, it was with an even heartier recommendation than his mother had granted them at the time of their preceding visit: [19]

[To the Duke of Mantua.]

My Cousin: I have desired to show you by this letter what contentment I have received from Lelio and Florinda, who have always behaved very well on their two trips to this kingdom. And if they have not returned to Italy sooner it is because I kept them to serve me with the other actors, their companions, as they continued to do, and if anything else is reported of them, I beg you will not believe it, but be assured they deserve the continuation of your good-will. And so I pray God, my Cousin, that he keep you in his holy and worthy protection.

Written at Paris, 3 February, 1622.

Louis.

At this point, then, Andreini must have been at the summit of his fame and of his powers. He was the leader of the most famous and best patronized company of actors in the world, the Fedeli, and he was an author of recognized importance. The favor he found at the French court he tried to attach permanently to himself by dedicating his numerous poetic and dramatic works to various personages prominent in Paris; moreover he usually saw to it that his plays, in order to have a favorable reception, should be first put on by his own company. In 1622, he published the five dramatic works in Paris already discussed, *La Sultana, L'Amor nello Specchio, La Ferinda, Li Due Leli Simili* and the bizarre extravaganza, *La Centaura.* No one of them, as has been said, offers anything amusing or even readable to a modern reader; all are full, like the author's numerous other works, of old material, tiresome type characters, poor and indecent jokes and the affectations of the prevailing academic literary style of the Seicento. Yet all Andreini's eighteen comedies were greatly admired by his contemporaries, probably because they were frequently performed by the Fedeli in the lively *commedia dell'arte* manner and because the staging and music used for them were beautiful and new.[20] Indeed these plays give an excellent idea of what the scenarios of the improvised plays must have been when they were filled out by their actors' wits. But there is nothing in any of them original enough or powerful or beautiful enough to give them any literary or poetic value.

Such tributes to the Muses, as Lelio would himself have called his works, brought him solid pecuniary reward for some of his dedications, and complimentary verses from his poetical contemporaries, a few of whom no more hesitated to call him the modern Homer and Virgil than they had to name his mother the modern Sappho. Moreover, "on account of his witty printed works," he was recognized as his mother had been by an election into an Academy, the highest honor that could come to an actor with poetical pretensions; after about 1605, Andreini signed himself "Accademico Spensierato," [21] showing that the Florentine Spensierati had elected him to membership, whether before or after he dedicated to them his defense of San Carlo is uncertain, probably before, as the practice of many poets at the time was to acknowledge such an honor by giving a dedication to their patrons. Andreini indeed in his long dedicatory preface to *L'Adamo* addresses Marie de' Medici with an admission of this aim:

I could not have been more favored by fate in this world, Most Christian Queen, than in the order which came to me to pass over into France with my Florinda and with our companions, to serve Your Majesty with the virtuous pastime of comedy, because, aside from the pleasure of obeying His Highness the Serene Duke of Mantua, our Lord, I, who was born under the most happy rule of the Illustrious Medici, shall see in the person of Your Majesty my own country glorified, and its most splendid sun (I speak of Your Majesty's self, splendor of your race) spreading the rays of its brilliance over the breadth of that so great kingdom . . . [I omit a still more complimentary sentence in which the Queen's mind

is extolled at length.]   But in order not to lose
myself in such a splendor . . . I present myself humbly before Your Majesty with this
work, a poetic imitation called *Adam,* composed by me during the freer hours of my
professional life; it seems to me that at least
the material, which being both great and
sacred suits with the greatness and piety of
Your Majesty, may serve me as magic shield
before your Most Christian Brightness, so that
I may be able to contemplate it without hurt
to my eyes, as before the rays of the sun observers protect themselves by interposing some
ingenious crystal.   So, while Your Majesty, as
I humbly beg you will, deigns to contemplate
in my book the marvels of God and his divine
works, I may rest in the contemplation of those
of Your Majesty, and of your wonderful son,
the Most Christian King, living image and example of both father and mother, from whose
superhuman virtues the kingdom will grow to
heights of glory, and the life of Christendom
will ever profit.   I have wished particularly to
dedicate this work to Your Majesty, because,
aside from the reason of having been born a
subject of Your Most Serene House, as I have
said, which obliges me to some tribute of vas-

salage, I have the reason of being the son of Isabella Andreini, so favored, as I know she was, by the kindness of Your Majesty, wherefore I all the more eagerly recognize the maternal debt, thus in some way procuring the continuance of Your Majesty's grace. So I beg in all humility that it may please you to pardon the boldness of my wish to eternize my work by linking it with your name, and to see in this but the will to lend it forever this honor, which belongs to Your Majesty. Whose Most Christian person, together with that of the unconquered King, your son, God guard and make happy; with which ending I bow myself humbly at your feet.

From Milan, 12 June, 1613.

Your Most Christian Majesty's most humble servant,

GIO. BATTISTA ANDREINI.[22]

A booklet dedicated to Richelieu,—"vermilion statue with angel's face and golden tongue,"—[23] together with various other records, shows that the Fedeli were again in Paris, in 1623 and later, and gives proof of new difficulties in the company. There are suggestions of a falling off in their skill and popularity at this time, and a little later, September 20, 1626, Flaminia, though again the leading lady, is reported "so ugly that it's unbearable to see her."

The next year while all or part of the troupe were in Germany and Hungary the news came to them of the disturbances in Mantua already alluded to, culminating in the terrible sack of the city in 1630. Andreini tried to secure himself in the favor of the most probably successful of the many claimants to the duchy by writing a fulsome letter to him,—the Duke of Nevers, one of the former friends of the Fedeli at the French court. The astuteness of the long-practiced actor in thus gambling on the future was justified by the result of the wars which ensued, for Nevers in 1631 actually succeeded to the title of Duke of Mantua under the name of Charles I, but so far as his "servants" were concerned he might as well have been unsuccessful; he either cared nothing for the theater and for the devotion of the Fedeli or, more probably, he cared so much for his own theater as to prefer a troupe of fresh young actors to these superannuated men and women. Fortunately Florinda did not live to see herself supplanted; she seems to have died in 1628 and a certain Lidia, possibly the Baldina of evil fame, to have taken her place shortly after, both as Giambattista's wife and as prima donna of the troupe.[24] But Andreini himself and most of his fellows lived on to suffer a neglect more poignant than disgrace to their proud spirits.

In 1632 begins a series of begging letters from Andreini to the new lords of Mantua, written in a tone of bitterness that makes clear enough his sense of the change from past favors to the present coldness of his patrons. A new company is engaged in place of the old one for the carnival of 1633, a terrible insult to pride as well as an infringement of privilege. In 1637, rewards not being forthcoming from the Duke for some services rendered, the Fedeli seem to have disbanded for good and all and their leader to have retired, not happily, either to his small property in the Mantuan countryside or more probably to some years of farther wandering in search of the fame he could not believe was dead. There are traces of him in Paris in 1643-4, though no definite proof,—only three tiny pamphlets published there of complimentary verses to Queen Anne, the Prince de Condé and the Duc d'Enghien, three probably despairing, certainly stiff and insincere, half-smothered cries for help from a sensitive and needy dependent. Later there are two more letters from Lelio to the Duke of Mantua which utter a confused rage of grief painful to overhear. The first, dated March 19, 1652, runs:

Most Serene Highness:

Since a long service to your most noble house, Most Serene my Lord, should have required, as indeed Your Highness' kindness recognized and of your own accord promised, a yearly pension of one hundred and fifty ducats for my good services; I, seeing these large promises empty of effect and needing to pay my debts in some way, resorted to the Grand Duke of Tuscany, my natural lord, that he would deign to ask Your Highness to arrange this without hateful dispute, for if with the possessions I find in Mantua, I should pay my debts, all contracted in the service of your most noble house, a pillage would be the only recompense given me. So may pity, which never sleeps in Your Highness, grow for Lelio, who during forty years has managed comedies for the noble Gonzaga and who is now helpless unless by two notes he may satisfy the greed of those who will not pay their just debts; so that by these notes may be ended forever the dispute over that which the Marquis Andreasio holds of mine, namely that little place I have never obtained possession of from the Illustrious Senate, for no one ever gives up another's belongings! It is now four years since

I told him, without lawsuits, to give it up but he continues to enjoy it and to draw the revenue from this place, while I languish. As for my notes, I confide so entirely in my much respected lord that I could wish it were the Most Illustrious Marquis Giulio Gonzaga to whom I have respectfully written. And so, not to bore Your Highness longer, I make my reverence to you, as also to your Most Serene Mother, whom I humbly petition for the favor I am begging, that is the concession without delay of the merest justice to me,—and so, kneeling to you both, I kiss your garments.

Your Serene Highness' servant, grown old in the Mantuan service, I would say without reward, but because I hope, I am silent.

LELIO, Comico Fedele.[25]

A sadder letter follows shortly:

Too few words, Most Serene Highness, occasion misunderstanding, wherefore lend a kind ear to the following facts:

Lelio, for a long time servant to your most illustrious house, in the course of his life believed his family, the Andreini, were most happy to be under so fortunate a patronage.

His parents of old served the Lord Guglielmo and his son Vincenzo, and were favored by being allowed to place one of their daughters at court and later to enter the same girl with a dowry given by the Lady Leonora, at the convent under the Reverend Mother Cantelma, so that the maid succeeded, thanks to her virtues, to the rank of Prioress among these noble and pious ladies.

Lelio, son of Isabella, followed in the service of the first Vincenzo and that of the second Vincenzo, his son, doing his duty with Florinda and their companions until the time of Duke Carlo of immortal memory. [d. 1637]

In those days of long and appreciated service, Florinda, Lelio's first wife, was thought worthy to sing *Arianna* when singers were scarce, and if I may be permitted to say so, she did it so admirably that the most noble Ferdinand, then Cardinal, said to Duke Vincenzo, his father, that Florinda ought not longer to tread the stage,—such a fine action was done for your noble house with great applause.

Joined in this most fortunate service, Domenico Andreini, brother to Lelio, after he had proved himself in arms, was honored by the Lord Ferdinand with the title of Captain and spent no less than ten years in this worthy duty, with no little praise. Also in that happy time, Pietro Enrico, son to the same Lelio, was looked upon with a favorable eye by Your Serene Highness.

Now Lelio alone remains to you, after long service, after many changes of fortune, little rewarded; even though he merited little or nothing himself, he nevertheless humbly recalls Your Highness' justice, not to add promises, to appoint him for the coming year (if it please God) to a life tenure of the Commission of Castles,—since small part of his life remains. And because the benefice is so meager, not more than 27 or 30 lire a month, and that uncertain, he begs some other sure succor, so that he may live and lend all his force to Your Highness.

Your Most Serene Highness'

Most Humble Subject and Servitor,

LELIO, Comico Fedele.[26]

The tone of disillusionment, of scarcely concealed scorn and hopelessness, makes the answer, unknown for certain though it be, all too probably unfavorable, perhaps nothing but neglect and silence, the usual recompense for the outworn servants of princes. Like Shakespeare's Adam, these abandoned creatures might generally expect nothing but "old dog" as their reward, a curse thrown contemptuously at them if they survived their youth and agility and beauty, no matter how many years they might have spent themselves in exhausting service.

NOTES

NOTES

CHAPTER I

[1] The often quoted proof dating the introduction of women on the Italian stage is found in a passage from P. M. Cecchini's *Brevi discorsi*, Napoli, 1616, p. 16: "Non sono cinquant' anni che si costumano donne in scena e vi si introdussero; poichè di necessità intervengono quasì in ogni importante caso, ch'al mondo succede: et se bene in suo luoco vi potevano giovanetti, tuttavia fù concluso esser assai meglio e di manco scandolo la donna, poichè ben guardata e dalla propria honestà e dall' interesse dell' honor del marito, si sarebbero fugiti quei scandali, che possono esser partoriti dalla libertà di quel garzone."

[2] Nashe, T., *Pierce Penilesse*. Cf. Scherillo, M., *La Commedia dell'Arte, Studj e Profilj*, chapter on Carlo Borromeo and the Gelosi; also Rennert, H., *The Spanish Stage, passim*.

[3] *La Supplica*, Bologna, 1636, pp. 126-7 and 223 ff.

[4] Barbieri, *op. cit.*, pp. 69-70.

[5] Rasi, L., *I Comici italiani, passim*.

[6] Barbieri, *op. cit.*, *passim*, and G. B. Andreini, *Il teatro celeste*.

CHAPTER II

[1] D'Ancona, A., *Origini del Teatro Italiano*, II, p. 134.

[2] Solerti, A., *Ferrara e la corte estense*, p. xvi f. Cf. also p. cvii.

[3] From a letter of 3 November, 1568, quoted Solerti, *op. cit.*, p. xci. Cf. Mic. C., *La Commedia dell'Arte* (1927), p. 205.

[4] In 1578. Cf. Solerti, *op. cit.*, p. xcvi.

[5] Romei, *Discorsi*, ed. Solerti, *op. cit.*, pp. 79 ff. Cf. the same volume for general information on the theater in Ferrara during the sixteenth century, pp. lxxxi ff.

[6] Printed by E. Cocco, in *Giornale storico della letteratura italiana*, 1915, pp. 57-8.

[7] Given in full by B. Croce, *Teatri di Napoli*, 1916, pp. 29-31.

[8] Neri, A., "Fra i comici dell' arte," in *Rivista teatrale italiana*, 1906, pp. 55-6.

ITALIAN ACTORS OF THE RENAISSANCE

[9] Molmenti, P., *Venise*, . . . II, p. 311.

[10] Valeri, A., *Gli scenari inediti di B. Locatelli*, p. 25.

[11] Baschet, A., *Les comédiens italiens à la cour de France*, pp. 19 ff.

[12] For the Gelosi the best history is in I. Sanesi's *La Commedia*, II, pp. 6 ff. A. Neri, *loc. cit.*, adds a number of interesting details.

[13] A. Bartoli, *Scenari inediti*, xc, and many contemporary descriptions of *intermedii*, similar to that in *La Confanaria di Fran. d' Ambra, con gl' intermedii di Giouan Battista Ciui, recitata nelle nozze dell' Illustro. Sig. principe Don Francesco de Medici et della Serena Regina Giouan. d'Austria.* Firenze, MDLXVI.

[14] Such defenses of the stage are numerous among the works of Italian actors, e.g. G. B. Andreini, P. M. Cecchini and N. Barbieri. Cf. especially Barbieri's *La Supplica*, p. 105.

[15] Solerti, A., *Ferrara e la corte estense*, p. xciii.

[16] This petition for a license to enable them to play in Genoa is printed by A. Neri, *loc. cit.*; for the long debate with Carlo Borromeo, cf. M. Scherillo, *op. cit.*, and d'Ancona, *Origini*, II, p. 498. Three articles in Italian reviews go into the matter of censorship, F. Barbieri, *Athenaeum*, Pavia, 1914; C. Levi, "La chiesa e i comici," *Emporium*, 1919; G. Sforza, "I comici italiani e la moralità del teatro," *Gazzetta letteraria*, 1890.

[17] Mic. C., *op. cit.*, Paris, 1927, p. 187.

CHAPTER III

[1] Rasi, *op. cit.*, II, under Piissimi, V. Cf. Solerti, *Ferrara*, pp. cii-ciii.

[2] *Acts of the Privy Council*, X, p. 144.

[3] D'Ancona, *Origini*, II, pp. 484-5. For Vincenzo's persecution of actresses he admired, cf. Ademollo, A., *La bell'Adriana*, ch. IV.

[4] D'Ancona, *ibid.*, p. 488.

[5] D'Ancona, *ibid.*, p. 489.

[6] *Lettere*, ed. of Venice, 1627, dedicatory letter to Carlo Emmanuele, Duke of Savoy, one of the patrons of the Gelosi. The letters form a series of semi-philosophical discussions of love and other emotions and problems in a style as artificial as that of the preface here quoted. They were probably in part used in Isabella's rôles on the stage.

[7] Barbieri, *op. cit.*, pp. 39-40.

NOTES

[8] F. Bartoli, *Notizie istoriche*, etc., I, p. 32.

[9] F. Andreini, *Bravure*, Rag. IV. Cf. for I. Andreini, Rasi, *op. cit.*, I, and Mignon, M., *Etudes sur le Théâtre français et italien de la Renaissance*, Paris, 1923.

[10] Her husband, Francesco Andreini, a Pistoian, had a notable career of great variety. At the age of twenty (1568) while a soldier in the Italian armies in Turkey he was captured by the Moslems and was held eight years as a slave; he finally made his escape and returned to Italy to act with the company of the Gelosi till his wife's death. Probably the Turkish atmosphere in the plots of some of Scala's scenarios for improvised plays reflect Francesco's adventures, for in the *Teatro delle favole rappresentative* published by Scala (1611), the repertory of the Gelosi is summed up, and in these pieces when first given there is little doubt that Andreini took the rôle of Flavio, a young lover, while his appearance suited the part, and when he grew older, of the Spanish Captain Spavento. Scala's book and Andreini's own volumes, *Bravure del Capitan Spavento*, Venice, 1607 and 1618, are the sources for a study of his character parts. Cf. the full synopsis of his work as well as of that of the Captains in improvised comedy earlier and later than his time in Senigaglia, *Il Capitan Spavento*. Cf. also Rasi, *I comici italiani*, under Andreini, F., and a brief note in *The Mask*, October, 1913. Andreini died in 1624, twenty years after quitting the stage to devote himself to literary work, living most of this time in Venice. The name of the family may originally have been Cerrachi, changed for some unknown reason. Cf. Bevilacqua, "G. B. Andreini e la compagnia dei Fedeli," *Gior. Stor.* xxiii, 1894, p. 82.

[11] G. B. A., *Comici Martiri e Penitenti*, Parigi, 1624. His sonnet to his mother's memory, published in a curious little volume of poems glorifying actors who had been also saints, runs as follows:

Tra le Scene più belle, ecco la *Bella*,
Splende *Accesa* d'honor, saggia *Andreina*,
Raggio nel Mondo, e'n Ciel pura Fiamella,
Che di sua Foco à'ncenerir destina.

Donna, dono fatal, opra divina,
Franca Penna Real *Intenta* appella;
Nè di tempo l'indomita rima,
Sua memoria immortal rode, o cancella.

[191]

ITALIAN ACTORS OF THE RENAISSANCE

D'ogni gloria maggior Scena fastosa,
Fatti Giardin d'un sempiterno Alloro,
Giardiniera bellissima Gelosa.

O qual di ricca Statua alto Lauoro
Fa Colonna poggiar ambizioza,
Di: Base fu d'un simulacro d'oro.

[12] Rasi, *op. cit.* Andreini, Isabella. But Ariosto, who died 29 years before Isabella's birth, was not one of her admirers, though Baschet and others have asserted he was.

[13] D'Ancona, *Origini*, II, 521.

[14] For the Gelosi and other Italian troupes in France during this period cf. A. Baschet, *op. cit.* The account of the Gelosi is on pp. 52 ff. For English parallels cf. V. C. Gildersleeve, *Government Regulation of the English Drama, passim*, N. Y., 1908; also Collier's edition of Northbrooke's *Treatise*, Shakes. Soc., 1843, introduction, p. xi,—a letter from the London Lord Mayor and aldermen, to Sussex, the Lord Chamberlain, declining to grant to a private person a license for appointing places for plays, because of "sondry inconveniences" bound to follow the "assemblying of multitudes of the Queen's people." Cf. too *The Alleyn Papers*, Shakes. Soc., 1843.

[15] Cf. Baschet, *op. cit.*, pp. 73-4. For the professional pride of the company, cf. F. Andreini's *Bravure del Cap. Spavento*, Venetia, 1624, Preface to the Readers, "The Gelosi for many years have showed the true method of composing and presenting comedies, tragicomedies, tragedies, pastorals, interludes," etc.

[16] Baschet, *op. cit.*, pp. 146-7.

[17] *Ibid.*, p. 147. Such recommendations were of course very common between princes. Cf. an interesting instance given by Rasi, *Comici italiani*, II, p. 243. There are also plenty of English records of the same custom, e.g. *Alleyn Papers*, ed. J. P. Collier for the Shakespeare Society, 1843, pp. 4-5, and Sir Robert Dudley's letter to Shrewsbury (1559) asking protection for his "servauntes . . . such as ar plaiers of interludes," "being honest men and suche as shall plaie none other matters (I trust) but tollerable and convenient," quoted in Collier's introduction to Northbrooke's *Treatise*, (1577), Shakes. Soc., 1843, p. vii.; T. W. Baldwin, in *The Organization and Personnel of Shakespeare's Company*, Princeton University, 1927, gives many other documents.

[18] *Histoire de France et des choses mémorables*, etc., quoted by

[192]

NOTES

Baschet, *op cit.*, pp. 147-8. There are many similar allusions in the *Mémoires* of Sully, Malherbe's works, etc.

[19] Solerti, *Ferrara*, xcix, note 4.

[20] *Ibid.* The ascription of this reference to Angelica is somewhat doubtful.

[21] Rasi, *op. cit.*, II, p. 95 ff. Rasi erroneously notes 1572 as the date of Drusiano's trip to England. Cf. for the Martinelli in Spain, Rennert's reference to them in his interesting book on *The Spanish Stage.*

[22] D'Ancona, *Origini*, II, pp. 504-6.

[23] For the identity of Margarita,—a vexed question,—cf. D'Ancona, *Origini*, II, p. 504, and Rasi, *op. cit.*, II, p. 104.

[24] D'Ancona, *Origini*, II, 508.

[25] D'Ancona, *ibid.*, II, 524 f.

[26] D'Ancona, *ibid.*, II, 526.

[27] D'Ancona, *ibid.*, II, 518 f.

[28] Baschet, *op. cit.*, pp. 107-108.

[29] Baschet, *op. cit.*, p. 114 ff.

[30] Jarro, *L'Epistolario*, p. 19; cf. C. Mic, *op. cit.*, p. 189 f., and Rasi, *op. cit.*, I, p. 637, for further details on the payment of actors.

[31] Ricci, C., *Teatri di Bologna*, pp. 12-13, from a record in a contemporary diary.

[32] *Ibid., p.* 37. Cf. the long letter from Tristano to his lord, translated by Baschet, *op. cit.*, pp. 277 ff. Also Appendix to the same book.

[33] Baschet, *op. cit.*, pp. 118-119.

CHAPTER IV

[1] Cf. E. Allodoli's edition of *L'Adamo*, Lanciano, Carrabba, 1913, for a summary of the history of this question and for a modern judgment of it.

[2] W. E. Flechsig, *Die Dekorationen der modernen Bühnen in Italien*, Dresden, 1894, p. 33, and Luzio-Renier, "Delle relazioni di Isabella d'Este Gonzaga con Ludovico e Beatrice Sforza," in *Archivio storico lombardo*, 1890, p. 941. Cf. L. B. Campbell, *Scenes and Machines* . . . Cambridge, 1923.

[3] A. Ademollo, *Alessandro VI, Giulio II e Leone X nel Carnevale di Roma*, Firenze, 1886, pp. 88-93. Also Flechsig, *op. cit.*, 65 ff.

[4] For one example among several that might be given, cf. the description of the "bellissima scenetta, la qual era finta Venezia,"

in Solerti-Lanza, "Il teatro ferrarese nella seconda metà del secolo XVI," *Giornale storico della letteratura italiano*, 1891, p. 172, n. 1.

[5] Leone de' Sommi, the talented Jewish actor-manager of the Duke of Mantua in the middle of the sixteenth century, says in one of his unpublished dialogues, quoted by A. d'Ancona, *Origini*, II, pp. 417 ff.: "io mi son trovato a condur una volta, tra le altre, una tragedia, et essendo la scena allumata giocondissamente, per tutto il tempo che i successi de la historia furono allegri, quando incominciò poi il primo caso dolente, della inopinata morte d'una reina, onde il coro esclamando stupiva, come il sole potesse patire di veder tanto male, feci (sì come havevo preparato) che in quello istante la maggior parte de i lumi de la scena, che non servivano alla prospettiva, furono velati o spenti: la qual cosa cagionò un profondissimo horrore nel petto degli spettatori. . . ."

F. Neri, *La tragedia italiano nel Cinquecento*, Firenze, 1904, p. 172, discusses this passage and others bearing on sixteenth-century tragedy.

[6] Andreini followed Ingegneri's advice in the use of much music in his plays; he also made occasions for his songs and choruses, just as Ingegneri suggested, and varied the style of them, introducing the echo refrain, for instance, in his pastorals, as his father had done in his pastoral, *L'Alterezza di Narciso*, Venezia, 1611.

[7] L. Rasi, *op. cit.*, I, p. 122.

[8] "A real Babel," says Bevilacqua of this comedy; cf. E. Bevilacqua, "Giambattista Andreini e la compagnia dei Fedeli," *Gior. Stor.*, 1895, p. 114.

[9] Flechsig, *op. cit.*, p. 33; cf. L. B. Campbell, *op. cit.*

[10] Cf. in the preface to *La Centaura* the sensible comments on the folly of a messenger's beginning his news with "Deh, perchè non son nato cieco? Deh, perchè non bevei latte avvelenate?" etc., for the poet says such speeches will sooner move an audience to laughter than to pity, for they will not fail to think the messenger out of his mind instead of broken-hearted.

[11] A. Perrucci, *Dell' arte rappresentativa premeditata ed al l'improvvisa*, Napoli, 1699, p. 26.

CHAPTER V

[1] Letter of 11 September, 1606, printed by Bevilacqua, *Gior. Stor.*, XXIII, p. 141 f.

[2] Bevilacqua, *Gior. Stor.*, XXIII, pp. 141 ff.

NOTES

3 D'Ancona, *Lettere de comici italiani*, pp. 6 ff. Andreini, in *Lo Specchio*, 1625, says that personal abuse of "neighbors" is no longer allowed in comedy.

4 Bevilacqua, *Gior. Stor.*, XXIII, 123 ff.; Cintio, "framed to make women false," the lover of Flaminia, seems to have been a handsome youth attached to the service of the Prince Alessandro Farnese, resented, therefore, as an interloper by the Duke of Mantua's servants as well as hated for his proud reflection of his mistress' airs. Cf. Rasi, *op. cit.*, I, p. 142. An unpublished letter from him to the Duke of Mantua, Archivio mantovano, E XXIV, No. 3, shows him out of favor in 1619.

5 Rasi, *op. cit.*, I, 145 f.

6 Solerti, A., *Albori del melodramma*, I, 16. The whole festival, on the occasion of the wedding of Vincenzo's eldest son, Francesco, to Margarita of Savoy, is described at length in a contemporary booklet *Compendio delle sontuose feste fatte l'anno MDCVIII . . . nella Città di Mantova*. Mantova, 1608. Cf. Vernon Lee's charming imaginative reconstruction of the celebration, *Ariadne in Mantua*.

7 Jarro, *L'Epistolario*, pp. 24-25.

8 The general custom was for a Capocomico to disband more or less entirely his company at the beginning of Lent, reforming his troupe, often with most of the old members, after Easter. Cf. E. Rè in *Gior. Stor.*, LXIII, p. 298.

9 Jarro, *L'Epistolario*, p. 24. Drusiano had died between 1606 and 1608, leaving a book of pious verses, which his brother gave to the library of the Grand Duke of Savoy in Turin, and which is the last record of its author.

10 *Comare* and *Compare* are terms that in sixteenth century English would be rendered by Gossip, as they named the relationship of fellow-sponsor, a relation very common between actors and their patrons. Cf. a letter from F. Alleyn to the Earl of Shrewsbury, Sept. 3, 1560, in which the writer says at the close, "My poor wife, your lordship's gossip, has her humbly commended, and your god-son Francis, I thank God, waxes a jolly boy." Quoted F. Mumby, *Elizabeth and Mary Stuart*, p. 139.

11 Jarro, *L'Epistolario*, pp. 50-51.

12 Jarro, *op cit.*, pp. 51-2.

13 Jarro, *op. cit.*, pp. 52-54.

14 D'Ancona, *Origini*, II, p. 405.

Leone de' Sommi was so greatly favored by Mantua that he dared in 1577 to petition as his reward for many efforts to please his patrons that he might be allowed to leave off the yellow badge which in Mantua Jews were forced to wear in order to distinguish them from Christians.

[15] Quoted Jarro, *op. cit.*, pp. 11-12; cf. D'Ancona, *Origini*, II, 527, n. 3. Croce, *Teatri di Napoli*, pp. 35-6 and 60 f., and Paglicci-Brozzi, *Il teatro a Milano*, 1891, pp. 14 ff.

[16] Jarro, *op. cit.*, pp. 57-8.

[17] Ed. P. J. Duchartre, Paris, Duchartre and Van Buggenhoudt, 1928.

[18] Jarro, *op. cit.*, p. 40. T. Martinelli died in 1630.

CHAPTER VI

[1] Bevilacqua, *Gior. Stor.*, XXIII, 132.

[2] Bevilacqua, *Gior. Stor.*, XXIV, 90.

[3] Baschet, *op. cit.*, pp. 254-5.

[4] For Pedrolino's misfortune see the account of his life in Rasi, *op. cit.*, II, p. 242.

[5] Cf. a letter of Virginia Andreini, D'Ancona, *Lettere*, etc., pp. 9 and 11.

[6] Both these sad affairs are recorded in documents quoted by A. Neri, *loc. cit.*, pp. 102 f. and 110-11.

[7] Cf. the account of a certain Antonio's unjust imprisonment, Rasi, *op. cit.*, II, 126; another letter of the same sort, Rasi, I, 638 ff., from Flaminia (Cecchini), complaining of her brother's imprisonment, 16 Feb. 1612; also the tale of Gianpaolo degli Agochj's two years' solitary confinement without any conviction, told by D'Ancona, *Origini*, II, 513.

[8] N. Barbieri, *op. cit.*, p. 42, says, "It is unnecessary to recount how many Princes and Princesses, Kings, Queens, Emperors and Empresses have held at the font the children of actors, and how they honor them with the name of Gossip . . . and how they have fed them with their own hands, . . ." etc. Barbieri, himself an actor, uses these facts to prove the worthiness of his fellows, who could not have been thus honored by the great had they been mean creatures! Barbieri was rewarded by a military position in the French guards, *ib*. p. 41.

[9] In a letter to the Duke of Mantua, October, 1613. Cf. Jarro, *L'Epistolario*, p. 59.

[10] P. M. Cecchini, *Lettere facete e morale*, Lettera VI. Cf. Rasi, *op. cit.*, I, p. 633. In B. Croce's *Teatri di Napoli*, the event

[196]

NOTES

is dated between 1616-1618. For Cecchini's serviceableness to his patron, cf. Bartoli, *Scenari inediti*, etc., cxxxvii, note.

[11] Baschet, *op. cit.*, p. 275. Cf. T. Martinelli's letter of 1620, cited Bartoli, *Scen. inediti*, CXLII, in which is given an account of Fritellino's objections to traveling in the same company with Lelio, and of his oaths, rage and curses on the occasion.

[12] Baschet, *op. cit.*, pp. 276 ff.

[13] Bevilacqua, *Gior. Stor.*, XXIV, p. 109.

[14] Baschet, *op. cit.*, 270.

[15] Baschet, *op. cit.*, pp. 286 and ff.; Tristano had threatened to leave the stage before this—notably after a severe illness, in 1606-7, probably about the time of his brother Drusiano's death.

[16] Cf. Henslowe's troubles with his company as recounted in the Articles of Grievance they drew up against him in 1612, *Alleyn Papers*, Sh. Soc. 1843, pp. 78 ff.

[17] From Jarro, *op. cit.*, p. 40.

[18] Baschet, *op. cit.*, p. 270; Bevilacqua, *Gior. Stor.*, XXIV, p. 105.

[19] Baschet, *op. cit.*, p. 304.

[20] Prunières, H., *L'opéra italien en France avant Lulli*. Paris, 1913, pp. xxxix and 67.

[21] Barbieri, *op. cit.*, p. 40.

[22] For a long discussion of *L'Adamo*, cf. Bevilacqua, *Gior. Stor.*, XXIII, 134 ff.

[23] *Il Teatro Celeste* (1624), commemorative verses on those actors who have also become saints.

[24] Rasi, *op. cit.*, I, under Andreini, Lidia. E. Picot, in *Rassegna bibliografia della letteratura italiana*, IX, 61, gives a documented account of Andreini's last years.

[25] D'Ancona, *Lettere*, pp. 27-8.

[26] D'Ancona, *Lettere*, pp. 27-29.

INDEX

INDEX

Accesi, 77, 85-6, 153.

Adami, B., 163.

Adamo, L', 87, 97 *ff.*, 101 *ff.*

Aminta, 18.

Andreini, D., 184.

Andreini, F., 43-4, 47, 53, 191, n. 10.

Andreini, G. B., 54, 87-125, 126 *ff.*, 140, 148, 158-166, 171-186, 191, n. 11.

Andreini, I., 46, 49-56, 58, 62, 133.

Andreini, L., 180.

Andreini, V., 96, 120, 128, 132-7, 140, 148, 158-166, 171-3, 180, 184.

Arlecchino, *cf.* Martinelli, D. and T.

Baldina, La, 171-2, 180.

Barbieri, N., 11, 32, 33, 169.

Beolco, Giulia, 42-3.

Borgia, Lucrezia, 15, 29.

Borromeo, Carlo, 28, 34, 189, n. 2.

Cecchini, O., 128, 134-5.

Cecchini, P. M., 80-85, 128-139, 142, 148, 161, 164-5, 171, 189, n. 1.

Celia, 13.

INDEX

INDEX